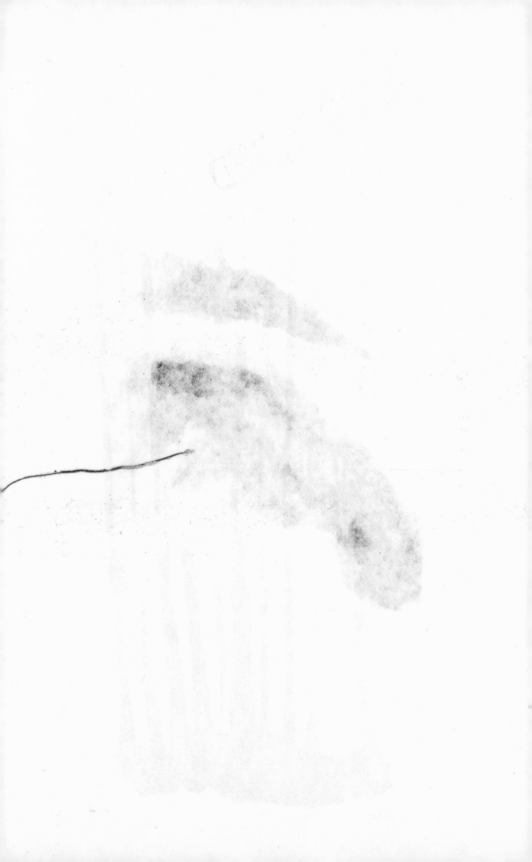

PROTESTANT CHURCHES

AND

INDUSTRIAL AMERICA

Protestant Churches
and
Industrial America

HENRY F. MAY

*With a new Introduction by
the Author*

OCTAGON BOOKS

A DIVISION OF FARRAR, STRAUS AND GIROUX

New York   1977

TO JEAN

CONTENTS

Introduction to the second edition   vii
Introduction   xvii

PART I. THE CONSERVATIVE MOLD, 1828-1861
1. The Battle with Radicalism   3
2. Protestantism and Reform   26

PART II. THE SUMMIT OF COMPLACENCY, 1861-1876
1. Triumph and Certainty   39
2. Progress and Its Price   51
3. Two Giants   64
4. Neglected Prophets   73
5. Theology and Social Opinion   80

PART III. SOURCES OF CHANGE, 1877-1895
1. Three Earthquakes   91
2. The Face of the City   112
3. New Moral Problems   125
4. Academic Precedents   136
5. Winds of Radicalism   148

PART IV. SOCIAL CHRISTIANITY, 1877-1895
1. Conservative Social Christianity   163
2. Progressive Social Christianity   170
   (The Social Gospel)
3. The Social Gospel and the Churches   182
4. The Social Gospel and American Progressivism   204
5. Radical Social Christianity   235
6. Christian Social Teaching and American Thought   263

Bibliography   267

Index   291

INTRODUCTION TO THE
SECOND EDITION

MOST of the work that led to this book was done before World War II, and a draft was completed in 1946-47. Since that time, new ideas and events have made us look differently at the whole American past. Nothing has shifted more than our perspectives on American religious history.[1]

Much more than I realized as I wrote it, this book was dominated by the assumptions about American religious history of the late Arthur M. Schlesinger, who directed the thesis out of which it grew. As the book's most acute critics have pointed out, it usually takes for granted Professor Schlesinger's organization of late nineteenth-century American religious history in terms of challenge and response. In this period, Schlesinger said, the churches were reacting to new ideas, particularly those implied by Darwinian science and Biblical criticism, and to social changes like the rise of the city, immigration, and labor conflict.[2] Nobody can deny either the power of these forces or the importance of the churches' reaction, but Professors Mead and Handy, among others, have argued that this is only part of the story, and that too close a concentration on external challenge tends to neglect the inner vitality and continuity of the religious tradition that shaped the response.[3] The best metaphor for this kind of criticism of sociological church history is that used by H. Richard Niebuhr in criticizing his own earlier work:

Though the sociological approach helped to explain why the religious stream flowed in these particular channels it did not account for the force of the stream itself . . .[4]

Since 1950 more and more writers of religious history have given emphasis to the theological stream as well as the sociological banks, to the great

[1] I have discussed this shift in "The Recovery of American Religious History," *American Historical Review*, XLL (1964-5), 79-92.

[2] Arthur M. Schlesinger, "A Critical Period in American Religion, 1875-1900," Massachusetts Historical Society, *Proceedings*, LXIV (1932), 523-547.

[3] Robert T. Handy and Sidney Mead, review in *The Journal of Religion*, XXX (1950), 67-69. For further interesting discussion of the Schlesinger thesis by Handy, see his "The Protestant Quest for a Christian America, 1830-1930," *Church History*, XXII (1953), 8-20.

[4] Niebuhr, *The Kingdom of God in America*, XX (New York, 1937; paperback edition, New York, 1959), ix.

enrichment of our understanding of the whole river, with its deeps and shallows, its complex tributaries and spreading delta. While I was working on this book I was aware (though doubtless insufficiently aware) that the optimistic social emphasis in recent American Christianity was being harshly criticized both by European theologians like W. A. Visser 'T Hooft and George Hammar and by Americans like the Niebuhr brothers. Since then neo–orthodoxy in its turn has been challenged and in some quarters replaced by a more radical humanism and a more activist social commitment than Washington Gladden or even George Herron could have imagined.

Well beyond the confines of American religious history, the whole progressive synthesis of American history is beginning to be challenged more radically than ever before by social and moral crisis. In the 1930's, it was almost impossible not to see American history as culminating in the apparently successful social and political adaptations of the New Deal, whose way had been prepared by a long series of social critics and reformers, many of them liberal Christian in motivation. Even World War II was assimilated into an optimistic organization of history by most practicing American historians, just as most Social Gospel preachers had managed to regard World War I as a temporary interruption to the triumph of social Christianity. Even today, of course, most historians like most ministers refuse to be Jeremiahs. Yet I am sure that both are being forced, like other Americans, to take account more deeply of the failures as well as the successes of the American past.

The most important way in which all these developments affect this book is that the story it tells, like much of the standard subject matter of American history, becomes the story of a group and not of the whole society. I deliberately limited my subject to the articulate, urban, middle-class section of American Protestantism. But, like the leaders of this group in their own time, and like most historians up to now, I accepted more completely than I realized the claim of such people to be the leaders and teachers of the increasingly heterogeneous society in which they lived. Whether conservatives or liberals in theology, whether defenders of the social status quo or prophets of change, the official, articulate leaders of this kind of American Protestantism agreed on one thing: their assumption that theirs was the task of uplifting the masses. Well after 1895, they voiced that assumption as frankly as their ancestors had in the days of Lyman Beecher—to look no further back.

The early leaders of American social Christianity failed, as I showed in this book, in their sincere if sometimes misguided attempt to speak to and even for industrial workers. They made no attempt of similar magnitude and intensity to deal with the acute social problems of farmers. Though not all feared recent immigrants as much as Josiah Strong, even the more generous regarded the newcomers as objects for uplift rather than as active participants in working out a new social and religious order. Toward Negroes, their benevolence was usually as offhand and indecisive as that of most lay progressives in the period between Reconstruction and the Civil Rights Movement.

These social limitations, of course, went hand in hand with religious ones. The Protestant social movement had only the most gingerly relations with the very different and important adjustment to urban society being carried on at the same time by American Catholics, who actually had the working-class constituency whose lack the Protestants constantly bewailed.[5] With regard to the Jews, whose major contribution to American social thought was also beginning, they were seldom hostile but often uninformed. Various barriers, social and theological, erected from both sides, separated liberal Protestantism from such groups as Lutherans, Mormons, Christian Scientists, premillenarians, and some kinds of popular revivalists.

Both the urban Protestants who preached social conservatism in the seventies and those who preached social progressivism in the nineties and later spoke for a part of the urban middle class. They spoke also as heirs of the alliance between modified Calvinism and moderate revivalism which had been formed in the early nineteenth century and had dominated the centers of Protestant power ever since. Leaders of this alliance maintained cordial relations with low-church Episcopalians and (once they had contained Boston liberalism) a polite tactical alliance with the more conservative of the Unitarians. Out of the religious and social grouping shaped by this system nineteenth-century America drew most of its political, economic, and intellectual leadership. But the power of this leadership to speak authoritatively for the whole society was more limited than its spokesmen could realize at the time, or than historians could see for some time afterwards.

It is in the light of this fundamental fact, by no means new to historians but newly impressed on our consciousness, that it may be worthwhile to look at some of the criticisms made of this book since it appeared. Timothy Smith, in his excellent *Revivalism and Social Reform*, criticizes all recent interpretations of the Social Gospel for neglecting the pre-Civil War revivalist and perfectionist roots of American social reform.[6] He is right that

[5] This development has been studied in Aaron I. Abell, *American Catholicism and Social Action* (New York, 1960; paperback edition, Notre Dame, Indiana, 1960).

[6] Smith, *Revivalism and Social Reform* (New York and Nashville, 1957), 148-9 and *passim*.

periodization, in American religious history and American history in general, has been too much dominated by major political events. He is right also that the Social Gospel had some conscious relation to pre-Civil War reform, particularly antislavery. Yet the relation was less direct than he implies, and the tradition somewhat distorted. The prewar movements for peace, "temperance," antislavery and other causes were very different in mood and method from the social criticism that began in the seventies and flourished from the nineties to World War I. Among prewar reform leaders coming from the major churches, and among church spokesmen in the decade after the Civil War, acute interest in the problems of capital and labor was rare, and fundamental doubt about the principles of political economy still rarer. These particular kinds of social involvement grew from a new social and intellectual milieu. New, but not unaffected by the past. Henry Ward Beecher was after all the son of Lyman Beecher and the brother of Harriet Beecher Stowe, and he was also the spiritual father of Washington Gladden and Lyman Abbott. Prewar reformers and postwar social critics shared many assumptions about the nature of American society and the power of evangelical religion to deal with social problems. Relations between the two periods need subtler exploration than they have yet been given.

The criticism of the book most often made, particularly by generally friendly reviewers from the new "church history" camp is that it neglects theological for social causation. They are surely right that the book tries to separate theological and social thought too sharply. Yet I believe that its principal conclusion about the particular group it deals with is correct. The movement of Protestant spokesmen from social complacency to social concern was immediately brought about by reaction to social crisis. The nature of this reaction was determined in part by the new theological tendencies and the whole intellectual climate of which these were a part. This is a point I tried to make in Chapter 5 of Part II, but one to which I would give more consistent emphasis throughout if I were rewriting this book.

Those who held the commanding pulpits, editorial offices, and seminary chairs in late nineteenth-century American Protestantism were fast moving toward a theology of immanence and evolution.[7] Drawing its prin-

[7] Since I wrote this book, liberal theology has been briefly but fruitfully discussed by Sydney E. Ahlstrom in his essay on "Theology in America" in James Ward Smith and A. Leland Jamison, *The Shaping of American Religion* (Princeton, 1961), 232-321; and by H. Shelton Smith, Robert T. Handy, and Lefferts A. Loetscher in *American Christianity* (New York, 1963), II, 255-308. This general tendency and its connection with social thought are handled with much penetration by Winthrop Hudson, in *The Great Tradition of the American Churches* (New York, 1953; paperback edition, New York, 1963), esp., 157-225.

cipal American support from Horace Bushnell, affected indirectly by Transcendentalism, American Christian liberalism of this period was not in its earlier phases derived from the European romanticism of Schleiermacher and the European social Christianity of Ritschl. It was rather a parallel movement, increasingly affected by its European analogues as it came of age. Evolution, tamed and assimilated to the idea of progressive revelation and the evidences of American progress seemed to fit exactly into domestic and foreign currents of liberal thought. To some young ministers of the eighties and nineties, a new view of God's purposes and man's destiny seemed to be dawning. The reality of democratic progress was a necessary part of the social thought of most middle–class Americans. To some liberal Christians it was more than this: it was the decisive evidence of God's work in the world.

Thus, slums and strikes and depressions challenged the central beliefs of those ministers whose work led them to the social battleground. Repentance and a new life were a traditional way of handling any kind of disaster, but repentance and reform had to be assimilated to the new evolutionary perspective. The answer seemed to emerge from a new reading of the central Christian message, with an emphasis on its social content. Thus social crisis not only produced social Christianity, but made it a necessary part of the unfolding religious view. By the early twentieth century, liberal theology and the social gospel, systematized and closely related to each other, were part of the standard doctrine of many of the most influential American preachers and teachers.

Both Christian liberalism and the social gospel have been riddled by the heavy guns of neo–orthodoxy, and both are enough out of fashion so that some of their content can be rescued. It is easy to realize that it will not do to subsume the difficult paradoxes of Christianity under a vast unfolding of Divine purpose, in which man ascends from fellowship with the brute to unity with God, and the Christian redemption becomes merely the clearest indication of the upward route. Yet, as Kenneth Cauthen has shown,[8] some of the insights of Christian liberalism retain their vitality, not least among the neo–orthodox. And a historian has only to reread Washington Gladden's *Recollections*[9] to feel the liberating power of the dawning realization that one need not wait in passive misery to be released from the paralyzing hatred of God.

Similarly, I think, the simplicities and superficialities of the social teachings of Gladden and his fellows are by now far enough in the past so that

[8] Cauthen, *The Impact of American Religious Liberalism* (New York and Evanston, 1962).

[9] (Boston, 1909), esp., pp. 32-39.

we can appreciate *their* liberating function. To break with the iron law of wages as well as the certainty of eternal punishment, to realize that poverty is no more a necessary evil than slavery, were surely both valid and important gains, and they were not easy to achieve. It is not strange that those who reached these conclusions, often with the emotional force of a conversion, thought that they pointed a clear path ahead—a path not without struggle but leading surely toward the kingdom of God on earth.

It is a commonplace of intellectual history that from a distance, active opponents often seem similar. American Unitarians and Trinitarians of 1820, seventeenth-century English Puritans and Anglicans, even sixteenth-century Lutherans and Catholics can be seen to have much in common. This is true for nineteenth-century American defenders and opponents of the social status quo, those who fulminated against strikes and those who defended them. Most of the principal characters of this book shared a belief that under the leadership of Anglo–Saxon Protestantism, the nation and the world were advancing in moral and physical well-being. Within this assumption, they differed mainly on one question: whether the process of advance was automatically controlled by economic law and Divine will, through the operation of individual human nature; or whether God and evolution made use of human agency also in the form of collective action.

Similarity and even essential agreement should not obscure nuance, and more could be made than is made in this book of differences even within the sector of opinion and society here described. Among some social conservatives and also among some social progressives one can find traces of the Calvinist iron. There are important differences between the churchly organicism of the Anglicans, the commitment to independency and voluntary organization of the Congregationalists, and the hortatory emotional enthusiasm characteristic of the evangelical mainstream, which transcended denominations. Yet most of the articulate American Protestants of this period shared a set of assumptions about religion and society, a set of assumptions which was shaken and redirected, but not fundamentally altered, by the period's social upheavals.

Of the Christian progressives, not all managed the difficult feat of talking about Christianity and leaving out the Cross. The Atonement had been the principal subject for a century of New England theology, and Bushnell had not made its meaning entirely educational. George Herron, for one, seldom forgot the sacrificial meaning of the central Christian symbol. And in the period right after that discussed here, the principal spokesman for the Social Gospel was Walter Rauschenbusch, who said in 1917 that "The cross forever puts a question—mark alongside of any easy treatment of sin."[10]

[10] *A Theology for the Social Gospel* (New York, 1917), 268.

Many treatments of the Social Gospel concentrate on the period of fruition rather than that of preparation, and have given their greatest attention to Rauschenbusch. This was the case with Howard Hopkins' valuable and authoritative treatment of the Social Gospel, which appeared while I was working on the present book.[11] If one is concerned with permanent religious value rather than influence on social opinion, the later period and particularly Rauschenbusch are the right place to center one's study. It is not surprising that later students of American religion have found Rauschenbusch the most attractive representative of the Social Gospel; some have argued that he is an exception to the optimism and the theological superficiality of the movement.

My principal reason for treating Rauschenbusch here only briefly is, of course, that he had not yet become a major national figure by 1895. But a reexamination of his earlier works convinces me that before 1917, there were fewer differences than similarities between him and the earlier Social Gospel leaders like Gladden, Strong, and Ely, whom he much admired. Like these men, Rauschenbusch formed his social opinions under the impact of social crisis, during his work in the New York slums from 1886 to 1897. Before this, he says, he "had no idea of social questions."

Then I began to work in New York and there, among the working people, my social education began. . . . When I began to apply my previous religious ideas to the conditions I found, I discovered they didn't fit.[12]

Rereading the Gospels and the prophets in the light of this experience Rauschenbusch found, like others before him, a profound social message. From this time on his religious emotions were centered in his vision of the Kingdom of God emerging through both evolution and history. He was a consistent and passionate opponent of any apocalyptic interpretation of Christianity, and he argued till the end of his life that this was only a minor and unessential element in the teaching of Jesus, a view being made more and more difficult to sustain by the biblical scholarship of Rauschenbusch's day.[13] Despite his roots in German culture, Rauschenbusch was as certain as Josiah Strong that leadership in the movement toward the Kingdom lay with Anglo-Saxon Protestantism. In the peak year of progressivism and of the Social Gospel, he argued that in America the family, the church, the schools,

[11] Hopkins, *The Rise of the Social Gospel in American Protestantism, 1865-1915*, (New Haven, 1940). As so often happens, I was dismayed when Hopkins' book appeared, since it had used a great deal of material which I thought I had discovered. Actually my book profited greatly from his complementary treatment, and he welcomed it with great generosity.

[12] Speech, undated, quoted in D. R. Sharpe, *Walter Rauschenbusch*, (New York, 1942), 232.

[13] e.g. in A *Theology for the Social Gospel*, 220.

and political life were already partly Christianized. Only the Christianizing of business remained, as the primary concern of the current generation.[14]

In his last book Rauschenbusch set about giving the Social Gospel which had, he said, become official, a theology. Here some of his deeper insights, observable though latent in the earlier books, receive fuller expression. Here, moreover, Rauschenbusch's confidence in the coming Kingdom is tempered, far more deeply than ever before, by his consciousness of the power of human and social evil. Rauschenbusch was utterly unable to see the war as many of his Social Gospel colleagues saw it—either as a purely German challenge to Christian social advance or as a purely temporary interruption of it. War clouds the book as it clouded the author's last years. Here, I think, the nature of the difference between Rauschenbusch and the earlier Social Gospel leaders becomes clear: it did not lie in doctrine, but in temperament and in emotional depth.

This story has been told from several perspectives, and others surely beckon. My main purpose, writing when I did, was to describe the effect of Christian social thought on what then seemed the American mainstream. For the assault on nineteenth-century social determinism, for the development of the kind of progressivism dominant in 1912 and still powerful in 1932, the work of the Social Gospel pioneers was clearly of great importance. It is as hard now as it was twenty years ago to assess the importance of this episode in the whole history of American culture or religion, still more in the history of religion in general. It may have some significance that of recent books, none has been more influential among young American ministers and seminary students than Harvey Cox's *The Secular City*.[15] Like Beecher or Gladden, Cox believes that the church has a responsibility for establishing social goals and pointing the way toward them—indeed he goes much farther and finds the definition and function of Christianity to be almost entirely in providing a theology and a leadership for social change. Like Rauschenbusch, Cox sees church history as a progressive and liberating unfolding of God's purpose. His popularity suggests—and the conclusion is hardly a surprising one—that many Americans, including American Christians, are still moralists and activists.

What a historian thinks this means for the future depends, I suppose, on the views historians like other people inescapably absorb from their environment. Finishing this book late one night in 1947 when I was, like most of my friends, full of worry about the bomb and the cold war and the

---

[14] *Christianizing the Social Order* (New York, 1912), 123-156. For a specific contrast between Anglo-American and European Christianity, ibid., 399.

[15] (New York, 1965.)

quandaries of American liberals, I found myself, to my surprise, writing that progressivism, and even religiously motivated progressivism, had dominated American history and would continue to do so. To my further surprise, I find that I still make this guess. But nobody can believe this now in the same way people believed it in 1895, 1912, or even 1947.

July, 1967
Berkeley, California

INTRODUCTION

IN THE late nineteenth century a series of painful shocks jolted the American people toward a realization of profound change. Suddenly or gradually, many were forced to realize that they were no longer living in an agrarian democracy, but in an industrial nation already increasingly dominated by giant corporations. The resulting readjustment of traditional social thought is, of course, by no means finished yet. Its first stages, however, were accomplished between 1877 and the middle nineties.

During this period of recurrent depression, doubt and struggle the Protestant churches still maintained, to a greater extent than is usually realized, their historic position of intellectual and moral leadership. It was natural for church opinion to play a major part in this national crisis, as it had in previous times of stress. Religious contributions to the central readjustment of this period left permanent effects on American social thinking.

The Social Gospel, perhaps the most characteristic and certainly the most spectacular development of Protestant thought in this period, has attracted increasing attention from recent students, among whom Professor C. H. Hopkins is outstanding for his thorough scholarship. No attempt has yet been made, however, to study the whole influence of church opinion, conservative as well as liberal, in close relation to the period's social history.

The present volume is not intended primarily as a contribution to religious history, but as a study of an important phase of American social thought. Thus theological problems, obviously of first importance to church thinkers of this or any period, are deliberately neglected except where they are essential to an understanding of social points of view.

Because of the immense mass of material on this subject, it has been necessary to impose several somewhat arbitrary limitations. First, the period of intensive study is limited to the three post-Civil War decades. Church concern with industrial problems was not entirely new in this period and it continued to increase in the twentieth century. It is in this first response to industrial problems, however, that it made its most crucial contributions.

Second, the attention of this study is concentrated on five major denominations, the Presbyterian, Congregationalist, Baptist, Methodist and Episcopalian groups. In them converge the principal early currents of American religious history, running from Calvinist, Independent, Pietist and Anglican sources. By the mid-century these churches, or at least their articulate leaders, formed a powerful body of Protestant opinion, remarkably united in its attitude toward society. Other religious groups, though by no means unimportant, differed from this well-established Protestant bloc, and form fitting objects for separate study. Some, like the Catholic, Lutheran and Reformed bodies need to be studied in connection with European developments. Others, like the Disciples of Christ, were cut off by their rural constituencies from the first shocks of large-scale industrial crisis. Important old groups like the Friends and new groups like the Christian Scientists were separated from historic Protestantism by their entirely different religious outlook.

Third, since a detailed investigation of such a subject by localities would hardly be practicable, research was limited to those expressions of church opinion which commanded some national attention. Geographically, therefore, the emphasis falls naturally on the urban areas of the east and the Middle West. These areas first felt the effects of large-scale industrial development, and from them still spoke the most authoritative voices of American Protestantism.

Thanks are due to the Social Science Research Council, which made possible a year's uninterrupted work on this project and to Harvard University for various fellowships which assisted at earlier stages. The author gained understanding of American religious history from a course in that subject given at Harvard by Professor P. G. E. Miller. Professor Henry Nash Smith provided valuable advice and encouragement. Professor C. H. Hopkins was extremely generous with his deep knowledge of American religious history and contributed a great many helpful suggestions. A special debt is owed to Professor A. M. Schlesinger who suggested the topic, supervised the research, and at all stages gave the author the benefit of his illuminating and patient criticism. Gratitude for many kinds of encouragement and assistance is expressed in the dedication. Needless to say, the opinions expressed in the text are those of the author alone.

In the interests of readability documentation has been considerably cut. A more thoroughly documented version, offering a denser sampling of church opinion, is deposited in Harvard College Library.

Claremont, California
August, 1948

I

THE CONSERVATIVE MOLD

1828-1861

 1

THE BATTLE WITH RADICALISM

ALEXIS DE TOCQUEVILLE, explaining the great democratic experiment to the world of 1835, stated an enduring paradox of American religious life. According to this acute observer, the New World's churches, divided, sectarian and lacking the authoritative backing of the state, yet managed to maintain a strict control of manners and morals. Religion in America was stronger, not weaker, than traditional, established European religion. Accepting the institutions of democracy, the churches were able to curb democratic excesses.[1]

It is not surprising if this system, unique in Tocqueville's day, proved puzzling to his European readers, for it was the product of two hundred years of gradual adjustment. Puritan theocracy, in so far as it had ever existed in America, had failed early. The New World's economic individualism, political localism and sectarian diversity had combined from the start to prevent the development of any disciplined and unified religious system. Recurrent revivals had weakened the hold of traditional doctrines and distinctions, spreading instead the ideal of the humble individual in direct contact with God. Finally the head-on conflict between traditional theology and eighteenth century liberal thought had forced even the most authoritarian churches to make a strategic retreat.

Yet the American people, except perhaps on the distant, barbarized frontier, retained their respect for traditional strict morality. The homely virtues, taught by the dissenting sects of sixteenth- and seventeenth-century England and reinforced by New World experience, were naturally under the guardianship of the churches. Organized religion had gradually surrendered its claims to direct control of political life. However reluctantly, it had relinquished the financial support of the state.[2] Here the churches had stopped; they consistently refused to surrender

[1] Alexis de Tocqueville, *Democracy in America*, Henry Reeve, trans. (4th ed.; New York, 1841), I, 328-343.
[2] The process of disestablishment ended in 1833 with the separation of Congregationalism and the state in Massachusetts. E. B. Greene, *Religion and the State. The Making of an American Tradition* (New York, 1941), p. 94.

their right to supervise the morals of the nation. This reservation was a large one, for few important questions were without their moral aspects. Throughout the century, ministers maintained their right to exhort and rebuke the public from the pulpit and in the press, to point out national duties and denounce national sins.

Imperceptibly, as the nation's diverse churches had worked out this adjustment to American society, old sectarian conflicts had become less vital.[3] Groups that had arrived from Europe determined to build a separate community of the saints, in America had found the world less hostile and their members harder to control. Congregationalists, in the course of their long rearguard defense of traditional theology, had gradually opened their doors to the nonelect. Baptists and Quakers, no longer persecuted, had ceased to shun and fear the state. Methodists, never really at odds with society, had proved admirably adapted to growth in the American environment with their simple tenets, revivalist techniques, and efficient organization.

On the other hand, churches which had once aspired to universal authority had been forced to accept a minority status. Presbyterians, in 1801, made a tactical alliance with their Congregational neighbors which, while it greatly increased their proselyting effectiveness, grieved the firm adherents of the unique Presbyterian polity. The Protestant Episcopal Church, forced to forego government support, was adapting itself to the techniques of voluntary religion without altogether abandoning its hopes of eventual leadership.

By the second quarter of the nineteenth century, spokesmen of the major churches, when they commented on the virtues and errors of American society, tended to sound increasingly alike. None, indeed, could claim to be an indisputably authoritative voice of American religion. On many subjects, worldly and religious, a Baptist congregation in Tennessee or a Methodist circuit rider in Indiana would be sure to disagree heartily with a Princeton theologian. But the disagreement would not extend to the fundamental moral duties of a Christian society. On such basic themes, opinion was largely formed by the leading Protestant pulpits, colleges, magazines and denominational gatherings of the northeast and older west.

In its most characteristic pronouncements, American Protestantism substantially approved the church-state status quo. Dangers still existed;

[3] Ernst Troeltsch, who has brilliantly distinguished between the various strains of European Protestantism, finds that "In North America . . . it is impossible to isolate Calvinistic, Puritan, and sectarian influence." *The Social Teaching of the Christian Churches*, Olive Wyon, trans. (New York, 1931), II, 687.

infidelity and immorality might, unless Protestantism was alert, capture the state. Democracy, particularly to New England clerics, remained at best a dubious proposition. But republican government and voluntary religion were heartily endorsed. Within the limits of these basic institutions Protestantism could fight its battles, struggling to make free religion stronger and the republic more Christian.

Clerical historians described with satisfaction the development of Christian America. To them God's plan for this continent was manifest in events as early as the Reformation, which constituted, in the words of a Presbyterian patriot, "the grand means employed by God in preparing a people who should lay the foundation of a Christian empire in the New World."[4] The colonists had been led to America and sustained through various trials so that a Christian republic might be built.

The Revolution, being a difficult point, received particular emphasis. Protestant historians had to admit that infidelity, profiting by the unfortunate French alliance and by the temporary prestige of English and American infidels, had almost succeeded "in obtaining credit for all that was good in a work which it only corrupted and marred. . . ."[5] Correctly viewed, however, the Revolution and its leaders were part of the Christian tradition:

> The fathers and leaders of the American struggle for freedom—excepting Tom Paine, the English Voltaire, who, however, by his infidelity, vices, and vulgar habits soon lost all influence, and was thrust out of all decent American society—were anything but radical reformers or wild destructionists, like the heroes of the French and German revolutions. They were men of sound practical judgment, of decidedly liberal, and yet sober, conservative, and constitutional views, and of the most honorable, moral, and in some instances even decidedly religious character.[6]

The basic Christianity of the republic was exhaustively proved not only by historical argument but by analysis of existing institutions. Con-

---

[4] Robert Baird, *Religion in America* (New York, 1844), p. 32.

[5] *Ibid.*, p. 286.

[6] Philip Schaff, *America* (New York, 1855), p. 39. Another example of Protestant historiography is R. H. Tyler, *The Bible and Social Reform* (Philadelphia, 1860), which traces all modern progress and prosperity to the free use of the Bible. Horace Bushnell, the great theologian, always an enemy of anything associated with "French" liberalism, traced all real progress in history to the Christian institutions of Rome, England and America. *Society and Religion: A Sermon for California* (Hartford, 1856), pp. 13-16. Even forty years later a church historian commenting on the Revolution could lump together and condemn "the catchpenny materialist morality of Franklin, the philosophic deism of men like Jefferson, and the popular ribaldry of Tom Paine. . . ." L. W. Bacon, *A History of American Christianity* ("The American Church History Series," XIII [New York, 1897]), 230.

gress, clerical spokesmen pointed out, appointed chaplains for itself, the army and the navy, and opened its sessions with prayer. Church property was exempt from taxation. Blasphemy, polygamy, Sabbathbreaking and other profanations of Christian precepts were punishable by state laws.[7] Such measures were part of the duty of government, in return for which government was entitled to the loyal support of good Christians. Philip Schaff, the thoroughly naturalized leader of American Lutheranism, explained the American compromise to a German audience in typical terms:

For it is by no means to be thought, that the separation of church and state there is a renunciation of Christianity by the nation; like the separation of the state and the school from the church, and the civil equality of Atheism with Christianity, which some members of the abortive Frankfurt Parliament were for introducing in Germany. . . . The nation, therefore, is still Christian, though it refuses to be governed in this deepest concern of the mind and heart by the temporal power. . . .[8]

Organized Protestantism supported the dominant economic beliefs and institutions even more unanimously than it accepted the existing form of government. Whatever the casual connection between the origins of capitalism and Protestantism, both were parts of the American inheritance. Calvinist doctrines of hard work and saving, Wesleyan exhortations to get for the sake of giving, complemented and reinforced the lessons of the American environment. On the other hand, those ingredients of early European Protestantism that seemed to lead in the direction of a regulated economy had long been cast aside even in New England. By the nineteenth century western and eastern Protestants might differ among themselves about the bank and the tariff, but both took for granted the sanctity of private property, the virtue of competitive enterprise, and the legitimacy of gain. Moreover the most articulate and influential sections of American religion were intimately associated with the mercantile wealth and financial conservation of the eastern seaboard.

Support for the moral, political and economic status quo was ingrained in American Protestantism by habit and history. When religion, the family, sound government and property rights seemed to be menaced by radical forces, Protestant conservatism became explicit and militant.

[7] Schaff, *op. cit.*, pp. 91-92; Baird, *Religion in America*, pp. 116-129; M. L. Edwards, "Religious Forces in the United States, 1815-1830," *Mississippi Valley Historical Review*, V (1909-10), 434-449; Greene, *Religion and the State*, pp. 94-98; W. A. Visser 'T Hooft, *The Background of the Social Gospel in America* (Haarlem, 1928), pp. 17-23.
[8] *America*, pp. 90-91.

The first battle in which Protestantism was placed on the defensive was, of course, its struggle with the Enlightenment.[9] Associated with the most suspect elements that took part in the American Revolution, still more deeply damned by its connection with the French upheaval, religious radicalism allied itself in the new republic with the forces of leveling democracy. The climax of orthodox fright came with the election of Thomas Jefferson who, in the words of a later church writer "in conversation, and by his writings, did more than any other man that ever lived among us to propagate irreligion in the most influential part of the community."[10]

Despite Jefferson's victory at the polls, orthodoxy won the battle for the nation's soul. Popular freethought temporarily died out in the great revivals that distinguished the turn of the century. Intellectual deism, denounced from New England pulpits, found refuge only among the Unitarian minority. But the churches were placed on guard. The Presbyterian-Congregationalist conservatives particularly, associated with the defeated Federalists, clung to their belief in the depravity of the masses and waited for further manifestations of combined religious and political radicalism.

It was the second struggle between the churches and radicalism, a complex encounter that took place during the period of Jacksonian democracy, that fixed for a generation the pattern of Protestant social conservatism.

Andrew Jackson himself, though a devout Christian supported by thousands of orthodox western Presbyterians and Baptists, became a target of New England pulpit artillery. Whig clerics charged the Democratic leader with militarism, breaking faith with Indians, tolerating official immorality, and many other sins. Worse, they found in the more radical Jacksonians a disposition to deny the Christian character of the Republic and, by implication, the churches' right to moral supervision. Philip Schaff expressed the typical fear:

There is a great deal of political atheism in that country, which practically denies the divine origin of civil government altogether, and makes the sovereign people not only the medium and instrumental cause but the ultimate source of all power. And this kind of democracy is generally only a decent name for social despotism, or downright mobocracy.[11]

[9] For an accurate account of this struggle see G. A. Koch, *Republican Religion* (New York, 1933).
[10] Baird, *Religion in America*, p. 286.
[11] *America*, p. xi.

Linked with the extreme left wing of Jacksonian democracy was a revival of specifically religious radicalism. Instead of a polite, tolerant Jeffersonian deism, the new movement was militant, popular and violently anticlerical.

Open infidelity, . . . has descended to the lower ranks. It now burrows in the narrow streets, and lanes, and purlieus of our large cities and towns, where it finds its proper aliment—the ignorant and the vicious to mislead and to destroy.[12]

Small but vigorous, the newer freethought boasted all the paraphernalia of an organized faith. In its own fairly widespread press, in meetings, debates, conventions, books and pamphlets, it attacked revealed religion and "priestcraft" in vigorous and sometimes scurrilous terms.[13]

In Frances Wright, the Scottish feminist and freethinker, were concentrated all the new dangers to orthodoxy. Her interest in the Owenite socialist experiments, her militant feminism, and especially her personal audacity in daring, though a female, to harangue public meetings were enough to condemn her. If any more counts were needed, the charge of believing in free love could be plausibly supported from her writings. And like other infidels, this "High Priestess of Beelzebub" made no effort to placate her clerical enemies. Clergymen, she stoutly alleged, were soothsayers hired by the "Moneylenders" to delude the masses. Churches should be, as one in New York had been, turned into halls of science.[14]

In 1829-30, Miss Wright, together with Robert Dale Owen and other freethinking intellectuals, helped to organize the New York Workingmen's Party. A considerable number of the hungry and discontented "Workies," conscious of vigorous clerical opposition to their movement, backed the freethought panacea, an anticlerical form of state-controlled education. Others endorsed the radical agrarian proposals of George Henry Evans, who combined freethought and agrarian propaganda in his *Working Men's Advocate*.[15]

To orthodox Protestants this determined coterie represented a concerted, culminating attack on the state, the family, private property and

[12] Baird, *op. cit.*, p. 286.
[13] See Albert Post, *Popular Freethought in America, 1825-1850* (New York, 1943).
[14] See W. R. Waterman, *Frances Wright* (New York, 1924), esp. pp. 138-144, 152 ff.; J. G. Perkins and Theresa Wolfson, *Frances Wright, Free Enquirer, The Study of a Temperament* (New York, 1939), pp. 210 ff. The atmosphere of the extreme radicalism of the period is well conveyed in R. W. Leopold, *Robert Dale Owen* (Cambridge, 1941), and in A. M. Schlesinger, Jr., *The Age of Jackson* (Boston, 1946).
[15] Post, *Popular Freethought*, pp. 70, 87-88; Leopold, *Owen*, pp. 85-102.

revealed religion. Some of Protestantism's heaviest guns were immediately unlimbered in a vigorous counterattack. Lyman Beecher, the redoubtable champion of modified orthodoxy, dedicated a powerful sermon to the specific purpose of rescuing the American laboring class from evil influences. Carefully distinguishing between Christian, or American, liberty and the new "atheistic liberty," the eminent theologian called the Workingmen's Party an "infidel trumpet-call to all the envious and vicious poor."[16]

This particular enemy was overcome quickly; the freethought leaders did not long retain their hold on organized labor. But the clerical campaign against radicalism lasted on.

Another movement tarred with the freethought brush was the widespread and varied attempt to found experimental communities on communist lines. One of the earliest and most prominent of these perfectionist associations, New Harmony, was a direct product of the anathematized Owen-Wright group. New Harmony was the site of Robert Owen's "Declaration of Mental Independence" from obsolete ideas of property, revealed religion and conventional marriage.[17] Other experiments were associated with liberal German immigrants, who tended toward anticlericalism and freethought.[18]

Not all, of course, of the Utopian experimenters were freethinkers. Indeed contemporary observation and recent research agree that the communities which were founded with primarily religious motives were in general more successful than those devoted to purely secular social reform.[19] Much of the perfectionist fervor of these experimenters seems a manifestation of the persistent tendency, as old as Christianity, for

[16] Lyman Beecher, *Lectures on Political Atheism and Kindred Subjects, together with Six Lectures on Intemperance* (*Works*, I, [Boston, 1852], 91-139.

[17] Post, *Popular Freethought*, pp. 178-180.

[18] *Ibid.*, pp. 72-74, 186.

[19] This is strongly stated by the veteran community leader J. H. Noyes, who also quotes Horace Greeley and Charles A. Dana very effectively as upholding the same point. *History of American Socialism* (Philadelphia, 1870), pp. 137-139. He finds a strong connection between communist experiments and apocalyptic revivalism. *Ibid.*, p. 229. Charles Nordhoff, in *The Communistic Societies of the United States* (New York, 1875), p. 387, thinks that, while some devout and common belief is necessary for harmonious communal life, it need not be specifically religious. E. S. Bates believes that religious motives were the sustaining force and Fourierism destructive. *American Faith* (New York, 1940), pp. 359-399. T. C. Hall thinks that the religious impulse came chiefly from Continental sects, since the American "dissenting" tradition is individualistic—a theory which seems to underrate the role of Unitarianism and Universalism. *The Religious Background of American Culture* (Boston, 1930), pp. 252-253.

radical religious sects to withdraw from the world and live a saintly life in common.[20]

Come-outer sects, however, have always been disliked by organized churches, well-adjusted to contemporary mores. Backers of the communities included all the least popular types of radical religion, from the Shakers to the small German and Swedish sects of "primitive Christians." Swedenborgianism was combined with Fourierism in the beliefs of Henry James the elder.[21] Universalism gave the communist movements one of their more successful leaders, Adin Ballou. Horace Greeley, who acted as a powerful publicist for the Fourierist movement, was also a Universalist.[22] The radical wing of Unitarianism contributed not only Brook Farm, but also one of the most stirring propagandists for Christian communism, William Henry Channing. Pleading for communities based on joint-stock ownership, co-operative labor, and a "Combined Dwelling," he called on the church in language typical of perfectionist sect spirit to "shake off at once her drowsy dislike of agitation, her prim decorum, her timid, non-committalism, her politic prudence, all forms of half-wayness, and, with decisive singleness of purpose, consecrate her energies to the labors of this transition-age."[23] Such appeals, coming from sects which were regarded by many orthodox Protestants as halfway houses to infidelity, naturally got little response.

The religious note was often struck by colonizers even when their experiments fell, as most of them eventually did, under the influence of Fourierism, the "foreign" and "atheistic" belief so often denounced by the pious. The National Convention of Associationists, an organization formed under Fourierist auspices, used religious ceremonial and language that reminds one of later Christian socialism:

An important branch of the divine mission of our Saviour Jesus Christ, was to establish the Kingdom of Heaven on earth. . . . Divine truths must be translated into actual life . . . . let the church adopt a truly associative organization, and the blessings so long promised it will be fulfilled.[24]

[20] As an example of religious fervor, demanding a complete change in society, see Adin Ballou's *Practical Christian Socialism* (Hopedale, 1854), a mixture of eccentricity and religious-social doctrines that has much in common with the work of later religious radicals such as Jesse H. Jones.

[21] See James, "Socialism and Civilization," in *Moralism and Christianity* (New York, 1850), pp. 39-94. According to E. S. Bates, a "considerable number" of Swedenborgians had similar interests. *American Faith*, 420.

[22] Long after his Fourierist activities were over, Greeley still believed that a "Christian Social Order" was possible. *Recollections of a Busy Life* (New York, 1868), p. 506.

[23] W. H. Channing, *The Christian Church and Social Reform* (pamphlet, Boston, 1848), p. 28.

[24] Quoted in Noyes, *American Socialism*, p. 219.

One Fourierist minister, writing in 1845, elaborately proved that Fourierism is not only compatible with Christianity, but practically necessary to it. Pointing out that existing social conditions debase men to the level of beasts, he damned the major churches for their hypocrisy in picturesque and violent language.[25]

Adherents of the major denominations were further alienated by the fact that some prominent associationists were renegades from orthodoxy. John Henry Noyes, notorious for his unorthodox theories of marriage, was originally drawn to a career of reform by Charles G. Finney's revivals. But he soon broke completely with this orthodox background. A writer in a Presbyterian periodical of 1870 laments:

As fellow-students in the same theological seminary, we were in frequent contact, and had much animated discussion over the first beginning and original genesis of the ultraisms which at last flowered out into that system of sanctimonious license.[26]

Dr. William Keil, founder of communistic communities in Missouri and Oregon, had successively abandoned the Lutheran and Methodist faiths.[27]

These brave little experiments offered a fundamental challenge to the economic and political institutions wholeheartedly accepted by Evangelical Protestantism. Sometimes they openly opposed prevailing conventions of property, marriage and family life; occasionally, in the true sect spirit, they proclaimed their contempt for worldly churches. It is small wonder that spokesmen of the major denominations condemned them wholeheartedly.

Not only communistic experiments, but socialism in general were recurrent targets for pulpit and tract criticism. Robert Baird, typifying clerical opinion on this as on other subjects, condemned "Owenism" and "Socialism" as "economic or political schemes, in which infidelity seeks to embody and sustain itself."[28] John W. Mears, a Presbyterian minister, contrasted Christianity, the true friend of the workingman with socialism, his false friend and actual enemy.[29]

A particular group of progressives specifically attacked by evangelical leaders were the refugees from the defeated European revolutions of 1848. Philip Schaff expressed a common attitude:

[25] H. H. Van Amringe, *Association and Christianity* (pamphlet, Pittsburg, 1845).
[26] *Biblical Repertory and Princeton Review*, XLII (1870), 329.
[27] R. J. Hendricks, *Bethel and Aurora* (New York, 1933), p. 3.
[28] Baird, *Religion in America*, pp. 286-287.
[29] John W. Mears, *The Bible in the Workshop; or, Christianity the Friend of Labor* (New York, 1857), pp. 331-334.

. . . the modern European heroes of liberty, or rather of licentiousness—too many of whom have unfortunately been set adrift upon us by the abortive revolution of 1848—become mightily undeceived in America, and begin at once, in beer-houses and infidel journals, to scoff at the intolerable tedium of the Jewish Sabbath, the pharisaical church-going, the tyrannical priestcraft, and whatever else they may call the pious habits and institutions of the United States.[30]

In the thirty years before the Civil War religious opinion, not without provocation, lumped together religious and social radicalism. Under its blanket condemnation fell left-wing Jacksonian democracy, the infant labor movement, experimental communism and other forms of socialism. Inevitably this antiradical alignment permanently strengthened the already strong conservatism of the churches.

For purposes of contrast with unsound radical doctrines, defenders of orthodoxy could call on an authoritative and well-knit body of conservative argument, derived from the highest academic quarters.[31] Collegiate education in America before the Civil War remained largely under the control not only of organized religion but of the most conservative sects. The oldest, most influential and most numerous colleges were those founded by Congregationalists and Presbyterians in New England, and, as a part of the struggle for the western soul, in the northwest.[32] Except for Harvard's Unitarian apostasy, denominational colleges had been strongholds of orthodoxy since the seventeenth century. Under the formidable leadership of President Dwight of Yale, they had participated in the counterattack against Jeffersonian deism. Not without hard-fought skirmishes, they had preserved the tradition of the endowed, denominational college against the Jeffersonian ideal of state-supported democratic education.[33] Partly in self-defense, partly from

[30] Schaff, *America*, p. 41.

[31] The clerical economists of this period have been thoroughly investigated by Joseph Dorfman, *The Economic Mind in American Civilization, 1606-1865* (New York, 1946), II, 512-835; and are still more exhaustively treated by Michael J. L. O'Connor, *Origins of Academic Economics in the United States* (New York, 1944). The treatment in the following pages owes much to these two accounts.

[32] Of 288 pre-Civil War college presidents, 262 were ordained ministers. Of these 156 were drawn from "Calvinist Protestantism in the narrower sense of the word," 30 were Baptists and 28 Methodists. G. P. Schmidt, *The Old Time College President* (New York, 1930), pp. 184-186. Davis lists colleges in existence in 1850 by denomination as follows: Baptist, 13; Episcopal, 10; Methodist, 13; Roman Catholic, 13; Congregational and Presbyterian, 71. Emerson Davis, *The Half Century* (Boston, 1851), p. 75.

[33] O'Connor treats the Dartmouth College Case of 1819 as the victorious culmination of this defense. *Origins*, p. 71.

earnest devotion to inherited patterns of thought, the colleges had long mixed conservative political and economic precepts with their religious and moral indoctrination. In the first quarter of the nineteenth century such principles were imbedded in the senior courses in moral philosophy. These culminating courses, often taught by the venerable white-bearded presidents themselves, instructed a generation of students in the sanctity of private property, checks and balances, limited suffrage and (as yet) free trade.[34]

Confronted by the increasing militancy and popularity of radical doctrine in the Jacksonian years, college administrations, like other bulwarks of orthodox Protestantism, found it necessary to develop a more systematic, up-to-date defense. Relying on Whig businessmen for moral and financial assistance, the colleges needed a subject which would appeal by its practical soundness to these new allies. To meet these needs they turned toward the rising science of political economy.

Although some of the doctrines of Adam Smith and his followers had long been included in clerical summaries of knowledge, the English school did not fully satisfy the needs of American colleges. Smith himself was associated with eighteenth-century anticlerical liberalism. His classification of ministers among unproductive workers was particularly resented. Moreover, such gloomy tenets as Ricardian rent theory and Malthusian population doctrine hardly squared with the American tradition of unlimited free land and insufficient population.

Part of the necessary revision of classical doctrines was accomplished in Britain. During the first quarter of the century, a number of British religious leaders and philanthropists became deeply convinced of the necessity of teaching correct notions of political economy to England's discontented industrial workers, hitherto left unacquainted with such new and suspect subjects. For this urgent task, it was necessary to purge the Gloomy Science of any radical associations and to combine it with approved religious and moral principles. The manuals produced in this process were considerably better adapted to American collegiate needs than the great originals.

Political economy became further cleansed by its association with the Scottish moral philosophy of the late eighteenth and early nineteenth century, especially with the teachings of Dugald Stewart, Smith's principal British popularizer.[35] The Scottish thinkers, defending religious

[34] See Schmidt, *Old Time College President*, pp. 127-135.

[35] For a discussion of the Scottish philosophers and their popularity in American colleges, see Woodbridge Riley, *American Thought from Puritanism to Pragmatism and Beyond* (New York, 1923), pp. 118-139.

and moral orthodoxy against Berkeleian idealism, Lockian materialistic psychology, deism and other heresies, expounded a simple acceptance of a series of common-sense postulates. These first principles, apprehended by self-conscious observation instead of mere sense reaction, always coincided with traditional cosmology and morality and with revealed religion. This "Scottish realism," increasingly accepted in American colleges by the 1820's, affected the teaching of political economy in two ways. First, by its reconciliation of natural and revealed religion it furthered orthodox acceptance of the propriety of spreading secular knowledge. Second, scholars nurtured in a philosophy which assumed its own "common-sense" postulates found it easy to assume further doctrines such as the wage-fund theory, a proposition which appealed to them by its obviousness, its easy deduction from common knowledge, and its tendency to promote social order, even though the leaders of European economic thought had already found it untrue.

From a combination of the original classical political economy, British and Scottish conservative adaptations, and their own need to combat Jacksonian radicalism, American scholars worked out a school of political economy which might well be labeled clerical laissez faire. For at least a generation and in many institutions far longer, this body of doctrine dominated American economic teaching.

The laws of political economy, as taught in the clerical texts, were not only compatible with natural religion, they were almost a part of it. The Reverend John McVickar of Columbia stated his basic postulate as follows: "That science and religion eventually teach the same lesson, is a necessary consequence of the unity of truth, but it is seldom that this union is so satisfactorily displayed as in the researches of Political Economy."[36] Henry Vethake of the University of Pennsylvania was unusual in that he was not an ordained minister, but his approach was equally pious: ". . . no branch of human knowledge exhibits to us more beautiful illustrations of the consistence of all truth, and of that unity of design which pervades the various provinces of creation."[37] Since God had clearly established the laws which governed economic life, it followed that these laws must not be tampered with. Francis Wayland, president of Brown and author of the most popular American text, stated this obvious deduction in semitheological terms:

[36] John McVickar, *Outlines of Political Economy* (New York, 1825), p. 69. This text is a revised version of the article on "Political Economy" in the Edinburgh Supplement to the *Encyclopedia Britannica* by J. B. McCulloch, an adherent of the revised classicism of the Scottish school. The quotation, however, is from a footnote by McVickar.

[37] Henry Vethake, *Principles of Political Economy* (Philadelphia, 1838), p. 15.

If God have made labor necessary to our well being, in our present state; if he have set before us sufficient rewards to stimulate us to labor; and if he have attached to idleness correspondent punishments, it is manifest that the intention of this constitution will not be accomplished, unless both of these classes of motives are allowed to operate upon man.[38]

From this simple proposition Wayland deduced the whole platform of the New England mercantile interest. In his logical pages it is made clear that the Divine plan demands that all property must be divided and none held in common, that no charity must be given to any but the afflicted, and that the government has no right to levy protective tariffs, alter the value of specie, or "oppress" banks.

The immutable laws propounded by these authors are nowhere more certain in their operation than in the realm of wages and labor problems. One and all, the clerical economists took over from the earlier English classics the doctrine that wages are paid from a fixed wage-fund whose amount cannot be altered by labor action. Alonzo Potter, later Episcopal bishop of Pennsylvania, writing in 1840 in response to the labor disturbances of the depression of 1837, made a particularly rigid exposition of this axiom. Trade-unions, according to Potter, were bound to injure the interests of their own members because they disregarded the laws of nature "which are nothing less than laws of God."[39] The interests of labor and capital, particularly in this country, were demonstrated by the clerical economists to be always inseparable. (This was to be the chief stock argument of opponents of trade-unionism for more than a century.) Trade-union action, they declared, if it "artificially" raises wages, simply cripples the capitalists who provide employment, or at best lessens the wage-fund and throws employees out of work.

Vethake and Potter, who wrote in a time of depression and discontent, did not confine themselves to calm demonstrations of the futility of labor organizations; they denounced them as a positive evil. Vethake, for instance, considered it unnecessary to argue the point: "No one will deny that the existence in a community of all combinations of the nature of the trades' unions is an evil of no little magnitude...."[40] Clearly anticipating the staple antiunion arguments of the later part of the century, Potter charged that unions were given to secrecy, that they

[38] Francis Wayland, *The Elements of Political Economy* (4th ed.; Boston, 1852), p. 118.

[39] Alonzo Potter, *Political Economy* (New York, 1840), p. 282. This text is partly a revision of G. P. Scrope's British text, but the supplementary chapter on labor, to which the citations on these pages refer, is entirely Potter's own. The authorship of various chapters is established by O'Connor, *Origins*, pp. 204-213.

[40] *Principles*, p. 326.

tended toward class antagonism, and that their leaders were often foreign and atheistic. They invaded the rights of employers, farmers, and especially of nonunion workingmen. In the United States their activities were always unnecessary and in time of depression disastrous. They forgot the highest interests of their members, courting disaster by working for their intellectual and physical well-being only.[41] In lurid terms Potter described the debasing activities of these organizations: "They congregate workmen night after night in tumultuous assemblies, where their passions are inflamed and their principles poisoned."[42]

Other forms of radical innovation shared the clerical ban. Vethake assured his readers that a ten-hour law would give the working population more time for vice and dissipation.[43] Potter condemned all experiments in common property holding, singling out the political and religious theories of Robert Owen for particular rebuke.[44] At times, like other conservatives of his day, this formidable champion of property rights tended to deprecate democratic government itself:

Of the disadvantages incident to a popular government, perhaps the most serious is that untiring spirit of change which is apt to possess the people, and which involves in uncertainty all investments of capital, and almost every description of industry.[45]

These simple dogmatists of the thirties and forties set the tone of American political economy for many years to come. Wayland's text alone reached a circulation of fifty thousand by 1867 and continued to be reprinted with slight revision until 1875.[46] Small wonder that those who drew their whole stock of economic theory from these authorities were certain that the laws of political economy were as fixed and known as any other canons of natural religion. Efforts to tamper with these laws, it was clear, were both impious and unwise.

The clerical proponents of laissez faire did not, indeed, secure a complete monopoly of American economic teaching. Protectionism, though less popular in academic circles than free trade, had powerful backing among the growing manufacturing interests. However, protectionist economists, themselves often clergymen, did not dissent from their free-

[41] Potter, *Political Economy*, pp. 259-281.
[42] *Ibid.*, p. 299.
[43] Vethake, *Principles*, pp. 332-335.
[44] Potter, *Political Economy*, pp. 244-251, 263.
[45] *Ibid.*, p. 241.
[46] Gladys Bryson, "The Emergence of the Social Sciences from Moral Philosophy," *International Journal of Ethics*, XLII (1931-1932), 311; O'Connor, *Origins*, p. 324.

trade colleagues in their general views of economic science.[47] Calvin Colton, the Presbyterian mainstay of Whig protectionism, shared to the full the prevailing dogmas regarding labor and capital.[48] Francis Bowen, Harvard's Unitarian philosopher and economist, denounced free trade but defended the rest of the current theory in the most rigorous terms: ". . . the sight of the two extremes of opulence and poverty,—the hope of rising to the one and the fear of falling into the other,—is the constant stimulus which keeps up that energy and activity of the human race. . . ."[49]

A somewhat deeper disagreement with the dominant clerical laissez faire stemmed from the teachings of Henry C. Carey, whose protectionist social science influenced an important minority of Protestant opinion both before and after the Civil War.[50] Influenced by the ideas of Alexander Hamilton and Friedrich List, and doubtless by the sentiments of the prosperous Philadelphia circle in which he lived, Carey was suddenly converted from free trade to protectionism in 1844. In his crowning work, *Principles of Social Science,* he made use of a ponderous apparatus of universal history, science and pseudo-science that was clearly influenced by both Comte and Fourier.

As became a contributor to the Comtian tradition, Carey denounced the classical economists for their overnarrow concern with one part of knowledge and for their pessimistic conclusions. The Deity, said this humane sociologist, could not possibly have intended any such laws as those promulgated by Malthus and Ricardo. The "great Architect of the universe was no blunderer such as modern political economy would make him."[51] Full of optimistic Americanism, Carey refused to allow for the New World, especially, the inevitable miseries decreed by economists of the Old.

Yet Carey had more in common with the classical advocates of laissez faire than a first glance would indicate. Like theirs, his method was fundamentally one of a priori dogmatism. The question for all science to ask was, he said, "what in a word, are the laws instituted by the Creator for the government of matter."[52] Carey showed even greater con-

[47] Potter himself, without deviating from his antiunion views, developed leanings toward protectionism after his first book. Dorfman, *Economic Mind,* II, 832.

[48] Calvin Colton, *Public Economy for the United States* (New York, 1848), pp. 319-321.

[49] Francis Bowen, *The Principles of Political Economy* (Boston, 1856), p. 499.

[50] Illuminating treatments of Carey are found in Dorfman, *op. cit.,* II, 789-805; and in L. L. and Jessie Bernard, *Origins of American Sociology* (New York, 1943), pp. 398-433, 689-702.

[51] Carey, *Principles of Social Science* (Philadelphia, 1858-9), I, 232.

[52] *Ibid.,* I, 11.

fidence than the free traders in his own ability to expound the Divine
plan, since his fundamental laws applied to all physical and social
science.

Obviously Carey made no complete break with the dominant teachings. With a slightly altered variant of the wage-fund theory he demonstrated that increasing profit is to the interest of labor. He opposed poor
laws or factory acts.[53] Making use of the ancient biological analogy, he
allowed the government, as the seat of intelligence in the body politic,
to intervene only "in that sphere of life which is nearest its central movements," leaving the rest to laissez faire.[54] The universal principle of
Association, a postulate which Carey shared with Fourier, led to little
but an unqualified endorsement of corporations, a protective tariff, and
the Bank of the United States.[55]

The first economist to put Carey's principles in a form which attracted wide clerical attention was Carey's friend and disciple, Stephen
Colwell, the Presbyterian industrialist and economist. Preaching substantially the same economic doctrines as Carey, Colwell, instead of
promulgating a new social science, put his argument in the then startling
form of an attack on the social teachings of American Protestantism.

Colwell, like other earlier and later critics of organized Christianity,
charged that the churches were neglecting to teach Christ's commandments regarding charity and brotherly love. He attacked the sins of existing society—its hardness, its fierce competition, the sanctity of property
but not of labor, the treatment of labor as a commodity, etc. The conventional political economy, Colwell declared, was merely an apology
for this state of things. Worse still, all contemporary churches, instead
of leading movements for the reform of these evils, were absorbed in
ritual and theology. They defended the un-Christian social order because
they thought that they profited by it.[56]

Colwell was surprisingly tolerant in his discussion of socialists and
other social reformers, though he left no doubt that they were wrong.

[53] See Dorfman, *Economic Mind*, II, 791-793.

[54] *Principles*, III, 105.

[55] *Ibid.*, II, 285-286, 441, 443; Dorfman, *op. cit.*, II, 789-805.

[56] *New Themes for the Protestant Clergy; Creeds without Charity; Theology without Humanity; and Protestantism without Christianity* (2nd ed.; Philadelphia, 1852),
passim. This element in Colwell's work has led students of the Social Gospel to depict
him as a direct forerunner of this late-nineteenth-century school of religious thought.
See James Dombrowski, *The Early Days of Christian Socialism in America* (New
York, 1936), pp. 31-34; C. H. Hopkins, *The Rise of the Social Gospel in American
Protestantism, 1865-1915* (New Haven, 1940), p. 6. While it is clear that Colwell
anticipates many later criticisms of conservative Christianity, this estimate needs to
be qualified by an examination of Colwell's role as a fundamentally conservative
high-tariff economist.

Radicals should, he urged, be met by churchmen not with derision and contempt but with patient friendly counsel, showing them that "in Christianity they can find the only hope of a better system of society, and the only solution of social problems."[57]

Colwell, like Carey, offered few concrete proposals for social change. Primarily, like many religious critics of society, he pled for individual, Christian regeneration as a solution for social problems and a substitute for other methods of social change. Like Carey, this Pennsylvania economist and manufacturer confined his proposals for social action to an endorsement of the tariff, which would in his view at once lighten the burden borne by labor and bring about general prosperity.[58]

It was evidently the general tone of Colwell's work and his denunciation of the churches, rather than any very radical economic doctrine, that caused the outbreak of a minor storm of controversy over his *New Themes*. Samuel Austen Allibone, a Philadelphia banker, made the sweeping charges that Colwell was an infidel and a socialist.[59] Colwell answered with another book restating and slightly toning down his earlier statements and cited, in an appendix, a number of favorable notices by eminent churchmen and religious periodicals.[60] William Henry Ruffner, a Presbyterian minister of Philadelphia, took a moderate position, denying the charge that Colwell was infidel but insisting on moderating the harshest part of Colwell's attack on the churches.[61] The controversy closed with an extremely vitriolic rebuttal by Allibone against Colwell and his apologists. The outraged author refused to believe that Ruffner, who wrote anonymously, was a clergyman "on the same ground that he should demand proof, of a forger, or burglar, who declared himself to be of some good family of our acquaintance."[62] Ruffner supplied thirty strongly hostile opinions from religious sources.

---

[57] *New Themes*, p. 221. See also pp. 359-364.

[58] This is the principal subject of Colwell's purely economic works, which are discussed by Dorfman, *Economic Mind*, II, 789-805 and Bernard, *American Sociology*, pp. 434-442.

[59] In *A Review by a Layman of a work Entitled "New Themes, etc."* (Philadelphia, 1852). Allibone's tracts, as well as Ruffner's, cited below, were published anonymously.

[60] Stephen Colwell, *Christianity for American Christians* (Philadelphia, 1852). It should be noted that some of the commendatory quotations are distinctly qualified and others suspiciously short. Colwell further restated this defense in his *Position of Christianity in the United States* (Philadelphia, 1853) and his preface to William Arnot's *The Race for Riches* (Philadelphia, 1853).

[61] *Charity and the Clergy; Being a Review by a Protestant Clergyman, of the 'New Themes' Controversy* (Philadelphia, 1853).

[62] *New Themes Condemned; or Thirty Opinions upon 'New Themes,' and its 'Reviewers'* (Philadelphia, 1853), pp. 152-153.

The violence of this controversy over a statement of essentially conservative economic opinion demonstrates the extreme novelty in Colwell's
day of such a departure from prevalent doctrine by a prominent lay
member of a major church. Colwell's pious protectionism was no
novelty, but his tolerant words for socialists and his denunciation of
church indifference were startling departures for a Presbyterian manufacturer of the 1850's.

An ostensibly far less radical departure from the classical norm, but
one which actually proved capable of more constructive development,
was contained in the prewar work of John Bascom. Bascom, trained in
both theology and law, was the pattern of a mid-nineteenth-century authority on human and divine affairs. His religious orthodoxy, his vigorous, oratorical style, and his successive presidency of Williams and
Wisconsin assured him of a respectful audience among organized Christians.

In the prewar period Bascom was still expounding the classical
economic dogmas in a manner reminiscent of Wayland: "The fewness
of its forces and the steadiness of their action, place the theories of
Political Economy on a footing well-nigh as safe as those of mechanical
powers."[63] Yet even in 1859 Bascom qualified his acceptance of the law
of human selfishness. This familiar force was, indeed, sufficient for the
present, "the lowest social state." To Bascom, however, the inevitable
operations of this motive would themselves raise men to a higher level,
and thus selfishness itself would automatically be displaced by higher
motives.[64] Bascom was to spend the next forty years elaborating and
altering his elaborate synthesis of the forces of selfish individualism and
Christian love. It was unusual in 1859 to feel any contradiction between
these two forces or to suggest that one of them might replace the other.

Even after political economy, branching out from moral philosophy,
became a separate study, its traditional doctrines affected the teaching
of ethics in American colleges. Wayland's very popular ethical textbook,
like his work on economics, gave Divine and moral sanction to the
rights of property and narrowly limited the rights of society. His moral
teachings included such concrete matters as a demonstration that debtors
do not become morally free of debt by passing through bankruptcy and
a statement of the impropriety of fixing rates of interest by law.[65] Joseph
Haven, in a similar ethics text first published in 1859, contrasted the

[63] John Bascom, *Political Economy* (Andover, 1859), p. 11.
[64] *Ibid.*, p. 136.
[65] Francis Wayland, *Elements of Moral Science* (5th ed.; Boston, 1841), pp. 257-
258, 246.

moral advantages of individual ownership with the evils of common property.[66]

The economic doctrines taught by clerical professors constituted part of a general view of a world regulated by Divine Law, much of it codified and easily comprehensible. It was natural, therefore, that these principles occasionally found their way out of the classroom into the pulpit. Sermons on the correct principles of political economy served to supplement direct attacks on social and religious radicalism.

Jonathan Wainwright, the Rector of Boston's Trinity Church, preaching an election sermon in 1835, chose the favorite text proclaiming that "The poor shall never cease out of the land."[67] Wainwright proved the necessity of inequality by a typical combination of theology and political economy, including among authorities cited Dr. Chalmers, the great Scottish preacher, and Professor McVickar. Some amelioration of social conditions was, he said, to be expected, but this would be accomplished through Divine methods and in God's own good time. Equalitarian schemes, communistic communities, agrarian proposals for tax reforms were all condemned in this typical sermon. Labor combinations might be permissible but must beware of irresponsibility. Misguided charity was an evil especially to be feared. If only the people of this country were well instructed in "sound principles of political economy" Wainwright assured his congregation, no danger could arise "from the false but plausible maxims of those who talk so loudly about equalizing the condition of man."[68]

Twenty years later William D. Haley, a Congregational pastor of Alton, Illinois, delivered a similar economic homily in a series of lectures addressed specifically to workingmen. Like many others he emphasized the community of interest between capital and labor and the Divine ordination of differences in wealth. Urging saving and temperance as the true way to improve one's station, Haley added the more original theory that if savings banks sometimes failed, it was the fault of the depositors for lacking sufficient confidence. Haley's words on interest demonstrate how far Protestantism had departed from the forgotten teachings of medieval Christendom.

The man who hoards his thousand dollars, or his one or two hundreds, who is afraid to place it in bank, and so over-conscientious that he will not take

[66] Joseph Haven, *Moral Philosophy* (New York, 1880), pp. 149-154.
[67] Jonathan M. Wainwright, *Inequality of Individual Wealth the Ordinance of Providence, and Essential to Civilization* (pamphlet, Boston, 1835).
[68] *Ibid.*, p. 47.

interest for it, is a greater injury to society than he who obtains an unusual interest for his capital; and he deserves to lose it.[69]

Prewar Protestantism, in its combat with social heresy, did not limit itself to theoretical argument. A network of militant organizations was also part of the clerical counteroffensive. The interdenominational organizations formed in the 1820's were not, indeed, originally concerned with political or economic problems, but rather with evangelical causes. They arose out of the spirit of reformed orthodoxy, accepting the theological changes which made missionary work compatible with Calvinism but rejecting other doctrinal and moral departures from the ways of the fathers. Deism, tippling, frontier ignorance, Sabbathbreaking and Unitarianism were all among the original enemies of this Protestant united front.[70]

The spark that actually touched off this explosion of religious militancy was the revival of the mid-twenties, led by Charles Grandison Finney.[71] Ordinarily, the recurrent revivalism which is so striking a feature of American religious history leads its followers away from organized movements and toward a personal search for salvation. Finney, however, held a special position in the great argument over the nature of a revival experience. To him a mystical conviction of salvation was to be understood as a fit beginning for religious effort, rather than as a mere assurance of election, passively received.[72] It was, according to Finney, proof of a "seared conscience" when one was apathetic to questions concerning one's own well-being or that of others. Such questions included "abolition of slavery, temperance, moral reform, politics, business principles, physiological and dietetic reform," etc.[73]

Full of revivalist zeal, Congregationalists and Presbyterians set up a network of societies, labeled by a historian "The Benevolent Empire."[74] Funds were provided by pious and wealthy merchants like the Tappan brothers. Nonparticipating churches were spurred by example to set up parallel organizations.[75] Ministers and laymen of all the principal Prot-

[69] William D. Haley, *Words for the Workers* (Boston, 1855), p. 38.

[70] See D. R. Fox, "The Protestant Counter-Reformation in America," *New York History*, XVI (1935), 19-35. This article treats the organizations primarily as a reaction to Unitarian gains.

[71] G. H. Barnes, *The Antislavery Impulse, 1838-1844* (New York, 1930), pp. 11-12, traces the connection between Finney's revivals and these organizations, as does W. W. Sweet, *The Story of Religions in America* (New York, 1930), pp. 410-411.

[72] Barnes, *op. cit.*, p. 11.

[73] *Oberlin Evangelist*, III, 65-66, quoted in C. F. Wright, *Charles Grandison Finney* (Boston, 1891), p. 171.

[74] See Barnes, *Antislavery Impulse*, pp. 17-28.

[75] A. I. Abell, "The Impact of the City on American Protestantism, 1850-1900" (MS thesis, Harvard, 1938), p. 28 ff.

estant churches spent large sums and considerable co-ordinated effort in promoting foreign and home missions, Bible and tract distribution, Sabbatarianism, and the spiritual rescue of sailors and prostitutes. Hand in hand with these evangelical movements went active work for temperance.[76]

This outbreak of reform has sometimes been seen as part of the humanitarian urge of early nineteenth-century liberalism. Actually, it was in many ways an expression of religious conservatism. Finney himself had set significant limits to his endorsement of worldly movements. All such impulses must, he insisted, be accompanied by the all-important experience of regeneration. Finney denounced young ministers who devoted themselves exclusively to any particular social issue which, while worthy in itself, distracted them from fundamental religious questions. Abolitionism, for instance, could be "infidel" if its spirit was wrong.[77] Like a true child of New England orthodoxy, Finney rejected the whole structure of social doctrine based on natural rights and suggested that the church, by insisting on high moral standards, could regulate both the commerce and the politics of the world.[78] This doctrine was alien to the spirit of contemporary liberal humanitarianism, and of course anathema to the anticlerical radicals.

Like earlier denominational enterprises, the interdenominational movements which stemmed partly from Finney's teachings continued untainted by any liberal notions of the perfectibility of man. They were rather concerned to save sinful humans from irreligion and from a few of the most pernicious moral errors into which they might be tempted. These allied evangelical endeavors offended the extremely conservative Calvinists who objected, on theological grounds, to any extra-church organizations or any holding out of hope to the nonelect. But they seemed to most Protestants to involve no break with American religious tradition. Certainly they implied no departure whatever from the prevalent clerical defense of the basic economic and social status quo.

Toward purely humanitarian endeavor, the Benevolent Empire offered the somewhat gingerly co-operation implied in Finney's precepts.[79] Individuals prominent in the great evangelistic societies were also to be found among the backers of some of the humanitarian move-

---

[76] See J. A. Krout, *The Origins of Prohibition* (New York, 1925), pp. 113, 300-301.

[77] Wright, *op. cit.*, pp. 152-153; C. G. Finney, *Sermons on Gospel Themes* (Oberlin, 1876), pp. 347-362.

[78] *Gospel Themes*, pp. 143, 382.

[79] Samuel Gridley Howe, for instance, was able to get the co-operation of the American Bible Society in his effort to put the Bible within the reach of the blind, though many orthodox ministers distrusted him for his religious liberalism. S. G. Howe, *Letters and Journals*, Laura E. Richards, ed. (Boston, 1909), II, 28.

ments of the day. It is significant, however, that antislavery, involving as it did a radical challenge to property institutions, received no cordial response from the moral reformers. Arthur Tappan, the leading financial supporter of the early antislavery movement as well as of the Benevolent Empire was deeply grieved to find that the latter refused to recognize the former:

> Notwithstanding the reiterated entreaties and remonstrances of those Christian abolitionists, who had been among the original founders and long-tried friends of these [evangelistic] societies, these institutions remained dumb and paralyzed before the American Moloch![80]

The American Board of Commissioners for Foreign Missions, the American Home Missionary Society, the American Bible Society, the American Tract Society—all these refused to have anything to do with antislavery until some of them were actually split by withdrawal of the antislavery minority.[81] Temperance reformers, similarly, could be thoroughly annoyed by attempts to link them with antislavery.[82]

To Fanny Wright and her hard-pressed cohorts, and indeed to many radical Jacksonian Democrats, the development of large, co-ordinated evangelistic organizations seemed by no means a manifestation of humane reform. Rather it seemed the climax of a priestly plot to throttle progress and freedom.[83] Although the Benevolent Empire was not the sinister conspiracy it appeared to them, and although its original purposes had been nonpolitical, it was quite ready to accept a challenge from freethinkers and "Jacobins." Inevitably, the organized forces of evangelical reforms, like many individual ministers, were drawn into the battle with social radicalism.

Both sides were in earnest. Home Missionary organizations saw it as their duty to rescue the nation, and particularly the West, from social and religious vagaries.[84] Freethinking societies in turn tried to counter

[80] Lewis Tappan, *The Life of Arthur Tappan* (New York, 1870), pp. 328-329.

[81] *Ibid.*, pp. 322-337; *The American Home Missionary Society and Slavery* (pamphlet, anon., 1859); R. V. Harlow, *Gerrit Smith, Philanthropist and Reformer* (New York, 1939). An examination of the tracts published by the American Tract Society (12 vols., New York, 18—?), fails to show any mention of problems other than those of infidelity, need for conversion, and vice. For a brief account of the divisions in the great mission and tract organizations, see A. C. Cole, *The Irrepressible Conflict, 1850-1865* ("A History of American Life," VII [New York, 1934]), 257.

[82] Krout, *Origins*, pp. 176-177.

[83] See A. M. Schlesinger, Jr., *Jackson*, pp. 150-160.

[84] R. L. Power, "A Crusade to Extend Yankee Culture, 1820-1865," *New England Quarterly*, XIII (1940), 638-653. The Home Missionaries appealed, for instance, to businessmen to make their investments safe by promoting Christianity, and hence financial conservatism, in the west. *Ibid.*, p. 642. See also C. B. Goodykoontz, *Home Missionaries on the American Frontier* (Caldwell, Idaho, 1938), pp. 425-426.

the offensives of the American Tract Society and the American Bible Society. The controversy moved into the field of national politics when Ezra Stiles Ely, in a Fourth-of-July sermon for 1827, called on members of the great denominations to unite their efforts and elect only believers.[85] To freethinkers and other radicals, this proposal of a "Christian Party in Politics" seemed to constitute the natural and horrifying climax of the machinations of reform organizations. To the evangelical reformers, on the other hand, radical resentment of their political efforts seemed additional proof of a conspiracy against all religion.[86]

The climax came in 1829-30 when the Sabbatarians, anticipating the tactics of later pressure groups, organized a campaign to end Sunday mail service.[87] The radical press raged as letters from ministers and laymen flooded Congress. The proposed reform was rejected in a strongly-worded anticlerical report by a Senate committee headed by Colonel Richard M. Johnson, thenceforth a hero of anticlericalism. For many years, this defeat rankled among the believers in conventional religious reform. A pious historian writing in 1850 denounced the report

. . . respecting which it has been said, "Satan never accomplished a greater temporary victory over the Sabbath, through any agency, in any country, than was accomplished by this report, if we except the abolition of the Sabbath in France, during the reign of infidelity."[88]

If either side won a victory in this warfare it was the organized defenders of orthodoxy. By 1850, militant freethought and many other forms of radicalism were on the decline. Some of the component organizations of the Benevolent Empire, however, had also weakened or even perished, victims of internal conflict over theology or slavery.[89] But these first large-scale clerical pressure groups left several important legacies. In them ministers and laymen first became thoroughly conscious of the power of organized religion in the framework of democratic politics. For some time religious reform activities followed much the same pattern as that set by these first interdenominational movements. Conservative social doctrine, and especially suspicion of organized labor, long remained part of this pattern.

[85] Post, *Popular Freethought*, pp. 122-131, 213; Schlesinger, *op. cit.*, p. 137.
[86] Lyman Beecher, for instance, denounced infidel pretenses that Bible societies, Sunday-school and tract organizations, etc., were part of a conspiracy to unite church and state. *Political Atheism*, pp. 127 ff.
[87] This incident is described in some detail in A. M. Schlesinger, Jr., *op. cit.*, pp. 137-140.
[88] Davis, *The Half Century*, p. 185. This book, filled with praises of the activities of the Benevolent Empire, may be taken as a sample of the orthodox point of view.
[89] See Barnes, *Antislavery Impulse*, pp. 162-163.

PROTESTANTISM AND REFORM

AS THE great theorists of religious history have made clear, the world-reforming impulse inherent in Christianity seldom dies out completely even in periods of church conservatism. Outside the orthodox fold, America in the pre-Civil War decades was filled with humanitarian enthusiasm. Naturally, many devout Protestants and even many ministers were stirred by this tide. Not all were confined within the narrow limits of specifically Protestant reform.

Some forms of the humanitarian impulse were, as we have seen, associated with "Jacobin" and anticlerical ideas and thus closed to the devout. However, a middle ground existed between radicalism and the Benevolent Empire. A group of reform movements, not controlled by evangelistic organizations, proclaimed humanitarian objectives and yet refrained from attacking the foundations of existing society and religion. To such causes, although denominations and individuals largely remained aloof, individuals of undoubted orthodoxy sometimes adhered.

Because its purposes could be linked closely and easily with the teachings of Christianity, the movement for international peace ranked high in respectability. More ministers held life memberships in the American Peace Society, founded in 1828, than did members of any other profession. In 1838 the Society claimed that more than a thousand ministers had pledged to preach on peace at least once a year.[1] An account of the organization's activities shows the names of some of the most respected leaders of conservative Protestant opinion occurring again and again: Francis Wayland, Calvin E. Stowe, Amasa Walker, Lewis Tappan, and that antiabolition rock, President Nathan Lord of Dartmouth.[2] According to one student, the movement was so strong in New England that by 1836 "most" of the churches in that region had passed peace resolu-

[1] M. E. Curti, *The American Peace Crusade, 1815-1860* (Durham, 1929), p. 48. It should be remembered that such statistics undoubtedly include many Unitarians.

[2] Edson C. Whitney, *The American Peace Society, a Centennial History* (Washington, 1928), *passim*.

tions.[3] Next to the Quakers and Unitarians, Congregational, Baptist and Methodist ministers seem to have been the most numerous clerical participants in the drive for peace.[4]

Yet even this relatively inoffensive movement never received official support from any major denomination. Over the nation, only a small minority of ministers ever took part in it.[5] Extreme theological conservatives were of course opposed to any such attempt to enter the sphere of earthly organization. Many more who were willing to work for moral causes found this movement outside the churches' mandate. Considerably less respectable than temperance agitation, it remained on about the same level as movements for better care of the insane, prison reform, etc. Purely humanitarian endeavors such as this remained open to ministers of the slightly more liberal wing of orthodoxy. They provided a valuable vent for the reform impulse and certainly involved no direct opposition to the central economic and social theories so widely prevalent.

Opposition to slavery, far more deeply than any other movement, strained the prevalent church adjustment to society.[6] To many northern ministers, slavery was not merely an evil to be opposed, like cruel prisons, by humanitarians. It was rather a national sin, to be stamped out, like Sabbathbreaking and intemperance, lest it blot the souls of Americans. One N. N. Eggleston, for instance, preaching a sermon for a Connecticut fast day, listed slavery as one among many doleful proofs that America was forgetting its responsibility to God.[7] Horace Bushnell, who had little use for political and social reform movements along humanitarian lines, felt obliged to endorse the moderate antislavery movement

[3] Christina Phelps, *The Anglo-American Peace Movement in the Mid-Nineteenth Century* (New York, 1930), p. 34.

[4] Curti, *Peace Crusade*, pp. 23, 49. C. S. Ellsworth, in his interesting study of "American Churches and the Mexican War," *American Historical Review*, XLV (1939-1940), 301-326, says that the attitude of churches in that crisis depended on a number of factors, including location, degree of centralized authority, theological traditions, etc., and finds, as one would expect, that the leaders in opposition to the war were Congregationalists, Unitarians, and Quakers, with the Presbyterian and Baptist groups divided.

[5] Curti, *op. cit.*, p. 48; Phelps, *op. cit.*, p. 33.

[6] For various insights into the problem of the relation of the churches and antislavery, see Barnes, *Antislavery Impulse*; E. A. Moore, *Robert J. Breckinridge and the Slavery Aspect of the Presbyterian Schism of 1837* (Chicago, 1932); J. N. Norwood, *The Schism in the Methodist Episcopal Church, 1844* (New York, 1923); Mary B. Putnam, "The Baptists and Slavery, 1840-1845" (MS. Master's thesis, Chicago, 1910); Charles B. Swaney, *Episcopal Methodism and Slavery* (Boston, 1926), as well as the works on general and denominational church history listed in the bibliography.

[7] Eggleston, *God Among the Nations* (pamphlet, Hartford, 1845).

on moral grounds.[8] Many ministers, scattered throughout the north and west, had enough of the come-outer spirit of their forefathers so that they could not resist the call.

Antislavery could be brought under the church's mandate to rebuke sin, yet it called into question a fundamental vested interest and threatened the stability of society. In the period before it became a political mass movement, plenty of northern ministers of every denomination fought hard against abolitionist agitation.[9] Some who became famous as antislavery leaders in the late fifties had been distinctly lukewarm to the earlier and less popular movement.[10] Others maintained to the end their objections to any agitation of such a dangerous issue.

It was inevitable that this fundamental conflict of duties should split some of the major churches. Between 1844 and 1853 the Baptists, Methodists and New School Presbyterians successively fell apart over various phases of the slavery question, with the Old School Presbyterians following suit in 1861.[11] Congregational and Unitarian churches, because of their looser organization and geographical location, managed to avoid an official division, but not to prevent controversy.[12] Only the Episcopalians were able to remain comparatively aloof.

Even after these splits had taken place, many northern ministers refused to take sides. As late as 1856 a large element in the New York Y.M.C.A. resigned simply because antislavery resolutions had been argued in the society, though they had been defeated.[13]

In the long run, however, the growth and eventual triumph of the antislavery crusade stirred churchmen more than any other prewar reform movement, and led them into more fundamental criticism of

---

[8] Bushnell, *A Discourse on the Slavery Question* (pamphlet, Hartford, 1839), *The Northern Iron* (pamphlet, Hartford, 1854); T. T. Munger, *Horace Bushnell, Theologian and Preacher* (Boston, 1879), pp. 61, 167.

[9] A strong indictment of organized religion from an abolitionist view is James G. Birney's *American Churches the Bulwarks of American Slavery* (3rd Amer. Ed.; Newburyport, 1842, pamphlet). Birney examines and slightly overstates the proslavery record of each of the great churches. See also C. R. Fish, *The Rise of the Common Man 1830-1850* ("A History of American Life," VI [New York, 1927]), 256; Barnes, *Antislavery Impulse*, pp. 93-97.

[10] See Lyman Abbott, *Henry Ward Beecher* (New York, 1903), p. 155, and Paxton Hibben, *Henry Ward Beecher: An American Portrait* (New York, 1927), pp. 148-150, for this phase of Beecher's career.

[11] See A. H. Newman, *A History of the Baptist Churches in the United States* ("American Church History Series," II [rev. ed.; New York, 1915]), 443-453; Sweet, *Methodism in American History* (New York, 1933), pp. 229-302; R. E. Thompson, *A History of the Presbyterian Church in the United States of America*, "American Church History Series," VI (New York, 1895), 135, 155-156.

[12] Barnes, *Antislavery Impulse*, pp. 92-99.

[13] L. L. Doggett, *Life of Robert McBurney* (Cleveland, 1902), pp. 41-42.

existing society. Especially since the churches later tended to exaggerate the part they had played in the early abolition struggles, the resultant tradition became a useful precedent for those who wanted the churches to espouse unpopular causes.[14]

Antislavery did not, however, directly involve any radical alteration in the economic views even of its adherents. Slavery had never been really compatible with the doctrines of Adam Smith, though the clerical revision of laissez faire had sometimes included a defense of America's anachronistic institution. More than any other reform movement, this moral crusade caused sincere Protestants to re-examine their comfortable adjustment to existing society. But as the antislavery forces grew and solidified, as the original prophetic radicals allied with hardheaded farmers and businessmen in the Republican party, emancipation became a vindication of existing Northern society, not a challenge to it. The long fight for freedom strained, but it did not fundamentally damage, the established relations of church and state in America.

Whatever their position with regard to humanitarian reform, the vast majority of Protestant spokesmen in prewar America heartily approved and upheld the central economic and political institutions of the country. They rejoiced that America was a Christian nation in which church and state, though separate, were allied. Despite several severe depressions, they were sure, like most of their countrymen, that national prosperity would continue to grow. When hungry workingmen and their radical allies attacked at once economic and religious orthodoxy, clerical complacency naturally turned to frightened reaction. Individual ministers, borrowing from religious professors, denounced social heresies and tried to explain to the disturbed classes the sanctity of economic law. Evangelical societies mobilized for defense. Few spokesmen of orthodox denominations questioned the propriety or importance of this widespread campaign and few escaped a conservative bias that lasted well beyond its immediate occasions.

Throughout the prewar period, evangelical Protestantism was deeply conscious of the parallel development of its rivals, the liberal sects. Unitarianism especially constituted a standing challenge not only to the dominant theology but to the social preachings of the orthodox denomi-

[14] However, this tradition could, like most traditions, be put to a variety of uses. An editorial in the *Independent*, July 26, 1877, p. 3, for instance, compared the railroad strikes of 1877 to the slavery question in a surprising manner: "Shall we, who have fought and conquered that we might forbid capital to rob and enforce labor, now allow labor to rob and enforce capital? Never!"

nations. The faith of Harvard maintained, of course, a strict distance from contemporary extremes of religious and social radicalism. Unitarian leaders had shared the Boston dislike of Jefferson and France. Yet, in their deepest assumptions, they were a product of the Enlightenment. Unitarians tended to accept notions of human perfectibility and the power of the human reason against which the older denominations were still waging a last-ditch resistance.

Instinctively hospitable to proposals for the improvement of society, they contributed far more than their proportional share of leadership to the movements for humanitarian reform.[15]

Unitarianism, moreover, was concentrated in industrial New England, whose spreading factory towns and old mercantile cities felt keenly the hard times of the forties. Full of enthusiasm for man, the essentially undefiled image of his Maker, Unitarians could not tolerate conditions degrading to humanity. Many Unitarian leaders, in their general comments on contemporary society, sounded a different note from that of the orthodox chorus.

William Ellery Channing, the great liberal leader, besides lending his prestige to many good causes, seemed at times to express a sweeping dissatisfaction with current social tendencies:

Society is not only disfigured but endangered by the poverty and ignorance, and vice of a multitude of its members; . . . A louder and louder cry is beginning to break forth through the civilized world for a social reform, which shall reach the most depressed ranks of the community.[16]

The reforms demanded by Channing, however, were primarily moral, not material.

There is but one elevation for the laborer and for all men. . . . The only elevation of a human being consists in the exercise, growth, energy of the higher principles and powers of his soul. . . . This elevation is indeed aided by an improvement in his outward condition, and in turn it greatly improves his outward lot; and thus connected, outward good is real and great;

[15] For short accounts of some of the principal leaders, listing their participation in various movements, see S. A. Eliot, *Heralds of a Liberal Faith* (Boston, 1910), especially Vols. II, III.

[16] W. E. Channing, "On Preaching the Gospel to the Poor," *Works* (17th ed.; Boston, 1866), V, 273. See W. M. Salter, *Channing as a Social Reformer* (pamphlet, 1892). C. R. Fish believes that "He was probably more influential than any one person in uniting the forces of religion with humanitarian reforms, and in developing the idea of social service by the churches which has become so characteristic of American Christianity." *Rise of the Common Man*, p. 197.

but supposing it to exist in separation from moral growth and life, it would be nothing worth nor would I raise a finger to promote it.[17]

To Channing, as to his orthodox rivals, the vices of the poor were to blame for much of their poverty.[18] A spokesman for the liberal optimism of the Enlightenment rather than for concrete contemporary discontent, Channing expressed a strong Jeffersonian fear of industrialism and specifically opposed the formation of class-conscious political parties.[19]

Channing's generous principles, coupled with greater experience of concrete urban problems, carried another Unitarian leader into a more vivid consciousness of the moral evil of poverty. Joseph Tuckerman, who devoted his life to a great pioneering work among the Boston poor, was concerned with physical as well as religious relief. Like so many young ministers a generation later, Tuckerman was deeply shocked by his first contact with the sordid conditions of early industrialism.[20] Not only did he demand an expansion of Christian charitable institutions but, breaking with prevalent economic thought, he urged employers to keep wages as high as possible as a part of their Christian duty.

Yet Tuckerman's conclusions about American society differed little from Channing's, and even agreed basically with those of the Trinitarian leaders. Tuckerman believed that poverty, and even dependence, were inevitable,[21] and saw the maintenance of the existing social order as one of the main purposes of his work:

It [my work] may bind the employed to the employer by stronger ties than any pecuniary compensation could form and in various ways . . . it may be made one at least of the strongest bonds which can be formed between the great classes of the rich and the poor. And on what other, I ask, than moral bonds, is any reliance to be placed in the great exigencies of our society.[22]

Spokesmen of the transcendentalist minority in Unitarianism followed the humanitarian current much further into radical social criticism than Channing and Tuckerman ventured. Theodore Parker, particularly, became the beacon of Boston's intellectual and religious radicalism. Going beyond most reformers of his time, he saw a connec-

---

[17] Channing, "On the Elevation of the Laboring Classes," *Works*, V, 166-167.

[18] *Ibid.*, p. 214.

[19] *Ibid.*, pp. 225-226, 164.

[20] Tuckerman, *Essay on the Wages Paid to Females for their Labor* (pamphlet, Philadelphia, 1830). A good account of Tuckerman's early work and of much other early and important Unitarian charitable effort is G. W. Cooke, *Unitarianism in America; A History of its Origin and Development* (Boston, 1902), pp. 322-342.

[21] Tuckerman, *The Principles and Results of the Ministry at Large, in Boston* (Boston, 1838), p. 286.

[22] *On the Elevation of the Poor* (Boston, 1874), pp. 28-29.

tion among separate social evils and raised questions that implied a criticism of basic contemporary beliefs. Like Tuckerman, Parker reacted vigorously to his observation of America's growing industrialism. Striking out against such modern evils as unemployment, bad housing, and low pay, he demanded that labor's grievances be settled on the basis of rights, not charity. Attracted by Fourierism, as by every other generous program for social improvement, Parker could raise the fundamental question of the rights and responsibilities of private property in the industrial age.[23]

Orestes A. Brownson, the tortured eccentric who passed through many and varied stages in his long journey to Catholicism, was, during his Universalist and Unitarian phases, perhaps more scathing than any contemporary social critic.[24] Brownson at his most radical demanded such fundamental changes as abolition of inheritance and placed the blame for the misery of industrial depressions squarely on the wage system. Naturally such views were denounced as strongly by the dominant spokesmen of liberal religion as by the evangelical conservatives. In his final Catholic phase, however, Brownson not only specifically repudiated socialism but went so far as to declare that worldly reform was of little importance and poverty not a real evil.[25] Despite his fervor and courage, Brownson forfeited by his erratic shifts any possibility of major influence on Christian social theory.

These earnest and vigorous, if sometimes eccentric, radicals, expressed, at most, the views of the extreme left wing of liberal religion. Most Unitarians and even many reformers of Unitarian and transcendentalist faith took pains to draw a distinction between themselves and the followers of Parker and Brownson. Sylvester Judd, for instance, participated actively in the peace, antislavery, temperance, penal reform, Indian rights and other movements. In one of his allegorical novels he showed considerable awareness of industrial problems, pleading, like Tuckerman, for an expansion of church philanthropic work to bind "Knuckle Lane" to "Victoria Square."[26] Yet Judd, thoroughly irritated at what he considered the unreasonable violence of radical reformers, urged them to return to "the recognition of the reasonable soul . . . or, in plainer words, to the simple letter of Scripture, which says, 'Provoke not, love one another, overcome evil with good.' "[27]

[23] See H. S. Commager, *Theodore Parker* (Boston, 1936), pp. 181-185, 163.
[24] See A. M. Schlesinger, Jr., *Orestes A. Brownson. A Pilgrim's Progress* (Boston, 1939), esp. pp. 90-108.
[25] *Ibid.*, pp. 102, 105-106, 204-205.
[26] See his *Richard Edney* (Boston, 1850).
[27] Quoted by Arethusa Hall, *Life and Character of the Reverend Sylvester Judd* (Boston, 1854), p. 294.

Orville Dewey, the pastor of a well-to-do New York church, represents a still far more conservative type of Unitarian reformer. Though Dewey himself preached against many of the evils of contemporary society, he was outraged at Horace Greeley's statement that the rich were responsible for the existence of poverty. Like most of his clerical contemporaries, Dewey was quite certain that it was, in almost all cases, the fault of the poor themselves. Though gulfs between classes were deeper than they ought to be most wealth, as well as most poverty, was earned and deserved.[28] In his respect for businessmen, Dewey yielded to none: "I say, therefore, that there is no being in the world for whom I feel a higher moral respect and admiration than for the upright man of business; no, not for the philanthropist, the missionary, or the martyr."[29]

At its most conservative, Harvard and Boston Unitarianism was as far from Dewey's moderate reformism as from Parker's radicalism. Harassed by its own left wing and shocked by the radical threats which distressed the orthodox conservatives, Unitarianism could and did contribute to the militant defense of the status quo. Francis Bowen, the stalwart Harvard protectionist, long typified the really conservative section of liberal religion.

Even more than Unitarianism, Universalism seems to have contributed disproportionately to reform causes. Adin Ballou, besides leading Hopedale community and taking an active part in the temperance, peace and antislavery movements, signed a manifesto that offers a perfect example of the come-outer sect spirit. In this document Ballou and several other ministers and laymen promised completely to eschew luxury, politics, violence, cruelty to men or animals, theatrical exhibitions, games of chance, elaborate clothing, swearing oaths, and even the overeager attempt to proselytize others.[30] Horace Greeley derived from his Universalist faith something of the optimistic zeal that determined his long series of reformist vagaries.[31] In 1846-7 the Massachusetts Convention of this liberal denomination formed "The Universalist General Reform Association" which interested itself officially in peace, prison reforms, antislavery, temperance, and "general philanthropy."[32]

[28] Dewey, *Autobiography and Letters of Orville Dewey, D.D.* (Boston, 1883), p. 91; *Moral Views of Commerce, Society and Politics, in Twelve Discourses* (New York, 1838), pp. 101-102.

[29] *Moral Views*, p. 71.

[30] Quoted in full in Adin Ballou, *Autobiography*, S. Heywood, ed. (Lowell, 1896), pp. 309-313.

[31] His socialist biographer calls Greeley a "devoted Christian Socialist" and emphasizes the Christian side of his ideas. Charles Sotheran, *Horace Greeley and other Pioneers of American Socialism* (New York, 1892), pp. 219-251.

[32] Richard Eddy, *Universalism in America* (Boston, 1886), I, 364.

Perhaps the man who, in the prewar period, anticipated most completely the later reactions of many Christians to industrial evils was the Universalist minister, E. H. Chapin.[33] In his work in the slums of Richmond, Boston and New York Chapin was even more deeply moved by the ugly realities of city life than Tuckerman. When he discussed sweatshops, for instance, he lost the calm, analytical tone characteristic of much liberal religious comment: "Perhaps this is treading upon the business interest of some. I can't help it if it is. Perhaps I don't know as much about it as I might; but I know enough to make me sick at heart."[34]

Chapin, drawing his conclusions from concrete experience rather than from a priori laws, seems to have broken sharply with many of the standard assumptions of his time. He could not share the prevailing exaltation of the merchant:

... the business of the Trader is thought to be more noble than the sweaty toil of the Producer. It is a great mistake. If there are any genuine distinctions, over and above those of character—and I do not believe there are—then he who makes a thing is greater than he who passes it to and fro and speculates upon it.[35]

Repeatedly, Chapin demanded mutual help, not "mere self-aggrandizement."[36] Still more startling was his venture, via the Universalist rejection of Original Sin, into social environmentalism:

Do I say that the guilt should be imputed to the conditioned—that it is all owing to circumstances? No: but I *do* say that, in nine cases out of ten, crime is no proof of *special* depravity apart from *general* depravity, and that the circumstances have just so much weight as this—that put you or me in those same circumstances, in nine cases out of ten, we should be criminals too.[37]

The role assigned to religion by this unique innovator was far more positive than the moral supervision prescribed by most of his contemporaries. Christianity was to rule our daily life and our national politics, to teach man the great ideas of self-government, human rights and peace —America would fulfill her duty only when she "makes Christianity

---

[33] See Anson Titus, *Edwin Hubbell Chapin, D.D., LL.D.* (reprinted from the *Historical and Genealogical Review* for April, 1884; Boston, 1884).
[34] E. H. Chapin, *Moral Aspects of City Life* (New York, 1853), p. 151.
[35] *Ibid.*, p. 42.
[36] *Ibid.*, p. 183.
[37] Chapin, *Humanity in the City* (New York, 1854), p. 202.

Practical." For the solution of pressing social problems religion must provide "Conviction," "Working Power," and "Interpretation."[38]

Like his contemporaries, Chapin occasionally expressed his suspicions of paternalistic interference by the state.[39] But the main emotional impact left by his pamphlets is like that of the Social Gospel tracts of a half-century later. In his own time, before most clergymen had experienced directly the agonies of industrialism, both Chapin's experiences and his reactions to them were too rare to gain him much of a hearing.

Despite their large proportion of articulate leaders, the liberal sects exerted only a limited influence on the great mass of Protestant social opinion. The solid structure of economic and social conservatism could not be easily damaged. Conservative Unitarians contributed to its defense as far as they could. Many conservative Protestants had little use for any Unitarian or Universalist opinion and most considered radical transcendentalism a variety of infidelity.

Unitarian thought had to wait until later for its full effect on the great evangelical denominations. Yet much of its content was dated. The glowing optimism, the passionate individualism, the belief in the omnipotence of education characteristic of the prewar Unitarian reformers could not outlast the Civil War. A few early pioneers like Tuckerman and Chapin sensed ugly realities which had not yet dawned on their contemporaries. But these realities had to be discovered by later Christians through their own bitter experience.[40]

The real impact of Unitarianism on Protestant social thought was indirect. Gradually, through its constant challenge to the dominant theology, through the humanitarian precepts and actions of its leaders, Unitarianism helped to alter Protestant ideas of the possibilities of mankind. Reinterpreted by one generation after another, humanistic religious ideas were eventually to be applied by some Protestants to society as well as to the individual.

Frederick Dan Huntington, who left Unitarianism in 1860 for an important career in the Episcopal church, epitomizes the effects and limitations of prewar Unitarian teachings. Huntington's own detailed views of contemporary problems, as he stated them just before his denominational change, were typical of the dominant social conservatism.

[38] *Ibid., The Responsibilities of a Republican Government* (sermon, Boston, 1841), p. 11; *Humanity*, pp. 225-252.
[39] See *The Relation of the Individual to the Republic* (sermon, Boston, 1844), pp. 8-9.
[40] It is significant that postwar Unitarianism shared the conservatism of the other churches, and that the Unitarians were not ahead of the other churches in turning toward the Social Gospel. See pp. 80-83.

He believed in the inevitable beneficence of laissez faire, chastened only by a "paternal" attitude on the part of employers. Like so many of his brethren, he specifically attacked socialism, trade-unions, labor legislation and strikes.[41]

In the same sermon, however, Huntington stated a general theoretical view of man and society that opened a way for quite different social doctrines. Instead of laws and relations fixed for all time as a part of a scheme of Divine government, Huntington preached a society appointed by God to be a school for man, to teach him among other things mutual help. In society as well as in the individual soul would much of God's will be worked out; society was "the Sphere of the Kingdom of Christ on Earth."[42] Such views were a striking departure from the prevalent individualism in religion and economics.

Huntington retained these germs of a social theology long after he left the Unitarian pulpit. Eventually, as a bishop, he was to be a part of a movement that took such theological views for granted and coupled them with a wide range of fairly specific social criticism.

In orthodox Protestant circles in 1860, however, liberal theology had only a limited and indirect effect. Fundamental criticism of existing society scarcely penetrated, except as an enemy to be overcome. The alliance between conservative religion and conservative economics held firm.

[41] F. D. Huntington, *Human Society: Its Providential Structure, Relations and Offices* (New York, 1860), pp. 82-83, 120-121, 143-189.
[42] *Ibid.*, pp. 107-141, 260-307.

II

THE SUMMIT OF COMPLACENCY

1861-1876

TRIUMPH AND CERTAINTY

TO PROTESTANTS of the Northern States, the years of the Civil War furnished the supreme vindication of American religious institutions. The churches entered the war on the crest of the Revival of 1859, apparently triumphant over their old enemies, sluggishness and infidelity. Throughout the war ordinary religious functions were not only maintained but expanded. War prosperity provided increased funds for home and foreign missions, Bible and tract distribution and the newer work of the Y.M.C.A. In 1863 still another revival swept the war-torn land.

Meanwhile organized religion undertook vast new tasks. Agencies representing all the major churches strove to safeguard the faith among the troops and to spread it among the freedmen. Northern ministers, accompanying the federal armies, took over the buildings and jurisdictions of their southern rivals. And with one voice, in pulpit and press, religious leaders prayed for the Christian republic and denounced the sins of its enemies.

In this final phase of the struggle against the sins of slavery and rebellion, spokesmen of all denominations proclaimed more sweepingly than ever the right of the churches to speak out on all moral issues. The Presbyterian General Assembly, always following a broad interpretation of its own responsibilities, declared in 1863 that although partisan politics should be eschewed by "church courts" yet

the sphere of the church is wider and more searching, touching matters of great public interest, than the sphere of the magistrate, *in this important respect*—that the civil authorities can take cognizance only of overt acts; while the law of which the church of God is the interpreter, searches the heart . . . and declares that man truly guilty, who allows himself to be alienated, in sympathy and feeling, from any lawful duty. . . .[1]

The Methodist General Conference, in addition to countless resolutions upholding the war and condemning the enemy, altered the church

[1] Presbyterian Church in the U.S.A., General Assembly, *Minutes*, 1863, p. 58.

discipline to make slaveholding itself a sin.[2] The most influential Baptist newspaper proclaimed the duty of preaching on the war:

It is quite fashionable with a certain class [this refers specifically to a statement in the Catholic *Boston Pilot*] to denominate sermons which show the application of the principles of Christianity to the affairs of government as political preaching. We insist that it is preaching Christ, and we cannot see how the Gospel in all its relations can be proclaimed without this. Any minister who during the rebellion did not develop the great truth that Christianity demanded obedience to a beneficent government, and that rebellion and treason were odious, failed of fulfilling his whole duty.[3]

The political influence of the Congregational clergy reached its peak in the activities of Henry Ward Beecher, the great pulpit orator. Already a national figure through his participation in the latest stage of the anti-slavery movement, Beecher in wartime became something that America had not seen in generations: a church political leader. In addition to delivering some highly publicized lectures in England in behalf of the Union cause, Beecher continually harangued his countrymen on emancipation, Reconstruction, immigration, the currency, local politics, taxes, a standing army, corruption, free trade, pacifism, presidential candidates and almost every other public question.[4] By 1862 he had decided that:

It is the duty of the minister of the Gospel to preach on every side of political life. I do not say that he *may;* I say that he *must.* That man is not a shepherd of his flock who fails to teach that flock how to apply moral truth to every phase of ordinary practical duty.[5]

The Episcopalians, having painfully preserved the church from schism by keeping clear of the slavery crisis, were far less willing to enter the wartime political sphere. Although even this church avowed its loyalty, declaring its sense of the "grievous wrong" the rebels were inflicting on church and country, it also stated its determination to "err on the safe side if we must err at all" and avoid entering the realm of secular politics.[6] Yet some Episcopalians refused to accept this hands-off stand.

[2] W. W. Sweet, *The Methodist Episcopal Church and the Civil War* (Cincinnati, 1912), pp. 39-40.

[3] Editorial on "Political Preaching," *Christian Watchman and Reflector,* September 20, 1866, p. 2.

[4] See especially H. W. Beecher, *Patriotic Addresses,* John R. Howard, ed. (New York, 1891).

[5] Beecher, "Speaking Evil of Dignities" in *Freedom and War. Discourses on Topics suggested by the Times* (Boston, 1863), pp. 294-310, 394-395.

[6] Protestant Episcopal Church, General Convention, *Journal,* 1862, pp. 51-53. For a defense of this position, see F. C. Ewer, *A Rector's Reply to Sundry Requests and Demands for a Political Sermon* (pamphlet, New York, 1864). The comparative aloofness of this church was sometimes attacked by other denominations, for instance in the *Congregationalist,* November 10, 1865, p. 178.

In 1860 C. S. Henry, a rector who had played a part in the prewar peace movement, defended the right to apply religion to politics as ardently as any Methodist. In a democratic country, he averred, "It is infinitely important . . . that the whole people should be enlightened in all that regards the just exercise of their political rights."[7] And in Philadelphia young Phillips Brooks added his golden voice to the support of the war, Lincoln, and Negro rights.[8]

When the triumph of the great cause came in sight, clerical exultation was unbounded. Editorials and sermons painted the war as a triumph of American Christianity, the instrument of God's will in blotting out the sin of slavery:

> How are the mighty fallen! Three fifths of their territory is wrested from them. . . . Hallelujah! the Lord God omnipotent reigneth! His right arm hath gotten Him the victory![9]

> No Christian can look upon the events of the last four years without being deeply impressed with the conviction that they have been ordered by God to produce great and lasting changes in the state of the country, and probably of the world.[10]

In this mood of triumph, church spokesmen were less than ever disposed to question the basic institutions that had come through the fiery furnace:

> What cause have we for gratitude to God for his gift of such institutions to us, and of renewed confidence in them. . . . No other country—not even that living under the most "limited" monarchy—could have gone through such a crisis, so much unmoved. . . . That only stands secure which stands broad and deep on the eternal foundations of human rights and the Divine law.[11]

Through the postwar years, despite the cynicism that pervaded some business and political circles, Protestant spokesmen maintained their tone of deep, exultant confidence in the future of the Christian republic. Evidence of corruption and materialism did not daunt them. These enemies, with threats like Mormonism, Catholicism and intemperance, would be overcome by Christian effort. One great encouraging fact remained; churchgoing was still a national habit, at least among the

---

[7] *Considerations on Some of the Elements and Conditions of Social Welfare and Human Progress* (New York, 1861), pp. 364-365.

[8] A. V. G. Allen, *Life and Letters of Phillips Brooks* (New York, 1900), I, 416 ff.

[9] Gilbert Haven, "The Great Election," *Methodist Quarterly Review*, XLVII (1865), 263.

[10] *Biblical Repertory and Princeton Review*, XXXVII (1865), 436.

[11] *Congregationalist*, April 28, 1866, p. 2.

prosperous, enlightened middle class that was America's special glory and hope.

Religious statistics in the Census of 1870 showed a gratifying gain in every index of church prosperity. Property held by churches swelled from $171,397,932 to $354,483,581 in a decade.[12] To a German audience, Joseph P. Thompson could boast that American Protestants, without state aid, had raised fifty million dollars for missions in 1872.[13] A triumphant summary of progress published in the centennial year estimated Protestant church members at over eight million.[14]

Religious fervency seemed to wax with numerical strength. In 1875 Dwight L. Moody and Ira D. Sankey, returning triumphant from their work in England, commenced their long series of American revivals, converting millions to simple, untheological "Bible religion." Though some fainthearted individuals were alarmed at the tide of Catholic immigration, a more typical attitude was one of sturdy, uncompromising confidence in the dominance of Protestant tradition:

> This is a Christian Republic, our Christianity being of the Protestant type. People who are not Christians, and people called Christians, but who are not Protestants, dwell among us; but they did not build this house. . . . If any one, coming among us, finds that this arrangement is uncomfortable, perhaps he will do well to try some other country.[15]

Protestant optimism extended outside the strictly religious sphere into a prophetic vision of the future greatness of the nation, now purged of its deepest sin. The swift opening of the Far West, the disclosure of vast new wealth, the bustling energy of industrialization all were cited as further evidence that "Our political and social mission may be sublime beyond that of any other contemporary people."[16]

To safeguard this great mission and the institutions which were to carry it out was still, as it had been in wartime, the task of the churches. One group of ultraconservatives, gathered in the National Reform Association, proposed to make sure of the republic's Christianity by passing a constitutional amendment stating the sovereignty of God and the supremacy of Revelation. This movement, formed in 1863, secured in the postwar decade the backing of the United Presbyterians, the Old

[12] *U. S. Ninth Census* (1870), I, 506. All religious statistics for this period should be accepted with caution, since they are drawn from optimistic church reports.

[13] Thompson, *Church and State in the United States* (Boston, 1873), p. 111.

[14] W. F. P. Noble, *1776-1876. A Century of Gospel-Work* (Philadelphia, 1876), p. 108.

[15] S. M. Campbell, "Christianity and Civil Liberty," *American Presbyterian and Theological Review*, V (1867), 390-391.

[16] *Christian Advocate*, July 7, 1870, p. 212.

School Presbyterian General Assembly and the Methodist General Conference.[17]

Most Protestant authorities, if they did not support this extreme proposal, upheld theories of church and state that were unaltered since the previous generation. The Methodist General Conference stated very clearly American religion's historic claims:

We do not assume for the Church the right to arraign "the powers that be"—powers which God has placed upon a ground of independent authority, and charged with peculiar functions; and yet from scriptural warrant we do claim for the Church the right and duty of speaking words of praise or censure, approval or condemnation, of the great principles of law and government, according as they harmonize or antagonize with the essential ethics of true religion.[18]

A Baptist writer condemned the Social Compact and all other theories of government that did not take account of the Christian basis of governmental authority and the essentially moral nature of society.[19] Speaking in less theoretical terms, a Presbyterian boasted that "the loyal churches of the North form a large army and wield a good deal of political influence—to say nothing now of their influence with the High and Mighty Ruler of the Universe."[20]

In theory, church political power was still used only to defend the interests of morality and religion. This continued to cover a wide ground. Retaining the use of the Bible in the schools and yet fighting the Catholic parochial school system was a difficult and important objective. Concern for the old American Sabbath increased with immigration and the temperance movement, set back by wartime laxity, went into a new and more militant phase. Vice and violence, especially the abomination of Mormon polygamy and the shame of brutality toward Indians, made the Far West an important field for church political efforts. Questions of city government and civil service reform could easily be related to Christian morality.

The first political concern of northern Christians remained, of course, the rounding out of the great antislavery task. Combining genuine, disinterested and important work for Negro welfare and uplift with an

[17] W. E. Garrison, *The March of Faith* (New York, 1933), p. 18; National Reform Convention, *Proceedings, 1874* (Philadelphia, 1874).

[18] "Report of the Committee on the State of the Country," Methodist Episcopal Church, General Conference, *Journal*, 1868, p. 628.

[19] William C. Conant, "The Bible and the State," *Baptist Quarterly*, V (1871), 276-293.

[20] George L. Prentiss, "The Political Situation," *American Presbyterian and Theological Review*, IV (1866), 330.

Old-Testament doctrine of vengeance, the churches were among the most influential forces working for a policy of radical reconstruction.[21] The religious press took a strong stand for a "sound" currency, which seemed to the clerical editors, as to most middle-class easterners, a matter of common honesty.[22] With their views on Reconstruction and the currency pointing the same way, many church papers left their readers little doubt which party to join:

> Were all parties, all platforms, and all candidates, in our judgment, equally honest, capable, and advantageous so that . . . the dues, in short, of that coming kingdom of God for which we labor, would be met and satisfied as well by the success of one as of another, no question of mere commercial or economical expediency would ever be raised by us. . . . But we are not yet living in the millennium. . . . And sincerely believing that, in the main, the Republican is more nearly the party of progress and justice, and the future, than the so-called Democracy, we have often advocated (but always from a moral stand point) the Republican measures and candidates.[23]

On all fronts, against all possible enemies, Protestantism still stood ready to defend the republic and its system. Its confidence in the prevailing order and its confidence in its own mandate were equally unimpaired.

Economic and social problems in the postwar era could still be solved, like political questions, by simple moral judgments. Protestant enquirers found little to shake their optimism when they turned to prevailing economic theories, still largely formulated under clerical auspices. In 1866 the Reverend George N. Boardman, appealing to such venerable authorities as Dr. Chalmers and Francis Wayland, could still urge ministers to study political economy as a branch of natural theology.[24] A. H. Strong, president of Rochester Theological Seminary, proclaimed the same well-tried belief: "I know of no better proof of the divine origin of Christianity than this, that her laws are little by little found to be the laws of nature. . . . This I believe to be already true of Political Economy."[25] And the *Congregationalist*, commenting on the brightening future of the South, could still refer as a matter of course

[21] See P. H. Buck, *The Road to Reunion 1865-1900* (Boston, 1937), pp. 12-13.

[22] *Christian Watchman and Reflector*, November 16, 1865, p. 2; *Congregationalist*, October 1, 1868, pp. 2-3; *Christian Advocate*, July 14, 1870, p. 220.

[23] *Congregationalist*, October 29, 1868, p. 348.

[24] "Political Economy and the Christian Ministry," *Bibliotheca Sacra*, LXXIX (1866), 73-107.

[25] "Christianity and Political Economy" (address, 1871), in *Philosophy and Religion* (New York, 1888), pp. 444-445.

to "the laws of political economy, which are but a part of God's providence in this world."[26]

For those who wished to study these laws in detail, the colleges still offered the doctrines, and often the texts, developed in the prewar era. Although in Europe new theories were rife, American institutions clung to the most conservative English texts.[27]

Perhaps the most influential American economist was Arthur Latham Perry, a minister's son and a strict adherent of the doctrines of Wayland and Bowen. Like his predecessors, Perry identified "the fundamental laws of society" with "the footsteps of providential intelligence."[28] These laws made it particularly plain that concerted action to raise wages was immoral and useless, since it could only act to lessen the wage-fund.

Amasa Walker, like Perry, was a layman in a field in which ordained ministers were still plentiful but he too aspired to "show how perfectly the laws of wealth accord with all those moral and social laws which appertain to the higher nature and aspirations of man."[29] Since wages depended on supply and demand, strikes were useless and dangerous. More liberal than some of his contemporaries, Walker believed labor organizations to be legal and congratulated them on turning toward the cause of co-operation.

The chief rival to these traditional teachings, at least in clerical circles, was still the essentially conservative protectionism of Carey and Colwell. This distinctive American school was carried on in the postwar period by Robert Ellis Thompson, an ordained minister who became professor at the University of Pennsylvania in 1874. Thompson cited Carey as his master and Colwell as another important influence.[30]

Like his predecessors, Thompson objected to the classical doctrines on idealistic, humanitarian and nationalist grounds. Malthusian and Ricardian doctrines he condemned as devices of the British upper class to prove social improvement impossible. Such doctrines were, he thought, particularly unsuitable to the hopeful and free society of the United States. Disagreeing still further with his contemporaries, Thompson attacked that great shibboleth, the wage-fund doctrine. A theory which

[26] January 19, 1866, p. 10.

[27] For the persistence of the clerical school see O'Connor, *Origins*, pp. 262-267; Bryson, "Emergence of the Social Sciences," *International Journal of Ethics*, XLII, 312-313. For a typical review of an English author (J. E. Cairnes, one of the last to cling to the wage-fund theory), see *Presbyterian Quarterly*, IV (1875), 189-191.

[28] Perry, *Elements of Political Economy* (New York, 1866), p. 26.

[29] Walker, *The Science of Wealth* (5th ed.; Boston, 1869), p. xi.

[30] Thompson, *Elements of Political Economy* (3rd ed. of his *Social Science and National Economy*; originally published 1875, Philadelphia, 1882), pp. 6-7. For comment on Thompson see Bernard, *American Sociology*, pp. 424-428, 695-698.

proclaimed the impossibility of raising wages under the capitalist system, he acutely pointed out, could give only comfort to socialists.[31]

Thompson's insistence on the possibility of improvement led him to an attitude toward labor unions that was slightly more tolerant than that of his laissez faire colleagues. Under some circumstances, organization might even effect a wage increase. However, Thompson appended to this unorthodox admission the conventional statements that capital and labor should find their interests common, that unions are unnecessary in a free country, and that they are often guilty of wrong practices. Thompson disapproved co-operation but endorsed profit-sharing schemes introduced by management.[32]

Like the doctrines of Carey and Colwell, Thompson's humanitarian rejection of laissez faire led principally to a plea for the use of the nation's power for social improvement. In concrete terms, this still meant an endorsement of the protective tariff.[33] Doubtless the reforming spirit of the Carey-Colwell school helped to soften the hard dogmas of laissez faire. But the school gave little concrete impetus to social reform. It is significant that later, in the age of the gaining Social Gospel, Thompson was to become one of the most articulate proponents of the conservative defense.[34]

Economic dogmas, formulated a priori on the basis of Divine Law or, less frequently, national interest, retained their supreme authority. American Protestantism in the postwar period was, however, beginning to become conscious of another body of social doctrine, the school of so-called "social science" or sociology stemming from Comte and Spencer. Comte himself, since publication of a condensed translation in 1853, had been known to American clerics as a dangerous infidel. Positivism had been repeatedly condemned by Protestant reviews for its rejection of theology and metaphysics. Though the furor had died down somewhat by the seventies, to accuse a book of being tinged with Positivism was still enough to damn it.[35] Yet the Comtian tendency toward complicated

---

[31] *Ibid.*, pp. 53-69, 93-117.   [32] *Ibid.*, pp. 132-139.

[33] This is clear throughout the *Elements*, for instance on pp. 64-65 where the tariff is presented as the best alternative to communism.

[34] See pp. 215-216.

[35] See Bernard, *American Sociology*, pp. 205-219, 224-236, 679-688, for a summary of the clerical denunciation of Comte with considerable quotation from the religious press. In 1871 the *Congregationalist* went so far as to hint that Comte was to blame for the Paris Commune and for other dreadful activities of the International, among which it included Fenianism. June 29, 1871, p. 204.

Since Carey and Thompson both admitted being influenced to some degree by Comte, both might be treated as a part of this school of sociologists. It seems more correct, however, to consider them as nationalist economists, drawing their inspiration from Hamilton, List and American manufacturers, and relying on Comtian social science chiefly as a source of impressive verbiage.

a priori classifications and formulations was essentially congenial to the habit of thought of the late nineteenth century. Many disciples of the French master were eventually to exert considerable influence over clerical social doctrine.

Darwinism, another principal ingredient in the growth of sociology, was replacing Comtism in the seventies as the main enemy of orthodoxy.[36] While the conflict over evolution was raging among the scientists, American religious opinion remained firmly set against the new doctrine. To earnest Christians, Darwinism seemed to challenge not only the biblical account of creation, but the concepts of God and man that underlay a whole civilization. Through the seventies, most Protestants (other than advanced religious liberals) held to the eventually damaging position that Darwin's thesis could *never* be reconciled with religion. Only a few far-sighted divines were saying that natural selection could, if proved true, be interpreted as a part of the Divine method.[37]

Darwinism's greatest influence on American social thought was exerted through the teachings of Herbert Spencer. Beginning in the middle sixties Spencer's works, pushed by an enterprising publisher, became the vogue among America's advanced intellectuals. His sales and his prestige grew steadily throughout the next two decades.

The pundit of Victorian optimism, preaching the benign and universal advance from simplicity to complexity, seemed in many ways suited to appeal to Protestant American opinion. His theories were as sweeping and comprehensive as those of the familiar formulations of Divine Law. They led to a still more rigid defense of private property and a more complete condemnation of state action, backed by the up-to-date authority of science. Spencer himself hoped for clerical approval and insisted that his views were reconcilable with religion. When he was called a Positivist by a ministerial reviewer he strongly denied the charge.[38]

[36] For illuminating summaries of clerical reception of Darwinism in this period, see Richard Hofstadter, *Social Darwinism in American Thought 1860-1915* (Philadelphia, 1945), pp. 11-17; B. J. Loewenberg, "Darwinism Comes to America, 1859-1900," *Mississippi Valley Historical Review*, XXVIII (1941-42), 339-368, and the same author's "The Controversy over Darwinism in New England 1859-1873," *New England Quarterly*, VIII (1935), 232-257.

[37] As an example of a book which denounced Positivism and other aspects of modern thought such as the theories of Mill, Spencer and Huxley, but yet·opened the door to a possible acceptance of modified evolutionary thought, see James McCosh, *Christianity and Positivism* (London, 1875).

[38] J. E. Barnes, "Herbert Spencer on Ultimate Religious Ideas," *New Englander*, XXII (1863), 692-728; "A Letter from Mr. Herbert Spencer," *New Englander*, XXIII (1864), 169-171. Both these sources are quoted by Bernard, *American Sociology*, pp. 152-153. See Spencer, *First Principles of a New System of Philosophy* (2nd ed.; New York, 1867), pp. 3-24, for an example of his effort to make his doctrines acceptable to contemporary religious opinion.

However, even aside from Spencer's evolutionism, his method of reconciling science and religion was not such as was acceptable to orthodox religious opinion in the sixties and seventies. While his own vast dogmatic structure was deducible from science, religion must for the present be assigned to the sphere of the "Unknowable," though its evidence might eventually lead to conclusions reconcilable with Spencerian truth:

Thus, however untenable may be any or all the existing religious creeds, however gross the absurdities associated with them, however irrational the arguments set forth in their defence, we must not ignore the verity which in all likelihood lies hidden within them.[39]

American Protestants were by no means ready to be patronized in this manner. Though Spencer, because of his thoroughly moral personal character, his reputation as an intellectual giant, and his acceptable social conclusions, was treated with more respect than Comte or Darwin, he too was condemned by most Protestant writers long after his American publication.

It was partly this rejection of the British Aristotle by American Protestants that caused John Fiske in 1869-1871 to develop, in his famous Harvard lectures, the theistic argument for Spencer's "Cosmic Philosophy." But even Fiske, partly because of Unitarian associations, was far too liberal for the mass of contemporary church opinion. A review of Fiske's lectures by John Bascom, himself no rock-ribbed conservative in either his theological or his social views, was typical of the prevailing Protestant attitude.[40] Though Bascom respected the morality taught both by Fiske and his master, he found that the Spencerian cosmos had insufficient place either for God or Man. Bascom objected, moreover, to the conceited tone with which Fiske dismissed ideas still dear to his orthodox countrymen. Spencerian sociology, in its purer forms, did not make its influence felt in Protestant circles until the next decade.

In the immediate postwar years, however, another type of social science, purged of Comtist or Darwinian associations, began to be formulated in America. The American Social Science Association, founded in 1865, meant by its name simply to proclaim its interest in all fields relating to the study of society, from history to jurisprudence. It included such highly respected figures as John Bascom, Carroll D. Wright, Charles Francis Adams and General Grant. Among its purposes it listed the

[39] *First Principles*, p. 17.
[40] Bascom, "The Synthetic or Cosmic Philosophy," *Bibliotheca Sacra*, XXXIII (1876), 618-655.

"Advancement of Education," the "Prevention and Repression of Crime," and the "Progress of Public Morality."[41] As a sociologist tolerantly describes it, "It represented humanitarian sentiment more distinctly than a desire for critical methodology."[42]

The extreme respectability of this organization helped to introduce it favorably to the religious public, hitherto suspicious of anything called social science. The *Christian Advocate*, for instance, carefully explained to its readers that the Association had nothing to do with either materialism or socialism.[43] Though it promoted no definite opinions, the Association doubtless helped to spread the idea of scientific investigation of society, as opposed to a priori dogmatism.

Meantime at least one of the older clerical authorities was turning toward the new discipline. President Bascom, already an accepted authority on theology, philosophy, science and economics, now added social science. Before the war Bascom, as we have seen, had been engaged in the difficult task of demonstrating that a future era of Christian love would arise automatically out of the present operation of private interest. Naturally some of the Spencerian concepts and vocabulary proved convenient. Belief in a vast, complex, automatic development pervaded Bascom's postwar writing.[44]

Interest, hidden as a seed by God in the dark, cold soil of society, initiates a growth it does not understand, pushes up into a higher region, and there finds and feels a heaven-descended warmth, which henceforth seizes upon it and draws it ever up, thirsting for that which is above.

For the sake of safeguarding this precious seed of the future, Bascom was as willing as Spencer to accept the action of "those natural forces, which sift and winnow savage society . . . with terrible waste of the worthless." For the present our efforts, Bascom thought, should be directed toward reaching only that "proximate" justice which is attainable "in this stage of the inevitable ascent." (This concept seems analogous to the Relative Natural Law of Catholic theology.)

In the sphere of labor, as elsewhere, inequality was necessary to the purpose of "natural selection." (Bascom actually used this controversial

41 Constitution, published in the *Radical*, III (1865), 106-108.
42 A. W. Small, "Fifty Years of Sociology in the United States (1865-1915)," *American Journal of Sociology*, XXI (1915-16), 729. See also Bernard, *American Sociology*, pp. 527-607.
43 January 24, 1869, p. 196. For other articles praising the Association see the *Independent*, June 19, 1869, p. 4; *Christian Union*, May 27, 1874, pp. 418-419.
44 An important series of articles was "The Natural Theology of Social Science," *Bibliotheca Sacra*, XCV (1868), 1-23, 270-315; 645-686. The quotation below is from p. 315.

phrase.)[45] However, the force of self-interest worked beyond its allotted time and sought the immediate rather than the ultimate good. When this happened, the lowest groups found themselves unable to continue their normal march upward and conflict between capital and labor ensued.

For the redress of these temporary wrongs, Bascom offered few concrete means. Not only socialism but also hours legislation and (in almost all cases) strikes were pronounced harmful, both from the viewpoint of evolutionary social science and from that of the older economic law. If the employee wanted higher wages, "he has but one test of the validity of his claim, but one method of constraining, and that is his ability to secure elsewhere the sum demanded."[46] Bascom urged labor to seek the peaceful alternatives of self-improvement and investment in co-operatives and called on capital to live up to its responsibilities. Both must remember that society had passed the stage of mere self-interest and was moving into the sphere of benevolence.

These theories, as typical as any of the intellectual atmosphere of Bascom's age, were applied to many current problems in the philosopher's prolific writings for the religious press.[47] Bascom consistently pleaded for enlightenment and unselfishness. Yet his theory, like Spencer's, offered the conservatively inclined every encouragement to assume that present evils were necessary to the automatic progress which Providence or (in more fashionable terminology) the laws of society provided.

Whether they consulted the old proponents of natural religion and economic law or the latest, more or less suspect, advocates of social science, Protestant inquirers found in contemporary social theory the same lessons of laissez faire. Tradition and analysis confirmed their confidence in the wisdom and beneficence of the prevailing order.

[45] *Ibid.*, p. 652.
[46] *Ibid.*, p. 675.
[47] The same series is continued in *Bibliotheca Sacra* XXVI (1869), 120-162, 401-442, 609-646. See also Bascom, "Labor," *Independent*, February 18, 1875, p. 5; "The Sphere of Civil Law in Social Reform," *American Presbyterian Review*, III (1871), 40-51.

2

PROGRESS AND ITS PRICE

THE lessons taught by scholars were reinforced in the postwar era by the practical experience of church leaders. On all sides business leaders, enriched by the operation of correct economic principles, were supporting religious and philanthropic enterprises on a new scale. Even the old evangelical churches, traditionally refuges for the lowly, began to blossom with Romanesque facades and munificent endowments. Wealthy laymen were finding their way into positions of influence in the churches as elsewhere. Yet the churchmen who sang the praises of industrial giants need not be accused of hypocrisy or servility. To most Americans, the men who were building the railroads and the steel mills were national heroes.

In this postwar period, as for several generations after, many Protestant spokesmen delighted to point out that the road to success led through Christian living. "Men who have tried it, have confidently declared that there is no sleeping partner in any business who can begin to compare with the Almighty."[1]

The Christian businessman, who by frugality had risen to great wealth, was pointed out again and again as an example to imitate. Political economy taught that his investments were themselves a service to the community and especially to labor. As the *Unitarian Review* put it:

There is not a poor man who has five dollars in a savings bank, or a laboring man who has a single productive share in a factory or a railroad, or who has a hundred dollars insured upon his furniture or his life, who is not under obligation to a class of men who usually receive small pay or thanks for the valuable and painstaking services which they render.[2]

[1] *Congregationalist*, June 21, 1876, p. 196.
[2] Editorial, "What We Owe to Business Men," *Unitarian Review*, VIII (1877), 564. See also Strong, *op. cit.*, in his *Philosophy and Religion*, p. 453, for an example of praise of the Christian investor who abstains from pleasure in order that he may employ labor.

In the *Baptist Quarterly* the son of Francis Wayland drew a series of moral lessons from the career of Thomas Brassey, the British railroad king. The *Congregationalist* used Amos Lawrence as its example of a Christian rich man. With still greater enthusiasm, the *Independent* proclaimed that "We need all the Jay Cookes we have and a thousand more."[3]

Constantly preaching the Christian uses of wealth, Protestant moralists occasionally found it necessary to qualify the more difficult Gospel passages on poverty and simplicity.

To "take no thought for the morrow" does not mean that we must live literally from hand to mouth, and give away everything we do not immediately need. . . . God has need of rich Christians, and He makes them, and He assigns particular duties to them.[4]

The preacher may not, then, indiscriminately inveigh against luxuries, for the sum of wealth cannot be too great, if well used, and luxuries are the only foundation of large wealth in any community.[5]

The *Christian Advocate* had no use for lilies of the field:

We fear for that young man's morality, who is content to live merely paying his current expenses. . . . No young man not already sufficiently endowed should be satisfied with his year's work who does not find himself a richer man at the end than he was at the beginning.[6]

To those who had succeeded the churches preached, of course, the excellence of charity. Often generosity, like morality and religion itself, was pronounced conducive to business success. Quite as often, however, it was proclaimed as a positive duty. The ancient Protestant doctrine of the stewardship of wealth was preached again and again, with warnings for those who neglected to use their gains in the Divine service. A university president, speaking before the Evangelical Alliance in 1873, after emphasizing the disastrous consequences of any interference by the state with wealth, insisted with equal force that "There are moral laws which govern the accumulation and management of property."[7]

[3] H. L. Wayland, "A Captain of Industry," *Baptist Quarterly*, VII (1873), 149-164; *Congregationalist*, August 2, 1876, p. 24; *Independent*, November 5, 1868, quoted in Garrison, *March of Faith*, p. 57.

[4] *Congregationalist*, July 14, 1869, p. 12.

[5] Boardman, *op. cit.*, in *Bibliotheca Sacra*, LXXXIX (1866), 84.

[6] May 21, 1874, p. 164.

[7] M. B. Anderson, "The Right Use of Wealth," in Evangelical Alliance, Sixth General Conference (1873), *History, Essays, Orations and other Documents* (New York, 1874), p. 360.

An Episcopalian rector coupled the threats of socialism and covetousness.[8] In general, however, most religious commentators struck a note of complacency rather than admonition; splendid examples of Christian benevolence were much more common than misuse of wealth.

Christian writers did not hesitate to set limits to the duty of charity in accordance with the individualist political economy of the day. Horace Bushnell, for instance, preaching on the duties proper to the high calling of the merchant, cautioned the Christian in commerce that he must carry on his business strictly according to the laws of trade "and never let his operations be mixed up with charities. . . ." As an example of the type of benevolence that is most fitting, Bushnell suggested that the merchant set aside "remnants, faded, and smirched, and smoked, and shelf-worn-goods, and styles of goods gone by," "all which he would otherwise put in auction, and sell at great loss to himself," and sell these carefully selected materials to the poor at low prices.[9]

Charity was further limited by the widespread belief in the unalterable depravity of the poor. Over and over religious writers insisted that poverty, like riches, was generally deserved. A staunch Calvinist could put this doctrine of reprobation in even more severe terms. Admitting that circumstances might have something to do with the origins of "ignorance, indolence, and immorality," the Reverend Charles Wood declared that

they soon become, exceptional cases aside, a necessary inheritance, an inborn, entailed evil, with all the force and regularity of law, transmitting their image from one generation to another, and creating conditions of life, which either discourage or crush out every ennobling aspiration. . . . Yet none are more exacting in their demands, none more arbitrary, none more unreasonable and at the same time more unconscious of unworthiness, than this very class.

For this doomed group, not much could be done. The same writer frankly stated that benevolent associations, missions, and the like, generally did more harm than good except when they were empowered by law "to take the children of the perishing classes, to care for them until they are of a suitable age to be apprenticed or bound out to some useful occupation beyond the reach of their immediate relatives or friends." As for other assistance to the poor,

[8] Edward Washburn, *The Social Law of God: Sermons on the Ten Commandments* (New York, 1875), pp. 198-211.

[9] Bushnell, "How to be a Christian in Trade," in *Sermons on Living Subjects* (New York, 1873), pp. 263-267.

the serpent is not cast out and slain. It is only fed and satisfied, and put to sleep, that it may gather power and venom in order to strike its deadly tooth all the deeper into the soil of its miserable victim. Pauperism and vagrancy are *crimes*, and should be *prevented* or *punished*.[10]

Such extremes of hostility to the unfortunate are not representative of the majority of Protestant opinion in the postwar period. Many church members believed heartily in the utility of working to alleviate distress. Yet even some of the most philanthropic agreed with the *Independent* that a permanent solution to the problem of poverty was not only impossible but undesirable:

The poor we have with us always; and this is not the greatest of our hardships, but the choicest of our blessings. If there is anything that a Christian may feel thankful for, it is the privilege of lifting a little of the load of some of his heavily-burdened neighbors.[11]

Protestant admiration of business magnates was challenged by the huge financial and railroad scandals of the Grant era. As the story of one fraud after another burst into light, the religious press carried out its duty of moral rebuke. Readers were warned that speculation, while not evil in itself, might easily be carried into dishonesty. Fraudulent corporations, especially railroads, were denounced in a good many editorials. Editors appealed to the consciences of shoddy manufacturers. Monopolies, especially the telegraph monopoly, were taken to task. Occasionally the death of a great capitalist whose personal or commercial faults were especially widely known called forth the opposite of a eulogy.[12]

Yet the basic complacency of religious spokesmen does not seem to have been shaken by the disclosures of the era's corruption. Indictments of particularly dishonest individuals were often coupled with reassuring statements, as for instance the *Watchman and Reflector's* assertion of its "high estimate of the honor of our business men as a class."[13] Protestant commentators, like most Americans, regarded the sins of Jim Fisk and the scandals of the *Crédit Mobilier* as unhappy departures from the norm. Respect for the rich, particularly the pious rich, was little shaken

[10] "The Pauperism of our Cities; Its Character, Conditions, Causes, and Relief," *Presbyterian Quarterly*, III (1874), 226. (Italics his.)

[11] *Independent*, November 26, 1874, p. 14.

[12] E.g. editorials in the *Watchman and Reflector* on Fisk, January 18, 1872, p. 6; and on Vanderbilt, January 18, 1877, p. 20.

[13] February 16, 1871, p. 6.

and confidence in prevailing economic doctrine was disturbed hardly at all.[14]

Nowhere did religious writers display more unanimity than in their discussions of wages and labor. Prevailing doctrines of academic economics squared exactly with the popular American belief in hard work and competition. There was one fundamental answer with which all discussions of the subject could be ended:

Labor is a commodity, and, like all other commodities, its condition is governed by the imperishable laws of demand and supply. It is all right to talk and declaim about the dignity of labor. . . . But when all has been said of it, what is labor but a matter of barter and sale?[15]

The *Congregationalist* was so certain of its ground that it insisted it was to everybody's interest to lower the cost of labor to "the lowest attainable point," even when a working-class subscriber wrote canceling his subscription.[16]

Interference with the workings of economic laws in order to raise wages was, according to religious editors, particularly unnecessary in America. The *Congregationalist* stated that very old and common belief later to be codified and debated as part of the "frontier theory":

. . . one thing is certain, that so long as thousands upon thousands of acres of magnificent soil can be secured beyond the Mississippi at a merely nominal price, no man who is blessed with health and willingness to work, be his family large or small, need come to the poorhouse.[17]

[14] A sidelight on the commercial morality of some of the religious press itself can be gained by a glance at its advertising. It was quite usual to print advertisements for railroad stocks in close proximity to articles extolling the progress of the railroad, explaining the reasons for its soundness, and even pointing to its moral beneficence. *Congregationalist*, November 7, 1867, p. 216; August 27, 1868, p. 276; *Watchman and Reflector*, January 19, 1871, p. 6; July 30, 1868, p. 2; December 31, 1868, p. 2; February 4, 1860, p. 2. Henry Ward Beecher as editor of the *Independent* was charged by the *Nation* with accepting bribes to puff the Northern Pacific, a charge which the paper hotly denied. October 22, 1874, p. 16. The *Independent* in 1885 took advertisements for "Coughs, Colds, Croup and Consumption" medicines that were "certainly curing in every case." July 2, 1885, p. 19. The *Christian Advocate* of October 14, 1886, carried advertising for a concern which implied that it could very probably find inherited fortunes hidden in Europe for anybody fortunate enough to have any one of fifty thousand surnames. Some of the families invited to try their luck were Johnson, Myers, McGregor, O'Hara, O'Neill, Schmidt, Smith, May and Zooch. Yet the same paper declared, on June 23, 1887, that it would admit no advertisement that did not come from respectable houses doing useful business.
[15] *Watchman and Reflector*, June 4, 1874, p. 6.
[16] July 21, 1870, p. 228.
[17] March 17, 1870, p. 4. Similarly, the *Watchman and Reflector* insisted that "In this country, every industrious, prudent, skillful, healthful laborer can acquire a handsome competence by the time he is fifty years old, if that is what he desires." November 16, 1871, p. 6.

The ill-organized, sporadic, idealistic labor movement of the postwar period, struggling against conditions as yet unrealized by most Americans, ran into head-on conflict with the beliefs of articulate religious leaders. Beside being useless in the light of the wage-fund theory, labor organization seemed destructive of traditions dear to Protestant America. Over and over spokesmen of all sects lamented that unionism would drag the energetic, ambitious, hard-working laborers who were America's pride down to the level of the lazy and the shiftless. Eventually labor organization would, it was said, give rise to the rigid class lines that had caused the decadence of Europe.[18]

When organized labor, under the passionate leadership of Ira Steward, began to center its demands on the eight-hour day, clerical commentators were especially irritated. The idea of getting "ten hours' pay" for "eight hours' work" seemed as obviously contrary to conventional moral precepts as did "tampering" with the dollar. Once again, old theological ideas of natural depravity were called on as religious spokesmen declared that an increase of leisure would be an increase of vice.[19]

Horace Bushnell, commenting on a demand for a restriction of the hours of women workers, sounded as grimly uncompromising as any of his more orthodox contemporaries:

It is nothing that in great poverty, single women or women having families are brought into conditions of unspeakable severity; the same is true of men, and we do not expect them to sink mournfully or moaningly under their lot, but to bravely bear, and dig, and climb till they are free. . . . Again, it is nothing that women, sewing women for example, are not helped directly in the matter of their wages by legal enactment, any more than that men are not—there is no such possibility as a legally appointed rate of wages; market price is the only scale of earnings possible for women as for men.[20]

The sternest condemnations, of course, were reserved for "Strikes," still a sufficiently unfamiliar phenomenon to be referred to with capitals and quotation marks. Some clerical authorities defended the right of an individual worker to stop work when he chose. But the slightest suspicion of coercion was hotly denounced. The consensus seemed to agree with the *Congregationalist* that in practice a strike, being "akin to vio-

[18] Examples of this individualist argument against labor unions are innumerable. See, for instance, *Watchman and Reflector*, January 30, 1868, p. 2; *Independent*, December 2, 1869, p. 6; *Christian Union*, January 29, 1870, p. 72; July 10, 1872, p. 51; *Congregationalist*, March 17, 1870, p. 4; Lyman H. Atwater, "The Labor Question in its Economic and Christian Aspects," *Presbyterian Quarterly*, I (1872), 465-495.

[19] *Congregationalist*, June 14, 1867, p. 94; *Independent*, June 13, 1872, p. 4.

[20] Bushnell, *Women's Suffrage, The Reform Against Nature* (New York, 1869), pp. 11-12.

lence in its very seminal idea," could hardly hope to avoid falling into the temptation of unlawful methods.[21] When this opinion was coupled with the prevalent belief that labor struggles could not possibly raise wages, it led to a vigorous hostility to almost every strike.

One particular labor crisis brought in a different series of arguments against unions. In 1870 a gang of Chinese laborers was brought to North Adams, Massachusetts. Since the newcomers worked for very low wages, under semiservile conditions, and especially since they had been imported specifically to replace union men, organized labor objected. To the religious press, this question seemed to involve the racial issues fought out by the war. Even the *Congregationalist*, usually comparatively mild in its language, became passionate on behalf of the Orientals, whom it described as "youthful, pliable, faithful, quiet, neat to a degree" and praised for their ability to exist on wages "considerably less than those for which the Anglo-Saxons, or the Celts, whom they have displaced, have refused to work."[22] The *Christian Advocate* stated the case against the unions with more than usual harshness:

The demand for labor is all the time in excess of the supply, and the result of this state of things has been to render the laboring classes capricious and despotic, and, in many cases, improvident. . . . This arrogance and inefficiency have at length produced their natural results, and employers of labor are looking about them for a better class of laborers, and, because the Chinaman seems likely to respond to this demand, the monopolists of labor raise an outcry against him.[23]

The North Adams conflict foreshadowed the growth of another major cause of misunderstanding between churches and trade-unions. The unions, believing that wage levels were deliberately smashed by the importation of contract laborers and other helpless immigrants, were placing increasing emphasis on immigration restriction. The churches, on the other hand, were continuing to judge this question, like all others, on the basis of traditional individual morality. Only when they came to believe that immigration constituted a moral and religious threat were the churches to move toward an endorsement of restrictions.

[21] June 6, 1872, p. 180.
[22] Editorial, "China at North Adams," June 30, 1870, p. 204. See also July 14, 1870, pp. 3-4.
[23] Editorial, "The Chinese at North Adams," July 14, 1870, p. 220. See also *Watchman and Reflector*, July 7, 1870, p. 6; July 14, 1870, p. 6; *Christian Union*, June 25, 1870, p. 408. Even Washington Gladden, later a leader in the explanation of labor's viewpoint, at this period took part rather uncritically in the defense of the Chinese and, by implication, of the practice of importing them in such situations. Gladden, "Thanksgiving among the Chinamen," *Congregationalist*, December 1, 1870, pp. 5-6.

Many church writers of this period and later, while condemning labor unions, had a good word to say for co-operation. Although it challenged some of the prevailing economic dogmas, the co-operative movement could hardly be said to involve violence or coercion. As labor conflicts became more acute, co-operation was often preached as a substitute for strikes. With amazing naïveté, religious commentators in a period of inflation advised discontented employees to avoid dissipation, save their wages and buy out the employer. Yet some clerical comment expressed doubt whether even co-operative movements were compatible with "economic laws."[24]

Discussion of socialism was less common. Occasionally, to be sure, religious spokesmen continued to blast the remaining experimental communities, but the tone was one of complacency rather than alarm.[25] Before 1871 European socialists were mentioned only occasionally, as "harmless theorizers," who "have really but few followers among the masses."[26] Few American Protestants realized that a group existed which was pledged to the systematic destruction of the existing order, until the Paris Commune burst forth into civil war. Naturally, few inquired into the rights and wrongs of this bloody episode; most condemned the Communards in terms as harsh as those used for Fanny Wright forty years before.[27]

Indignation mounted higher when it was discovered that the First International had spread its machinations to this peaceful and contented land. Alone among clerical commentators, Edward Beecher realized that the questions raised by the International were "the great questions of the age," and urged that, as Christ cared for the working classes, "His church ought to do the same, and to study the principles involved in their elevation. If this work is left to infidels and atheists, it may result in revolutions, bloodshed, earthquakes."[28] Far more typically, the *Watchman and Reflector* confidently assured its readers that the ambitious, property-owning working classes of America

[24] The *Congregationalist* urged co-operation as a solution for the North Adams conflict and also for a strike at Fall River in the same year. June 30, 1870, p. 204; September 1, 1870, p. 276. The *Independent* expressed slight hostility to co-operatives. July 11, 1867, pp. 3-4.

[25] The *Independent* attacked Wallingford and Oneida communities, October 11, 1866, p. 2; September 27, 1877, p. 2. The *Watchman and Reflector* denounced all such attempts, November 18, 1868, p. 2. The *Christian Advocate* commented unfavorably on the founding of a new community at Brockton May 20, 1869, p. 156.

[26] George C. Comfort, "Liberalism in Europe," *Methodist Quarterly Review*, XLVIII (1866), 267.

[27] E.g. *Watchman and Reflector*, July 6, 1871, p. 6; *Congregationalist* June 1, 1871, pp. 172-173; *Independent*, July 4, 1872, p. 6.

[28] Beecher, "The International," *Christian Union*, February 14, 1872, p. 155.

are by no means desirous of making a division of their possessions for the benefit of the vagabonds and tramps, the drunkards and drones, the shiftless and criminal classes, who alone furnish permanent followers to ridiculous foreigners who have contrived to "loaf" from Europe to America.[29]

Protestant confidence in the prevailing economic theories and the soundness of existing society was put to a severe test in the dark years following 1873. Yet even when respected companies were closing their doors and unemployed laborers were roaming the highways, clerical comment lost little of its complacency. According to the Presbyterian General Assembly, church revenues suffered surprisingly little:

Amid trials that have pressed hard upon many—the rich as well as those in humbler circumstances,—church-worship has been maintained not only, but our various beneficent and missionary enterprises have been carried forward without serious disturbance.[30]

Like most papers in most depressions, the religious press appealed for confidence in the nation's financial institutions. As the gloomy winter wore on, appeals for charity became more frequent. Yet those who always took a stern attitude toward the poor still stuck to their demand that society succor the unemployed only "as paupers, in the name and on the footing and proper fare of paupers."[31]

Above all, Protestant spokesmen, assured by the dominant political economy that recovery could only come about through automatic deflationary processes, counseled the poor to be patient. A speaker at the Episcopal Church Congress, for instance, assuring the nation that society was gradually moving toward a Christian ideal, pleaded with the poor to

be content with your wages; work for what you can get, but work; . . . deserve more, and in the Lord's good time you will get more if you deserve it. Doubtless your wages, in some cases, at least, are not what they ought to be. But you know, as Christians—if not, it is our pleasure and privilege to teach you—that whatever you suffer here from the injustice of others will turn to your account hereafter. Be quiet. Whatsoever your hands can find to do, do it, and be content with your wages. God will take care of the rest.[32]

Sincerely believing that the solution of hard times lay in such quiescence, Protestant spokesmen naturally redoubled their denuncia-

[29] January 29, 1874, p. 6.
[30] Presbyterian Church in the U.S.A., General Assembly, *Minutes,* 1877, p. 590.
[31] L. H. Atwater, "Our Industrial and Financial Situation," *Presbyterian Quarterly,* IV (1875), 520.
[32] W. D. Wilson, "The Mutual Obligations of Capital and Labor," Church Congress, *Papers, Addresses and Debates,* 1874, pp. 53-54.

tions of strikes. Not only, said one cleric after another, were labor conflicts always senseless and subversive of American ideas, they were also likely to deepen the depression. In time of unemployment a strike

must be either a suicidal mistake or a premeditated one. To choose idleness and dependence instead of low wages is a blunder; to prevent, by violence, another man who is strong from earning his daily bread in the place where you have refused to work is but a felony.[33]

All other "disturbances" met equal condemnation. The *Independent* praised the New York police for prompt suppression of an unemployed parade.[34] A resolution passed by the International in New York asking President Grant to call a special session to deal with the depression was ridiculed by the *Watchman and Reflector*. Such a request proved its makers "ignorant, not only of the first principles of political economy, but of the purpose for which the national government exists. That government is not bound to find work for any man."[35] The unemployed that wandered from town to town in these years also alarmed religious commentators, who usually demanded that they be forced to settle down.[36]

Throughout the postwar decade, most religious commentators found in each contemporary tendency or event another illustration of the old, all-sufficient dogmas of laissez faire. Only occasionally, scattered voices expressed a hesitancy to swallow these doctrines whole. Such dissent as existed, outside of a few neglected radical coteries, was expressed in moral terms and focussed only on the more extreme manifestations of greed or callousness. For instance George N. Boardman, in a long article generally in support of contemporary economic theories, reverted to an earlier Christian view when he suggested that individualism needed to be qualified by regard for the family. Some slight exertion of social power

[33] *Independent*, December 16, 1874, p. 14. For similar views see June 11, 1874, pp. 15-16; *Watchman and Reflector*, May 1, 1873, p. 6; *Christian Union*, July 1, 1874, pp. 518-519.

[34] January 22, 1874, p. 17. This is probably the "Tompkins Square Massacre" that deeply stirred other witnesses, such as Samuel Gompers, to quite different reactions. Gompers, *Seventy Years of Life and Labor* (New York, 1925), I, 94-97.

[35] *Watchman and Reflector*, November 20, 1873, p. 6. This paper similarly condemned the farmers' movement of the seventies, a topic mentioned less often than strikes in the religious press. August 7, 1873, p. 6.

[36] E. g. *Congregationalist*, October 21, 1875, p. 332. The *Churchman*, often rather grandiose in its idea of the status of the Episcopal church, believed that the solution was for honest wanderers to carry letters from their rectors. October 30, 1875, p. 478. The *Christian Union* was unusual in saying that the reason for the tramps' shiftlessness was discouragement, and that the way to cure it was to employ them. November 10, 1873, p. 586.

might, he thought, be necessary to protect those who could not protect themselves in the day's commercial warfare. Christians were not necessarily to condemn such devices as poor laws or free schools; these really represented an increase of wages on behalf of the family.[37] An anonymous writer in the *Christian Advocate*, in the course of stating the fairly conservative doctrine that the employer must determine the wage in the light of conscience, referred to academic economics in somewhat unusual terms: "Those who substitute the so-called laws of political economy for the laws of God will have an account to render to him."[38] (It is perhaps significant that the editors thought it necessary to disclaim responsibility for this unusually forthright statement.)

Such uneasy caviling at the accepted views arose, perhaps, from the survival of some half-forgotten traditions of a godly society or, more likely, from an instinctive response to basic Christian teaching. It can never have been entirely easy to reconcile unadulterated laissez faire with some passages in the Old and New Testaments. These rare murmurs of dissent indicate, at most, that religion never completely loses its critical potential. Their rarity indicates still more clearly that most Protestants found little to criticize in prevailing ideas or conditions.

As in the prewar period, the most important objections to the prevailing optimism came not from dissenting moralists but from those few ministers who had already experienced firsthand the conditions in the nation's growing slums. Largely unseen and unrealized by the prosperous, churchgoing middle class, living conditions in the immigrant cities and industrial towns were often unspeakable. Crowded in tenements and cellars, racked by epidemics, the urban poor of this individualistic age often lacked even the elementary aid of charitable institutions.

Already one consequence of these conditions was beginning to be brought to clerical attention. Observant churchmen noticed, with alarming regularity, that the city working class was not attending Protestant services.[39] In response to this startling fact, the churches were already being drawn increasingly into evangelical and thence into charitable work. By the end of the seventies a rudimentary network of city missions and church philanthropic institutions already existed, backed by in-

[37] *Op. cit.*, in *Bibliotheca Sacra*, LXXXIX (1866), 73-107.
[38] Editorial, signed J. A., February 22, 1872, p. 60.
[39] See discussion of "The Ministrations of the Church to the Working Classes," Protestant Episcopal Church, Church Congress, *Papers, Addresses and Debates*, 1875, pp. 39-73; also "The Church for the People," *Ladies' Repository*, XXX (1870), 134-139; "Preaching the Gospel to the Poor," *Biblical Repertory and Princeton Review*, XLIII (1871), 83-95; "The Church and the Working Class," *Watchman and Reflector*, October 31, 1872, p. 6.

dividual congregations, by denominations, and even by interchurch charitable organizations.[40] This great expansion of religious effort, still in its embryo stage, was eventually to have a profound effect on the social opinions of many church workers.

As yet, however, the prevailing complacency was often impenetrable even by facts. Some church comment on the alienation of the working class sounded, in fact, almost congratulatory. The *Christian Advocate*, organ of a church which traditionally spoke for the poor, prided itself that

by virtue of the habits which religion inculcates and cherishes, our Church members have as a body risen in the social scale, and thus become socially removed from the great body out of which most of them were originally gathered. This tendency of things is natural and universal, and in its results unavoidable; perhaps we might add, also, not undesirable.[41]

Where church spokesmen were forced to admit that bad conditions existed, a traditional scapegoat was at hand. The Presbyterian General Assembly could still blame urban falling-away on the fact that "The immigration from Europe, so greatly stimulated of late years, is deeply popish, or as sadly infidel."[42]

Only here and there firsthand experience of urban evils was producing the beginnings of a more fundamental analysis. In 1872 Charles Loring Brace published a realistic description of New York conditions that was the beginning of a long and influential series of clerical exposés.[43] Even the *Presbyterian Quarterly* in general commented favorably on this work, although it took occasion in doing so to insist that "here, as a general rule, poverty comes from vice, rather than vice from poverty."[44] Another reviewer, however, already agreed with Brace that crime and vice must be blamed on overcrowding as well as on drink and immigration.[45] But such realism was exceptional. City experience, like other causes of change, was only beginning to show its effect on Protestant social opinion.

Buttressed by the nearly unanimous opinion of academic authorities,

[40] A. I. Abell, *The Urban Impact on American Protestantism, 1865-1900* (Cambridge, 1938), pp. 27-56.

[41] "Methodism and our City Masses," *Christian Advocate*, February 8, 1866, p. 44. The *Christian Union* similarly boasted that "Most of the readers of this paper are undoubtedly, compared with the mass of the community, in the current depression, in comfortable circumstances." October 27, 1875, p. 346.

[42] *Minutes*, 1868, p. 18.

[43] *The Dangerous Classes of New York and Twenty Years Work among Them* (New York, 1872). For further discussion of Brace and his work, see pp. 112-113.

[44] II (1873), 89.

[45] J. F. Richmond, "The Dangerous Classes and Their Treatment," *Methodist Quarterly Review*, LV (1873), 455-474.

sustained by the growing wealth and power of the churchgoing middle class, American Protestantism maintained its support of the combined social and religious orthodoxy developed in the prewar period. Christian America was still being guided by the Unseen Hand; church and nation were sound. Greed at the top could be ignored or accepted as a tool of progress. Misery at the bottom could be waved aside as inevitable or, at most, treated by a program of guarded and labeled philanthropy. The only vigorous dissent came from isolated and ineffective radicals. Until they were shocked by a series of violent social conflicts, most Protestant spokesmen continued to insist that all was well.

3

TWO GIANTS

T HE conservative and optimistic tendencies of Protestant thought in the postwar period extended beyond the sphere of church comment on concrete social issues. These traits pervaded much of the general religious teaching of the day and were reflected in the work of the period's great preachers. Phillips Brooks, the eloquent and inspiring rector of Trinity Church and bishop of Massachusetts, and Henry Ward Beecher, the pulpit orator of Plymouth Church, Brooklyn, were the religious giants of their day. Opposites in many ways, both reflected throughout their postwar careers the conservative social outlook of the seventies, the period of Brooks' ripening greatness and Beecher's mature power. Neither changed his opinions much during the next two troubled decades.

When Brooks was called to Trinity in 1869, he rather surprised his crowded congregation by preaching little on social and political matters. During the war, in Philadelphia, he had lent his already great eloquence to the cause of Negro rights, and Boston was used to reforming ministers. Certainly his conception of his duty did not preclude social preaching; he had stated his attitude to pulpit antislavery in terms that could be widely extended: "I preach what I was ordained to preach—the gospel, nothing else: but as a part of the gospel I will accept the rebuking of sins, and public sins as well as private."[1]

Endowed with great eloquence, a warm heart, and a personality whose spiritual power left a deep impression on all who came in contact with him, Brooks could have achieved wide mundane influence if he had chosen to emphasize the rebuke of public sins. But the great preacher was primarily concerned with personal religion. He even deplored the fact that English Episcopalians were turning some of their attention from spiritual to social questions.[2] In the first place, social reform was not the primary duty of the church, and in the second, as we can gather from his few economic pronouncements, contemporary society did not seem to need a great deal of reform.

[1] Brooks to his father, December 19, 1864, in Allen, *Phillips Brooks*, I, 523.
[2] *Ibid.*, II, 224-225.

Like many of his contemporaries, Brooks believed that social inequality was both inevitable and desirable:

There can be no doubt, I think, whatever puzzling questions it may bring with it, that it is the fact of privilege and inequalities among men for which they do not seem to be responsible, which makes a large part of the interest and richness of human existence. . . . I believe that the more we think, the more we become convinced that the instinct which asks for equality is a low one, and that equality, if it were completely brought about, would furnish play only for the lower instincts and impulses of man.[3]

To Brooks it was not wealth in itself but only the *misuse* of great riches that was wrong and dangerous in "a community where poor men and rich men live side by side."[4] Like aristocrats of all ages, Brooks deeply believed that education, wealth and social position were deliberate gifts of God, and that their accompanying responsibilities must not be ignored, either through modesty or cowardice.[5]

Poverty (though Brooks, unlike some of his contemporaries, made it clear that he was not terming it a positive blessing) had also its special virtues—dignity and self-respect, avoidance of servility or envy. It had its sources of special happiness—a closeness to reality, a mutual dependence, the development of deeper faith.[6] And Boston's bishop, whose sincerity was perhaps greater than his experience, did not believe that great need was widespread in America during his time. "Excessive poverty," he said, "actual suffering for the necessities of life, terrible as it is, is comparatively rare."[7]

"Communism," which in Brooks' vocabulary seemed still to mean the radical egalitarianism of the experimental communities rather than the doctrines of Marx, was un-Christian: "Nowhere is there any communism in Jesus. The waste of power which communism involves would find no tolerance from Him."[8] Yet Brooks, living in the light of his mystical faith, was not as perturbed by the central social problems of his time as were some of his contemporaries.

We wrestle with the problem of socialism and individualism, the problem of the many and the one; and we wonder which of the two must be sacrificed to the other. . . . Let us be sure that to Christ, to God, there is no

---

[3] Brooks, "The Duties of Privilege," in *New Starts in Life and Other Sermons,* Eighth Series (New York, 1897), p. 88.

[4] "How to Abound," in *Sermons,* Sixth Series (New York, 1893), p. 151.

[5] "The Duties of Privilege," p. 93.

[6] "How to Be Abased," in *Sermons,* Sixth Series, p. 159-176.

[7] "The Man with Two Talents," in *Twenty Sermons,* Fourth Series (New York, 1887), p. 194.

[8] "The Duties of Privilege," p. 89.

problem. . . . When society shall be complete, it shall perfectly develop the freedom of the individual. When the individual shall be perfect, he will make in his free and original life his appointed contribution to society.[9]

About the eventual solution of the labor problem itself Brooks was equally confident. As the problem got more serious, new light would be vouchsafed.[10] Meanwhile his advice to working people was, like that of his contemporaries, patience and self-improvement:

> . . . if the workmen of our country can live worthier and nobler lives they will not merely do something to conquer the enemies I have just been speaking of, but they will do something to help the solution of these great problems that seem to loom up with such danger in the future.[11]

Brooks did not oppose social change with the panic, the stubborn reiteration, the violent denunciation of his contemporaries.[12] His conservatism came neither from the pat generalities of classical economics nor from class prejudice, but from his happy temperament, worked upon by the optimistic atmosphere of his time. Brooks, full of natural vigor as well as untroubled faith, living in the "interesting inequality" of Boston society and perhaps slightly detached from its worst aspects, shared the prevailing satisfaction with the times. Puzzling events did not shake his confidence that "It will get settled somehow, and things will be juster than they are to-day."[13]

Not especially from the standpoint of a Spencerian or a classical economist (for Brooks was not particularly an academic) but on traditional religious grounds, Brooks was an individualist. He strongly disliked any tendency to think of men in groups or classes:

> Here is where all party spirit shows its viciousness. Here is where all socialism shows its weakness. Here is where all the weak idolatry of organic methods fails. It loses sight of the final unit in its watch over some of the accidental and temporary combinations of mankind. The final unit is the man.[14]

[9] "Individual and Collective Humanity," in *Seeking Life and Other Sermons*, Tenth Series (New York, 1904), p. 138.

[10] "The New and Greater Miracle," in *The Light of the World and Other Sermons*, Fifth Series (New York, 1891), p. 31.

[11] "Address at the Laying of the Cornerstone of the Wells Memorial Working-Men's Club and Institute, Boston, Mass., May 30, 1882," in *Essays and Addresses* (New York, 1895), p. 371. See also Allen, *Phillips Brooks*, II, 786-787.

[12] It is interesting that W. D. P. Bliss, the Christian Socialist, admired Brooks deeply and tried to prove that he was at heart a socialist. Brooks endorsed Bliss' radical Church of the Carpenter, visited it, and contributed to it. *The Dawn*, May, 1892, pp. 5-6; January 23, 1893, p. 2.

[13] Undated letter on the labor question, quoted in Allen, *op. cit.*, II, 787.

[14] Brooks, *The Influence of Jesus* (Bohlen Lectures, New York, 1879), p. 112.

The church must stick to her vital business with the individual soul, and not become entangled in "second causes" and machinery.[15] In an address on "The Duties of the Christian Business Man"[16] Brooks told his audience, typically, that he could not tell them in detail what they should do. (Many of his contemporaries would have been glad to.) Businessmen, like others, should learn and discharge their duties with the aid of prayer, the Bible, and the Church.

Perhaps Brooks is most easily understood as a combination of the Catholic and the revivalist. His calm, dignified eloquence seems far removed from the warm exhortation of Moody. Yet both believed that their sole duty was to effect a spiritual change in their hearers. It may be significant that Brooks admired Moody deeply, and thought Henry Ward Beecher "the greatest preacher of America and the Century."[17] Nothing in his social teaching disagreed essentially with the opinions of either. Though he transcended it, Brooks did not in any particular conflict with his time.

Henry Ward Beecher reached a far larger audience even than Brooks and was much less reluctant to express specific opinions on worldly matters. Sentimental, self-indulgent, egotistical, immensely warmhearted but sometimes callous, Beecher was as much the embodiment of nineteenth-century America as Walt Whitman. As one of his less worshiping biographers points out: "He was not in advance of his day, but precisely abreast of his day. . . . his inner experience was identical with that of millions of his countrymen. His gift was merely that he was articulate while they were not."[18]

By giving his countrymen the kind of preaching they wanted, Beecher made himself more than the most famous son of a great clerical family. From his call to Plymouth Church in 1847 until his death almost fifty years later he was the most influential minister in America and one of the leading molders of public opinion of his day. Through his large and wealthy Brooklyn congregation, through the sermons that were published in many newspapers and finally in book form, through his speeches and addresses and essays on all sorts of subjects, through his successive control of two extremely influential religious newspapers, the *Independent* and the *Christian Union*, and finally through the publicity, some of it extremely unpleasant, which surrounded his whole spectacular

[15] *Lectures on Preaching* (New York, 1877), p. 240.
[16] *Essays and Addresses*, pp. 71-96.
[17] Allen, *Phillips Brooks*, II, 148-149; Brooks, "Address at the Installation of Rev. Lyman Abbott, D.D.," in *Essays and Addresses*, p. 176.
[18] Hibben, *Henry Ward Beecher*, p. viii.

career, Beecher achieved an influence and a notoriety unknown to ministers today.

Since boyhood Beecher's exuberant nature had strained against the inherited Calvinist bonds. In his maturity, responding gladly to the liberal theological currents which were abroad, he evolved an emotional, optimistic theology that exactly suited his needs and talents. Unconcerned about dogmatic controversy, testing his beliefs by the way they made him feel, he was in touch with the ordinary American as very few church leaders ever have been. At the same time he was a liberating influence on some of the most important of the next generation's liberal church leaders.

Adhering exactly to the historic American compromise between church and state, Beecher denounced a "theocracy" in standard liberal terms, yet took a very high view of the minister's function as a moral guide. It was not only the preacher's right, but his duty, to speak out on all subjects that could remotely be connected with moral questions:

. . . when ministers meddle with practical life, with ethical questions and relations, they are meddling with just what they do understand, or ought to. . . . There is nothing . . . more untrue than that every man understands his business best, if by that you mean that he understands it in its largest relation—in its results upon the general welfare; and more particularly if you mean that he understands his own business best in its moral influence upon himself, upon his fellows, and upon society. . . . The moment a man so conducts his profession that it touches the question of right and wrong, he comes into my sphere.[19]

No popular heresy, Beecher insisted, was more hopelessly mistaken than the idea that men have a right to follow their worst impulses without being disturbed by Christian ministers. It was the duty of the church to root out selfishness, not only from the individual heart, but from the family, business and social life. The state needed instruction and moral guidance as much as did individuals. When the church neglected the questions which the community wanted discussed, or discussed them in an unintelligible, "philosophic" way, it forfeited its influence over the masses.[20]

Beecher himself ran no risk of making this mistake. In his participa-

[19] Beecher, "The Sphere of the Christian Minister," quoted in *Patriotic Addresses* (New York, 1891), pp. 79-80.

[20] "Authority of Right over Wrong," *Plymouth Pulpit*, Second Series (New York, 1870), pp. 421-438; "Scope and Function of a Christian Life," *Ibid.* pp. 91-108; "The Duty of Living Peaceably," *Plymouth Pulpit*, Ninth Series (New York, 1873), pp. 7-22; "The Church's Duty to Slavery," *Freedom and War* (Boston, 1863), p. 207.

tion in the antislavery movement of the fifties, and in his enormous patriotic endeavor during the Civil War he had started speaking freely on political issues, and he never ceased. Not only did he orate freely and often on standard questions such as immigration, the currency, war, taxes, corruption, and so forth; he was also a considerable power in Republican party politics, local and national.

In the fervent patriotism of the war and postwar years nobody could outdo Beecher. Democracy was the final form of government, a product of the progress of Christianity through the ages, destined to spread from America over the earth. And by democracy Beecher meant, of course, "equitable opportunity" and not compulsory equality: "No government has a right to thrust a strong man down to the level of weakness. No institution has a right to force a weak man up to the level of a strong."[21]

Beecher accepted the dominant economic theory with his usual gusto: "The things required for prosperous labor, prosperous manufactures, and prosperous commerce are three. First, liberty; second, liberty; and third, liberty.[22] Of course, the great preacher's warm heart was filled with sympathy for the poor. Particularly in his Civil War days, he loved to proclaim the uplift of the poor as the Church's primary mission, and the measure of the nation's moral welfare. But, he made clear, he was referring to *moral* uplift, to the healing of spiritual rather than economic ravages. Almsgiving, he believed, had wrought the destruction of England and of every other nation where it had been widely practiced.[23]

In the postwar years Beecher fell into line with his contemporaries, proclaiming that poverty in America was either nonexistent or the product of vice:

Even in the most compact and closely-populated portions of the East, he that will be frugal, and save continuously, living every day within the bounds of his means, can scarcely help accumulating.[24]

There may be reasons of poverty which do not involve wrong; but looking comprehensively through city and town and village and country, the general truth will stand, that no man in this land suffers from poverty unless it be more than his fault—unless it be his *sin*.[25]

[21] "National Unity," in *Patriotic Addresses*, p. 759.
[22] "Speech in the Philharmonic Hall, Liverpool," *Ibid.*, p. 519.
[23] "The Bible to be Spiritually Interpreted," in *Plymouth Pulpit*, Ninth Series, p. 226.
[24] "Practical Ethics for the Young," *Plymouth Pulpit*, Seventh Series (New York, 1872), p. 281.
[25] "Economy in Small Things," *Plymouth Pulpit*, New Series, III (New York, 1874-5), 263.

When he turned to the subject of wealth Beecher stated the prevalent theories with unusual authority. The great preacher, with his liberal salary and large royalties, could speak on this topic with the authority of one who was himself the nation's outstanding success in his field. In a sermon on "The Deceitfulness of Riches" he warned young men against wealth's incidental temptations, but painted a brilliant picture of the power of riches for refinement, civilization, morality, virtue and for the world-wide work of the church. With these possibilities in mind "we are not," he concluded, "to stand and inveigh against riches, and we are not to warn young men against becoming or desiring to become, rich."[26] Like many of his contemporaries, he explained that the Bible was not to be taken too literally on this point:

> In different places throughout the Scriptures it is taught that riches are evil and mischievous. But would civilization be helped, if all capital were dispersed? . . . Now, take the true meaning of this precept. It is designed to relieve men from miseries. It is intended to keep them from an inordinate love of money. It is meant to give them a higher conception of wealth.[27]

Beecher, like his fellows, believed that success and morality ordinarily went hand in hand. He could not help believing, as he looked around his Brooklyn congregation of well-to-do and pious merchants, that "generally the proposition is true, that where you find the most religion there you will find the most worldly prosperity—in communities, I mean; not in single persons."[28] With his usual vigor, Beecher denounced the stock frauds and corporate swindles of his day. He deplored these episodes, however, for a sound conservative reason; they brought into disrepute "indispensable elements of property in this land." And more than ever such scandals made it clear to him that "commercial prosperity stands indissolubly connected with public morals."[29]

Perceptive, sensitive to social currents, and caring little for consistency, Beecher occasionally suggested that American society held the germ of future diseases, that "The distance is becoming wider in every decade of years between the cultured and the uncultured; between the rich and the poor; between the different sections of society."[30] But such infrequent gloomy notes cannot have brought much more than a pleasant shudder to the Plymouth Church congregation. Any moments of doubt were lost in hours of glowing optimism. Mechanical progress was making the poor

[26] *Plymouth Pulpit,* Eighth Series (New York, 1873), p. 19.
[27] "The Bible to Be Spiritually Interpreted," *Plymouth Pulpit,* Ninth Series, p. 229.
[28] "The Temporal Advantages of Religion," *Ibid.,* p. 366.
[29] "Lessons for the Times," in *New Star Papers* (New York, 1859), pp. 95, 98.
[30] "Signs of the Times," *Plymouth Pulpit,* Eighth Series, p. 195.

more contented; wealth was steadily being Christianized and put into the service of society.[31] Confidence and exuberance flowed from Plymouth pulpit in a steady stream.

A familiar oratorical device much used by Beecher was to give his hearers a sudden, temporary shock by *seeming* to espouse unorthodox views, then to explain his meaning in reassuring terms. His views on labor unions follow this pattern. At a time when any mention of such organizations still alarmed many of his contemporaries, Beecher welcomed them as a sign of the inevitable upward movement of the lower classes:

And although it will bring sore disturbance, and create sore revolutions, and lead to a great many errors, and entail a great deal of mischief, nevertheless, I thank God that there is a rising of men from the bottom of society toward the top. My heart goes with the men who are poor and ignorant and who are working for liberty to be larger and richer.[32]

But Beecher's humanitarian emotions did not carry him into sympathy with any *existing* labor organizations. No union was good which contained a core of selfishness, which followed "glittering social theories," which regarded work as an evil, which tended toward irreligion, or which set aside "the great law of subordination."[33] It is difficult to see any function for a good labor union after Beecher has pointed out the dangers of a bad one. The eight-hour movement he repeatedly condemned.[34] Men must regard work as good, not evil; the more hours the better. Equalization of wages negated the "law of intelligence and skill," it was "a rebellion against Jehovah."[35] Opposition to the immigration of unskilled labor was contrary to the interests of the country.[36] Finally, the great strikes of 1877, ending the period in which organized labor could be regarded as an interesting novelty, drew from Beecher, as from many of his brethren, denunciations of unbelievable violence.[37]

Beecher used the same technique when he shocked his hearers by admitting some sympathy with the "Internationals." Welcoming their existence as another symptom of the upward struggle, he quickly ex-

[31] See for instance "The Ground and Forms of Government," *Patriotic Addresses,* pp. 392-393; "The Tendencies of American Progress," *Plymouth Pulpit,* Fifth Series (New York, 1871), pp. 203-220.
[32] "Signs of the Times," *Plymouth Pulpit,* Eighth Series, p. 191. See also "The Tendencies of American Progress," pp. 207-208.
[33] "Signs of the Times," pp. 199-200.
[34] "Practical Ethics for the Young," *Plymouth Pulpit,* Seventh Series, p. 279. "Cuba and the Brotherhood of Nations," *Plymouth Pulpit,* New Series, I, 199.
[35] "War and Peace," *Plymouth Pulpit,* Ninth Series, p. 229.
[36] "The Tendencies of American Progress," pp. 209-210.
[37] See pp. 93-94.

plained that their "creed" was "heretical," and many of their characteristics "atrocious and detestable."[38] Their "grand blunder," like that of the
labor unions, was "the supposition that men can be made to stand on the
same level, whom God did not make of the same force. . . ."[39] Beecher,
like his contemporaries, denounced the Paris Commune in fiery terms
but was confident that America's religion and her "cheap land, that will
not fail for many generations to come," would save us from similar
dangers.[40] Only later, when social crisis had reached America, did he
change his tone from calm to terror, calling for the use of the regular
army against "socialist riots."[41]

There was, in fact, nothing at all extraordinary in the social and
economic opinions of Beecher except the vigor, enthusiasm, and
frequency with which they were expressed. In his fervent patriotism, his
sweeping optimism, his belief in democracy, his frank attachment to
individualism and competition, he typified the well-to-do American of
his time. Like most of his contemporaries, lay and clerical, he saw social
and economic problems as essentially simple. Protect the rights of the
individual, support morality, and everything in this fortunate country
would go more than well. Beecher was as exuberantly successful in his
sphere as any railroad king. Even his involvement in the most publicized
divorce scandal of his time failed finally to dislodge him from his pedestal.
Surrounded by adoring and wealthy parishioners, buoyed by an exuberant
temperament, he was not likely to dwell on the less happy aspects of
American society except when some violent upheaval brought them
momentarily to his attention. In such crises his reaction was instant
and emotional.

Like his vastly different contemporary, Phillips Brooks, Beecher by his
magnetism and warm personal religion attracted many men of very
different social views. His type of religion—untheological, emotional,
humanitarian—was to become very common in American. In a different
environment, some of Beecher's direct disciples were to use his views and
methods for the criticism of society. But Beecher himself was and remained a sturdy defender of freedom, prosperity and the status quo.

[38] "War and Peace," pp. 227-228.
[39] "Earning a Livelihood," *Plymouth Pulpit*, Ninth Series, p. 189.
[40] "The Lesson from Paris," *Plymouth Pulpit*, Sixth Series (New York, 1872), pp.
244-245.
[41] "Address before the Society of the Army of the Potomac" (1878), *Patriotic
Addresses*, pp. 819-821.

4

NEGLECTED PROPHETS

D ESPITE the comfortable picture painted by nearly all Protestant comment, despite the evidence of luxury and vigor, the postwar years were not a period of universal content. Farmers were struggling with falling prices, inflated interest burdens and crushing railway rates. The real wages of labor had been declining even before the onset of depression in 1873. But the churches, as some of their keener leaders were soon to discover, had to a large extent lost touch with these discontented groups. The isolated critics of society, lay and clerical, who stood at the fringes of organized religion, could not make their voices heard above the swelling chorus of exultation.

Many of the fervent perfectionists who, in the prewar period, had called for a Christian reorganization of society proved unable to direct their enthusiasm into postwar channels. Adin Ballou, the venerable founder of Hopedale, describes with superb insight and pathos the plight of the old reforming generation as it confronted an altered nation:

As to special reformers, they had mostly fallen away from my high ideals of Practical Christianity. The Non-resistants, with few exceptions, had failed in the hour of trial and yielded allegiance to the war-god when with his battle-axe he cleft asunder the fetters of the slave. . . . Anti-slavery had become apotheosized by its war-power triumph and rested from its labors. All that could be done in its behalf was to carry relief to the freedmen, to which I contributed by words and deeds. The temperance cause called for devotees, and I gave it the support I could without involving myself in its reliance upon penal laws, arbitrary exactions, and final resort to violence. The same was true of the cause of women's rights. . . . Finally, the working people's movement flung its standard to the breeze and called for recruits to its heterogeneous ranks. I was interested in its objects and professed claims, as I had been in similar movements in America and England for many years, and I studied and watched it with sympathetic desire and hope. But I found in it little of the spirit of fraternity, of co-operation between the strong and the weak; little of the spirit of Christian brotherhood. It sought to level down but not up. Its trust was in legislation and governmental coercion. The sword was its dernier resort. It belonged to a moral and social sphere and to a field of reform from which I had withdrawn forever.[1]

Even at its prewar height the idealistic, uncompromising reform spirit represented by Ballou had never greatly affected the major churches. But the antislavery cause had finally become that of northern Protestantism. The movement and its remaining leaders had achieved, in the postwar period, something of the prestige and sanctity usually attached to successful revolutions. It is all the more significant that even Wendell Phillips, the silver-tongued champion of Boston abolition, failed to shake Protestant complacency when, in his sixties, he issued a ringing challenge to the dominant economic views.

Unlike most of his aging antislavery colleagues, Phillips saw in the labor movement the logical successor of abolition and gave to it his remaining eloquence and power.[2] Not only did he endorse the eight-hour campaign, the co-operative movement, and other labor causes, he also immersed himself in the sporadic, ill-organized labor political movement of the seventies. The Labor Reform party of Massachusetts was tainted, in orthodox eyes, not only with unsound ideas on wages and hours but also with Greenbackery. It was further disliked because of its links with Ben Butler, whose spectacular and erratic career in politics and the army had alienated much respectable opinion. Yet Phillips, in 1870, accepted its nomination for governor. At the party's 1871 convention, which nominated Butler, he presented a resolution that seemed to echo the ideas of contemporary European socialists:

We affirm, as a fundamental principle, that labor, the creator of wealth, is entitled to all it creates. Affirming this, we avow ourselves willing to accept the final results of the operation of a principle so radical, such as the overthrow of the whole profit-making system.

He even referred to the Paris Commune in friendly, though moderate terms: "I, for one, honor Paris, but in the name of Heaven and with the ballot in our right hands, we shall not need to write our record in fire and blood; we write it in the orderly majorities at the ballot-box."[3] When the new party was attacked by the Reverend Samuel A. Johnson in the *Radical*, organ of liberal Unitarianism, Phillips answered in a speech at the Boston Music Hall. Terming Johnson "the best critic which the labor movement has met," he answered his standard criticisms of the

[1] Ballou, *Autobiography*, pp. 462-463.
[2] For information on this phase of Phillips' career, see G. L. Austin, *The Life and Times of Wendell Phillips* (Boston, 1888), pp. 257-267; Carlos Martyn, *Wendell Phillips: the Agitator* (New York, 1890), pp. 377-398. An interesting letter from Phillips regarding the labor question is printed in *Equity*, December, 1874, p. 71.
[3] Phillips, *The Labor Question* (pamphlet, Boston, 1884), pp. 5, 6.

labor movement one by one. To Johnson's shocked assertion that the new party's platform tended toward an "equalization of property," Phillips responded with a proud assertion that such was indeed the case.[4]

After describing the new and grim conditions that disgraced the Bay State's industrial towns, Phillips in his peroration attacked Protestant apologists on their own grounds. Commenting on the proposed building of a model town by A. T. Stewart, the New York magnate, he repudiated the sort of philanthropy admired by his contemporaries: "The civilization which alone can look the New Testament in the face is a civilization where one man could not build, and another man would not need, that sort of refuge."[5]

Yet even this home thrust did not pierce the armor of postwar Protestantism. Comment in the church press deplored, in a tone of complacent patronage, the fact that a man who had once been a great leader could fall prey, in his old age, to eccentricity.[6] Later, when Phillips spoke a good word for the Russian nihilists in a Phi Beta Kappa oration, the tone of church criticism naturally became considerably more scathing.[7] But when the old reformer died in 1884 most of the religious press reverted to its earlier attitude, praising his earlier leadership and alluding briefly but sorrowfully to "those vagaries of his later life."[8]

Isolated, mystical radicals exist in all ages of Christian history. Among the more interesting specimens of this type in the postwar period was the Reverend Jesse H. Jones, an eccentric, devoted figure who has received more notice from recent historians than he did from contemporaries.[9] A Harvard and Andover graduate and a Congregational minister, Jones devoted his life to preaching Christian communism, writing on the subject, founding small, short-lived organizations of like-minded people, and editing two Christian communist newspapers. Though his work began after the war, Jones was as much an expression of the prewar perfectionist spirit as Adin Ballou.

[4] Johnson, "Labor Parties and Labor Reform," *Radical*, IX (1871), 244-265; Phillips, *Labor Question*, pp. 5-21.

[5] *Labor Question*, p. 21.

[6] *Christian Advocate*, September 22, 1870, p. 300; *Watchman and Reflector*, October 13, 1870, p. 2; *Independent*, October 19, 1871, p. 4; *Christian Union*, September 19, 1877, pp. 222-223.

[7] The *Congregationalist* directly blamed Phillips and other spokesmen of "mawkish sentiment and maudlin philanthropy" for Garfield's assassination. July 6, 1881, p. 218; August 3, 1881, p. 280.

[8] *Andover Review*, I (1884), 309-316; *Congregationalist*, February 7, 1884, p. 46; *Watchman*, February 7, 1884, p. 1.

[9] See Dombrowski, *Early Days*, pp. 77-83; Hopkins, *Social Gospel*, pp. 43-49. For biographical detail see the sketch by Halah H. Loud in Jones, *Joshua Davidson, Christian* (New York, 1907, published posthumously), pp. vii, xvi; also the account with portrait in *Dawn*, April, 1893, p. 1.

Jones, like many sectarian mystics of other ages, drew from the Gospels the lesson that the Kingdom of Heaven prophesied by Christ was "an entirely new kind of temporal, political government which he would establish on earth," and that this perfect community was to be based on common property.[10] The communistic practices of the primitive church, the principle of Christian love, the Mosaic law, and logic all seemed to Jones to prove this point. The coming social organization was to be one of small, self-governing, self-sufficient communities in which each member had a small homestead, and the right of use in the rest of the land. Exchange was to be cut to a minimum and was to be entirely for cash and in the medium of the time-dollar.[11] Jones' program was not designed, like contemporary European socialism, to change industrial society, but, like older Utopias, to reject it.

Despite his somewhat fantastic proposals, Jones had perceived some of the evils of existing American society to which many Christians would awaken in the next quarter-century. His idealism was outraged by the power and ruthlessness of the "money-kings," the misery of the slums, the bolstering of selfishness by codes of law and even etiquette, the "selfish" practices of bankers, manufacturers and landlords. The only solution was, he said, "a system of communital life in which the people shall own the money, . . . the railroads, . . . the manufactories, . . . the houses, . . . the lands; and shall conduct them as the people choose. . . ."[12]

This happy order was to be developed in America; Jones was as patriotic as Beecher. Like other Protestants, Jones believed that God's plan for America was demonstrated in its founding, in the Revolution and in its subsequent history. With Divine help, America had achieved democracy in governmental life and must go on to carry it in to her "work-life" in the form of communism.[13] Carrying his interpretation of America's mission even further than his contemporaries dared, Jones announced his central discovery in huge fancy type with a full-page floral border:

THE UNITED STATES OF AMERICA
IS THE KINGDOM OF HEAVEN WHICH JESUS CHRIST
CAME TO ESTABLISH UPON THE EARTH.[14]

Jones' method of achieving his Utopian goal had a great deal in common with the 'means used by earlier and contemporary Protestant

[10] Jones, *The Kingdom of Heaven* (Boston, 1871), p. 63 and *passim*.
[11] The most detailed description of Jones' program is his *The Bible Plan for the Abolition of Poverty* (Boston, 1873).
[12] *Kingdom of Heaven*, p. 282.
[13] *Ibid.*, pp. 186-194, 274, 278.
[14] *Ibid.*, opposite p. 214.

movements. Among existing parties he made the same choice as other clerics; "I never knew but one Sabbath-school man who was a Democrat."[15] For the future, however, Jones proposed to organize a new party to be called "Jesus Christ's Party," "The Christian Party," or "The Friends of Jesus." Working for the establishment of Christian communism as an ultimate goal this organization was to include among its immediate aims woman suffrage, the Bible in the schools, prohibition, penny postage and other comparatively conventional projects. The Methodist church, because of its size, organization and democratic sympathies, was to take the lead. And the location of the first nucleus of the life in common could be taken for granted: "Intelligence agrees with density of population in pointing to the neighborhood of Boston as the place where to found the True Christian Society."[16]

Jones spent his life in a fruitless, devoted effort to forward this program. In 1872 he founded, in Boston, the Christian Labor Union, an organization doubtless seen by him as the nucleus of the Christian party. It met once a month, backed public lectures by Jones and others, and published two small, short-lived papers, *Equity* and *Labor Balance*.[17] The circulation of these forlorn sheets never reached five hundred, publication was sporadic, and the last few numbers were pages in Henry George's *Standard*. As courageous as they were unsuccessful, Jones' papers attacked such shibboleths as orthodox political economy and heavy expenditures for foreign missions. They backed the eight-hour movement, most contemporary strikes including the railroad strike of 1877, co-operation, the Granger and Greenback movements, and women and child-labor reform. In 1878 *Labor Balance* endorsed most of the platform of the Socialist Labor party.

The spirit and sources of Jones' struggling movement were demonstrated by the men he gathered round him. His best-known colleague was Josiah Warren, the philosophical anarchist whose theories emphasized money based on labor hours.[18] Warren had been a member of New Harmony, he had established a "Time-Store" in Cincinnati in the late twenties and, with his colleague Stephen P. Andrews, had headed Modern Times, a Long Island community based on his own theories. In

[15] *Ibid.*, p. 205.
[16] *Bible Plan*, p. 188.
[17] Published respectively April, 1874-December, 1875 and October, 1877-February, 1879. The program of the C.L.U., which follows that suggested by Jones' books except that its communism is less specific, can be found in *Equity*, April, 1874, p. 8. All its activities can best be followed in this paper.
[18] Warren is rather fully treated by Bernard, *American Sociology*, pp. 315-320; 326-330. See also William Bailie, *Josiah Warren, the First American Anarchist, a Sociological Study* (Boston, 1906); Noyes, *American Socialism*, pp. 42, 92, 94-101; R. T. Ely, *The Labor Movement in America* (N.Y., 1886), pp. 238-240.

Jones' movement he found a congenial fellowship and plenty of opportunity in the two papers to set forth his own system.

Another disciple of Jones was Edward H. Rogers, a Methodist laborer who in 1891 was called by W. D. P. Bliss "a type of the New England workingman of fifty years ago."[19] Rogers supported Jones' views on socialism, labor and the church and believed in his complicated, prophetic biblical interpretation. He emphasized especially that the coming of Christ's earthly kingdom would outlaw all interest, that labor was the only legitimate means of existence.[20]

T. Wharton Collens, a Roman Catholic from New Orleans, was the group's financial backer. His socialist Utopia, *The Eden of Labor,*[21] reflects a strange mixture of biblical lore, millenarianism, and currency theories, expressing a stern contempt for piecemeal reform devices such as labor unions, co-operatives, etc. Lost in the scramble of postwar life, it was natural for such earnest souls to seek refuge in the Christian Labor Union.

Even more than similar groups before the war, Jones' thoroughly Christian movement remained cut off from the main Protestant bodies. The principal weekly of his own church published one editorial deploring his activities, and, half a year later, an article by Jones with an accompanying editorial praising his sincerity and refuting his views in a tone of tolerant amusement. The *Presbyterian Quarterly* condemned Rogers' tracts for misinterpretation of the Bible.[22] But few took seriously Jones' indictment of existing society. As *Equity* sadly admitted, the Christian Labor Union was approved by only one minister aside from its members, a Negro preacher in Arkansas.[23]

It is significant that later, when social criticism was sweeping through the churches, Jones received a little overdue recognition. A few church magazines published his views and Rogers, in 1887, was given a chance to state the C.L.U.'s ideas before the Evangelical Alliance.[24] But Jones,

---

[19] Quoted in the front of Rogers, *Natural Life in the Spirit World* (Boston, 1891).

[20] See his various tracts and pamphlets, *The Relation of Christianity to Labor and Capital* (Boston, 1870), *The Church of the Laborers* (Boston, 1873), *Like unto Me* (Boston, 1876), *The Hope of the Republic* (Boston, 1886), and *Natural Life.*

[21] Philadelphia, 1876.

[22] Editorial, "A Few Thoughts on Labor," *Congregationalist,* December 28, 1871; Jones, "The New Political Economy," July 11, 1872, p. 218. Editorial, p. 220. *Presbyterian Quarterly,* IV (1875), 191-192.

[23] *Equity,* last issue, December, 1875, p. 28.

[24] *Social Economist,* II (1892), 179-187; IX (1895), 184-190; XII (1897), 169-175. The *Kingdom,* (a social Christian newspaper discussed below), July 13, 1894, p. 5; July 27, p. 4; Evangelical Alliance for the U.S.A., *National Perils and Opportunities* (New York, 1887), pp. 234-246.

basically a come-outer, could never achieve a working relation with official Protestantism. Even in 1893 the eulogy of Jones printed in the Christian Socialist *Dawn* had to draw a dismal conclusion: "Since May, 1890, he has been without a church, his experience having demonstrated the fact that the Christian church will not retain a man as pastor who is strenuously faithful to the Master in Christian Reform."[25]

Another isolated and still more eccentric Christian radical of this period was R. J. Wright, a professor of philosophy and church history who published in 1875 his pretentious scheme for the reorganization of society.[26] Wright's program looked forward to the establishment of "limited" communism organized in a complicated series of local and corporate units. His complex presentation made use of arguments from Comte, Spencer, numerology, theology and prewar associationism. Most of the religious press praised Wright's Christian spirit and made light of his social doctrines.[27]

Theorists like Jones or Wright are common in the unfrequented byways of American social science. Religious radicals, spinning plans for a perfect society out of their reading of the Gospels and prophets or out of their own troubled consciences, are found in every age. In periods of widespread discussion of social change, such theorists sometimes receive a hearing and, consequently, adapt their proposals to contemporary possibilities. But in periods of complacency, meeting only ridicule and hostility, they are forced to withdraw into tiny coteries, from which they can continue to issue their brave defiance of the existing world.

Jones and his followers were not, as they are sometimes called, the direct ancestors of the Social Gospel. The men who were finally to open the eyes of many Protestants to social criticism drew their support from events, not from largely forgotten precursors. Only after the achievements of later generations did progressive Christians begin to look back on these unheard heralds with respect.

[25] *Dawn*, April, 1893, p. 1.
[26] *Principia: or the Basis of Social Science* (Philadelphia, 1875). Wright is treated in detail in Bernard, *American Sociology*, pp. 274-303.
[27] *Churchman*, October 23, 1875, p. 462; *Bibliotheca Sacra*, XXIII (1876), 783; *Presbyterian Quarterly*, IV (1876), 561-562; *Methodist Quarterly Review*, LIX (1877), 367.

5

THEOLOGY AND SOCIAL OPINION

LITTLE middle ground existed, in the postwar years, between complacent optimism and frustrated, eccentric radicalism. The great homogeneous, conventional mass of middle-class Protestantism was well insulated against critics like Jones. Yet even in the sixties and seventies, Protestant conservatism was under attack from a potentially more powerful quarter. The stern theology that underlay much social conservatism was being eroded away. In the long run, indirectly, this change in religious thought was to contribute toward a change in social opinion.

It must be emphasized that no direct relation existed, in the postwar period or later, between liberal theology and progressive social thought. This fact is evident, for example, in the postwar attitudes of Unitarianism. Even more than in the prewar period, this officially liberal church shared the social complacency that prevailed among the orthodox denominations. As always, the church of Chapin and Tuckerman was a leader in philanthropic and charitable endeavor.[1] However, as in the case of the evangelical groups, such activity by no means implied serious criticism of the social order.

The columns of the *Unitarian Review*, in their discussions of the Chinese question, the limits of charity, the morality of a sound currency, etc., reflected the same complacency as the organs of orthodoxy. One writer, during the depths of the depression, described the misery of "very large masses" in moving terms. His only suggestions for improvement were, however, the further study of social science, more application of the golden rule, and "the united action of the disinterested class."[2] This essential conservatism, often accompanied by a somewhat condescending appeal to the "better element" to interest itself in social problems, remained typical of official Unitarianism until well after 1877.

---

[1] Abell, *Urban Impact*, pp. 32-39.

[2] C. W. Buck, "Social Reform," *Unitarian Review*, IV (1875), 575-577. Even in the early eighties this periodical contained only three articles tending toward social reform, including two asking for increased church interest in social problems in very moderate terms and one praising Ruskin's economic views. XVII (1882), 481-499; XXIV (1885), 385-410; XXIII (1885), 241-257.

Wealthy, respectable Boston Unitarianism always agreed with the orthodox denominations in everything but theology. But before the war the humanitarian impulse had expressed itself in the radicalism of the denomination's left wing; men like Parker and Brownson had raised the flag of revolt against conservative theology and conservative society at once. In the inhospitable atmosphere of the late sixties and seventies, even the religious radicals expressed little social discontent.

The *Radical*, organ of extreme theological liberalism from 1865 to 1873, devoted to the vivid memory of Parker and the fading presence of Emerson, dedicated its energies almost entirely to the doctrinal battle with official Unitarianism. Only three articles on labor appeared in this short-lived journal. Of these, the first criticized the International, the second pleaded for the interdependence of labor and capital and opposed "artificial" interference with wages, and the third called for moral education for workingmen.[3]

In 1876 a group of liberal intellectuals, mostly rebels against official Unitarianism, founded the Free Religious Association.[4] Well out in the vanguard of contemporary religious thought, its members tried to combine transcendentalism with an idealistic, ethical version of Darwinism. Its members spoke for human solidarity, progress and the golden rule. Its evolutionist optimism, however, made it unable to perceive the new problems that confronted American society, and its progressivism produced no concrete program. Liberal science still brought its adherents, by a very different route, to the same destination as the old-fashioned clerical economics: to the dogma of the certain, foreordained progress of mankind and thence to laissez faire. The recognized leaders of religious radicalism did not come to grips with industrial problems until the end of the seventies, when the Ethical Culture movement had displaced the Free Religious Association as the liberal banner bearer.[5] By that time even the orthodox were beginning to realize that something was amiss.

The principal manifesto of advanced religious thinkers in the postwar decade was O. B. Frothingham's *The Religion of Humanity*.[6] Despite the author's typical plea for mankind's unity and mutual love, despite his specific criticism of the prevailing ethic of "Watching out for number

---

[3] The *Radical*, V (1869), 115-122; IX (1871), 244-265; X (1873), 76-103.

[4] For a full account of this organization see Stow Persons, *Free Religion:An American Faith* (New Haven, 1947), also Loewenberg, "Darwinism comes to America," pp. 352-355.

[5] For the social attitudes of Ethical Culture, see Abell, *Urban Impact*, pp. 101-103, and Hopkins, *Social Gospel*, p. 58. This semireligious group seems to have had little influence on the opinions of the main Protestant bodies.

[6] New York, 1873.

one," his implied views on concrete social problems were those of his contemporaries:

If the artisan, forgetting the apparent discord between himself and the man who employs him, could be made to appreciate the accumulated treasure of patient heroism expressed by that hated word "Capital" . . . if the sinful could have it borne in upon them that that social order they regard as their persecutor, their tyrant, their tormenter, is in truth their best friend . . . the tough old heart would begin to throb and bleed again.[7]

The chief agency of Providence is wealth. . . .

Though the rich man be a miser, he is none the less, though unintentionally, a providence.[8]

As in the prewar period, opinions of sects or radical groups who had cut themselves off from the main body of orthodox Protestantism remained matters of little concern to most American Christians. Although the theology of major churches was altering fast, lines were still firm enough to exclude Unitarians, let alone semitheistic Darwinians. But even if an occasional Methodist or Presbyterian did hear a humanist voice, he heard no ringing prophetic words like Theodore Parker's, challenging every aspect of existing society. He heard his own social conclusions backed by some possibly startling texts.

Far more important to most Protestants was the more gradual undermining of the old theology inside the major churches. Like the religious radicals, the leaders of this more moderate theological revolution were often conservative in their own social and economic views. Horace Bushnell, the greatest theological liberator, had nothing but contempt for political libertarianism, and particularly for all theories constructed from a basis of natural rights or social contract.[9] His economic opinions echoed the justification of the status quo promulgated by the clerical professors. Henry Ward Beecher, who must be counted as a major popularizer of the new theology, was, as we have seen the epitome of his conservative milieu. Yet the work of both these men, and of all the moderate theological liberals who remained within the great denominations, was indirectly essential to a change of social opinion among Protestants.

Until 1865 the Congregational and Presbyterian churches, and to some extent the other large denominations, had held fast to the essentials

[7] *Religion of Humanity* (New York, 1873), p. 147.
[8] *Ibid.*, p. 196.
[9] See his *Society and Religion; Women's Suffrage;* "Popular Government by Divine Right," in *Building Eras in Religion* (New York, 1881), pp. 286-318.

of Calvinist theology.[10] Doctrines of election and reprobation had been defended by a series of brilliant theological advocates against the successive menaces of Arminianism and Unitarianism, and, with still greater difficulty, against the instinctive optimism and humanism of most Americans. In the course of this defense the grand old doctrines had been altered and twisted until they were sustained only by a complex and delicate framework of legalistic argument. Yet most Americans still subscribed, at least in form, to the old belief in a helpless humanity redeemed only by God's arbitrary act.

The conventional clerical view of society was deeply entwined with this theology. Just as sinful man could not debate the justice of eternal punishment, he was not permitted to criticize the laws by which God governed society. Neither salvation nor social well-being could be attained by human schemes. Poverty, like sin, was part of the structure of the universe.

Revivalism, the other great ingredient in traditional American religion, was as hostile as traditional Calvinism to the development of social criticism. Though revivalistic doctrines were less deadening to the will, they usually implied an extreme of religious individualism which left little ground for the reform of worldly society. Dwight L. Moody, greatest of evangelists, did not indeed rely for his conversions upon the preaching of hell's terrors. His powerful appeal was based on acceptance of the love of God and left considerable room for individual social service. Moody himself was a lifelong worker for good causes, particularly that of Christian education. But Moody, like his fellows, remained aloof from any discussion of the basic ills of society.[11]

A lesser evangelist of Moody's day put religious individualism in extreme terms:

Separate yourself from all your kind, make of the world a solitude, depopulate the globe, and think of yourself as the only living soul upon which the attention of Heaven and Hell is fixed tonight. . . .

Undue importance, as it appears to me, is attached to the connection of

---

[10] Among the most helpful accounts of American theological development for the nonexpert are the following: F. H. Foster, *A Genetic History of the New England Theology* (Chicago, 1907), and *The Modern Movement in American Theology* (New York, 1939); J. W. Buckham, *Progressive Religious Thought in America* (New York, 1919); George Harris, *A Century's Change in Religion* (Boston, 1914); G. B. Smith, "Theological Thinking in America," in *Religious Thought in the Last Quarter Century* (Chicago, 1927), pp. 95-115; and Visser 'T Hooft, *Background of the Social Gospel.*

[11] Gamaliel Bradford, *D. L. Moody, A Worker in Souls* (New York, 1927), pp 227-228. Moody was later criticized by Social Gospel advocates for this lack of interest. W. R. Moody, *D. L. Moody* (New York, 1930), p. 177.

Christians one with another, and to the good or bad effect such connection has upon individual growth.[12]

From before the Civil War until the end of the century, the whole system of American religious thought, both Calvinist and evangelistic, underwent a profound internal struggle as well as a series of external attacks. Many of the decisive battles of this revolution were being fought in seminaries and pulpits during the postwar period of social complacency.

By far the most effective of the internal innovators was Horace Bushnell. This great preacher, speaking a compelling emotional language, helped more than any other to reduce the distance between sinful man and perfect God. Bushnell's doctrine of "Christian Nurture" for children as against a sole reliance on conversion went a long way toward admitting the innate goodness of man. A growing emphasis on Christ and an insistence on his human characteristics implied a tremendous ideal for humanity. In his doctrine of the "Atonement" Bushnell thrust aside the precise and legal doctrines in which theologians had debated that central Christian event. To Bushnell the sacrifice of Christ expressed his essential humanity, and the world would be redeemed only as all men should imitate Christ's act. More and more of the powers of God were, in Bushnell's teachings, manifested through man.

To Bushnell, who everywhere narrowed the break between nature and the supernatural, earthly concerns were never unimportant: "There is . . . a *fixed relation between the temporal and the eternal, such that we shall best realize the eternal by rightly using the temporal.*"[13] The aim of temporal society was a high one: "To make every man as valuable as possible to himself and his country."[14] Bushnell himself believed that this aim was best achieved through laissez faire, but some of his disciples, accepting his view of the lofty purpose, prescribed quite different means.[15]

Doctrines similar to Bushnell's were debated in many churches as the humanistic optimism which had long pervaded American political

---

[12] W. H. H. Murray, "Burden-bearing," in *Music-Hall Sermons* (Boston, 1870), pp. 102, 106.

[13] Bushnell, "In and by Things Temporal are given Things Spiritual," *Sermons on Living Subjects*, p. 270 (underlining Bushnell's). For an interpretation of Bushnell's work see H. R. Heininger, *The Theological Technique of a Mediatorial Theologian—Horace Bushnell* (pamphlet, Chicago, 1935).

[14] "The Day of Roads," in *Work and Play* (New York, 1866), p. 434.

[15] For an appreciation of Bushnell by the greatest early spokesman for social Christianity, see Washington Gladden, *Pioneers of Religious Liberty in America* (Boston, 1903), 227-263. In a letter to Theodore Munger, Gladden says of Bushnell: "It is no exaggeration to say that had it not been for the relief he brought to them on theological questions, many of the ablest young men in Congregational pulpits could not or would not have remained in them." Quoted in Munger, *Horace Bushnell*, p. 372.

thought flowed over at last into religion. The new interpretation of the Atonement made it possible to introduce less rigid interpretations of God's justice. Eternal punishment, even for the heathen, became intolerable and the doctrine of future probation offered a way out. By the time the new currents reached Henry Ward Beecher and his thousands of followers God's mercy had almost entirely replaced His justice.

As the increasingly humanistic theology of Bushnell and his successors raised man's nature to a level with God's, the slowly penetrating disclosures of science seemed to reduce both to a less transcendent level. While the churches were still only beginning to assimilate the doctrines of evolution, conservative Christianity was further jolted by the application of European historical scholarship to the critical study of the Bible. More and more theology and especially preaching took on an apologetic character, minimizing the miraculous content of religion and reconciling the old doctrines wherever possible with science and common sense.

These two currents, humanism and evolutionary science determined the climate of advanced religious thought, even inside the older churches, by the postwar era. Beginning in esoteric language and restricted arenas, the struggle between these forces and the inherited faith emerged into the public view. Congregations split, ministers quarreled with their flocks, and the conservative denominations tried and ousted daring modernists. During the eighties the new doctrines were effectively combined with the remnants of the old in the school of progressive orthodoxy, centering in Andover Seminary.

Young ministers of liberal tendencies entering their work in the seventies were likely to be affected to one degree or another by several of the common doctrines of the new theology. They were almost certain to feel the impact of the new science and the necessity of reconciling religion with its discoveries. They were likely to insist on judging the old doctrines from the standpoint of nineteenth-century morality. Often they centered their religious emotions on a new study of the example of Christ. Finally, to one degree or another, consciously or not, they looked at God and the universe less in terms of transcendence and more in terms of immanence.

These new tendencies could not but affect the social opinions of many of their protagonists. The basic change was the new conception of man. Huge possibilities seemed to open before human beings who, instead of accepting salvation or the opposite from an inscrutable God, could participate in the work of redemption. As Protestants ceased to devote themselves to an intense examination of their own spiritual states, the habit of extreme religious individualism weakened. The idea of brotherhood, long neglected in Protestant theology, received a re-emphasis.

New ideas on the nature of the universe made it difficult to believe in fixed laws of society. As God's actions in the sphere of eternal judgment became amenable to human ethical standards, it became more difficult to explain inequality and injustice as part of natural law. In a universe of vast changes, the social structure as well as the cosmos became increasingly subject to evolution. In the optimistic dawn of the new theology, possibilities open to humanity appeared boundless.

The new doctrines worked negatively as well as positively to change the direction of Protestant social thought. As the intricacies of theological debate ceased to command clerical energies, as an unquestioning surrender to Christ in a mystical experience grew to be a less all-compelling goal, a new outlet for Christian energy became necessary. When the passionate self-discipline and the zeal for reforming others characteristic of America's religious inheritance ceased to find their nourishment in battling for salvation, they were bound to turn toward the reshaping of society.

It is necessary to reiterate that theological change did not inevitably or directly bring about a re-examination of social beliefs. In the sermons of Beecher, for instance, the new theology seemed at times to consist of nothing but a vague and easy optimism. Some of his preaching made it appear that spiritual truth was whatever one liked, that for salvation good intentions were the chief necessity:

I gradually formed a theology by practice—by trying it on, and the things that really did God's work in the hearts of men I set down as good theology, and the things that did not, *whether they were true or not, they were not true to me.*[16]

The Christian religion is not a system of laws, it is a state of the heart.[17]

In the opinion of many later American Protestants, religion lost, by such facile doctrines, much of its motive power, power that could have been used for social as well as spiritual leadership. In losing sight of sin, it lost its power to explain or attack evil. From being impossible, betterment of the world became too easy. With the old search and struggle for salvation, religion sacrificed some of its emotional depth.

Certainly in Beecher's case and in that of many others, humanitarian

[16] Beecher, *Statement before the Congregational Association of New York and Brooklyn, etc.* (New York, 1882), p. 13. (Italics mine.) This whole statement is a landmark in the breakdown of the old theology.

[17] "The Substance of Christianity," *Plymouth Pulpit,* Third Series (New York, 1869), p. 352.

theology led to no change in the fashionable social complacency. Beecher's reassuring theological platitudes combined very easily with his assertions, in times of misery and strife, that all was well. No religious newspaper was quite as vigorous in its defense of the social status quo as the *Independent,* an organ of popular theological liberalism edited by Beecher until 1863 and then by Theodore Tilton, Beecher's colleague and (until the great divorce suit) friend.[18]

Yet, in the early postwar years when any admixture of humanism or humanitarianism with orthodox religion was revolutionary, even Beecher played an important part in liberating his fellow Christians from a view of the world that had long paralyzed their social energies. When Beecher died, Lyman Abbott, a leader of moderate social Christianity, was among those who expressed their debt: "From Mr. Beecher I first learned that God is love, that law is redemption, and that love, not conscience, is the soul's primate."[19] In the *Christian Union,* which he took over from Beecher, Abbott was to express a consistent if rather timid program of social reform, combined with a liberal theology.

Eventually believers in the application of Christianity to society were to carry the teachings of Bushnell and Beecher further and develop a so-called social theology. But this was to take place only after dissent from conservative postwar economic doctrine had become widespread. In the postwar age, theological change had hardly begun to show its effect on social thought. Gradually, the new world view was to make it easier for religious Americans to believe in the possibility and desirability of social change. Humanistic religion in the seventies was already making it increasingly possible for Protestants to turn their eyes toward the world; what they saw there was to alter their whole conception of society during the next generation.

[18] Editorial, "Henry Ward Beecher," *Christian Union,* March 10, 1887, pp. 3-4.

[19] The theologically conservative *Congregationalist* was slightly less rigid in its social opinions than the *Independent.* On the other hand the theologically liberal *Andover Review* was much more open to new social ideas than either. In the religious press, as elsewhere, no *direct* correlation between theological and social opinion can be proven.

III

SOURCES OF CHANGE

1877-1895

THREE EARTHQUAKES

IN 1876 Protestantism presented a massive, almost unbroken front in its defense of the social status quo. Two decades later social criticism had penetrated deeply into each major church. Some of the most prominent Protestant leaders were calling for social reform; Christian radicals, not unheard, were demanding complete reorganization of society. The immediate cause of this important change lay neither in theological innovation nor in the world "climate of opinion" but in the resistless intrusion of social crisis, and particularly in a series of large-scale, violent labor conflicts.

For a generation slums and depressions, farmer protests and labor parties had been pictured by church theorists as necessary, incidental flaws in the inevitable improvement of society. The events of 1877, of 1886, and of 1892-94 were, however, impossible to ignore and difficult to explain away. Optimistic theory had to be reconsidered in the light of burning freight cars. Spokesmen of religion were forced, like editors and professors, to answer the question why, in the home of Christian progress, desperate men were refusing well-meant advice, defying authority, organizing and battling with the determination of despair.

To ministers nurtured in the pat theories of Francis Wayland the sudden outbreak of large-scale labor warfare was at first completely unexplainable, except in terms of human depravity. Little in their experience fitted them to understand the motives of non-Protestant, slum-dwelling wage earners.

In these years of rapid industrialization free men, heirs of the self-reliant tradition of agrarian America, were suddenly finding themselves at the mercy of distant corporation executives. To such men, and to the immigrants who worked by their sides, passive endurance was not acceptable advice. Threatened with unemployment and faced with drastic cuts in already low wages, labor's instinct was to fight. Hardworking, self-made owners and managers of industry, long praised as public benefactors in pulpit and press, determined that no walking delegate should interfere with their imperial control, were ready for a showdown. In the resulting series of conflicts religious onlookers reacted at first with dismay and hysteria. Gradually, however, as labor war died down and revived, some Protestant thinkers began, tentatively and gingerly, to formulate answers for the questions thus drastically presented. In the momentary, untheoretical reactions of Protestant commentators, especially in the religious press, to these upheavals one can understand the increasing necessity for new Christian social doctrine.

Since the crash of 1873, a crisis had been on the way. Unemployed men roamed the cities and roads, labor unions were growing desperate in a series of minor defeats, and Marxian socialism was winning its first few converts in the United States. In July of 1877 a sudden 10 per cent wage cut on the majority of railroads east of the Mississippi precipitated the most destructive labor battle in American history. Trains were halted; troops fought with angry mobs; bloodshed and fire mounted in Baltimore, Pittsburgh and other railroad centers.

The religious press reacted promptly and energetically, in terms of the period's theoretical certainties. The *Independent* asserted that, once laborers started to coerce others into stopping work,

then the question ceases to be one of allowable conflict between capital and labor, and instantly becomes an issue between law and anarchy. Laborers are then criminals in intent and criminals in fact. They are rioters and public enemies, and worse than wild beasts turned loose upon society.

Rioters, no matter what their grievances, must first be warned, and then, unless they promptly stop their rioting, "the remedy of bullets and bayonets should be applied to them, without hesitation and with an energy and force that will be quickly felt. . . ." Putting down the mob, the editors insisted further, was not enough. "The safety of society demands punishment." As to the questions in dispute, the *Independent* hoped only "that no company will make any compromise with rioters. Compromises are not in order when men are *fighting* for higher wages or against a reduction of wages."[1]

As the struggle continued, the *Independent's* tone changed from condemnation to hysteria:

If the club of the policeman, knocking out the brains of the rioter, will answer, then well and good; but if it does not promptly meet the exigency, then bullets and bayonets, canister and grape—with no sham or pretense, in order to frighten men, but with fearful and destructive reality—constitute

[1] July 26, 1877, p. 16.

the one remedy and the one duty of the hour. . . . Napoleon was right when he said that the way to deal with a mob was to exterminate it.[2]

The *Congregationalist* warned its readers of the probable identity of the strike leaders:

Very likely scores, if not hundreds of those reckless desperadoes to whom the most fiendish excesses of the days of the Commune in Paris were due, may now be here, fervid apostles of the same red-handed and blazing license.

Like the *Independent* it called for drastic measures:

Bring on then the troops—the armed police—in overwhelming numbers. Bring out the Gatling guns. Let there be no fooling with blank cartridges. But let the mob know, everywhere, that for it to stand one moment after it has been ordered by proper authorities to disperse, will be to be shot down in its tracks. . . . A little of the vigor of the first Napoleon is the thing we now need.

Compromise would simply sow the wind for "future whirlwind-reaping."[3]

The *Christian Union*, later to become the main organ of moderate social Christianity, agreed that "There are times when mercy is a mistake, and this is one of them" and appealed to the standard economic dogmas:

If the trainmen knew a little more of political economy they would not fall so easy a prey to men who never earn a dollar of wages by good solid work. . . . What a sorry set of ignoramuses they must be who imagine that they are fighting for the rights of labor in combining together to prevent other men from working for low wages because, forsooth, they are discontented with them.[4]

R. E. Thompson, by no means one of the most rigid of contemporary ministerial economists, issued a pamphlet warning workingmen against walking delegates who, he said, lived in luxury and stirred up trouble for completely selfish reasons. Like his predecessors for fifty years he appealed to the discontented to shun radicalism, to save, work hard, and avoid liquor and tobacco.[5]

Henry Ward Beecher, stating similar principles in his usual vivid terms, condemned the strikes in two sermons.[6] Beecher, whose large salary and still more handsome royalties and newspaper revenues enabled him to indulge his exuberant tastes for driving fine horses and carrying handfuls

[2] August 2, 1877, p. 16.
[3] *Congregationalist*, July 25, 1877, p. 236.
[4] July 25, p. 62. Also August 1, p. 82.
[5] Thompson, *Hard Times and What to Learn from them. A Plain Talk with Working People* (pamphlet, Philadelphia, 1877).
[6] Published in the *Christian Union*, August 1, 1877, pp. 92-94; August 8, 1877, pp. 112-114.

of uncut gems in his pockets, denounced the railroad employees for not being willing to bear their poverty more nobly:

It is said that a dollar a day is not enough for a wife and five or six children. No, not if the man smokes or drinks beer. It is not enough if they are to live as he would be glad to have them live. It is not enough to enable them to live as perhaps they would have a right to live in prosperous times. But is not a dollar a day enough to buy bread with? Water costs nothing; and a man who cannot live on bread is not fit to live. What is the use of a civilization that simply makes men incompetent to live under the conditions which exist. . . .[7]

After each of the crises of the period, once the immediate shock of horror had begun to wear off, religious commentators cast about for some remedy. While the fires of 1877 were hardly out, the *Watchman*, for instance, called for "a more serious and earnest attempt, in all kindness of spirit, to enlighten the minds of those who have been so deplorably deceived" into thinking themselves "victims of wrong." It even suggested the need of "a quickened feeling of responsibility and a purified moral sensibility on the part of those who manage capital and employ labor" and wondered whether no salaries could have borne reduction.[8] Many similar articles suggested that railroad companies, by no means the most popular type of corporations in any circles, might not be without fault.

Protestant opinion agreed, however, that strikes were not the answer. The *Congregationalist* was "not prepared to deny" that workmen had the right to cease work simultaneously. But it did not believe "there ever was, or ever will be, a case in which to exercise this right is not the most foolish thing possible for workmen to do." This concession, it said, was the "extreme limit"; no suspicion of coercion by either party was allowable.[9] This remained the most common doctrine: strikes *might* be legal when they involved no suspicion of force, but they were always foolish.

The drastic shock of 1877 effected a change in the volume and pitch, rather than the content, of church comment on labor. The Boston Y.M.C.A., for instance, offered a prize for an essay on this question of the hour. The winner, Joseph Nash, devoted himself to setting forth the inutility of labor unions and strikes according to the rules of classical

[7] *Christian Union*, August 1, 1877, p. 93. It is reassuring to find that this statement, which Beecher repeated at intervals despite some unfavorable reactions, was refuted by the *Christian Advocate*, which proved conclusively that it was impossible to support a family, save, maintain decency, and provide minimum funds for education and sickness on a dollar a day. December 16, 1880, p. 801.

[8] August 9, 1877, p. 252.

[9] August 1, 1877, p. 244.

economy. There was nothing new in Nash's plea for abstinence and hard work nor in his half-hearted endorsement of co-operation and arbitration. Nash, however, did not share the complacency of the calm postwar theorists; he believed that the recent conflicts marked "a new phase in our social order."[10]

The events of 1877 cast a shadow of alarm over the rest of the decade. T. DeWitt Talmage, the evangelist, in one of his few references to worldly events, vividly recalled in his autobiography his impressions of the aftermath:

> For hundreds of miles along the track leading from the great West I saw stretched out and coiled up the great reptile which, after crushing the free locomotive of passengers and trade, would have twisted itself around our republican institutions, and left them in strangulation and blood along the pathway of nations.[11]

The year 1877 remained a symbol of shock, of the possible crumbling of society. As late as 1886, in the midst of another crisis, a spokesman of social Christianity warned his readers that "another 1877 may be the prelude to another 1793."[12]

Naturally enough, in the years after this staggering blow the religious press devoted a great deal of space to "Communism," which included all forms of socialism and sometimes trade-unionism as well. Many gradually seemed to recover their confidence that such doctrines could never present a serious threat to this fortunate country. Others remained alarmist. More often than ever, it seemed necessary to insist that in America the "average distribution among men" was "as near the rule of equity as it is in human power to make it."[13] Readers were warned against the apparently socialistic implications of certain biblical passages in increasingly strong language:

> Take the law of charity, "Give to him that asketh thee, and from him that would borrow of thee turn thou not away," interpret it literally, and undertake to put it into practice in New York; it would be a great deal better to burn down the city.[14]

Pure trade-unionism continued to be regarded by most religious opinion

[10] Joseph Nash, *The Relations between Capital and Labor in the United States* (pamphlet, Boston, 1878), pp. 7-8.

[11] Talmage, *T. DeWitt Talmage, D.D.* (London, 1912), p. 84.

[12] T. Edwin Brown, *Studies in Modern Socialism and Labor Problems* (N.Y., 1886), p. 67.

[13] *Independent*, October 31, 1878, p. 15.

[14] *Christian Union*, January 22, 1879, p. 74.

as one degree more acceptable than communism but some organs, like the *Christian Advocate*, refused to make this distinction:

> The Trades' Unions are despotic and revolutionary in tendency. . . . The worst doctrines of Communism are involved in these unions. . . . Legislate Trades' Unions out of existence, making it a crime to starve a poor man, or rob a rich one.[15]

When a reader objected to this extreme view, the editors qualified it only slightly, insisting that, if trade-unions and communism were not identical, "the foundation assumptions of each are the same," and that "Neither can exist in peace with the Republic."

In the late seventies alarm was kept alive by the formation of labor parties. These struggling, ill-organized ventures, formed by inflationist farmers, Knights of Labor and other discontented groups toward the end of a heavy depression, seemed to the religious press the creation of foreign agitators. The *Congregationalist* termed Ben Butler's Greenback-Labor candidacy for the Massachusetts governorship a contest between "the good old Anglo-Saxon civilization" and "French Communism."[16] The strongest denunciation was reserved for Dennis Kearney, the sand-lot agitator of San Francisco, who seemed to the religious press to combine Irish labor-union violence and western anti-Chinese lawlessness.[17]

In the years after the great strike, Christian editors were uneasy about the wandering unemployed. Most had little doubt about the character of the migrants:

> . . . they are profane, licentious, filthy, vermin-swarming thieves, petty robbers, and sometimes murderers, social pests and perambulatory nuisances; which require the immediate and stringent attention of the community. . . . We confess a strong feeling in favor toward the idea . . . that it might be well to revive for use in this connection the long obsolete whipping-post.[18]

During the revival of prosperity and decrease of strife that marked the early eighties, the fears of religious editors tended to subside. They continued frequently to expound the dogmas of classical economics, to

---

[15] *Christian Advocate*, May 2, 1878, p. 280; June 13, p. 376.

[16] October 30, 1878, p. 348.

[17] Typical editorials on Kearney are found in the *Unitarian Review*, X (1878), 170-186; *Independent*, July 4, 1878, p. 15; *Congregationalist*, August 7, 1878, p. 252; *Christian Advocate*, May 15, 1879, p. 20.

[18] *Congregationalist*, February 27, 1878, p. 68. The *Christian Union* characterizes tramps similarly and recommends compulsory workhouses, November 7, 1877, p. 392. The *Christian Advocate* urges cities to provide work at subsistence levels and treat as criminals those who refuse it—this is the only suggestion I have seen that treats the problem as an economic rather than a moral one. August 7, 1878, p. 520.

denounce communism, strikes and the eight-hour movement, but the tone of confidence predominated over that of alarm. More important, occasional writers, once more searching for an answer to the labor problem, began to shift away from the extreme rigidities of clerical laissez faire.

The *Christian Advocate* expressed concern over the fact that Philadelphia streetcar men worked eighteen hours a day and averaged less than four hours sleep.[19] It praised welfare work by employers and endorsed arbitration.[20] Discussing child labor, the *Independent*, while it declared itself "no friend to laws which shut the factory against children," hoped that they would not "get too early into toil, or spend in work so much of the time as to lose the discipline and acquirements of common school education."[21]

Regarding labor unions, the *Congregationalist* concluded that "The days are gone in which these organizations were regarded by the general public, as well as by capitalists in particular, as wholly evil." In the future, the editors believed, unions would either die out gradually or undergo reforms which would render them more worthy of respect.[22] One strike during this calm interval actually came close to receiving general support from the religious press, a fact as yet without parallel. The telegraphers' strike occurred in the fairly prosperous year 1883; it was conducted peaceably, and above all it was directed against a very unpopular monopoly, the Western Union, controlled at that time by the unscrupulous Jay Gould. The company was prosperous (though its financial conduct had not been above reproach); it had twice cut the wages of its skilled workers; it paid less to women for equal work; it insisted on Sunday labor; and it had refused to negotiate. In view of all these conditions, even the *Independent*, sticking to its belief that strikes in general were to be deplored and wages should be regulated by supply and demand, concluded that "There are, however, cases in which great and merciless monopolists . . . leave to their employees no other remedy."[23]

Even after the onset of depression and during the upward curve of labor troubles in the middle eighties, the religious press maintained a tone of comparative calm. In fact, just before the outbreak of the second great crisis in 1886, some religious papers had begun to take a far more friendly tone toward organized labor. The *Christian Union* already was

[19] February 23, 1882, p. 14.
[20] March 1, 1883, p. 130; October 18, 1883, pp. 3-4.
[21] May 31, 1883, p. 7.
[22] September 13, 1883, pp. 3-4.
[23] July 26, 1883, p. 16.

receptive to the views of the early Social Gospel movement, though this had scarcely started to color the reactions of most Protestant organs. This advanced paper, commenting on a Chicago horsecar strike, presented novel views regarding public utilities. The company had, it stated, the legal right to discharge employees without notice or cause. However, because of the special status of horsecars the community might well modify the law so that "it shall not confer upon the corporation the *legal* right to do a *moral* wrong."[24] Such a mixture of morality with "political economy" in a major religious publication would have been unthinkable ten years before and was still rare.

When the Cleveland Rolling Mill Company imported contract laborers to break a strike, the *Congregationalist* called the action evidence of a "heartless, arbitrary, imperious spirit."[25] Two Cleveland ministers preached sermons on the strike which were published in the *Independent*.[26] Both denounced "communism" but pleaded for profit-sharing, co-operation, and the application of the golden rule. The *Independent's* editors, however, repeatedly defended the importation of contract labor in itself, insisting that "The right to make such contracts . . . is, indeed, one of the fundamental principles of human liberty" and denouncing the Republican plank opposing the practice.[27] The *Christian Advocate's* attitude toward the strikes of this period was not so much hostile as gloomy. It saddened the editors that a year of depression should also be a year of strikes and suggested that, "after all, the struggle has its grounds in corrupt human-nature."[28]

In discussing the depression itself only the *Christian Union* seemed to realize that unemployment in a period of big industry represented a fundamental, unanswered problem: "It is no longer true in America that an able-bodied man, with average health and average intelligence, need ask no pity of his brothers, but can bake his own bread and find his own butter."[29] The *Congregationalists*, in an editorial with curious, Malthusian implications, found "Christian progress" responsible for the increasing problem of the depraved poor because it had stopped their extermination by plague and war.[30] The *Christian Advocate* devoted an

[24] July 9, 1885, pp. 2-3.
[25] July 30, 1885, p. 256.
[26] George T. Dowling and Hyram C. Haydn, "Lessons of the Strike, Two Sermons Preached in Cleveland," *Independent*, August 6, 1885, pp. 7-9.
[27] July 31, 1884, pp. 17-18.
[28] July 23, 1885, p. 470.
[29] November 26, 1885, pp. 5-6.
[30] June 10, 1884, p. 12.

editorial to "Methodist Mechanics Out of Work," urging them to make a "desperate effort" to keep up their subscriptions:

Will you sit about stores, and run the risk of being drawn into saloons? If ever good reading is needed—reading that will divert your mind, give your wife and children something to talk about besides grinding care—it is when the husband and father is out of work.[31]

Surprising enough, this editorial, patronizing as it seems to a modern reader, was reprinted a year later because of a favorable response from unemployed laborers, who, according to the editors, had found it "a cure for low spirits." It was also praised and imitated by the *Watchman*.[32]

As the critical year 1886 approached, the religious press was divided in its attitude toward the growing, amorphous, idealistic Order of the Knights of Labor. Among the Knights were Greenbackers and a few socialists, and Protestant critics often objected to its original secret character. On the whole, however, they approved of Grand Master Terence V. Powderly, the most well-intentioned and bungling of labor leaders. Powderly opposed secrecy and preferred the development of co-operatives to strikes. When, following two successful struggles with Jay Gould, the Knights suddenly received a huge influx of unskilled labor, Powderly was more disconcerted than delighted with the Order's new size and power. In February, 1886, before the third, disastrous strike against Gould's railroad had broken out, even the *Independent* considered Powderly "an excellent as well as an able man."[33] In March, when Powderly was still trying to curb his more militant western subordinates, the *Independent's* praise was less wholehearted. It still said, however, that if we must have "a sultan of satraps and slaves," Powderly was a "moderate and sensible ruler."[34]

As the Gould strike became more and more bitter, as traffic was halted and business supplies were held up, the religious press became more hostile. Denunciation of the strikers still did not reach the frenzied pitch of 1877; few church commentators denied the abstract right to strike and most of them blamed the outbreak partly on low wages and unscrupulous capitalists. But by April even the *Christian Union* was insisting that "Every man who owns a house and lot or has a dollar in the savings bank is interested to maintain the right of a freeman to work without fear of a mob."[35] More and more frequently, religious commen-

[31] January 31, 1884, p. 1.
[32] *Christian Advocate*, January 14, 1885, p. 1; *Watchman*, January 22, 1885, p. 1.
[33] February 18, 1885, p. 17.
[34] March 25, 1886, p. 17.
[35] April 1, 1886, pp. 52-53.

tators, despairing at the increase of social conflict, concluded that the only solution lay in spiritual regeneration.[36]

The southwestern railroad strike, ending in utter defeat for the Knights, was only the most serious of many conflicts in the spring of 1886. A horsecar strike in New York increased the tension. The *Christian Union* approved the orderliness of the strikers while the *Watchman* rebuked them for their violence.[37] The *Independent* strongly denounced the bakers' boycott, calling the Knights in somewhat confused metaphor a "virtual imperium in imperio in the bosom of the body politic."[38] In general the religious press opposed the eight-hour campaign which the new American Federation of Labor was vigorously promoting.[39]

In the stormy weeks immediately before the Haymarket disaster church spokesmen were filled with fear and foreboding. C. O. Brown of Dubuque gave a series of *Talks on Labor Troubles* pointing out the dangers of the times.[40] Too many workers were listening to Henry George. Anarchist groups were growing more dangerous. Clergymen must persuade labor of the old truths—that economy, hard work and individualism were the causes of America's prosperity. The *Christian Union*, considering itself a proved friend of labor, appealed to the unions themselves to mend their ways: "Order your warriors to the rear; order your peace-makers to the front; and put on your white flag the motto of your largest and most potent order: THE SUBSTITUTION OF ARBITRATION FOR STRIKES."[41] Echoing a very widespread feeling of impending crisis, the *Christian Advocate* compared the spring of '86 with America's blackest hour:

We regard the elements at work in the United States to-day as more fraught with peril to our institutions than all the merely political and personal discussions, conflicts, and agitations which culminated in the late war. . . . We are not frightened . . . but in the darkest hours of the Civil War we never felt more sober than to-day. . . .[42]

This spring of conflict and increasing tension culminated in the disastrous Haymarket affair. The bomb thrown at the Chicago police on

[36] E.g. *Christian Advocate*, April 1, p. 199; *Baptist Quarterly Review*, VIII (1886), 377-382.

[37] *Christian Union*, March 11, p. 3; *Watchman*, March 11, p. 1.

[38] April 29, p. 17. The *Independent* had, however, given John Swinton space for a defense of the boycott. April 8, p. 4.

[39] E.g. *Watchman*, May 6, p. 1. The *Christian Union*, however, was in favor of the movement. January 21, p. 3.

[40] Chicago, 1886.

[41] April 22, pp. 3-4.

[42] March 11, p. 19.

May 4 represented everything that the churches most hated and feared. The meeting grew out of a strike, it took place in a polyglot city. The bomb seemed a direct threat to property, order and the state. The small group of direct-action anarchists accused of responsibility had undoubtedly been given to violent language. It was not surprising that in approving the fate given the arrested anarchists the religious press did not consider all the facts. In the mood of hysteria that swept lay and religious circles alike it was useless to point out that the meeting had been peaceful until marched on by the police, that several strikers had been shot a few days before, or, more important, that the men condemned to hang were not accused of throwing the bomb. Again, as in 1877, few church papers balked at salutary bloodshed:

A mob should be crushed by knocking down or shooting down the men engaged in it; and the more promptly this is done the better.[43]
. . . when anarchy gathers its deluded disciples into a mob, as at Chicago, a Gatling gun or two, swiftly brought into position and well served, offers, on the whole, the most merciful as well as effectual remedy.[44]

When the court decided that the revolutionary editorials of the Chicago anarchists had caused some person unknown to throw the bomb, and that the arrested men were therefore guilty of conspiracy to murder, the religious press heartily approved the death sentences. Protests by liberals were denounced:

To talk about pity, sympathy or delay in connection with such demons, is to encourage their kind; to speak of their offenses as *political*, is to hide their character and engender the sentiment which breeds them.[45]

After the executions had been attended to, the preaching of anarchism must be suppressed.[46]

Dissent appeared only on the fringes of Protestantism. W. M. Salter, a Chicago Ethical Culturist, called for life imprisonment rather than hanging.[47] Hugh O. Pentecost, a radical Congregationalist minister who said the anarchists had been murdered, was bitterly attacked by his brethren. By this time Pentecost was already on the road which was to take him out of the church altogether.[48]

[43] *Independent*, May 13, pp. 16-17.
[44] *Congregationalist*, May 13, p. 162.
[45] *Christian Advocate*, October 6, 1887, p. 641.
[46] This opinion was apparently unanimous in the religious press, including even the *Christian Union*, May 13, 1886, p. 295.
[47] *What Shall Be Done with the Anarchists?* (pamphlet, Chicago, 1887).
[48] See pp. 237-239.

Not all church commentators allowed their horror to take them all the way back to the opinions of 1877. The *Congregationalist* took pains to point out that men and women who were laboring gradually to improve society were not to be confused with anarchists.[49] The *Churchman* praised profit-sharing as a means of preventing such outbreaks.[50] And, as in all the crises of the period, many religious spokesmen heightened their pleas for increased evangelistic effort and for the preaching of the golden rule in labor relations.[51]

The most striking immediate effect of the bomb, however, was to revive and increase hostility to labor in lay and clerical circles. It is significant, for instance, that the *Churchman*, which before the tragedy had been reasonably calm in its comment on the year's strikes, on May 29 regretted that a mob of dissatisfied strikers who had threatened Martin Irons, leader of the southwestern strike, had not finished off "that truculent impostor."[52]

Further heightened by the Henry George mayoralty campaign in New York, hostility to unions once more clung on for several years after the crisis, although the late eighties were not a particularly troubled time in labor history. Professor Arthur T. Hadley very competently discussed labor's fall from grace in the *Independent*.[53] Two years before, he said, the prevalent suspicion of great wealth and the conservative tactics of the Knights had produced a public opinion more friendly to labor than any in previous history. Then the Knights had grown rapidly and the new membership had forced the Order to endorse boycotts, large strikes, and radical politics. Hadley doubted whether labor would ever recover the esteem of the public, especially as its most able leaders were certain to acquire capital and join the other side.

By this time opponents of organized labor, still overwhelmingly dominant in the religious press, had forsaken the frank and sweeping condemnations of the prewar economists. Ordinarily they expressed some sort of qualified, abstract approval of union objectives, criticizing union methods in terms of traditional individual morality. Violence against strikebreakers was, of course, the most common complaint. Editors of the *Congregationalist*, hearing that some union leaders were urging

[49] August 26, 1886, p. 284.
[50] May 15, 1886, p. 535.
[51] The Presbyterian General Assembly, as well as many papers and individuals, referred to the bombing as proof of the need for evangelism. "Report of the Standing Committee on Home Missions," General Assembly, *Minutes*, 1886, p. 183.
[52] *Churchman*, May 29, 1886, p. 592.
[53] Hadley, "The reaction against Labor Organizations," *Independent*, July 28, 1887, pp. 1-2.

strikers to suspend payment of rents, warned against striking "under the mistaken idea that your doing so will abolish the Decalogue." The *Churchman* blamed the decline of the Knights on "the attempt to substitute economical [sic] theories for personal righteousness." The *Watchman* similarly contrasted Christianity's ethical methods with reliance on "oath-bound and confederated secular and merely human organizations." As usual, the *Independent* went a good deal further in its reaction against unions, declaring in a moment of anger that "The most withering and outrageous despotism that has yet shown itself in the world is this of the strike and the boycott."[54]

Most actual strikes in this period encountered the familiar clerical hostility, ordinarily coupled by now with a statement that all strikes were not necessarily evil. The New York coal-handlers' strike of 1887 and the C. B. & Q. strike of 1888 were specifically denounced.[55] The New York Central strike of 1890 was condemned with special severity since, in the first place, it inconvenienced the public, and, second, it was said to involve an attempt to control the company's hiring and firing policy. Only the *Christian Union* believed that employees were justified in striking if men were fired for union membership.[56]

On the other hand the long-drawn-out coal struggle starting at Spring Valley in 1888 received more sympathetic treatment. Some Protestant opinion was affected by Henry D. Lloyd's *A Strike of Millionaires against Miners*, with its burning descriptions of wage cuts, evictions, and blacklists. Father J. O. S. Huntington, the Episcopalian radical, covered the coal regions for the *Chicago News*.[57] The *Christian Union*, impressed by Lloyd's account, sent its own correspondent to the mining regions and published his conclusions that the monopolistic employers were largely to blame, defending such opinions against an attack in the *Evening Post* on "anarchistic ministers." Even the *Independent* criticized the Reading Railroad for threatening to boycott any company that raised wages.[58] The far-off London dock strike, approved by many British prelates and

[54] *Congregationalist*, February 10, 1887, p. 46; *Churchmen*, June 19, 1888, p. 691; *Watchman*, February 17, 1887, p. 1; *Independent*, February 3, 1887, p. 17.

[55] For the first, see *Christian Union*, "The Great Strike," February 3, 1887; *Independent*, June 26, 1887, p. 17; for the second, see *Independent*, March 8, 1888, p. 11; *Watchman*, March 15, 1888, p. 1; *Congregationalist*, March 8, 1888, pp. 3-4.

[56] *Andover Review*, XIV (1890), 413-416; *Congregationalist*, August 14, 1890, p. 278; *Independent*, August 14, 1890, p. 10; *Christian Union*, August 28, 1890, p. 261.

[57] See Lloyd, *Millionaires against Miners* (Chicago, 1890), pp. 71-73.

[58] *Christian Union*, February 2, 1888, pp. 134-136; *Independent*, June 12, 1888, p. 11.

also undertaken against a monopoly, was still more favorably treated by the American religious press.[59]

By the end of the decade some of the bitterness of the Haymarket year was dying down. Religious journals, for the first time, had moderated their hostility toward the eight-hour movement. The *Christian Union* and the *Andover Review* definitely favored the shorter day. The *Independent*, however, insisted that there be no interference with those who wanted to work longer, and the *Watchman* called for unprejudiced inquiry into the needs of specific industries instead of the general "tyrannical" eight-hour drive.[60]

A number of religious journals once more tried to deal analytically with the labor problem in general. By now such analyses ordinarily assumed the permanence of labor organization. The *Christian Union*, accurately anticipating actual tendencies, proposed the creation of impartial courts for railroad labor and the requirement of a week's notice for strikes on common carriers. It published comment on this scheme not only by leading religious publicists and economists but also by Powderly and by P. M. Arthur of the Locomotive Engineers. The *Independent* conducted symposia, also with labor representation, on railroad strikes and government ownership. The *Congregationalist* hopefully praised profit-sharing as a remedy for the errors of labor and the *Watchman* somewhat half-heartedly approved co-operation.[61]

American optimism, in religious circles as elsewhere, was still so great that a few years without major crises almost convinced some observers that the problem was solved. Six years after the frenzy of the Haymarket, the *Independent* could greet the last decade of the marvelous century with a paean of hope and praise. Right on the eve of the next major labor battle at least two religious journals editorially celebrated the dawn of a new era of mutual confidence between capital and labor.[62] Such superficial optimism, alternating with periods of alarm, indicated the continuing superficiality of the religious editors in their approach to labor problems. Yet there is little doubt that, from crisis to crisis, the old, rigid, certainties had lost some of their strength. Each interval of calmness

[59] *Independent*, September 5, 1889, p. 11; *Christian Union*, September 5, 1889, pp. 264-265; *Andover Review*, XII (1889), 422-426.

[60] *Christian Union*, April 17, 1890, p. 546; *Andover Review*, XIII (1890), 661-664; *Independent*, May 1, 1890, p. 11; *Watchman*, September 12, 1889, p. 5.

[61] *Christian Union*, February 21, 1889, pp. 230-232; *Independent*, August 28, 1890, p. 18; October 2, 1890, pp. 1-6, 14; *Congregationalist*, September 4, 1890, p. 5; *Watchman*, January 2, 1890, p. 16.

[62] *Independent*, January 2, 1890, p. 16; *Churchman*, April 23, 1892, p. 513; *Congregationalist*, July 14, 1892, p. 12.

found the religious press slightly more willing to accept organization and slightly more convinced of the problem's complexity.

The third crisis, a series of events from 1890 to 1894, was in many ways the most serious. It started in the spring of 1892 when the new and enormous Carnegie Steel Corporation proposed a new contract with its employees, including a considerable wage reduction. When the union objected General Manager H. C. Frick refused to confer and shut down the plant. On July 5 two boatloads of armed Pinkerton detectives, sent by Frick to guard the mills, were driven off in a pitched battle with the strikers. Eventually state militia reasserted control for the company and the mill was reopened with nonunion labor.

A considerable fraction of the religious press condemned the union in the old whole-hog manner, accusing union members of coercing fellow employees and attempting to "control" the plant. This group of papers defended the company's right to employ Pinkerton men. The *Independent* demonstrated most clearly its conception of the status of labor: "They have no more right to decide how the mills shall be operated, or by whom, than a coachman has to bar his employer out of his own carriages."[63] The *Christian Advocate* was shocked by the theory that the company had an obligation to confer with its employees: "Extend the rights of the state to the compelling of men or corporations to confer with representatives of labor, and you have despotism or Bellamyism forthwith. . . ."[64]

When a half-crazy anarchist, not a striker, attempted to assassinate Frick, anger mounted among these more conservative papers exactly as it had in 1877 or 1886:

> This is no time to arbitrate. The battle of law and order must be fought to the end. . . . Despotism would settle this matter better than we can. . . . Every patriot should hope for the best, and say only those words which will tend to the maintenance of law. If he has any abstract theories for bettering the human race, this is no time to ventilate them.[65]

The *Watchman*, which up to this point had tried to maintain neutrality, now swung around to complete support of the company, including approval of the use of Pinkerton men. The *Churchman* demanded punishment for strikers, stating that no treatment would be too severe for "men who, in a country like the United States, instigate or aid such a revolution."[66]

[63] July 14, 1892, p. 18.
[64] July 14, 1892, pp. 460-461.
[65] *Christian Advocate*, July 28, p. 507.
[66] *Watchman*, June 14, p. 1; July 28, p. 1; *Churchman*, October 28, p. 496.

In this crisis, however, those journals which sided completely with the employers found among the strike sympathizers whom they denounced a few clergymen. The *Churchman* argued with J. O. S. Huntington, embarrassingly a priest of its church and the son of a leading bishop. The *Independent* received a letter from a Pennsylvania minister who said that the employers were responsible for the bloodshed and that private police forces violated the principles of American government. (The editors found in this letter "revolutionary, not to say anarchist, ideas.") The *Christian Advocate* deplored the fact that "Certain ministers in the midst of the strike preached in such a way that the entire community should have risen up and suppressed them by exhibitions of public sentiment."[67]

Still more important than these rare indications of outright clerical support of the strike, another large fraction of the church press made an effort, even during the conflict, at impartial examination of its issues. The *Andover Review* criticized the violence of both sides but, very surprisingly for its time, suggested as a remedy that a worker should have an equity in his job.[68] Permanent employment, unless there was cause for discharge, should be the unwritten law. In the future, the editors continued, workingmen must receive whatever assurance of their rights the present industrial system "can be made to allow":

Otherwise the wage system will certainly and justly lose its place as the accredited method of industrial business, and something will be devised which will express in larger degree than wages the interest of labor in the means and agencies of production.

No other clerical comment approached this editorial for revolutionary implications but many challenged traditional ideas to some degree. Even the *Congregationalist*, appealing for arbitration, urged that "these great business enterprises" built up in the last few years by the labor of many thousands "are not merely private property," and that their skilled laborers could not be "arbitrarily" discharged any more than the operations of the companies could be "arbitrarily" hindered by labor organizations.[69] The *Christian Union* demanded suppression of labor violence but also attacked the company's use of blacklists, wage cuts and a private army. It too believed that employees should be treated as partners in a common enterprise, though it saw no legal way of enforcing this partnership.

[67] *Churchman*, September 10, p. 307; *Independent*, July 28, p. 10; *Christian Advocate*, November 24, p. 783.
[68] *Andover Review*, XVIII (1892), 272-278.
[69] August 4, 1892, p. 248.

The dispute was, it concluded, an incident in "the transition from an aristocratic to a democratic industrial organization."[70] The *Baptist Quarterly Review*, blaming both sides, declared that such major labor struggles involved principles that brought into question the present organization of society in which four thousand men were said to control two-thirds of the nation's wealth and many laborers believed the laws to be unjustly weighted against them.[71]

Such views as these do not represent the permanent conversion of any major portion of the religious press to a Social Gospel point of view, though this reformist school of thought was already attracting a number of advanced individual ministers. Yet it was a striking novelty for major church organs to discuss such fundamental questions *during* a bloody crisis.

This slowly dawning liberalism was to be tried further. In 1893 a serious panic hit the nation, followed by a prolonged industrial depression. In many ways this crisis was the most serious challenge to American political and economic institutions between the Civil War and the depression of 1929-37. Well before the panic farmers, seriously distressed for decades, had organized a radical party to press their demands for redress.[72] With the onset of depression the possible meaning of wage cuts and layoffs was underlined by the recent example of Homestead. By now industrial America was complex and interdependent enough to suffer deeply from the slump, and few thoughtful people expected it to be light or brief. Yet no economic or political agency seemed able to take the most elementary curative or palliative measures. Men from many classes and professions, including the clergy, pondered deeply the corruption and incompetence which the depression widely revealed. Remedies were suggested by socialists as well as silverites; liberals listened with some interest, and conservatives took renewed alarm.

The tragic movement toward Washington of the unemployed "armies" of 1894, helped on their way by many of the stricken cities and states through which they passed, received clerical support only from the radical fringes of religion. Carlo Browne, an eccentric theosophist, was one of the migrants' leaders.[73] Henry Frank, a liberal clergyman of San

---

[70] July 30, 1892, pp. 196-197.

[71] *Baptist Quarterly Review*, XIV (1892), 497-503.

[72] The religious press ordinarily disapproved and ridiculed the manifestations of farmer unrest throughout the period. But Protestant spokesmen, through the early nineties, were considerably more disturbed by labor conflicts than by agrarian uprisings. The relation of Protestant religion to the development of Populism, a subject outside the scope of this study, would be a rewarding subject for investigation.

[73] D. L. McMurry, *Coxey's Army* (Boston, 1929), p. 37.

Francisco, defended the armies in the *Arena*.[74] The spokesmen of the major churches, however, condemned the movement. "General" Coxey's proposed method of handling the depression, financing a work-relief project by controlled inflation, seemed in 1894 beneath direct comment. The *Churchman* pointed out, however, that "By far the most serious danger" of the crisis was "hasty legislation, which can never be reversed, and which would amount to a social revolution." The *Watchman* reminded the unemployed that they were already represented in Washington.[75]

The strikes of 1894 were more widespread than any in American experience. Originating usually in desperate efforts to sustain falling wages, they were fought out with great energy and tenacity. In most cases the giant corporations, backed by the courts, the federal executive and the middle-class public, were able to beat down the determined but essentially ill-prepared forces of labor. In this upheaval, climaxing several years of depression and turmoil, the religious press, including its more liberal segment, forgot the calm analysis it had tried to foster in 1892. For instance, the strike which was the 1894 stage of the long, intermittent struggle to unionize coal was condemned even by the *Christian Union*. The *Watchman* demanded that troops put "a pitiless stop" to such outbreaks.[76]

The climax of the period's labor war arose first in the model town of Pullman, Illinois. Pullman's neat and highly-publicized cottages represented the sort of employer-paternalism in which religious writers had long placed considerable hope. When the company reduced wages 25 per cent the employees protested, and when George Pullman dismissed some members of the protesting committee the men struck. The Pullman employees had recently affiliated with the new American Railway Union, a depression-born industrial organization. Against the advice of its leader, Eugene V. Debs, the A.R.U. declared a nationwide boycott of the struck company. As Pullman cars were cut out of trains all over the country, the conflict developed into an all-out war between Debs' union and the still more powerful General Managers' Association. The strike was defeated by a sweeping injunction which resulted in the imprisonment of its leaders, and by the dispatch of federal troops to Chicago, a move whose propriety and necessity have been keenly debated ever since.

No strike had so alarmed the middle-class public. The principal religious papers were unanimously and wholeheartedly hostile to the

[74] "The Crusade of the Unemployed," *Arena*, X (1894), 239-244.
[75] *Churchman*, January 20, 1894, p. 66; *Watchman*, April 12, 1893, p. 1.
[76] *Christian Union*, June 16, 1894, p. 1080; *Watchman*, June 7, p. 1.

A.R.U. Almost all of them made the point that, whatever the grievances of Pullman employees, a sympathetic railway strike was not to be tolerated. The violent language of former crises was repeated: "The inhuman and brutal selfishness of the leaders of the American Railway Union is something which disgraces modern civilization. . . ."[77] Even the *Outlook*, which, as the *Christian Union*, had often shown a comparatively friendly attitude toward organized labor, called the railway strike "monstrous" and "preposterous," denounced the idea of the "solidarity of labor" and urged that unions should be confined to one trade. Insisting that corporations, however maligned, were a step toward a wider distribution of property, the *Outlook* in traditional accents urged working men to "make it their ambition, not to get the better of capitalists, but themselves to become capitalists."[78]

Church opinion wholeheartedly approved the injunction and the use of federal troops, and demanded stringent punishment for Debs and the other leaders. The *Independent* suggested life imprisonment.[79]

As in 1892, a few dissenters from the dominant religious conservatism made themselves heard. The organ of the recently organized Christian Socialists, of course, supported the strikers and blamed the resultant violence on employer methods, but this group had little influence on majority opinion.[80] More striking was the defense of the strikers by William H. Carwardine, the Methodist minister of Pullman, Illinois.

This remarkably courageous critic seems to have had no connection with the growth of liberal and radical social theory in American Christianity. His opinions came from firsthand experience. Despite Pullman's attractive buildings and parks, the atmosphere of the town, as Carwardine described it, was one of espionage and petty tyranny. Press stories of high earnings and company contributions to relief he denounced as lies. In the recent crisis, dividends, salaries and rents on company houses remained high, while wages were cut by a third or more. Carwardine's conclusion on the town shows the effect of years of exasperation.

It is a civilized relic of European serfdom. We all enjoy living here because there is an equality of interest, and we have a common enemy, the Company, but our daily prayer is, "Lord, keep us from dying here."[81]

[77] *Churchman*, July 7, p. 7.
[78] *Outlook*, July 4, pp. 8-9; July 14, p. 49; July 21, p. 89; July 28, p. 130; August 4, pp. 169-170.
[79] July 12, 1894, p. 896. A typical example of the dominant clerical opinion is Z. S. Holbrook, *The American Republic and the Debs Insurrection* (Oberlin, 1895).
[80] *Dawn*, July-August, 1894, pp. 97-99.
[81] Carwardine, *The Pullman Strike* (4th ed.; Chicago, 1894), p. 25.

Carwardine not only sympathized with the strike, blaming it on the company's tyranny, but played an important part himself in persuading the A.R.U. to declare their sympathetic boycott.[82] His views were set forth in a public sermon in Chicago which, though widely denounced, was approved by at least one other clergyman of the city.[83]

Carwardine's conclusions on the strike were those of a man who had been stirred to earnest thought. Agreeing with his clerical contemporaries that mobs must be quelled, by force if necessary, Carwardine attributed the strike principally to dangerous inequalities and class gulfs. Like other Christians, he appealed for a new spirit of brotherly love and for the use of the ballot to right labor's wrongs. In addition, however, he demanded practical steps remarkably radical for the time, including compulsory arbitration and, in case of refusal by management, seizure of the plants for operation in the interests of the people.[84]

It is perhaps significant that this lonely and untheoretical clergyman was drawn by his immediate experience of conditions in Pullman into a position more radical than that of most of the more advanced Christian social theorists of the time. As one would expect, his book was reviewed very unfavorably by the chief newspaper of his denomination.[85]

As the strikes of 1894 were suppressed, the religious press once more pondered solutions for the problem of labor. The *Independent* suggested nothing more fundamental than that employers treat their men with more courtesy. The *Outlook* called again for compulsory arbitration and the requirement of advance notice of strikes.[86] Repeating a hope which clerical optimists had been expressing for a generation, this liberal organ looked forward to a day when railroad companies, already owned by many stockholders, should gradually be bought by their employees: ". . . without any wrench, any revolution, simply by thrift, industry, economy and practical wisdom—they will become their own employers. . . ."[87] The three great social crises of 1877, 1886 and 1892-4 had forced clerical observers to admit the existence of problems ignored, or waved aside, by the pat theorists of earlier times. Despite free government and free religion, class gulfs had somehow grown up, and in a period of intermittent labor warfare it was increasingly difficult to believe in the auto-

[82] Harry Barnard, *Eagle Forgotten, The Life of John Peter Altgeld* (Indianapolis, 1938), p. 282.

[83] Carwardine, *Pullman Strike*, pp. 118-119. This sermon was published in part in *Twentieth Century*, July 12, 1894, pp. 2-3, and in the Chicago *Herald*.

[84] *Ibid.*, pp. 118-126.

[85] *Christian Advocate*, October 4, 1894, p. 648.

[86] *Independent*, August 9, 1894, pp. 10-11; *Outlook*, July 21, 1894, pp. 89-90.

[87] *Outlook*, August 4, 1894, p. 170.

matic, benevolent operation of Divine or cosmic laws. First shocked out of their complacency into frenzied denunciation of labor uprisings, ministers were gradually beginning to search for solutions of new problems. The tentative efforts at analysis produced by the religious press in the intervals of hostilities made, indeed, no very significant contribution to social knowledge. Many Protestant editors still forgot their efforts at moderation and impartiality when a new conflict shook the social order.

Meanwhile, however, new schools of Christian social theory were growing up. Already each major outbreak of labor controversy was followed by publication of an increasing number of books which attempted to formulate a Christian solution for the general problems posed by strikes. The Christian social movement, already a major influence on American thought in 1895, owed its existence to the impact of labor conflict more than to any other single cause. Its formulations reflected many other influences, theoretical and concrete, but it could never have arisen had not the all-sufficient, optimistic formulae of Francis Wayland and Henry Ward Beecher been shattered by unanswerable events. In the day-to-day reactions of the religious press to these formidable challenges are reflected both the major cause for the development of social Christianity and something of its early direction.

THE FACE OF THE CITY

LABOR conflicts provided the drastic, sudden shocks that were necessary to shatter Protestant complacency. An almost equally powerful,
though more gradual influence on church opinion was the rapid growth
of great cities.

Industrial and commercial centers of a new scale, drawing their
millions not only from Europe and Asia but also from America's rural
population, were changing the nature of American society in countless
ways during the last two decades of the century.[1] As the cities became the
centers of progress in the arts, sciences, business, industry and philanthropy, they developed also as breeding grounds of poverty, misery, vice
and crime. In the contrast between Fifth Avenue and the disease-ridden
Lower East Side, class gulfs were dramatized as never before in America.
In the prewar and early postwar periods, only a small minority of the
clergy had realized the menace of city conditions. Now more and more
found them impossible to ignore.

In the eighties and nineties a series of religious writers, themselves
overwhelmed by city realities, set themselves to the task of awakening
their brethren. Charles Loring Brace, the Congregationalist reformer
who devoted his life to the welfare of city children, had already published
one of the first of the city exposés. In his next book Brace ventured
further into analysis and increased his demand for action, charging that
the church was neglecting a humanitarian tradition that had belonged to
it throughout the ages.[2]

Beside appealing for an expansion of charitable work, Brace, shocked
by the evidence of extreme inequality, called for a more just distribution
of wealth. Pursuing this topic, he found much in common between
Christianity and socialism, citing the early communism of the Disciples,
the agrarianism of Jewish land laws, and even "a certain tone throughout

[1] See A. M. Schlesinger, *The Rise of the City* ("A History of American Life," X
[New York, 1933]).
[2] *Gesta Christi: or a History of Humane Progress under Christianity* (New York,
1882).

112

the gospels, if not of 'communism,' at least in favor of greater distribution of wealth than would suit modern ideas."[3]

By no means a radical, Brace rejected socialism on many counts. Since he was absorbed in the direct, immediate needs of the city poor for relief, he had little to say about the labor movement, though it is interesting to note the moderation of his reaction to 1877: "I believe myself that, in general, the laboring classes do not receive their fair share. Strikes are one of their means of getting more."[4]

For some audiences, social criticism incidentally contained in such humanitarian appeals was particularly effective. Stated in terms of concrete experience and coupled with a plea for church action along comparatively familiar lines, Brace's opinions were comparatively well-received even in a period when Christians were still overwhelmingly conservative.[5]

In the middle eighties, perhaps because of the effects of depression and labor struggle, Protestant concern with urban problems rapidly increased. The conservative *Churchman* commented favorably on W. C. Preston's *The Bitter Cry of Outcast London*, insisting, however, that reform must be "slow and patient," since if every poor family in New York were now given a good dwelling, they would be as wretched as ever in six months.[6]

With less insistence on traditional dogma, William W. Adams described a New England factory town in the *Andover Review*.[7] His description makes the reader see clearly the dirty brick buildings, the rows of little gray-white ramshackle houses, the swarm of hungry children, the pale, dull faces, the crowd around the saloon on payday. The only remedy he suggested, however, was a recognition by the employer of his moral responsibility.

The most stirring of all books on the problem of the city were those by Josiah Strong, a Congregationalist minister who developed strong social-Christian views. Like many of his fellows, Strong had in his youth forsaken the stern old theology, after an exhausting mental struggle, for Bushnell's more optimistic doctrines.[8] Yet it is clear that theology alone

[3] *Ibid.*, p. 95.

[4] Letter undated, to Miss G. Schuyler concerning the 1877 strikes. Emma Brace, *The Life of Charles Loring Brace* (New York, 1894), pp. 354-355.

[5] E.g. *Christian Union*, January 11, 1883, pp. 33-34; January 25, 1883, p. 72.

[6] January 12, 1884, p. 32. This book is also quoted at length by Josiah Strong, *Our Country, Its Possible Future and its Present Crisis* (New York, 1885), pp. 130-132.

[7] Adams, "The Spiritual Problem of the Manufacturing Town," *Andover Review*, V (1886), 117-131, 341-359, 611-631.

[8] See *My Religion in Everyday Life* (New York, 1910), pp. 18-37 ff.

did not determine the direction of his thought. Strong himself, discussing the end-of-the-century development of a belief in the salvation of society as well as the individual, attributed this tendency to two main causes. These were, first, "the change in civilization, during the past century, from an individual to a social type," and "the progress of science, which has revealed the interdependence of body and mind, and the influence of physical conditions on spiritual life."[9] It is this appreciation of the importance of the environment, drawn largely from his knowledge of the new urban conditions, that gave his works their striking power.

Strong's message was conveyed in two powerful and early studies of the effects of the city.[10] In *Our Country*, especially, Strong created a sense of momentous and immediate crisis. This crisis was important partly because it was taking place in America; Strong was full of a jingoism surpassing even Beecher's, and prophetic of imperial expansion:

Then this race of unequaled energy, with all the majesty of numbers and the might of wealth behind it—the representative, let us hope, of the largest liberty, the purest Christianity, the highest civilization—having developed peculiarly aggressive traits calculated to impress its institutions upon mankind, will spread itself over the earth. If I read not amiss, this powerful race will move down upon Mexico, down upon Central and South America, out upon the islands of the sea, over upon Africa and beyond. And can any one doubt that the result of this competition of races will be the "survival of the fittest"?[11]

Despite this magnificent destiny, America's present state as described by Strong was by no means rosy. Like his contemporaries he deeply feared mass immigration, especially of Catholics. The most serious danger of all was the development in America of deep class distinctions, expressed in declining real wages and in the "feudal" brutality of some capitalists. All these dangers were at their worst in cities, where renegade Catholics, beset by poverty, made the best recruits to socialism and revolution.

In vigorous terms Strong insisted that palliative measures were not enough:

The slums are the "putrefying sores" of the city. They may be mollified with the ointment of missions and altogether closed at one point, but it will

[9] Strong, *Religious Movements for Social Betterment* (Monographs on American Social Economy, XIV, [New York, 1900]), 4-6.

[10] *Our Country;* and *The New Era, or the Coming Kingdom* (New York, 1893). Also important in its time was *The Twentieth Century City* (New York, 1898), later expanded into *The Challenge of the City* (New York, 1911).

[11] *Our Country*, p. 175, quoted with the geographical references omitted in *New Era*, pp. 79-80.

be only to break out at another until there is a constitutional treatment which shall purge the poison of the social system.[12]

Modern capitalists, with their power to control prices and employment, were as powerful and more irresponsible than feudal lords; their rule was "a despotism vastly more oppressive and more exasperating than that against which the thirteen colonies rebelled." The industrious laborer, not getting his share of the wealth he helped to produce, "ought not to be satisfied until justice is done him."[13]

Strong prophesied an immediate, climactic crisis which would test our institutions gravely. This supreme peril would come when free land was exhausted. Industries and cities would be greater, class differences deeper, and eventually a terrible depression would throw millions out of work.

. . . then, with the opportunity, the means, the fit agents, the motive, the temptation to destroy, all brought into evil conjunction, THEN will come the real test of our institutions, then will appear whether we are capable of self-government.[14]

Despite these apocalyptic predictions, Strong was essentially neither radical nor pessimistic. Socialism and individualism, social responsibility and property rights could be reconciled if the church took up her proper mission and became "the controlling conscience of the social organism."[15] If this came about, all problems would be solved—socialism would disappear, Christian principles of private property would be reaffirmed, the struggle of capital and labor would be ended by co-operation and commercial dishonesty would disappear.

This was the alternative which Strong continually presented, catastrophe or regeneration. And, for all his dire warnings, Strong was enough of an American optimist to be confident that the nation would choose the road of salvation. His fervent, evangelistic appeal, pointing to fearful perils and offering bright hopes, was cut in a pattern calculated to appeal to thousands of Christians. *Our Country* was, appropriately, published by the American Home Missionary Society, a fact regretted by the *Christian Union* only because "Its circulation ought not to be confined to Congregationalists, nor to the clergy, nor even to church

[12] *New Era*, p. 332.
[13] *Our Country*, p. 106; *New Era*, p. 151.
[14] *Our Country*, pp. 143-144. Strong fully believed in the safety-valve role which later historians ascribed to the frontier.
[15] *New Era*, p. 313. See throughout for this optimistic prophecy.

people."[16] A repeated best seller, *Our Country* was the *Uncle Tom's Cabin* of city reform.

Two years later it was followed by a similar city exposé, S. L. Loomis' *Modern Cities*. Loomis shared to the full Strong's virulent suspicion of the foreign-born and especially the Catholic workingman:

> With some important exceptions those who come from foreign lands, both Catholics and Protestants, bring with them most crude and imperfect notions of religious truth. No Christian culture lies behind them. They have never breathed a Christian atmosphere. Ideas with which all Americans, whether of pious parentage or not, have been familiar from childhood, are strange to them. . . . The whole method of our services, adapted to the cultured, Christianized elements of our society, is so far above them that it fails to secure their interest and attention. When one of them strays into a church, the chances are that he finds nothing there for him.[17]

As an aspect of his discussion of evangelistic difficulties, Loomis pointed out that the industrial worker often received low wages, worked long hours, and was subject to recurrent unemployment. The breach between employer and employee was widened by trade-unions, for which Loomis had little use. Partly because of the class feeling developed by unions, immigrant laborers avoided Protestant city churches. Because these institutions were "usually attended and sustained by persons of means and intelligence," the misguided workingmen considered them "the churches of the capitalists."[18] It was this separation from good influences that, to Loomis, explained the serious growth of corruption, drink, crime, pauperism and anarchism, all of which *Modern Cities* described in frightening terms.

Like Strong, Loomis confined his proposals for a solution to an increase in Christian evangelism, especially for the lower classes. To be effective, city evangelists must, he urged, know the conditions of the urban poor and give a respectful hearing to their complaints and proposed remedies, no matter how misguided these might be.[19]

Loomis' book, more conventional in its approach than Strong's and

[16] August 19, 1886, p. 22. For other laudatory reviews see *Congregationalist*, February 18, 1886; July 16, 1891 (review of second edition). For similar reviews of *The New Era* see the *Presbyterian and Reformed Review*, IV (1893), 697; *Christian Union*, August 5, 1893, p. 274. Only the *Nation*, always hostile to humanitarian uplift, found in Strong's remedies for radicalism "the one-sidedness and narrowness of an exclusively religious view." *Nation*, XLIII (1886), 228-229.

[17] S. L. Loomis, *Modern Cities and their Religious Problems*, introd. by Josiah Strong (New York, 1887), p. 91.

[18] *Ibid.*, p. 99.

[19] *Ibid.*, pp. 209-210.

somewhat less startling in its language, was also well received by the church press.[20] The drastic impact of Strong and Loomis on contemporary Protestant opinion was further demonstrated by one of their few adversaries, a southern Methodist minister named John B. Robins. Robins, admitting that the two books had been "generally read and universally commended,"[21] attacked them for presenting too gloomy a prospect. Great wealth, he said, was not a curse but a blessing, the natural result of Christian progress; immigrants and even their church would be altered for the better by the spirit of the time.

As for socialism, Robins pointed out, correctly, that Strong had given a disproportionate emphasis to the doctrine of small anarchist groups, disregarding moderate and gradualist socialist schools. Less conservative than his opponents, Robins believed that the existing order, with its inequality and oppression, was intolerable, and approved the discontent that had produced socialism. In time, he predicted, socialism's "selfish" elements would vanish under the beneficent influences of Christian American institutions and "This movement, with its obnoxious qualities eliminated, exalted by human sympathy, and glorified by human compassion, will yet reform, bless and crown our industrial and social systems.[22]

Full of the spirit of the new theology, Robins rested his confidence in the future on God's guidance of the world through the Immanent Christ. Though he was more receptive than his opponents to new social ideas, his mystical optimism made the total effect of his book almost quietistic. For the public of the eighties, Strong's mixture of vivid exaggeration and strenuous evangelism was undoubtedly more effective.

At the end of the decade a number of books on city conditions made some impression on clerical readers. In 1889 Helen Campbell's striking *Prisoners of Poverty* attacked hardhearted clergymen who ascribed poverty to vice and confined their preaching to "thou shalt nots": "To souls that sit at ease and leave to 'the power that works for righteousness' the evolution of humanity from its prison of poverty and ignorance and pain, it is quite useless to speak."[23] Jacob Riis' stirring and widely-read

[20] Some of it was originally published in the *Andover Review*, beginning VII (1887), 1-35. It was favorably reviewed in the *Independent*, November 10, 1887, p. 17, and the *Methodist Review*, LXXI (1889), 167.

[21] Robins, *Christ and Our Country: or, a Hopeful View of Christianity in the Present Day* (Nashville, 1889), p. 5.

[22] *Ibid.*, p. 63.

[23] *Prisoners of Poverty* (New York, 1889), p. 79.

How the Other Half Lives appeared in condensed form in the *Christian Union*, immediately following a condensation of Booth's *In Darkest England*.²⁴

In 1891 Louis A. Banks, a Boston Methodist minister, described to his congregation the disgusting conditions prevalent in the city's sweat-shops. Banks' concrete details were so shocking and his indignation so telling that the sermons aroused something of a storm. A sample letter from a member of his congregation cited standard economic doctrine to prove that the sweaters were doing a favor to the women and children they employed and warned Banks against arousing class hatred.²⁵

W. T. Stead, a British journalist of strong Protestant beliefs and reformist social convictions, published in 1894 a plea for city reform that had almost as great an impact on religious circles as *Our Country*. In language even more sensational than Strong's, Stead described Chicago's miserable present and exalted future.²⁶ Agreeing with many of its citizens, Stead believed that the Windy City was the future world's capital. This gave increased point to his vivid descriptions of police brutality and venality, protected vice, corrupt politicians, inadequate charities, taxes that fleeced the poor and other present evils.

Stead's proposed remedy was typical of the evangelist approach. The city was to be regenerated through a new "Church Catholic and Civic." Since existing Protestant churches were rich men's clubs, the new civic church would arise out of the city government which, whatever its shortcomings, at least recognized the principle of human brotherhood by its inclusion of all citizens. Administrative reforms would be made, the "Devils" of Plutocracy, Intolerance, and Intemperance would be cast out, and close relations would be established between the church and labor unions, to the benefit of both.

Stead wound up his book with a prophetic description of twentieth-century Chicago that might stand as a monument to the hopes of the nineteenth-century reformer.²⁷ In his picture of the future the Church of Chicago, with the Catholic archbishop as president and Jenkin Lloyd Jones, a liberal Unitarian minister, as vice-president, rules the city by

²⁴ *Christian Union*, November 20, 1890, pp. 622, 684; November 27, 1890, pp. 706-707. Editorial on both books, November 27, 1890, p. 703.
²⁵ Banks, *White Slaves, or, the Oppression of the Worthy Poor* (Boston, 1891). The letter referred to is on pp. 47-51.
²⁶ *If Christ Came to Chicago! A Plea for the Union of All Who Love in the Service of All Who Suffer* (2nd ed.; London, 1894).
²⁷ *Ibid.*, pp. 409-431.

the golden rule. "On the word of a patrolman" has become the standard phrase to express complete honesty. Marshall Field and Siegel, Cooper and Co. have both been given to the city with their complete stocks. The churches in the working-class districts are surrounded at the dinner hour by "grimy" workmen listening to organ recitals over their dinner pails. In a rousing climax, the book describes a civic reception to the German Emperor, who has crossed the ocean to see for himself Chicago, the ideal city of the twentieth-century world.

Stead's book did not bring all Chicago immediately to the mourner's bench, and the most loyal Chicagoan must admit that twentieth-century realities have fallen short of his dream. Yet the book was not entirely without concrete results. Its message was first delivered to a huge mass meeting, theoretically representing all classes. From this meeting stemmed the Civic Federation of Chicago, a powerful reform pressure group. Some slight temporary success was achieved by efforts for church-labor co-operation, and the city's ministers federated for district social work. An organization arising out of labor unions and calling itself "The Modern Church" preached a crusade for humanity once a fortnight in the Labor Temple. The book was roundly damned by the city's secular newspapers, while local religious journals remained half impressed and half indignant. Perhaps the greatest single tribute to its effectiveness was the sudden disappearance of the stocks of the first edition, evidently bought up by "the interests." Stead helped to open the eyes of religious and social-minded people to urban evils and played some part in the development of the semireligious reform spirit that was rife in the Chicago of Jane Addams and Florence Kelley.[28]

Like *Uncle Tom's Cabin* or *The Jungle*, these dramatic exposures of city evils were effective, not because of any originality, but because they described conditions which many people knew something about. Thousands of ministers were experiencing at firsthand the conditions described by Strong or Stead.

To many Christians the most shocking fact was that which was simplest and most easily realized; that city wage earners were staying away from church. Even in the early seventies, realistic Protestants had pointed to this gloomy fact. Now the problem of the "unchurched masses," usually linked to the threats of drink, Romanism and radicalism,

---

[28] For descriptions of the book's effect and aftermath, see London edition of *If Christ*, pp. 383-451; also Graham Taylor, *Pioneering on Social Frontiers* (Chicago, 1930), pp. 28-36.

dominated the discussions of many denominational and interdenominational groups[29] and was widely argued in the religious press.

Some Protestant writers still refused to admit the reality of the menace, denying that the church was losing ground with a touchy indignation that seemed to make the failure all the more obvious. In 1881 Daniel Dorchester published a volume designed to refute any idea that all was not well, concluding from his interpretation of census figures that the churches were increasing three times as fast as the population.[30] These conclusions were gleefully attacked by the always somewhat anticlerical *Nation*, which pointed out that Dorchester and other optimistic clerics were guilty of such statistical lapses as counting children among church members, and then multiplying members by four to account for "children and other adherents."[31] The argument was widely taken up by optimists and pessimists alike.[32]

Other church comment, admitting the fact of the lack of working-class attendance, tended still to accept the loss complacently. In 1883, for instance, a Protestant spokesman answering a critic turned the argument around:

It does not need proof that the classes which are eminently non-intelligent or non-respectable, are . . . like our friend, almost to a man, non-church-goers. . . . Church members average much more moral, intelligent, and wealthy than non-church-members. This is the natural result of their church-training.[33]

The *Andover Review* also considered it

. . . by no means a result altogether of evil that the churches stand for what is respectable and even refined, nor within proper limits, that certain lines

[29] See for instance, Presbyterian Church in the U.S.A., General Assembly, *Minutes, 1885*, p. 757; "Statement of the American Home Missionary Society," National Council of Congregational Churches, *Minutes, 1886*, pp. 119-124. In 1886 the American branch of the Evangelical Alliance, a powerful interdenominational organization, impressed by *Our Country* and similar books, called Josiah Strong to be its general secretary. He organized a spectacular series of conferences, dealing mainly with city problems, which had a very considerable effect on Protestant opinion. See Evangelical Alliance for the U.S.A., *National Perils and Opportunities* (New York, 1887); *National Needs and Remedies* (New York, 1890).

[30] *The Problem of Religious Progress* (New York, 1881), pp. 447-448.

[31] *Nation*, XXXVII (1883), 443-444.

[32] The *Nation* attacked again, XL (1885), 274-275. For typical optimistic articles in the same year in the *Independent*, see April 23, p. 14; April 30, p. 14; May 7, p. 14. Washington Gladden, who had polled the workingmen of Columbus with disheartening results, disagreed with the *Independent's* stand in that paper's issues of July 23, 1885, pp. 2-4; July 30, pp. 4-5. The *Christian Union* also took a pessimistic stand, June 11, 1885, p. 3. Yet four years later the *Christian Advocate* was still denying that any problem existed. February 21, 1889, p. 113.

[33] William Hayes Ward in a symposium on "Church Attendance," *North American Review*, CXXXVII (1883), 81.

of social cleavage appear in the group of people in denominations and in the several churches. . . . Let the fact be recognized, then that as the church includes the better classes of society, it will be disliked by the worse classes who are yet outside. . . .[34]

Most clerical opinion, however, by now both admitted and deplored the fact of working-class alienation and sought for diagnosis and remedy. By the middle eighties only a few Protestants were suggesting an explanation that later seemed obvious: that workingmen stayed away from church because the churches were indifferent or hostile to labor's most pressing demands. This sweeping answer was suggested in 1884 by a letter to the *Homiletic Review* from John Swinton, a radical but Christian labor journalist.[35] It is not surprising that the editors felt obliged to apologize for printing Swinton's "severe, and, as we think, undeserved, censure upon the clergy as a body." The letter, one of the first of many similar attacks from labor spokesmen, indicted ministers for indifference to suffering and injustice, claiming that in a long career of fighting the battles of the poor the author had never encountered a clergyman on the side of reform. Church philanthropy he dismissed as an emphasis on superficial at the expense of basic evils. The first thing for the churches to do, Swinton bitterly concluded, was to learn something of the conditions of the poor. "Whether they would reach the masses then seems a vain question; for I do not think that one-tenth of the wage-earning classes in New York believe in Christianity at all: but let them try."

The *Homiletic Review's* reply demonstrated complete unfamiliarity with the point of view which prompted this attack.[36] In answer to Swinton's charge that church philanthropic enterprise was either futile or of secondary importance from *labor's point of view*, the editors cited instance after instance of charity, evangelism, and even work for the causes of antiobscenity and antidivorce.

Yet some more social-minded ministers were wondering whether there might not be a grain of truth in such charges as Swinton's. Undoubtedly the realization of working-class alienation caused many Protestant leaders to re-examine their social attitudes.

The most immediate and concrete result of the challenging disclosures was, however, a tremendous expansion of the evangelical and welfare work already under way. Snobbish congregations were urged to be more hospitable to ill-dressed worshipers; churches that had moved to new

[34] II (1884), 291-293.
[35] VIII (1884), pp. 648-650.
[36] *Loc. cit.*, pp. 650-655.

residential neighborhoods established missions in the slums; revival meetings were directed specifically at city workers. More important, the social settlement movement, started in America in the eighties and flourishing by the nineties, brought knowledge of the lives of city populations to young ministers. Institutional churches with their club-rooms and gymnasiums, co-operative city missions, young people's organizations, brotherhood and deaconess societies and all the familiar paraphernalia of American Protestant welfare work grew and flourished during these years. The Salvation Army, imported in 1880, brought city poverty to the attention of many by its spectacular methods.[37]

The whole movement of institutional expansion arose from the evangelical and humanitarian problems of the city. Essentially untheoretical in itself, it nevertheless exerted an important indirect influence on church social theory. In the long run, welfare work was bound to bring into question the traditional dogmas on the nature of poverty and wealth.

These dogmas did not give in without a fight. Some opponents of the new institutions still pointed out the peculiar blessings of poverty or its indispensability to progress and civilization; others continued to insist that misery was always a punishment for vice.[38] Still others, like a writer in the *Independent,* insisted

> Let one half the money now given to temporal aid be expended in spiritual work in preaching the Gospel, and the poor will be better provided for and suffer less than they would, if ten times that amount were bestowed upon them in charity.[39]

Even some of those who accepted the new movements reconciled them with the old doctrines. Urban ills and institutional methods could be seen as new versions of poverty and charity, both of which might still be considered as part of God's plan rather than as manifestations of social failure. New methods of social work were seen by some as new means for the traditional Christian duty of giving alms; almsgiving promoted religion and prevented unrest.[40] Conservatively interpreted, church philanthropy could serve as an antidote to social criticism rather than as a cause of it.

[37] See Abell, *Urban Impact,* pp. 88-223, for a detailed examination of all these developments.

[38] A typical example is Bishop Samuel Smith Harris of Michigan, *The Relation of Christianity to Civil Society* (New York, 1883). Also *Congregationalist,* October 15, 1891, p. 348; *Christian Advocate,* March 13, 1890, pp. 160-161.

[39] James A. Hoadley, "The Gospel for the Poor," *Independent,* April 26, 1888, pp. 2-3.

[40] This very common attitude is expressed by the Reverend Alfred Yeomans, in "The Right of the Poor," *Methodist Review,* IX (1889), 17-25.

Inevitably, however, some of the sensitive young ministers and laymen who spent grim years in city missions, trying to relieve poverty that seemed to increase, learning to know as individuals people whom the last generation had labeled "the vicious poor," found themselves unable to accept the conventional complacent explanations of poverty.

Charles L. White, describing the work of the American Baptist Home Missionary Society among urban immigrants in the nineties, stated that the missionaries usually "have taken the part of labor, contending for its rights," although they have maintained a firm stand against "violence."[41] Graham Taylor, one of the leading exponents of settlement training for ministers, explained his own early and doubtless typical reaction to this kind of experience:

> As men came up from the pitfalls dug by themselves and others, they taught me, on the one hand, that the fallen could rise, and, on the other hand, that the conditions under which they fell could and should be changed, so as to make it easier to live right and harder to go wrong in every community.[42]

In 1896 the College Settlement Association sent to the residents in its settlements a questionnaire which asked, among other things, whether the recipients' "attitude toward social and industrial questions" had undergone any changes during settlement residence.[43] Some answered that they had become more conservative, "convinced that spiritual evils were far worse than temporal," or that "the social question will in no degree be solved by sympathy toward one class to the exclusion of another." Others were perplexed, stirred without having reached conclusions. A third group became definitely more sympathetic to the efforts of working people to better their own condition, convinced even "that the only weapon of the poor against the oppression of competition was in organization to maintain their rights." These three groups probably represented adequately the reactions of church settlement workers. Which was the largest group cannot be determined.

A by-product of church experience in cities was a changed attitude toward immigration. Despite widespread clerical hostility to some immigrant groups, church writers up to the early eighties usually opposed restriction, particularly when it was demanded by organized labor. Church papers continued especially to defend the Chinese, praising their thrift and docility, contrasting them unfavorably with their union

---

[41] Charles L. White, *A Century of Faith* (Philadelphia, 1932), p. 129.
[42] Taylor, *Pioneering*, p. 366.
[43] Christian Social Union, *Publications*, 29 (Boston, 1896).

opponents. The *Congregationalist* in 1884 still represented prevailing church opinion when it opposed restriction except for Mormon converts and socialist-anarchists.[44]

Gradually, however, fear of the effects of immigration became more powerful than the traditional reasons for opposing restriction. The Irish had never been as hospitably received as the Chinese. In 1881 the *Watchman* complained of their radical influence on the American working class.[45] Southern and eastern Europeans, often painted as free-thinkers and socialists, were no more popular among Protestant spokesmen.[46] As writers like Strong depicted urban centers of radicalism and irreligion swarming with immigrants, church attitudes toward immigration altered. By the end of the decade even conservative Protestants were beginning to agree with labor's demand for restriction, though different grounds were urged.[47]

In many ways, both tacit and expressed, American Protestants in the eighties and nineties were stirred and shaken by the great changes in American life which cities made manifest. Washington Gladden, describing the effect of his early experience in Brooklyn, spoke for a generation:

One could not help wondering whether in liberating the force which gathers men into cities, and equipping it with steam and electricity, a power had not been created which was stronger than the intelligence which seeks to control it; whether such aggregations of humanity, with wills no better socialized than those of the average nineteenth-century American, are not by their own action self-destructive. I do not mean that I reasoned out this query, at that time; but some sense of the appalling nature of the municipal problem was certainly present with me.[48]

[44] July 10, 1884, p. 230.
[45] October 27, 1881, p. 337. This editorial also accused the Irish of exaggerating their grievances at home, insisting dogmatically that "The woes of Ireland to-day proceed from bad whiskey and a bad church."
[46] Southern Europeans are specifically contrasted unfavorably with Chinese by Addison Parker, "The Exclusion of the Chinese from the United States, and the Immigration Problem," *Baptist Quarterly Review*, XII (1890), 460-475.
[47] For instance, editorials against restriction appeared in the *Congregationalist*, July 10, 1884, p. 230, and September 22, 1887, p. 320. An editorial in favor of restriction appeared June 11, 1891, p. 200.
[48] Gladden, *Recollections* (Boston, 1909), pp. 90-91.

NEW MORAL PROBLEMS

SOCIAL changes, during the eighties and nineties, forced several important extensions of Protestantism's traditional areas of influence. The familiar claim to moral supervision of public affairs, hitherto used largely in opposition to radicalism, now became itself a source of novel social doctrine. Many a clerical conservative, battling to uphold the traditional prerogatives of the church, defending its right to express opinions on various issues, failed to realize that he was preparing the way for church criticism of existing society.

Up to the end of the century, organized religion surrendered few if any of its historic claims to moral supervision. In 1888, for instance, Philip Schaff was still insisting as he had in prewar years that

the American system differs radically from the infidel and red-republican theory of religious freedom. . . . The American separation of church and state rests on respect for the church; the infidel separation, on indifference and hatred of the church, and of religion itself.[1]

The opening speech at the 1893 meeting of the Evangelical Alliance sounded a still bolder note of defiance:

It is still the fundamental belief of Americans that *the majority has no right to do what it pleases except when it pleases to do what is right*. We believe in a moral law that underlies and should override all statute laws. . . . And the foundation of this national belief is laid in the Christian faith of the majority of the American people.[2]

The campaign of 1884, in which the churches took more active part than in any since the war, demonstrated the continuing willingness of organized religion to intervene in politics when it considered moral questions involved. Ordinarily the church press was strongly Republican because of the antislavery tradition, the money question (on which a dogmatic defense of the gold standard was almost universal in leading

[1] Schaff, *Church and State in the United States* (New York, 1888), p. 15.
[2] President M. E. Gates, "The Significance of the Discovery of America," Evangelical Alliance for the U. S. A., *Christianity Practically Applied*, 2 v. (New York, 1894), pp. 48-49. (Italics Gates'.)

religious circles), and the party's general respectability. Like much of the reform element, however, church editors were tired of Republican corruption and repelled by Blaine's own connection with railroad and other scandals. Just when many of them were veering to support Cleveland, the reform governor of New York, it was disclosed that he was the father of an illegitimate child. This seemed to leave the religious press a choice between Republican corruption and Democratic immorality. Most, horrified at the possibility of seeming to condone personal failings, turned either toward Blaine or toward Governor St. John of Kansas, the Prohibition candidate.[3] The *Christian Union* tried to escape the dilemma by calling for the formation of a new third party based on standard reform demands such as national support for education, railroad regulation, opposition to Mormon polygamy, honest currency, an end of "subsidies to capital" but a tariff for the protection of labor, and local control of the liquor traffic. This platform drew many approving letters from well-known ministers, but in the end this paper too went for St. John.[4]

Many church proponents of moral intervention in politics stopped with such comparatively respectable issues as these. It was possible, however, for defenders of the church's traditional claims to extend them quite naturally, almost unconsciously, into still more controversial areas. The *Methodist Review*, for instance, listing the moral aspects of the 1884 campaign, mentioned not only the protection of Chinese and Negroes, the railroad and telegraph corruption, and sound money, but also "the relations of labor and capital, in which are involved some of the highest and most delicate interests, and also the greatest perils of the nation."[5]

This was, of course, a problem on which the church had long taken for granted its right to make pronouncements. *Opposition* to organized labor had been seen as a matter of morality and common sense, not needing any specific assertion of the church's duties. *Support* of organized labor would not seem to involve any great extension of church powers. Yet, since pro-labor doctrines involved opposition to the great

[3] The *Methodist Review* concentrated its denunciations against the Democrats. LXVII (1885), 118-121. The *Christian Advocate*, claiming neutrality, dwelt on the bad effects of personal "wickedness" in high places. September 25, 1884, p. 625. The *Independent* backed St. John, October 30, 1884, pp. 17-18; while the *Congregationalist*, after hesitating between the two major candidates, sadly left the choice to the consciences of its readers. July 17, 1884, p. 238; July 31, 1884, p. 254; August 28, 1884, p. 286.

[4] August 28, 1884, p. 196; September 11, 1884, pp. 245-246; October 30, 1884, p. 412.

[5] LXVII (1885), 118-121.

mass of standard authority, the proponents of Christian social reform, when they started to appear, usually failed to cite precedents of church moral supervision and wrote as if Protestant intervention in public affairs were something new.

The connection between the old moral-religious movements and the new demands for social reform was clearer and more direct through the expanded, militant temperance movement, which was defended by some of its early leaders on both moral and social grounds. Frances E. Willard, widely respected in church circles for her militant leadership of the Women's Christian Temperance Union, was especially early and influential in her championship of new social forces.

At the surprisingly early date 1874, the W.C.T.U. Declaration of Principles, drafted by Miss Willard, endorsed labor's demands for a living wage and the eight-hour day.[6] Throughout her early career, Miss Willard cordially co-operated with Terence Powderly of the Knights of Labor, who shared her temperance views. The Grand Master's picture had a place on her desk with those of other leading reformers.[7] Even in the stormy climate of 1886 an official letter from the W.C.T.U. to "all Knights of Labor, Trade Unions, and other Labor Organizations" approved the Order's efforts for co-operation, arbitration and the elevation of women, declaring "we come to you naturally as to our friends and allies," though it lectured the Knights a little for some of their alleged tactics.[8] In the same year Miss Willard defended the Knights in the *Independent*, where they received nothing but condemnation from other writers.[9] From 1886 forward the W.C.T.U. and the Knights exchanged fraternal delegates and Miss Willard herself was initiated into the Order in 1887.[10] In 1889 she also became an active participant in the Christian Socialist movement and an associate editor of its organ, the *Dawn*.[11]

In the nineties Miss Willard continued her sympathy with labor, participating especially in the demand for equal pay for women. She was not, however, able to sympathize entirely with most large strikes, calling for arbitration of the Homestead dispute and disapproving the Pullman strike because she had heard the rumor that Debs was "under

[6] L. J. Trowbridge, *Frances Willard of Evanston* (Chicago, 1938), p. 82.
[7] Frances E. Willard, *Glimpses of Fifty Years* (Boston, 1889), pp. 422-423; Trowbridge, *Willard*, pp. 134-138.
[8] Willard, *Glimpses*, pp. 413-415.
[9] "A Christian Woman's View of the Labor Movement," *Independent*, December 23, 1886, p. 1.
[10] Mary Earhart, *Frances Willard, From Prayers to Politics* (Chicago, 1944), pp. 247-250.
[11] See *Dawn*, June 15, 1889, p. 5; September 15, 1889, pp. 1-2; May, 1890, pp. 6-8.

the domination of whiskey" during it.[12] She came out wholeheartedly for an eight-hour law and for national ownership of railroads and telephone lines. Henry D. Lloyd, the radical writer, impressed her so much that she wished he could become President.[13]

In 1894 Miss Willard issued a statement that clearly demonstrates how far she had moved from a narrow moralistic interest toward a more searching analysis of social problems. As early as 1887 she had been taken to task by labor spokesmen (including Edward H. Rogers of the Christian Labor Union) for saying that the labor movement should concentrate on the correct use of present wages, especially attacking expenditure for liquor rather than striving first to raise wages. Although this view was shared by a great many religious reformers of the time, Miss Willard repudiated it in 1894. At the W.C.T.U. convention in that year she forthrightly stated that poverty must be wiped out first, drink second. Admitting her earlier lack of realism, she explained:

It was only our ignorance of the industrial classes that magnified a single propaganda and minimized every other so that Temperance people in earlier days believed that if men and women were temperate all other material good would follow in the train of the great grace.[14]

Naturally this long movement toward an increasingly pro-labor position had not been unanimously supported by Miss Willard's colleagues. Her friend Lucy Stone, equally active in the women's rights and prohibition movements, wrote to her in 1887 protesting her friendliness toward the Knights, who, said Miss Stone, "carry seeds of the disruption of all business as the very kernel of their creed."[15] Even the mildly liberal *Outlook* (formerly *Christian Union*) complained in 1894 that "For some time past the speeches of Miss Willard and Lady Henry Somerset have been as saturated with Christian Socialism as the platforms of Western Prohibitionists have been with a temperate form of Populism."[16]

Yet the influence of the temperance movement in developing a new social outlook was not a matter entirely of personalities. Frank C. Haddock, a strong conservative in matters of religion and morals, writing in the *Methodist Review* in 1887, indicated the effect which prohibitionism might have in breaking down laissez faire doctrines. Denouncing the suggestion that sumptuary laws were contrary to personal liberty, Had-

[12] Earhart, *Willard*, pp. 250-253.
[13] *Ibid.*, pp. 254-256.
[14] Quoted in Earhart, *Willard*, p. 257.
[15] *Ibid.*, pp. 246-247. Stone to Willard, March 28, 1887.
[16] November 24, 1894, p. 842.

dock asserted: "The justice or injustice of any given laws depends upon the character of the state; and in a Christian government no laws can be accounted oppressive which seek simply the furtherance of the underlying Christian principles."[17] It is doubtful whether he realized all the implications of this sweeping statement.

Sabbatarianism, another of Protestantism's traditional moral crusades, was also working out a new relation to the labor movement. Ever since Jacksonian days Sabbatarians had fought for the Sabbath on strictly religious and moral grounds, often in direct opposition to freethinking labor and radical groups. In the last decades of the century the Sabbath was still intact, enforced by state laws against most forms of Sunday labor and recreation, and church-connected organizations were still its most active defenders.[18]

By the early eighties, however, church Sabbatarians were already beginning to mix humanitarian with religious arguments and even to hold out the right hand of fellowship toward the labor movement, concurrently struggling against a seven-day work week. Julius H. Ward, an Episcopalian priest, admitted in an article in the *Atlantic Monthly* in 1881 that the old Puritan Sunday with its wearying compulsory round of churchgoing and religious study was obsolete. Modern conditions of labor rendered it necessary that Sunday become a day of rest, he conceded, urging that the Sunday laws, out of date in most respects, be "drawn out, like the heavy artillery, whenever soulless corporations attempt to snatch the day of rest from the great army of the working classes."[19]

The climax of church-labor co-operation on the Sabbath question came in 1889, when a giant petition for a national Sunday Rest Law regulating the post office and other federal activities was presented to Congress. The petition was backed by such diverse groups and individuals as the Central Labor Union of New York, the Brotherhood of Locomotive Engineers, the General Association of the Knights of Labor, Cardinal Gibbons, and the W.C.T.U. as well as by the church Sabbatarians.[20]

Backers of such co-operative church-labor campaigns probably included only the more progressive groups in organized religion, since

[17] Haddock, "Christianity and Our National Institutions," *Methodist Review*, LXIX (1887), 95.
[18] See A. M. Schlesinger, *Rise of the City*, pp. 333-335.
[19] Ward, "The New Sunday," *Atlantic Monthly*, XLVII (1881), 526-537.
[20] Wilbur F. Crafts, "A Strategic Year in Sabbath Reform," *Our Day*, III (1889), 310. See also Schlesinger, *op. cit.*, p. 335. The campaign was not successful.

there is plenty of evidence that not all Sabbatarians would accept labor allies.[21] Even some liberal Sabbatarians who were glad to co-operate with workingmen in opposing work on Sunday disagreed with them in regard to recreation. Wilbur F. Crafts, for instance, supported the Sunday Rest Law campaign of 1889, and rejoiced that "Christians tunnelling from one side of the mountain for the glory of God, and workingmen tunnelling from the other for their own good, meet at the Fourth Commandment." But he warned labor that it must not use the time gained from work for purposes of amusement.[22]

Some Sabbatarians, wishing the Sabbath kept free of both work and play but forced to recognize labor's demands for rest and recreation, brought themselves to favor a Saturday half holiday as a time for enjoyment. The *Watchman*, which in 1887 had denounced the half holiday as an "interference with the industrial interests of the community," withdrew its opposition with some misgivings in 1890. The *Christian Union* had long favored the half holiday and it was one of the issues on which the W.C.T.U. heartily co-operated with the Knights of Labor.[23]

The application of traditional morality to the growing problems of riches and business ethics was a more complex matter. Despite recurrent disclosures of corporate robbery, openhanded and enterprising captains of industry remained heroes to most Americans throughout the century. A large fraction of church opinion staunchly continued its unqualified defense of business and its leaders.

As in the previous period, a flood of literature for the guidance of youth reconciled Christianity with the aggressive virtues. "Young men are preached to on the evils of acquisitiveness; they should also be exhorted to cultivate it. . . . For even industrious selfishness is a benediction upon others, in spite of itself."[24] Wilbur H. Crafts polled successful men on the reasons for their success, finding it in their faithfulness to religion.[25] H. J. Latham tried to prove the converse relation also, urging

---

[21] Richard T. Ely cites examples of clerical refusal to co-operate with labor groups in campaigning against Sunday work, contrasting this with church eagerness in such causes as preventing Sunday opening of public conservatories. Ely, *Social Aspects of Christianity* (rev. ed.; New York, 1889), pp. 44-45.

[22] Crafts, "Valid Ground for Sabbath Observance," *Our Day*, II (1888), 261-262.

[23] *Watchman*, May 19, 1887, p. 5; August 28, 1890, p. 5; *Christian Union*, July 19, 1883, p. 43; Earhart, *Willard*, p. 248.

[24] *Christian Union*, January 8, 1885, p. 5. The *Congregationalist* published in 1883 a series of articles on the subject "Fidelity to Christ Helpful to Success in Business," beginning November 15, p. 389.

[25] Crafts, *Successful Men of To-day and What They Say of Success* (rev. ed.; New York, 1905, [cop. 1883]).

his readers to look each morning at the published list of failures and ask "How many men in that list honor God in their business, and give him his share of the profits." The correct answer was "Not one in five hundred. Sterling Christians seldom fail."[26] Somewhat less often, free spending, as well as vigorous acquisition, was linked to morality: ". . . there is no truer charity, whether designed or not . . . than generous living."[27]

Even some of the least popular of big business' practices and individuals were warmly defended. More than once the religious press defended the moral rectitude of Wall Street against its "ignorant" traducers.[28] The *Unitarian Review* deplored the injustice done to the outstanding philanthropist, Oakes Ames, in the investigation of railroad bribery.[29] The *Christian Union* used Cornelius Vanderbilt as an example of a rich man who owed his success to public contributions and the evangelist T. DeWitt Talmage, talking of the Vanderbilt gifts, rejoiced that "a railroad king could also be a Christian king."[30] A. H. Strong dedicated a book to Rockefeller, already becoming a bitterly hated man, as "The friend and helper of every good cause."[31]

An increasing number of religious commentators, however, found it necessary at least to qualify their praise of big business and its leaders. As always, many reconciled private gain and Christianity by preaching the old doctrine of the rich man as a steward or trustee, obligated to use his wealth for the glory of God or even, in a new age, for the welfare of mankind. The *Congregationalist* urged that "entire dedication" to the service of humanity was the "one possible justification" for the possession of great wealth.[32] William Reed Huntington, a prominent Epis-

---

[26] H. J. Latham, *God in Business* (New York, 1887), p. iv.

[27] A. P. Peabody, "Wealth," *Andover Review*, XIX (1893), 321-328.

[28] *Christian Union*, September 22, 1880, pp. 223-224; *Independent*, July 29, 1886, p. 4.

[29] VIII (1877), 564-565; XVI (1881), 561-563.

[30] *Christian Union*, August 3, 1882, p. 82; Talmage, *T. DeWitt Talmage*, p. 141. In 1884 a letter to the New York *Sun* criticized the Church of the Stranger for a plaque which dedicated the church to the "Glory of God" and the memory of Cornelius Vanderbilt, with Vanderbilt's name in much larger letters than the rest of the dedication. Quoted in Theodore Bourne, *Money and Labor. Corporation and Co-operation* (pamphlet, New York, 1884), p. 9.

[31] Strong, *Philosophy and Religion*, dedication. For the outpouring of praise for Rockefeller's first great gifts to Baptist enterprises in 1889, see Henry D. Lloyd, *Wealth against Commonwealth* (New York, 1902), pp. 348-351. A famous and vigorous reaction to pulpit praises of the rich in this period is Mark Twain's classic description of the clerical response to Jay Gould's contribution to yellow-fever sufferers. *Mark Twain in Eruption*, Bernard de Voto, ed. (New York, 1940), pp. 73-74.

[32] April 17, 1899, p. 134.

copalian, put the obligation less strongly: "If a government by wealth be inevitable (and perhaps it is), let us at least do what we can to spread the maxim that *richesse* as well as *noblesse oblige.*"[33]

More and more churchmen became unable to accept with complacency the revelations of financial dishonesty and corporate oppression. By the eighties attacks on speculation, unprincipled finance, and disregard of social obligation were no longer rare.[34] Occasionally a spokesman of one of the theologically more conservative denominations, harking back perhaps to the economic precepts of earlier centuries, made a general statement on business practice that accorded ill with the doctrines of laissez faire economics: "The man who trades or attempts to, for the purpose of 'getting the best of a bargain' in such a sense that he gains something while the other man loses, is no honest man."[35]

More and more frequently, religious writers as well as others discussed the question of regulation of corporations. The *Congregationalist* and the *Watchman* were deeply concerned over the power for evil of these great combinations and definitely favored regulation. The *Independent*, on the other hand, stoutly defended the trusts and denounced President Cleveland's "intemperate arraignment" in his famous tariff message of 1888 of "the most considerate, generous, and beneficent class of capitalists to be found in any country of the world."[36] Much church comment on this subject tended to be cautious and inconclusive. Yet this argument also was forcing religious thinkers to realize that the application of traditional morality to society was, in an age of combination, no longer a simple matter.

In 1889 the whole question of church attitudes toward private riches was brought to a sharp focus by the *North American Review's* publication of Andrew Carnegie's essay on "Wealth."[37] This article by the great ironmaster and philanthropist set forth in authoritative form the ideas that many Christian authors and most of the church press had been preaching for at least a generation. Its varied reception demonstrated that by 1889 some Protestants, moving for various reasons toward new economic views, could no longer accept these plausible theories.

[33] Huntington, *The Religious Use of Wealth* (pamphlet, New York, 1887), p. 16.
[34] *Independent*, January 3, 1884, pp. 2-3; *Andover Review*, V (1886), 633-639; *Methodist Review*, LXX (1888), 452-459.
[35] *Congregationalist*, January 23, 1878, p. 28.
[36] *Congregationalist*, March 21, 1889, p. 92; *Watchman*, February 7, 1889, p. 5; February 18, 1892, p. 1; *Independent*, December 13, 1888, pp. 2-3. In 1890 the Episcopal Church Congress discussed the problem at length, presenting both criticism and defense of the great combinations. Church Congress, *Papers, Addresses and Debates*, 1890, pp. 70-95.
[37] CXLVIII (1889), 653-664.

From the standpoint of a steelmaster of the eighties, the Gospel of Wealth was undoubtedly a liberal document. Almost apologetically, Carnegie argued that extreme inequality was an inevitable part of the wealth-producing factory system, that the development of riches and poverty was the high but necessary price which society paid for progress. Great organizing talent always and necessarily must have great rewards. The socialist or anarchist who sought to tear down existing society with its inequalities was really attacking civilization.

Assuming then, that he had proved the necessity of great private wealth, Carnegie asked himself what were the duties of very rich individuals. Leaving fortunes to descendants would simply result in waste. Bequests to society involved too much delay. Surprisingly, Carnegie came out for high inheritance taxes. But his principal conclusion was that rich men were obligated to give away what they had earned during their lifetimes. This giving must be done carefully and systematically, avoiding private charity which only pauperized its recipients and aiming at the promotion of such public interests as education, medicine, the arts and religion. To die rich, Carnegie concluded sweepingly, was to die disgraced. The rich man was a trustee who would administer the funds entrusted to him by the community far better than it could ever administer them for itself.[38]

The first important reaction to Carnegie's pronouncement came from England, where his generosity was enthusiastically praised by Gladstone, Cardinal Manning and Rabbi Herman Adler in the *Nineteenth Century*. A dissenting note was struck, however, by Hugh Price Hughes, the leader of the Christian social movement in English Methodism.[39] Expressing respect for Carnegie as an individual, "and without holding him in the least responsible for his unfortunate circumstances," Hughes considered him nevertheless "an anti-Christian phenomenon, a social monstrosity and a grave political peril." Hughes agreed with Henry George that progress and poverty were growing simultaneously, that very rich men like Carnegie at one end of the social scale meant poverty at the other. A program including free trade, free land and a progressive

[38] These ideas are further developed in later articles reprinted in Carnegie, *The Gospel of Wealth and Other Essays* (New York, 1933). Carnegie was more tolerant of labor unions, at least in theory, than any but the most advanced church authors of the eighties. See his "An Employer's View of the Labor Question" in this volume, pp. 97-111, and "Results of the Labor Struggle," pp. 115-133, both reprinted from the *Forum* for 1886.

[39] W. E. Gladstone, "Mr. Carnegie's Gospel of Wealth," *Nineteenth Century*, XXVIII (1890), 677-693; for Manning, Adler and Hughes, symposium on "Irresponsible Wealth," same volume, pp. 876-900.

income tax as well as an inheritance tax would, he said, relieve Carnegie of his burden by preventing its acquisition.

Stung, as one would expect, by this unexpected criticism, Carnegie answered in the following year.[40] He particularly objected to Hughes' statement, drawn from George, that developing private wealth meant the production of poverty also. Calling the highest authority to his support, Carnegie said that Herbert Spencer, after reading a few pages of George's work, had thrown it in the fire as trash. "I know of no writer or thinker of recognized authority, except Mr. Hughes," said the angry philanthropist, "who differs with the philosopher in this judgment." In fact the growth of private wealth necessarily *improved* the condition of the masses.

By this time the controversy had attracted the attention of American churchmen. Carnegie's benevolent doctrines, which echoed those long endorsed by most religious organs, were praised by Bishop Henry C. Potter, then considered one of the leading liberal and even pro-labor figures in the Episcopal church.[41] The *Churchman* also applauded Carnegie's essay, stating that while some of its doctrines sounded socialistic, yet "if Mr. Carnegie's socialism were practiced there would be no political socialism."[42]

Significantly, however, American clerics were not unanimous in accepting Carnegie's benevolence at face value. Professor William Jewett Tucker of Andover Theological Seminary rejected, like Hughes, the assumption that great riches were a permanent necessity.[43] Calling Carnegie's precepts a gospel of patronage, he pointed out that they would at best affect only the benevolent minority, not the "much greater amount of irresponsible and really dangerous wealth." For a more valid solution Tucker hailed the growing ethical tendency in political economy and approved such measures as franchise revision, increased municipal expenditure, heavy inheritance and income taxes, co-operation and profit-sharing. Naturally the small group of American Christian Socialists damned still more wholeheartedly this "pure paternalism, Carnegie's Gospel of Wealth—that blasphemous libel on Christ's Gospel of Brotherhood."[44]

[40] His reply, "The Advantages of Poverty," reprinted from the *Nineteenth Century* for March, 1891, appears in *The Gospel of Wealth and Other Essays*, pp. 43-73.
[41] Potter, "The Gospel for Wealth," *North American Review*, XLII (1891), 513-522.
[42] February 8, 1890, p. 138.
[43] Tucker, "The Gospel of Wealth," *Andover Review*, XV (1891), 631-645.
[44] W. D. P. Bliss, "What to Do Now," *Dawn*, July-August, 1890, pp. 109-114. Bliss insists elsewhere that such men as Carnegie are the ones really guilty of "paternalism," a charge frequently thrown at socialists. Bliss, *Handbook of Socialism* (New York, 1895), p. 197.

Traditional morality alone would not, of course, have destroyed by itself the marriage between religion and classical economics. Yet the relation had never been entirely easy. Whenever an individual, perplexed by new conditions and challenged by the evidence of dishonesty or injustice, applied to new problems a stricter and older moral code than that of Henry Ward Beecher, the result was likely to be another nail in the coffin of laissez faire.

ACADEMIC PRECEDENTS

DURING these troubled decades secular thinkers were looking for answers to the same new problems that troubled churchmen. As in earlier periods professors and preachers greatly influenced each other. At the end of the seventies both economics and sociology still taught the permanent moral and scientific necessity of laissez faire. By the middle nineties both disciplines were sharply divided, with a fraction of each calling for increased solidarity, partly on ethical and religious grounds.

In 1880, as an English writer pointed out, American political economy was especially distinguished for "the conspicuousness of the theological element" and for its optimistic tendency.[1] Teaching was still, to a large extent, under clerical control.[2] Francis Wayland's textbook, the epitome of prewar clerical laissez faire, was recast in 1878 by the Reverend Aaron L. Chapin, president of Beloit. The revised text, its piety and dogmatism undiminished, went into eight more editions.[3] Chapin's own popular high-school text, published in 1880, held to the established view of labor relations:

Experience shows that combinations on either side, to prevent free competition, cannot, for any long time, materially influence the rates of wages. Such attempts interfere with the natural law of supply and demand, which is the grand regulator of wages for the best interest of all concerned.[4]

Until 1885 the only rival to classicism in clerical circles was still the school of humanitarian protectionism deriving from Carey, Colwell and Robert E. Thompson. In 1882 and 1883 Thompson published new editions of his principal work.[5] A new member of the school, the Reverend George M. Steele, issued a secondary-school text in 1889. Like

[1] T. E. C. Leslie, "Political Economy in the United States," *Fortnightly Review*, XXVIII (1880-1881), 488-501.
[2] In 1884 there were 309 denominational and 61 nondenominational colleges. Garrison, *March of Faith*, p. 133.
[3] O'Connor, *Origins*, p. 324.
[4] Aaron L. Chapin, *First Principles of Political Economy* (New York, 1880), p. 83.
[5] *Elements of Political Economy.*

his masters, Steele rejected the rigid wage-fund theory and was somewhat more tolerant of labor unions than the Wayland school, though he held out little hope of success for labor's program.[6]

Lay professors of economics were influenced by the clerical school to a surprising extent. The influential textbook first published in 1887 by Professor J. Lawrence Laughlin of Harvard was full of the old language of theological certainty and insisted, as ministerial authorities had for a generation, that wages must be raised by saving and good habits, not by organized or state action.[7]

Most conservative of all the academic authorities was Simon Newcomb, an important astronomer whose avocation was political economy. Newcomb's textbook stated the dogmas of laissez faire and summarily refuted collectivist criticism in the conventional manner.[8]

In the troubled year 1886 Newcomb published in the *Independent* a long series of homilies to workingmen couched in a homely, colloquial style.[9] The "Plain Talks" were principally a vigorous attack on the Knights of Labor, including also a defense of the public benefits of great wealth and an argument that railroad corruption was negligible.

Francis Amasa Walker, son of Amasa Walker, was more aware than many of his colleagues of the new and critical forces that were capturing European economics. He attracted great attention by his attack on the sacrosanct wage-fund theory, asserting that the fund available for wages was not entirely predetermined by the existing capital but was affected by current productivity.[10] Still more surprising, Walker specifically opposed the subjection of economics to natural theology.[11] Yet this transitional writer failed to break completely with the traditional views. In his discussion of labor Walker opined that organization might have been necessary in the early industrial period in England, but that in enlightened contemporary America it could only disturb the delicate and correct balance between labor and capital, and would be "a wholly destructive agency." Walker's discussion of existing unions, especially the Knights,

[6] Steele, *Outline Study of Political Economy* (New York, 1889).

[7] J. Lawrence Laughlin, *Elements of Political Economy* (rev. ed.; New York, 1902), p. 369. The introduction lists the chapters altered since the original publication in 1887; that on labor is not among them. pp. vii-viii.

[8] Newcomb, *Principles of Political Economy* (New York, 1885).

[9] "A Plain Man's Talk on the Labor Question" (first two entitled "The Labor Question"), seventeen numbers, beginning March 25, 1886, p. 1; ending September 16, 1886, p. 3.

[10] Walker, *Political Economy* (rev. ed.; New York, 1887), pp. 248-258; pp. 364-370.

[11] *Ibid.*, pp. 25-26.

was actually more bitter in its hostility than the views of most of his colleagues.[12]

Not until 1885 were the dominant classical theories effectively challenged. American economic teaching had long been rendered obsolete by a host of European developments, including English neoclassicism, the marginal utility school, German historical economics and Marxian socialism. The American Economic Association, committed to a revolt against the classical dogmas, was formed under the leadership of a group of young men just back from German universities.[13] These innovators at once rejected the classical doctrines as unscientific and denounced them on humane and religious grounds. The Association's platform, drawn up by Richard T. Ely, declared

We hold that the conflict of labor and capital has brought into prominence a vast number of social problems, whose solution requires the united efforts, each in its own sphere, of *the church*, of the state, and of science.[14]

The movement represented by the Association was at once an effect and a cause of the new social tendencies in Christianity. Before the founding of the A.E.A., the first clerical exponents of social Christianity had already declared their opposition to the dominant academic school. Washington Gladden, Lyman Abbott, and twenty-one other ministers were among the original members of the Association.[15] Naturally the more liberal organs of Christian opinion greeted the new departure with approval.

A strong religious emphasis can be found in the works of almost all the leaders of the new economic movement. Many, in fact, became important contributors to the social Christian movement in the churches. Carroll D. Wright, one of the ablest and first of America's professional statisticians, had been head of the Massachusetts Bureau of Labor Statistics from 1873 until 1885, when he became chief of the Bureau of Labor in the United States Department of the Interior. His careful and

---

[12] *Ibid.*, pp. 378, 387-394.

[13] Francis A. Walker was the first president, but, as Richard T. Ely says, "He was not selected because we necessarily agreed with his views, but because we looked upon him as a champion of emancipation." Ely, *Ground Under Our Feet, An Autobiography* (New York, 1938), p. 163. The best account of the founding of the A.E.A. is in *ibid.*, pp. 121-149. A stimulating treatment of three prominent members of the new school, Clark, Ely and Patten, with emphasis on their relation to religious currents, is F. R. Everett, *Religion in Economics* (New York, 1946). The following treatment of Ely and Clark is influenced by Everett's; Patten affected religious opinion in this period comparatively little.

[14] Quoted in Ely, *Ground Under Our Feet*, p. 141. (Italics mine.)

[15] Everett, *Religion in Economics*, p. 86.

impartial reports of actual conditions among wage earners had been an early stimulus to religious opinion. Wright, who as early as 1882 had appealed for a more ameliorative and ethical school of economics, found his true place in the new Association.[16]

John Bates Clark was another of the early leaders of ethical economics, though his teaching later became increasingly conservative. Like many academic economists, he had been educated for the ministry. Clark, somewhat resembling Bascom in his argument for Christian evolution, believed that a noncompetitive, co-operative order was gradually replacing competition through God's providence. The transition was being made slowly, however, and a good Christian might still continue, during the life of the present system, "to buy, sell, and get gain, as well as give thanks and worship, with his eyes uplifted to the hills whence cometh his help."[17] Clark urged the church to conserve moral power and work to improve human relations even in our imperfect society, so that this residue of human goodness might be transmitted to the new order.

John R. Commons, later the dean of American labor historians and an important figure in Wisconsin Progressivism, took an important though somewhat later part in the rapprochement between religion and the new economics. Commons set forth his view on the duties of the church in a volume collected largely from his addresses before various Christian bodies.[18]

Christianity, Commons believed, was responsible for creating social problems by making men conscious of them. Because Christians, including ministers, failed to live by their beliefs, these problems remained unsolved. Ministers, he urged, should study sociology and give one-half their pulpit time to expounding it; they should labor to give Christians a conviction of social responsibility and social sin. In order to understand the viewpoint of the "neglected classes" it would be well for ministers to join the Knights of Labor. This was, to much of Commons' audience, a new and startling language.[19]

E. Benjamin Andrews, another of the ethical economists, had, like Clark, been educated in theology. Andrews was successively president

---

[16] For Wright's views see his *The Relation of Political Economy to the Labor Question* (pamphlet, Boston, 1882). For sample comment on the Massachusetts Bureau's reports, see *Congregationalist*, March 22, 1876, p. 92; August 21, 1884, p. 278.

[17] Clark, *The Philosophy of Wealth* (Boston, 1887, [cop. 1885]), p. 220.

[18] Commons, *Social Reform and the Church* (New York, 1894).

[19] The book was condemned as an "inversion of the Gospel" by the *Churchman*, June 23, 1894, p. 761.

of Brown, where his mildly bimetallist views created a great stir, and of the University of Nebraska. He continually called for an extension of the religious spirit into social life in books and articles addressed to churchmen.[20]

E. W. Bemis, a University of Chicago economist, served with Commons and Bascom as an editor of the social Christian *Kingdom* and wrote a tract published under the auspices of the Christian Socialist *Dawn*. Bemis himself was not a socialist, Christian or otherwise, but he believed that there was much truth in the socialist indictment of present society and that the socialist ideal was "noble." In 1894 Bemis was dismissed from the University of Chicago, allegedly because of a speech at the First Presbyterian church in which he criticized the railroads as well as the strikers for their actions in the Pullman conflict.[21]

Far more important than any other member of the group was Richard T. Ely, who was, in fact, one of the most important single influences on Christian social thought. Ely's revolt against the classical formulae was a product of his study in Germany, where he came into contact with the historical school. The direction of this revolt, however, was determined by Ely's shocked reaction to the labor crisis of the middle eighties.[22] The principal founder of the American Economic Association, a professor at Johns Hopkins and Wisconsin in the greatest periods of each of these universities, Ely was in a position of great academic influence. Though he was by no means a radical, he was the target of conservative attack throughout his early career.[23]

Ely's teachings were exactly fitted to appeal to the liberal church public. Not a theorist by temperament, he rejected both socialism and social Darwinism, calling on a new ethical and Christian spirit to set the goals of economic thought. Ely was, in fact, more a preacher than an economist. His best-selling textbooks resembled those of Francis Way-

---

[20] "The Duty of a Public Spirit," in Brooklyn Ethical Association, *Man and the State* (New York, 1892), pp. 3-19; *Wealth and the Moral Law* (Lectures at the Hartford Theological Seminary, Hartford, 1894); "Political Economy, Old and New," *Andover Review*, VI (1886), 730-748; "The Social Plaint," *New World*, I (1892), 2.

[21] For Bemis' views see his "Socialism and State Action," *Journal of Social Science*, XXI (September, 1886), 33-68; "The Relation of the Church and Social Problems," (*Dawn* Library, Tract No. 2, Boston, 1890?). For his dismissal, John T. Flynn, *God's Gold, the Story of Rockefeller and His Times* (New York, 1932), pp. 307-309.

[22] Ely, *Ground Under Our Feet*, pp. 65-72.

[23] The most bitter attack came in 1894, when Ely had to prove to an investigating committee of the University of Wisconsin that he was *not* a socialist and did not associate with strikers. *Op. cit.*, pp. 218-233; *Outlook*, September 29, 1894, p. 494.

land in their simple, dogmatic method, if not in their conclusions. Typical chapter headings, conveying much of Ely's message, include "Society an Organism," "The Economist Not Confined to the Material Life," "The Economic Life Not for Self," "Dependence of Man upon Man," "Private Not Identical with Public Welfare," "Ethical Aims an Essential of Economic Teaching," "Ethics and Political Economy," "Political Economy and Religion," and "Christianity."[24]

Beside backing such reforms as the public ownership of certain utilities, the income tax, etc., Ely made a sincere effort to understand and appreciate the labor movement. Breaking sharply with his academic and religious predecessors, he ridiculed some of their well-worn precepts about the all-sufficiency of hard work and saving:

> If you tell a single concrete workingman on the Baltimore and Ohio Railroad that he may yet be the president of the company, it is not demonstrable that you have told him what is not true, although it is within bounds to say that he is far more likely to be killed by a stroke of lightning. . . .[25]

Instead of patronizing the labor movement as a misguided but laudable struggle, as many of his religious contemporaries were in the habit of doing, he recognized it as "the strongest force outside the Christian Church making for the practical recognition of human brotherhood."[26]

Ely's appeal to the churches was based on the beliefs which liberal Christians were now willing to accept. Underlying all his teachings were the assumptions of the new theology, the freedom and brotherhood of man, the fatherhood of God, the imitation of Christ. Thus he could not be ignored when he flatly declared that "Christianity minus philanthropy is not Christianity at all. On the contrary, it is a monstrosity."[27] Naturally, Ely became a favorite speaker before church groups, including the Evangelical Alliance and the Parliament of Religions at the World's Fair. He was a member of pro-labor Episcopalian organizations and a close collaborator of the social-minded leaders in that church.[28] His writings for the religious press were voluminous, and sometimes produced considerable controversy. Ordinarily his books were favorably

[24] *Outlines of Economics* (New York, 1893).
[25] *Social Aspects of Christianity* (New York, 1889), pp. 97-98.
[26] *Labor Movement*, p. 138.
[27] *Social Aspects*, p. 85.
[28] Evangelical Alliance for the U.S.A., *National Needs and Remedies*, pp. 43-46; *Neely's History of the Parliament of Religions, etc.*, W. R. Houghton, ed. (Chicago, 1894), II, 550-554; *Ground Under Our Feet*, p. 78.

received by church opinion, though the *Independent* found in him "a curiously Germanic twist" and "a tone of demagogic appeal."[29]

Ely's doctrines, like those of the other ethical economists, were by no means profound. For the solution of vast and complex problems, the whole group tended to rely on a simple ethical appeal. This very simplicity partly explains their important effect on church opinion. These economists were reacting to perils which many churchmen had already observed; their appeals for reform were couched in the familiar language of ethics and religion. In place of the long-established dogmas of Wayland or Perry they offered equally simple formulae with different meanings. To those who had already reached reformist conclusions through their own experience, these professional economists offered valuable support.

Because of their preoccupation with the evolution debate, ministers in the eighties and nineties were profoundly influenced by Spencerian social science.[30] Most clerical opinion remained set against the British pundit, both for his acceptance of evolution and for his patronizing way of relegating religion to the "Unknowable." Theological opposition to Spencer was, however, fighting a losing battle. An increasing number of Protestant leaders were finding Darwinism and its social interpretations compatible with theism. The watershed was the conversion of Henry Ward Beecher, characteristically dramatic and characteristically well timed. In 1882 at a banquet for Spencer, Beecher in an eloquent oration announced that he had read and admired the British philosopher for twenty years.[31] By the next year, calling himself a "cordial Christian evolutionist," Beecher was leading the pro-Darwin forces in the church. There could be no surer sign that evolution, with its theological formulations, was widely accepted. The Immanent God working in many ways toward more complex and universal harmony, had become the God of American liberal religion.

[29] In a review of *The Labor Movement in America*, May 12, 1887, pp. 9-10. As uncompromising as ever, the *Independent* denounced Ely for saying that "it cuts him to the heart" to see laboring men shot down in the street. If there is a riot, said the *Independent*, they have no business to be in the street. For samples of the great mass of favorable reviews, see those of the same volume in *Churchman*, October 30, 1886, p. 517; *American Church Review*, L (1887), 108-109; *Congregationalist*, December 9, 1886, p. 416; *Watchman*, October 28, 1886, p. 7; *Christian Union*, November 25, 1886, p. 24.

[30] For excellent reviews of this subject, see Hofstadter, *Social Darwinism in American Thought 1860-1915*, pp. 1-36; Loewenberg, *op. cit.*, in *Mississippi Valley Historical Review*, XXVIII (1941-42), 339-368.

[31] Henry Holt, *Garrulities of an Octogenarian Editor* (Boston, 1923), pp. 14, 51; Abbott, *Henry Ward Beecher*, pp. 151-152.

With the theological barriers down, many Protestants discovered that Darwinism and Spencerianism seemed to put the well-entrenched belief in laissez faire on an even firmer theoretical ground than that of classical authority. Most religious opinion willingly accepted the new justification of individualist struggle.

Social Darwinism at the height of its prestige found able expression in the works of William Graham Sumner.[32] Ordained an Episcopalian priest, Sumner moved steadily away from the religious interpretation of society after he was appointed to a Yale chair in 1872.[33] He became, in fact, the most vigorous opponent of any admixture of ethics or "sentimental" humanitarianism, let alone religious dogma, with what he considered scientific sociology. Nevertheless, he remained in good Episcopal standing. Perhaps this partly explains why many church critics accepted his naturalistic theories.

After winning a hard battle in which he defended the use of Spencer's books against Yale's religious conservatism, Sumner developed evolutionary social science in a direction slightly different from Spencer's own. Evolutionary forces to Sumner were resistless, but not necessarily beneficent. The course for humanity was intelligent adaptation. Acceptance of things as they were was natural and therefore moral; "interference" ridiculous and mischief making.

Assuming that the natural order was one of competition, Sumner defended the dream of a completely competitive and individualistic order with rare and admirable consistency. Trusts and tariffs, as well as child-labor laws, were to Sumner presumptuous and unscientific interferences. The obvious cruelty of the existing order was acceptable as part of the scheme of things. Happiness as well as morality was equated with success, and success with adaptation to "natural" competitive evolution.

It is not surprising that Sumner's cool and honest formulae found frequent expression and cordial praise in the religious press.[34] He offered a new backing to the traditional Protestant economic doctrines at a time when backing was needed. The "Protestant ethic" of thrift, hard work and success, once preached as a means of testifying to God's glory and again defended on the basis of natural economic law, could now rest

[32] An illuminating treatment of Sumner is found in Everett, *Religion in Economics*, pp. 12-21. See also Bernard, *American Sociology*, pp. 500-509; Hofstadter, *op. cit.*, pp. 37-51.

[33] This point is abundantly demonstrated by Everett, *op. cit.*, pp. 13-14.

[34] Especially the *Independent*, e.g. August 25, 1887, p. 1; April 19, 1888, pp. 2-3; and the *Princeton Review*, e.g. November, 1882 (no volume number), pp. 241-262.

firmly on the latest science. Sumner might have become as great and lasting an authority in church circles as Wayland in the previous generation. Even as he wrote, however, critics were undermining his science, sociology, theology and economics from a new point of view.

In Europe and America, social thinkers were already beginning to go beyond the substitution of Spencerian dogma for traditional dogma. Scientists were questioning the universal reality of evolution through the survival of the fittest. Skeptics, seeing through Spencer's essentially anthropocentric formulae, were asking how it could be proved, even if struggle was nature's way, that this scheme of things worked for the benefit of humanity. Others were demanding that society, as well as species, be viewed as part of natural evolutionary development.

While a number of European thinkers were asking such questions, John Fiske, who had long been trying to reconcile Spencer with American religion, increased his emphasis on man's co-operative traits.[35] These characteristics, evidenced especially in human family life, might prove the final co-operative direction of evolution.

Among professional sociologists, the opposition to Spencer and Sumner was more vigorously formulated. Lester F. Ward, whose important and original work was barely beginning to be recognized, broke completely with the Spencerian inevitabilities. Pointing to the unnecessary waste of life in nature, Ward spoke for a reassertion of the human will and predicted the increasing development of purposive co-operation. In his attack on prevailing beliefs in nature's inevitable benevolence, Ward, of course, ran afoul of natural religion and lost the possibility of attaining much influence in clerical circles.

Ward's disciples, however, were not thus debarred. Albion W. Small, who took over Ward's humanistic tendencies, was moderately religious and ethical in his interpretation. Small's own successor, Charles R. Henderson, was one of the leaders of specifically Christian sociology and prominent in the social Christian movement at the end of the century. Both Ward and Small spoke at the Parliament of Religions in 1893.[36]

The Ward school of sociologists was, however, only one of many scientific and sociological tendencies which led to the downfall of social Darwinism and especially of Herbert Spencer's impressive structure.

[35] See his The Destiny of Man (Boston, 1884).
[36] C. R. Henderson, "Individual Effort at Reform Not Sufficient," Neely's History of the Parliament of Religions, etc., II, 448-564; A. W. Small, "Churches and City Problems," ibid., II, 587-595. See also Shailer Mathews, "The Development of Social Christianity in America," Religious Thought in the Last Quarter-Century, pp. 232-233.

By the end of the century Spencer's vogue had run out; leading thinkers in many fields had concluded that a continued insistence on individualist struggle as the inevitable, predestined ordinance of nature was little but the newest form of superstition.

Religious opinion, however, had not waited for science to repudiate evolutionary individualism. No sooner had theological opposition to social Darwinism begun to wane, than religious critics began attacking Spencer and his followers on humanitarian and moral grounds. Never entirely at ease with Spencer's mechanistic tendencies, many Protestants had been attracted partly by his reassuring justification of the status quo. As experience made it difficult for some clerics to believe in the perfect rightness of contemporary society, they willingly abandoned Spencerianism. More and more of the most advanced religious writers, their eyes newly opened, were finding the philosophy of social Darwinism cruel and anti-Christian.

As early as 1883 J. Monroe Gibson, writing in the *Independent*, had insisted that Christianity demanded the application of the law of love to all life and specifically rejected Spencer's belief that altruism was necessarily harmful.[37] A more thorough criticism was presented by John Bascom, still working out his combination of sociology and theology. Bascom, a mirror of the moderately advanced section of religious opinion since prewar times, had early accepted much of Spencer's method. He had, however, steadily increased the ethical qualifications to his acceptance of individualist struggle.

In 1887 Bascom insisted more specifically than before that society must advance out of Spencer's industrial stage to "a moral stage." Though he still believed the doctrines of laissez faire to represent economic truth, he now limited their validity to the economic sphere. "Ethical law" was as valid in its realm as "economic law" in its: "Economics and ethics play against each other, and make each other effective, as gravity and cohesion on the one side, and muscular force on the other, give the interlacing actions of life."[38]

Perhaps more important than this somewhat pretentious formula, Bascom's practical judgments of contemporary affairs showed considerable change of emphasis, particularly in relation to labor. Though he continued to dwell on the abuses of which labor unions were guilty, his acceptance of the principle of organization was by now forthright. Strikes and violence were incidental characteristics of an "absolutely

[37] August 16, 1883, pp. 6-8.
[38] Bascom, *Sociology* (New York, 1887), p. 148. See also *Social Theory* (New York, 1895), p. 152.

essential" movement. Bascom's rebuke to overcritical ministers was all the more telling because he had himself been guilty of the errors he attacked:

> There is a kind of criticism, heard in the pulpit as well as elsewhere, from which we can hope very little, a criticism that sees clearly the evils which accompany the convulsions of labor seeking its own, . . . and brings to these a sharp condemnation, and that without entering profoundly either into the burdens borne by workmen or the difficulties which obstruct every effort for their removal. . . . Workmen will listen to those who feel the hardships of their position, not to those who disparage these hardships; not to those who are always impressed with the mischiefs of the remedy, and forever renew the counsel of patience, as if it were given to children.[39]

In 1895 Bascom, coming full-circle from his prewar condemnation of unions, declared that "The labor-movement, in spite of its many evils, remains the most comprehensive and significant social ferment of our time."[40]

As earlier, Bascom expounded his changing views frequently in the religious press, which applauded his books as they appeared.[41] With his broad learning, his prolific writing, his respectability (attested not only by his academic position but by his early and more conservative writings), Bascom remained one of the most influential academic authorities for religious readers, providing successive formulations which were widely imitated.

Often the same Protestant liberals who had done most to welcome evolution as a liberating influence, and led in its theological formulation, themselves led the way toward the rejection of social Darwinism on humane and moral grounds. Some of these thinkers, trying to justify belief in evolution without accepting the Spencer-Sumner version of its social consequences, increased Fiske's emphasis on a further stage for evolution, a development of a co-operative society out of individualism.[42] Others followed Bascom in separating the spheres of evolutionary science and social ethics.[43] The most effective of the social Christians, however,

[39] *Sociology*, p. 237.
[40] *Social Theory*, p. 236.
[41] For sample reviews of his works, see *Independent*, August 11, 1887, p. 9; *Christian Union*, July 14, 1887, p. 41; *Outlook*, December 14, 1895, p. 1026.
[42] E.g. see Newman Smyth, *Christian Ethics* (International Theological Library Edition, New York, 1914, [cop. 1892]), p. 248.
[43] A keen critic points out that this separation was often too facile, that optimistic Social Gospel reconcilers of religion and science demanded concessions and limitations that neither side was prepared to grant. Visser 'T Hooft, *Background of the Social Gospel*, pp. 145-168.

did not feel the need of any labored philosophical defense for their rejection of Spencer. They simply decided that the dogmas of individualist struggle did not square with social experience or human emotions.

Washington Gladden, for instance, while he referred to Spencer as "the most distinguished living sociologist" took him to task for assuming his own omniscience and for failing to recognize that new circumstances demanded new adaptations by society. "We may yet go far beyond Mr. Spencer's limits," Gladden asserted, "and yet stop a great way this side of socialism."[44]

Finally, George D. Herron, the fiery Christian radical, rejected Spencer and his disciples lock, stock and barrel. Of Professor Sumner's doctrine of "enlightened self-interest" Herron declared:

This is a gospel which would have caused the proclaimer to be mobbed in the streets of Athens in the days of Pericles; a gospel which would have astounded Moses, and seemed ancient and barbarous to Abraham. The supremacy of the law of self-interest is the conclusion of Herbert Spencer's materialistic philosophy; and of the wretched pessimism of Hartmann and Schopenhauer. It is the principle upon which Cain slew his brother. It was the seductive whisper of the serpent in Eve's ear. . . . the law of self-interest is the eternal falsehood which mothers all social and private woes; for sin is pure individualism—the assertion of self against God and humanity.[45]

In a generation, social Darwinism developed from a shocking piece of "atheism" to the principal justification for existing society, promulgated from platform and pulpit. Just as it reached the summit of acceptance, however, it underwent a new attack. The new dual offensive, which finally succeeded in discrediting Spencerian science and sociology, came at once from scientists and from social Christians.[46]

[44] Gladden, *Applied Christianity* (Boston, 1886), p. 100. For further disagreement with Spencer, see also Gladden, *Tools and the Man* (Boston, 1893), pp. 249-251; 287-288.

[45] Herron, *The Christian Society* (New York, 1895), pp. 108-110.

[46] C. A. Elwood, in a review of Hopkins' *Rise of the Social Gospel*, criticizes that author for not giving more attention to the "sociological movement" as a positive influence on the Social Gospel. *American Historical Review*, XLVI (1940-41), 945-946. As indicated above, the chief importance of the Darwinian sociologists in relation to the Social Gospel was negative. Darwinism itself had contributed to the liberal theology which in turn influenced the Social Gospel. But sociologists of Sumner's type furnished a powerful support to the doctrines against which the Social Gospel revolted. On the other hand sociologists of a more collectivist stripe such as Ward offered only one among many formulations of a general collectivist response to social conditions; the Social Gospel was a parallel rather than a derivative movement.

WINDS OF RADICALISM

B Y THE late nineteenth century, radical movements throughout
the world were calling attention to the failures of industrial capitalism and urging its abolition or drastic alteration. American Protestants, themselves shocked by some of the more obvious shortcomings of
the existing order, could not remain entirely ignorant of these movements. To some they reacted with indignation, others they sought to
supplant, and from still others they drew, however cautiously, some
new weapons for their own arsenal.

The earliest radical movement to influence American churchmen
other than negatively was English Christian Socialism.[1] Thirty years
before the events of 1877 had startled American clerics, a fraction of
British religion had already been deeply stirred by the horrors of early
Victorian industrialism. When the disfranchised British lower classes
lost their battle for the Charter in 1848, Christian Socialism came forward with a substitute. Conscious of the theories of French Utopian
socialism, the movement was more profoundly influenced by the English Romantic indictment of industrial society. Under the ardent leadership of Frederick Denison Maurice and Charles Kingsley, the Christian
Socialists published tracts, founded co-operatives, and hailed the dawn
of a new Christian order. Their idealistic attack on capitalism failed of
its objectives; the co-operatives withered in a few years and the working
class did not enlist under the banner offered to it.

During the long heyday of British industrialism and empire from the
fifties to the mid-seventies, the sun shone so brightly that its rays penetrated even the lowest strata, and radicalism of all sorts withered. Yet
social criticism continued to flourish in nooks and crannies of the Established and dissenting churches. After Christian Socialism's first trumpet
call, England was never without a small group of parsons who sympa-

[1] For a valuable new interpretation of this development see Maurice B. Reckitt,
Maurice to Temple. A Century of the Social Movement in the Church of England
(London, 1948); another good brief account can be found in Spencer Miller, Jr.,
and J. F. Fletcher, *The Church and Industry* (New York, 1930).

thized with organized labor's hard struggle for existence, and the British labor movement never lacked a Christian and ethical strain.

When the depression, starting in 1875, ended this interim of relative content, British social protest revived, already filled with the special, gradualistic, ethical character that has distinguished it ever since. In such groups as the Fabian Society, the indirect influence of Christian thought was always strong. Moreover, the church produced at least two protest groups specifically its own. The Guild of St. Matthew, founded in 1884, carried on a militant socialist mission and the Christian Social Union fostered a moderate discussion of collectivist reform in leading church circles. Though both remained small, neither was without influence on the direction taken by the Church of England, until in the twentieth century semisocialist doctrines received official sanction. While these organizations of the eighties worked within the Establishment, British Methodism was influenced in a similar direction by the work of men like Hugh Price Hughes.

American Protestants, especially after social Christianity had begun its native development, were influenced by all phases of the older British movement. Almost no important religious writer on social problems failed to mention the English precedents. Kingsley and Maurice, particularly, were continually praised and denounced in the American church press.[2]

At least two of the small radical organizations that grew up in the American churches were of British origin. The influential (Episcopalian) Christian Social Union, founded 1891, was inspired by the British group of the same name. Herbert N. Casson's Labor Church of Lynn, Massachusetts, founded 1894, was intended to be a member of the system of labor churches founded in England by John Trevor. Toynbee Hall, Britain's pioneer social settlement, influenced by Maurice and Ruskin among others, was an important stimulus to American church philanthropy and affected the social philosophy of settlement workers.[3]

[2] See for instance Brown, *Studies in Modern Socialism*, pp. 25-26; H. W. Cadman, *The Christian Unity of Capital and Labor* (New York, 1888), pp. 35-41. The *Christian Union* published a series of articles by Richard T. Ely on "Christian Socialism in England," May 28, June 4 and June 11, 1884, pp. 7-8 in each issue. W. D. P. Bliss discussed "Socialism in the Church of England" for the *Andover Review*, X (1888), 491-496. The school was elaborately condemned by James McGregor in the *Presbyterian and Reformed Review*, III (1892), 35-63, but defended by Charles A. Aiken in the same issue, pp. 64-82.

[3] C. H. Brent, *The Spirit and Work of the Early Christian Socialists* (Christian Social Union, *Publications*, Series A, No. 11, Boston, 1896). John Trevor, "The Labor Church: Religion of the Labor Movement," *Forum*, XVIII (1894-1895), 597-601. Toynbee Hall is especially stressed by M. E. Curti in his account of the American Social Gospel. Curti, *The Growth of American Thought* (New York, 1943), p. 630.

The effect of the English movement on the Episcopal church in the United States was especially important and sometimes took official form. In 1888 a Pan-Anglican committee of bishops with some American representatives stated that there was no essential contradiction between Christianity and socialism except in the methods of some socialists. It is a tribute to the prestige of the source that this fairly advanced statement drew favorable comment even from the *Independent*.[4]

Several British books of Christian social comment stirred Protestant opinion on both sides of the ocean. The development of humanistic theology in this country had already been profoundly influenced by such books as Sir John Seeley's *Ecce Homo*. Later Christian liberals continued to find a stirring message in this examination of Christ's human characteristics and earthly mission.[5]

Canon W. F. Fremantle's *The World as the Subject of Redemption*, a plea for the salvation of society through Christian teaching, exercised a similar influence twenty years later.[6] Many other works produced by English churchmen contained some of the ideas found later in American social Christianity and were read by men who helped to develop the American school.[7]

Yet the social movement that finally, from many sources, developed within American Christianity was far from an echo of British Christian Socialism. It was not, from the start, handicapped by ties with an aristocratic and partly feudal Establishment. On the other hand, it was not supported by the prestige of an Establishment, or by the Church of England's unique inheritance of social influence. The occasional radical churchman in America seldom had the nearly immune and sacrosanct status that was and is offered by some ancient and well-endowed British benefices; he almost always had a board and congregation to deal with.

[4] August 30, 1888, p. 11.

[5] Vida D. Scudder said that Seeley's book, published in 1866, was "still recalled by men and women of long memories as one of the most stirring and disturbing books of their youth," *Father Huntington* (New York, 1940), p. 63. Francis G. Peabody called it the beginning of the "new appreciation of the social teachings of Jesus." *Jesus Christ and the Social Question* (New York, 1901), p. 38.

[6] Published London, 1885. For its influence in America, see Mathews, *op. cit.* in *Religious Thought in the Last Quarter-Century*, p. 231. Fremantle was attacked by the *Presbyterian Review* for too liberal and purely moralistic theology. VII (1886), 186-187.

[7] English publications that had some influence in America included Alexander McLeod, *Christus Consolator* (Wales, 1870); Mrs. Elizabeth Linn Linton, *The True History of Joshua Davidson, Communist* (Am. ed.; Philadelphia, 1873); J. Ll. Davies, *The Gospel of Modern Life* (London, 1875); and *Social Questions* (1885); J. E. Hopkins, *Work among Workingmen* (New York, 1884); Bishop B. F. Westcott, *Social Aspects of Christianity* (New York, 1887); Wilfrid Richmond, *Christian Economics* (New York, 1888); H. P. Hughes, *Social Christianity* (London, 1889).

Finally, American churchmen had to face the fact that, to a far greater extent than was true in England, the working class was outside the Protestant fold. Thus American social Christianity, when it appeared and grew in its time, was a movement arising primarily out of American conditions and following American patterns of action.

Less deeply and less often than by Christian Socialism, American Protestant leaders were occasionally influenced by the British labor movement and the nonreligious forms of British socialism. The work of Thorold Rogers, showing that British real wages had declined since the fifteenth century and urging the ameliorative effects of labor unions, was a shock to devout American believers in inevitable progress and economic law.[8] The moderate and gradualist theories of the Fabians attracted some United States Christians who were repelled by the little they knew of other forms of socialism.[9]

Even during these decades of questioning, much of the vast and complex development of European radical theory remained almost unknown to American Protestants. Socialism, particularly, like Positivism to a previous generation, was a matter for vague alarm rather than serious study. From Marx and Bakunin to guild or Catholic socialism, European protest reached American Christians principally in a series of brief and superficial summaries.

The first of these, by President Theodore D. Woolsey of Yale, appeared originally in the *Independent*.[10] Woolsey, like many academic authorities, had started his career with a theological education, rejecting the ministerial calling only after a spiritual struggle. His critique of the various forms of contemporary radicalism, despite the troubled year in which it appeared, was not immoderate in its hostility to socialism. It raised the usual optimistic and individualistic objections to collectivism and received considerable praise in the religious press.[11]

John Rae's *Contemporary Socialism*, a considerably less detached

[8] J. E. T. Rogers, *Six Centuries of Work and Wages* (New York, 1884). For U.S. comment, see for instance J. O. S. Huntington, "Philanthropy, Its Success and Failure," in *Philanthropy and Social Progress* (various authors, New York, 1893), p. 147.

[9] E.g., Gladden, *Recollections*, pp. 307-308. An editorial, "Socialism in England," *Congregationalist*, July 11, 1889, approved some but not all points of the Fabian program.

[10] "Remarks on Socialism and Communism," beginning December 19, 1878, pp. 1-2; ending August 21, 1879, pp. 4-5. Later published as *Communism and Socialism in Their History and Theory* (New York, 1880).

[11] *Independent*, August 28, 1879, p. 17; *Bibliotheca Sacra*, XXXVII (1880), 397-399; *Congregationalist*, February 25, 1880, p. 62; *Presbyterian Review*, I (1880), 411-412; *Christian Advocate*, January 29, 1880, p. 74.

criticism, refuted all radical theories from Christian Socialism to the single tax in orderly fashion, from the standpoint of laissez faire. Emile, Baron de Laveleye, a believer in slow Christian reform, criticized existing socialist and anarchist schools almost as sweepingly. Both of these forgotten manuals were surprisingly popular authorities among American Protestants of the eighties and nineties.[12]

Richard T. Ely's *French and German Socialism in Modern Times* was somewhat less condemnatory, stating that socialism had accomplished a worthy purpose in exposing existing evils, though all branches except Christian Socialism were mistaken in their methods. Ely, like the other summarizers, devoted an unduly large amount of space to small and unrepresentative anarchist bodies.[13]

Church readers of all these early handbooks were forced at least to recognize the existence of new economic outlooks in considerable strength and variety. In such cursory examination, however, they developed more alarm than understanding. Occasionally events in Europe pointed up their fears. Russian nihilist assassinations and the actions of French anarchists caused American Protestants to shiver briefly. German socialism, when it was noticed at all, seemed somewhat less alarming, but even the social insurance program of Bismarck was far too paternalistic.[14]

French and German Christian socialism apparently did not exert a positive influence on American Protestants until after the American social movement was well established, when scholars drew on European theory to support opinions already arrived at.

All American reception of Continental thought was colored by deep Protestant prejudices against the customs and religion of Europe.

[12] Rae, *Contemporary Socialism* (London, 1884); De Laveleye, *Le Socialisme Contemporain* (Bruxelles, 1881), translated as *The Socialism of Today* (London, 1885). Rae was highly praised, for instance, in the *Christian Advocate*, October 23, 1884. Laveleye was the chief source for D. H. MacVickar, "Social Discontent," *Presbyterian Review*, VIII (1887), 262-281. Both were praised by the periodical, VI (1885), 761-763 and by William Jewett Tucker in the *Andover Review*, II (1884), 621-622. They are the sources of James MacGregor, "Socialism," *Presbyterian and Reformed Review*, III (1892), 35-63, and for Edward S. Parsons, "A Christian Critique of Socialism," *Andover Review*, XI (1889), 597-610. They are the principal sources for the chapter on socialism in T. Edwin Brown, *Studies*, and for similar chapters in many other Social Gospel books.

[13] This book, published New York, 1883, was favorably reviewed by the *Churchman*, October 6, 1883, p. 377, and the *Methodist Quarterly Review*, LXVIII (1885), 387.

[14] For nihilists, *Churchman*, April 26, 1879, p. 450; *Congregationalist*, February 4, 1880, pp. 3-4; for anarchists, *Independent*, November 7, 1882, p. 17; for German socialism, *Independent*, August 20, 1890, pp. 2-3; for Bismarck, *Congregationalist*, May 16, 1889, p. 164.

Greatly irritated when a papal pronouncement linked Protestantism and socialism as errors, the *Watchman* retorted: "The fact is that everything which promotes ignorance and infidelity promotes Socialism. And Romanism promotes both."[15] In 1891 the papal pronouncements on social questions in *Rerum Novarum* attracted slightly more favorable attention. The *Methodist Review*, however, complacently deduced that the pope was afraid of the labor unions.[16]

One radical thinker whom few church writers found it possible to ignore was Leo Tolstoi. Organized religion has always been challenged and troubled by "eccentric" writers who demand literal, personal acceptance of the teachings of the New Testament and the Epistles regarding poverty, labor and communal ownership of goods. In Tolstoi biblical and philosophical argument was supplemented by almost overwhelming emotional power. Many American church critics were forced to take refuge in patronizing approval. A common argument admitted that Tolstoi was a great soul but assumed that his writings were not to be taken seriously as a social program. Readers were reminded that Tolstoi spoke only for conditions of life in despotic and superstitious Russia: ". . . his present work, which would be noteworthy in Germany or England, as it comes from Russia is a marvel of ethical insight."[17]

On the other hand a large minority of the religious press could not waive its opposition to radicalism even for a gifted and "eccentric" Russian. To the most enthusiastic admirers of wealthy, bustling capitalistic America, Tolstoi's espousal of poverty seemed an irritating anachronism. The *Independent's* review, still speaking in the accents of the seventies or earlier, lamented that

amid the riches and splendors of our Christian day the maudlin voice of one who would reduce our civilization to abject squalor finds admiring welcome and is re-echoed in the pulpit and in the religious journals of a country whose unparalleled happiness and freedom are due not to poverty but to wealth.[18]

Far more important than the distant echoes of European movements

[15] March 13, 1884, p. 1.
[16] *Methodist Review*, LXXIII (1891), 787-794. For favorable comment, *Andover Review*, XVI (1891), 175-178.
[17] Review of *My Religion*, *Andover Review*, V (1886), 554-556. The same patronizing near-approval is shown in reviews of Tolstoi's various works in most of the religious press. Only the *Christian Union* praised Tolstoi without qualification in an editorial February 27, 1892, p. 393.
[18] Maurice Thompson, "Christianity and Poverty," *Independent*, November 7, 1889, p. 6. A considerable number of the more conservative publications regularly abused Tolstoi's ideas and conduct.

were the voices of native radicalism. Few churchmen of the eighties and nineties could completely ignore the new spokesmen of dissent, especially those that spoke in semireligious language.

The greatest radical influence on Protestant thinkers, as on most middle-class Americans of his time, was Henry George.[19] It could not be denied that George was profoundly religious, opposed to violence, and sincere to the point of saintliness. His demand for taxing the unearned increment checked with American experience in this era of unparalleled speculation and profiteering in the land and its resources. It seemed to offer an alternative to the demands of the socialists, with whom George was in constant disagreement.

On the other hand, private property in land, from the tiny homestead to the millions of acres granted to railroads, was still sacred to most Americans. And the exuberant optimism that still pervaded middle-class America, lay and clerical, was deeply shocked by George's well-documented assertion that progress and poverty had somehow, unnecessarily, developed side by side.

From the time of *Progress and Poverty's* publication in 1879, most church critics explicitly rejected George's proposals. His picture of society was too dark; the single tax was Utopian and confiscatory. Nevertheless, the tone of church reviewers was almost always serious and respectful. The *Christian Union's* reluctant condemnation was typical:

No! Mr. George may be right; we are inclined to think that in his fundamental principles he is right. . . . But the accomplishment of so radical a change in the organization of society and industry cannot be brought about by any stroke of the legislative pen without at once the grossest injustices and the greatest disorder. . . .[20]

In 1884 a number of prominent clergymen attended a dinner honoring George, in a spirit of "admiration for the man but not indorsement of his doctrines."[21]

When George ventured into practical politics, discussion of his theories increased both in volume and in heat. In 1886, a year of turmoil and class feeling, the United Labor party persuaded George to become its candidate for the New York mayoralty. Sacrificing with some misgivings his undiluted championship of the single tax, George ran on a platform containing many union demands. His candidacy became a

[19] Religious aspects of George and Bellamy are emphasized in Dombrowski, *Early Days of Christian Socialism*, pp. 35-49, 84-95.

[20] May 4, 1881, p. 428. See also *Churchman*, March 27, 1880, p. 349; *Congregationalist*, June 22, 1881, p. 204; J. M. Sturtevant, "The Private Ownership of Land," *Princeton Review*, March, 1882, pp. 125-247; *Independent*, October 2, 1884, p. 17.

[21] *Christian Union*, May 8, 1884, p. 450.

symbol of protest, attracting the support of a wide variety of radicals, liberals and reformers. Despite alleged miscounting of ballots, he finished a strong second, outrunning Theodore Roosevelt. In 1888 the United Labor party, still claiming George as a leader, made a far less successful effort to enter national politics.

Some church spokesmen denounced the United Labor party in tones they had not used toward the theoretical proponents of the single tax.[22] The Reverend Howard Crosby, still insisting that poverty was caused by vice, said of George's followers that they were motivated only by "sheer envy." "Give any of them a million or two," Crosby lavishly suggested, and he would soon "extinguish his farthing light of philosophy."[23]

A small group of radical clergymen, including Father James O. S. Huntington, the most fiery of the early Episcopalian radicals, attracted considerable attention by ardently supporting George's candidacy. The *Churchman* editorially regretted that clergymen should so let their generosity run away with their judgment.[24]

A considerable fraction of the religious press, neither denouncing nor praising, managed to maintain a surprisingly tolerant attitude toward the United Labor party. The *Christian Union*, though it hoped no permanent class party would grow up, deplored the intemperate criticism George had drawn during the campaign and concluded that "No better fortune has happened to the city for many a day than his candidacy."[25] As George ceased to take an active part in politics, the tone of church comment became once more increasingly friendly.

Both before and after the campaign, George himself commanded more of a hearing in church circles than any previous radical. He presented his stirring indictment of existing society in person before leading denominational and interdenominational bodies. Other such gatherings discussed his theories with respect, and he was given space to defend his views in the religious press.[26]

Almost all the principal exponents of the new social Christian move-

[22] E.g. *Independent*, September 30, 1886, p. 17; *New Princeton Review*, III (1887), 258-265; *Christian Advocate*, July 28, 1887, pp. 477-478.

[23] Crosby, "The Forgotten Cause of Poverty," *Forum*, III (1887), 568-577.

[24] December 18, 1886, p. 742. See also *Christian Union*, November 11, 1886, pp. 1-2.

[25] November 11, 1886, pp. 1-2. For other tolerant accounts, see *Methodist Review*, LXIX (1887), 763-769; *Baptist Quarterly Review*, IX (1887), 502-507.

[26] For speeches by George, see Church Congress, *Papers, Addresses and Debates*, 1884, pp. 135-139; report of the 1886 meeting of the American Congress of Churches in *Labor: Its Rights and Wrongs* (Washington, 1886), pp. 261-268. George was respectfully discussed at the Baptist Congress for the Discussion of Current Questions. *Proceedings*, 1887, pp. 26-42, 47-71. He explained "The Single-Tax and What It Really Is and Why We Urge It" in the *Christian Advocate*, July 24, 1890, p. 481.

ment were deeply influenced by George.[27] Walter Rauschenbusch, perhaps the most important of the later church social theorists, supported him in 1886 and recorded, twenty years later, that he owed to that campaign his "first awakening to the world of social problems."[28]

George's revelation of the grim realities of industrial society was delivered with the authority of a compelling personality. Throughout his career and even after his death, his lay and clerical supporters showed a zeal that had almost a religious element. W. T. Harris, speaking to the National Social Science Association, described the impact of this social Messiah:

. . . in some of these Anti-Poverty meetings one feels that the people as a mass are not only groping after, but grasping the first principles of a national religion—very simple principles; but thoroughly and fundamentally Christian.[29]

One episode of the 1886 campaign was complicated by an extraneous issue. Among the spokesmen of discontent who supported George in that troubled year was Father Edward McGlynn. Because of his wide following among Irish laborers, normally Democratic adherents of Tammany, Father McGlynn was a most important recruit. A storm of discussion was stirred up when his American hierarchical superiors ordered him to stop attacking private property in land. Finally he was ordered to Rome and, when he refused to go, excommunicated. Despite this drastic action, much of his labor following stuck by him and he remained the second, if not the first, figure in the United Labor party and its offshoot, the Anti-Poverty Society. Eventually, through papal intervention, he was accepted back into the church without abandoning his social views.

The Protestant press, commenting on the McGlynn affair, had a hard time making up its mind between its old and strong antipopery and its antiradicalism. To some even of the more conservative editors, McGlynn became a hero of free speech whose American rights were menaced by an Italian potentate.[30] The *Independent*, on the other hand, was unable to make up its mind whether the pope or the single tax was the greater enemy. The *Watchman* ingeniously argued that the case did not involve

[27] See, for instance, Strong, *Our Country*, pp. 91-92; Abbott, *Christianity and Social Problems* (Boston, 1896), p. 87.

[28] Rauschenbusch, *Christianity and the Social Crisis* (New York, 1907), p. 394, quoted in D. R. Sharpe, *Walter Rauschenbusch* (New York, 1942), pp. 61-62.

[29] Quoted by George Monro Grant, "Progress and Poverty," *Presbyterian Review*, IX (1887), 188.

[30] *Churchman*, December 18, 1886, p. 741; *American Church Review*, XLIX (1887), 620-634; *Andover Review*, VII (1887), 308-325; *Methodist Review*, LXIX (1887), 775-777.

papal interference in American politics because McGlynn's politics were not American. Regretting a cordial reception given McGlynn by a group of Methodist pastors in New York, the *Methodist Review* rather surprisingly declared that, had Father McGlynn been a member of the Methodist itineracy instead of a priest, he would never have been allowed to preach communism under a high-sounding disguise.[31]

The furor over McGlynn was briefly revived in 1888 when the fiery priest, speaking before the Anti-Poverty Society, quoted Cardinal Manning's statement that "Necessity knows no law, and a starving man has a right to his neighbor's bread." Chicago clergymen, denouncing this revolutionary sentiment, drew from Governor John P. Altgeld a dry rejoinder. Pointing out that Christ and his disciples ate another man's corn without asking his permission Altgeld commented:

> When one thinks of this, and then reads some of the letters of the clergy of this city published in the Sunday *Times* holding that a starving man should die rather than touch his neighbor's bread, one cannot doubt that it is a long time since Christ was on earth, for we are evidently much more advanced in morals than He was.[32]

Edward Bellamy, America's most important Utopian socialist, was as deeply Christian as George in his background and beliefs. In *Looking Backward*, Bellamy's famous dream of the year 2000, the transition to socialism has been achieved peacefully. In the new, happy, society where every aspect of American civilization is transformed for the better, men find themselves able to appreciate Christ's teachings for the first time through their actual experience of Christian love.

A small group of ardent Christian radicals found in Bellamy's romance the formula they had been seeking and became active adherents of the short-lived "Nationalist" movement the book inspired. In Boston, particularly, the Nationalist Club was largely identical with the Christian Socialist group.[33] One of the strong critics of Nationalism derided the movement because the Boston club included thirteen clergymen and only one businessman.[34]

[31] *Independent*, December 16, 1886, pp. 2-3, and later; *Watchman*, June 2, 1887, p. 5; *Methodist Review*, LXX (1888), 129-133.

[32] J. P. Altgeld, "The Rich Man's Bread and the Poor—Cardinal Manning's Position," *Live Questions* (New York, 1890), p. 66. The incident is described by Barnard, *Eagle Forgotten*, p. 128.

[33] Letter to the *Christian Union* on "The Nationalist Movement," February 28, 1889, p. 275. W. D. P. Bliss, "Nationalism and Christianity," The *Nationalist*, I (1889), 97-99.

[34] N. P. Gilman, "Nationalism in the United States," *Quarterly Journal of Economics*, IV (1890-91), 64-65.

Bellamy was, however, too radical to penetrate as deeply as George into dominant church circles. By 1888 many Protestant leaders were willing to give a serious hearing to social reform, but hardly to socialism, even of the most visionary and innocuous variety. The editor of the *Nationalist* must have been dreaming when he said that "more generally . . . the religious press sees that Nationalism is the application to industrial life of the social ethics of Christianity."[35] In reality most of the religious press received Bellamy's idealistic proposals either with ridicule or hostility. The *Methodist Review*, for instance, reacted to *Looking Backward* with one of the strongest expressions of class hatred to be found in a religious magazine in the entire period:

It is time that culture, refinement, and the spirit of unity, order, and progress should combine against the ignorance, jealousy, hatred, and lust of the laboring classes; for the vices of the land inhere in these classes.[36]

Those religious writers who found any good in Bellamy mixed their praise with disclaimers. The *Churchman*, for instance, thought the book full of misconceptions but "inspiring." It reminded its readers that "astrology led the way to astronomy and alchemy to chemistry." The *Christian Union*, agreeing with only a few points of Bellamy's program, allowed him a reply in its pages.[37]

To most churchmen private property was sacred and government action still suspect. Yet, though only a few Christian radicals followed Bellamy, thousands of good Protestants read and discussed him. To many, *Looking Backward* was their first socialist reading of any kind.

Another radical writer who made a considerable impression on religious opinion was that fiery crusader against monopoly, Henry Demarest Lloyd. Usually remembered for *Wealth against Commonwealth*, his passionate indictment of Standard Oil, Lloyd also attracted considerable attention for his long struggles in behalf of midwestern coal miners and his successive connection with the Populist, Socialist Labor and Socialist parties. This indefatigable idealist perhaps typified the American radicalism of his time, a tangled and frustrated, yet vigorous combination of the old agrarian dissent and the new socialism.[38]

[35] Quoted by Dombrowski, *Early Days*, p. 94.
[36] XLII (1891), 280-286. For other strong attacks on Bellamy see for instance *Watchman*, May 15, 1890, p. 5; *Andover Review*, XIV (1890), 236-253.
[37] *Churchman*, February 1, 1890, pp. 109-110; *Christian Union*, November 13, 1890, p. 627.
[38] Dombrowski considers Lloyd a part of the "Christian Socialist" movement. *Early Days*, pp. 121-131. Lloyd's central position in American radicalism and his connections with social Christianity are both emphasized by C. McA. Destler, *American Radicalism 1865-1900. Essays and Documents* (Connecticut College Monograph No. 3, New London, 1946), *passim*.

Religion played quite as large a part in Lloyd's life and work as in those of George and Bellamy. His upbringing was strongly Calvinist and, like so many of his contemporaries, he was first set free from the iron bonds of the ancient faith by Beecher. His works are permeated with a mystical and almost prophetic vision of a new order of brotherhood.

Lloyd, moreover, maintained close personal touch with the developing social movement in the churches. He corresponded with leaders of liberal Christian opinion and asked their advice. He was deeply interested in some of the surviving Christian communist experiments. Both his exposure of mine conditions and his attack on Standard Oil greatly impressed the most liberal sections of church opinion. He attended meetings of the Brotherhood of the Kingdom, one of the earliest organizations of social Christianity, and helped to found the Brotherhood of the Co-operative Commonwealth, an influential radical organization with a strong Christian bent.[39]

Yet Lloyd, though perhaps closer to liberal church circles than any other major American radical, remained essentially outside the distinctively Protestant movement of social criticism. For one thing, he eventually went further along the socialist road than any but a few church leaders would accompany him. Also, his religious views were more and more completely displaced by environmentalism and humanism. At the very end, after a lifetime of combating church conservatism and prodding church inertia, he concluded: "Christianity is the religion that was, socialism is the religion that is to be."[40] Yet Lloyd helped to stir the social consciences of many Christians and, for a time, worked alongside the leaders of the distinctive social movement of American Protestantism.

The broad movement toward social criticism that developed and flourished inside American Protestantism was not unique. It was not primarily a spontaneous development from the new theology or the new Bible interpretation. Radical social doctrine had always been a part of the Christian heritage, but the few who had pointed this out had received scant attention in the prewar or immediate postwar periods.

Before new types of social criticism could get a hearing in any section of the American middle class, the old, powerful insistence that all was well had to receive a devastating rebuttal. This was provided primarily by

[39] For all this information on Lloyd's activities, see Caro Lloyd, *Henry Demarest Lloyd* (2 v., New York, 1912), *passim*. For favorable reviews of his works see *Christian Union*, November 27, 1890, p. 720; *Outlook*, April 6, 1895, pp. 565-566; *Kingdom*, June 7, 1895, pp. 8-9. The Brotherhood of the Co-operative Commonwealth and Lloyd's connection with the most radical section of Christian opinion are discussed on pp. 259-260.

[40] Quoted in Lloyd, *Lloyd*, II, p. 255.

the outbreak of serious labor conflict. With a sudden shock, comfortable citizens, religious leaders among them, realized the meaning of slums and unemployment. They were forced to recognize that many of their countrymen did not accept the doctrines of individualist effort and inevitable progress, that some had even been driven to desperation.

Once this shock took effect, social criticism developed in many quarters. Economists, sociologists and independent radical critics all offered their responses to the now obvious challenge, and most of these responses took a more or less ethical or religious form. Spokesmen of religion, influenced by all these groups and others, but more by their own close experience of misery and unrest, developed their own schools of social theory. The movement of social Christianity, developing as early as any American response to industrial crisis, became in turn a strong influence on all varieties of American social opinion.

IV

SOCIAL CHRISTIANITY

1877-1895

CONSERVATIVE SOCIAL CHRISTIANITY

THE social movement in American Protestantism appeared as a wide-spread, spontaneous response to the challenge of industrial society. Many of its early theorists, not realizing that their own experiences were part of a common, inevitable, readjustment, saw themselves as lonely heralds. Naturally, preachers of social Christianity spoke in different terms, influenced by various theologies, reaching different diagnoses for the ills of society. They shared, however, two characteristics: all were moved by a sense of social crisis, and all believed in the necessity and possibility of a Christian solution.

A large wing of the social movement was consistently conservative in its analysis and prescriptions. The conservative social Christians looked at current social unrest with fear and horror; they devoted a major part of their energies to pointing out the evils of socialism. Usually they were at least skeptical of trade-unions and some of them were overtly hostile. The solutions they urged, ranging from consumers' co-operatives to savings banks, involved no practical challenge to contemporary economic assumptions. The conservative social Christians echoed, in fact, many of the hoary theories of clerical laissez faire.

Yet this group differed from previous conservatives and their surviving followers in one obvious characteristic: they were not complacent. Their conservatism was defensive and apologetic. The earlier generation, despite occasional alarms, had insisted that all was fundamentally well; the con-servative social Christians viewed the conditions of society with deeper concern. The older conservatives had harshly insisted that some suffering was and always would be an economic and spiritual necessity; the new conservative school urged the poor to be patient in the hope of eventual improvement. Since the beginning of the century, conservative Protes-tants, though they had defended the church's right to make pronounce-ments on a wide variety of topics, had damned as sentimentality all interference on "Christian" grounds with the laws of individualistic laissez faire. The right-wing social Christians retained the old dislike of "machinery" for betterment, but called for a certain degree of reform on a voluntary, individual basis. Instead of repeating the iron law of wages, for instance, the new group urged employers to grant higher pay as a Christian act, thereby heading off socialism and trade-unions.

One of the earliest and most typical of this group was Joseph Cook, famous for his Boston Monday lectures. Stressing the opposition to liberal theology, Cook lectured on everything from Asia to biology, winning wide applause and the attention of an eager, cultivated, influential audience.[1] In the late seventies and eighties Cook, like other universal experts, turned to problems of labor and socialism.

Like most of his clerical contemporaries, Cook condemned not only the socialists, but the members of "oath-bound secret societies" such as the Knights of Labor. Though not all American labor unions were yet socialistic, Cook feared that they might become so. Strikes were "the most barbaric" of labor's weapons. Dennis Kearney and his Massachusetts imitators drew some of Cook's loudest thunders, and the income tax seemed to him a proposal to encourage improvidence.[2]

No equalitarian, Cook believed that in a free society those with merit would always rise, and therefore that the worthless would always form a separate class at the bottom. Urging a reading test for the suffrage, Cook asserted that America must seek "theocratic" and not "democratic" equality.[3]

The Monday lecturer repeatedly thrilled his audience with dark threats of retaliatory violence in case socialism spread in America: "Caesar was Rome's escape from Communism; and the day that a socialist revolution shall succeed in the United States, you will find on our map a Rubicon, and a man on horseback ready to cross it." (Applause.)[4]

Cook clung firmly to a large part of the traditional economic theory, repeatedly sounding the trumpet of self-help. Yet despite so many agreements with his conservative predecessors, he was a part of the new movement. Instead of asserting the all-sufficiency of natural forces, he called

---

[1] He had to move twice to larger auditoriums. Among his admirers were many of the period's leading college presidents, preachers and professors. See Cook, *Labor, with Preludes on Current Events* ("Boston Monday Lectures," VII [Boston, 1880]), iii-v. His lectures were widely reported and reprinted in America and England. *Bibliotheca Sacra* estimated that newspapers published each lecture in full in 100,000 copies and printed excerpts in 300,000 copies. *Bibliotheca Sacra*, XXXVII (1880), 381-391.

[2] These views are expressed throughout Cook's works, especially in *Labor, etc.*, and in *Socialism, with Preludes on Current Events* ("Boston Monday Lectures," VIII [Boston, 1880]).

[3] "The Infidel Attack on Property," *Independent*, November 14, 1878, pp. 4-6.

[4] *Socialism, etc.*, p. 57.

for the solution of the labor problem on Christian principles, and without a victory of either contestant. As ameliorative measures to stem the tide of socialism, he endorsed co-operation, arbitration, and factory legislation for the protection of women and children.[5]

Cook departed most sharply from the older conservatism in his ideas concerning wages. Praising the younger British economists, he rejected the classic wage-fund theory, under which clerics for two generations had demonstrated the impossibility of raising pay. Cook spoke for the view that wages and profits were alike potentially unlimited and were not in competition with each other, a theory that served equally well to demonstrate the inutility of labor action, but seemed to hold out some hope of a rising standard of living.

Since he repudiated the traditional assertion that wages are determined by forces outside human control, Cook had to work out his own rule of thumb to determine just wages. He concluded that, to support a family according to the American standard, the laborer must earn twice the cost of his unprepared food. This modest level, he insisted, must be imposed not by law but by public opinion, since "Only the Golden Rule can bring the golden age."[6]

The Boston Monday lectures, very widely reprinted in the church press, usually pleased their large and respectable audience. It is worth noting, however, that Cook was too radical for some of his readers. A detailed criticism in the *Baptist Quarterly Review* defines exactly the difference between the older conservatism and the new movement of conservative social Christianity which Cook represented. Admitting that Cook's work was not without merit, the editors took sharp exception to his doctrine of wages, which, however much the lecturer might dislike such a result, tended to further socialistic and communistic thinking. Wages, the *Review* insisted, can be determined only by labor's willingness to work and capital's willingness to invest. "Of course, there will be temporary phenomena not in seeming accord with these statements, but that the above is the general law is as little doubtful as the laws of Euclid." Such proposals of Cook as vacations with pay for women workers, were "nothing less than legislating money from the pockets of the rich into those of the poor, precisely what Communism proposes." Comment-

---

[5] "Cooperation the Help of the Poor," *Socialism*, pp. 93-118; "Co-operative Savings Banks in Germany," *ibid.*, pp. 121-144; "Mrs. Browning's Cry of the Children," *Labor*, pp. 98-119; "Sex in Industry," *ibid.*, pp. 132-145, 157-182. Significantly, one of Cook's grounds for approving the protection of workingmen is that low wages lead to a danger of "moral death" as well as physical death. "Sex in Industry," p. 180.

[6] *Labor*, pp. 227-228.

ing on Cook's statement that the question of capital and labor should be settled according to the ideas of a Christian commonwealth, the editors echoed at least two generations of authority:

> Very well, provided it is the ideal commonwealth, wherein perfect respect is paid to economic laws. That would, indeed, be so far a Christian commonwealth, for, as Frederic Bastiat said, the laws of political economy are the laws of God. Humanitarian measures, call them Christian or by what name you will, if found to favor the laborer as against the capitalist beyond what the working of natural laws would, are Communistic measures.[7]

When he spoke to the Protestant audiences of 1880, even Cook represented a new departure.

Since conservative social Christianity was essentially a defensive doctrine, it is understandable that the crisis of the late seventies produced a number of writings of this school. In the year after the great railway strikes, for instance, President Roswell D. Hitchcock of Union Theological Seminary issued a little volume on *Socialism* quite similar to those of Cook. Hitchcock used most of his space conventionally enough in denouncing radicalism and restating the usual laissez faire theories. Like Cook, however, he departed from the old conservative pattern when he dealt with wages, urging the Christian capitalist to pay more than the minimum possible.[8]

In the same year Joseph P. Thompson issued a tract which came to similar conclusions. After a detailed catalogue of the working man's "False Friends," Thompson admitted among labor's "True Friends" the traditional virtues, the spirit of Christianity and, with considerable hesitation, the co-operative movement.[9]

These doctrines of conservative social Christianity were to some extent new departures in the late seventies. Their mildly reformist outlook had become much more commonplace by the middle eighties, when they received their most authoritative and influential formulation from A. J. F. Behrends.[10] Behrends, a Brooklyn minister, was chiefly concerned to

[7] *Baptist Quarterly Review*, II (1880), 285-292.

[8] Hitchcock, *Socialism* (rev. ed.; New York, 1879). This book was in general well received by the religious press. A rebuttal by "A Socialist," pointing out that Hitchcock and most other church writers misstated the socialist idea, confusing it with a proposal for an immediate equal redistribution of wealth, was ignored by Protestant journals. *A Reply to Roswell D. Hitchcock, D.D. on Socialism* (pamphlet, New York, 1879).

[9] Thompson, *The Workman: His False Friends and His True Friends* (pamphlet, New York, 1879).

[10] Behrends, *Socialism and Christianity* (New York, 1886).

arouse Christianity to its great duty of overcoming socialism. His description of socialism, drawn from the handbooks of Laveleye and Ely, charged
the socialists with a mechanistic view of humanity and an unnecessarily
pessimistic analysis of American society. Behrends, however, admitted
at the end of this description that "the working classes have not shared
in the advance of the present century as they ought to have done," a
concession that sharply separates him from his truly conservative predecessors and contemporaries.[11]

In a discussion of "The Rights of Labor" Behrends, like many others,
devoted himself principally to showing what those rights were not.
Inequality and hard work were to be accepted as inevitable. Trade-
unionism, while not positively condemned, was narrowly restricted in
function. Producers' co-operation, according to Behrends, was impractical.

Like his predecessors, Behrends demonstrated at considerable length
the justice of great wealth and high profits. In pointing out the corresponding responsibilities of the rich, however, he went beyond Carnegie's
prescription of systematic charity. Good wages, the restriction of child
labor, industrial insurance, and a free Sabbath all were suggested as
suitable expressions of the good will of the wealthy. Behrends' discussion
of poverty is, similarly, a combination of old and new views. While he
asserted that the poor are a permanent and necessary phenomenon, and
that faults of character are the chief causes of poverty, he admitted that
some hardship is the result of social conditions and suggested such cures
as public education, liquor control and (more surprisingly) cheap
housing.[12]

In the exact spirit of the newer conservatism, Behrends ended his book
with an eloquent denunciation of socialism and "selfish" political economy
at once. Christianity alone, he asserted, would solve the time's social ills
and conserve private property.[13]

Behrends seems to have expressed fairly accurately the opinion of a
large number of Protestants in 1886. The *Baptist Quarterly Review*,
however, found the book too lenient toward radicals. More important,
a number of criticisms from the left indicated that by 1886 a social
movement existed which had gone beyond Behrends' conservative
reformism.[14]

[11] *Ibid.*, p. 94.
[12] *Ibid.*, pp. 139-158, 182-242.
[13] *Ibid.*, pp. 258-308.
[14] For disapproval from the right, see *Baptist Quarterly Review*, VIII (1886),
571-573; from the left, *Christian Union*, August 26, 1886, p. 23. Most other
leading Protestant organs heartily approved Behrends.

Similar and less widely publicized expressions of the new type of conservative doctrine were fairly common from the middle eighties on. Differing in detail, all writers of this school admitted that some improvement of existing conditions was necessary, and all laid their main stress on the value of voluntary or "Christian" methods as against "Socialism" or "Materialism."[15]

Spokesmen of conservative social Christianity were especially common among Unitarians. Perhaps it was natural that this church, drawing on an old tradition of reform but influenced by the high social and economic position of many of its members, should produce a number of limited and tentative programs for social harmony. Unitarian spokesmen of this school, perhaps more than their orthodox Protestant colleagues, seemed to see the task of reform somewhat in terms of *noblesse oblige*. George Batchelor, for instance, believed that "The wiser and better part of the minority are now leading in the way which all must follow" and said of "the multitude" that "For a long time to come, they will be on the hands of civilization, the majority to be instructed, guided, and cared for."[16]

By this time, theological differences seemed sometimes less important than agreement on social principles. The *Churchman*, for instance, commenting on Minot J. Savage's *Social Problems*, a typical Unitarian work contrasting Christianity's method of reform with all others, hoped that its readers might get "a little sound political economy, which they would reject from another source. The jelly of Unitarianism may thus disguise the quinine of common sense."[17]

Needless to say, some Unitarians as well as some orthodox Protestants were responding to the current challenge in different terms. Yet even the cautious and patronizing prescriptions of Batchelor or Behrends were a break with the past. It is a measure of the time's unrest that clergymen

[15] For examples, see D. J. Hill, *The Social Influence of Christianity with Special Reference to Contemporary Problems* (Boston, 1888); William DeWitt Hyde, "The New Economic Man," *Independent*, November 5, 1885, pp. 1-2; A. E. Waffle, "The Christian Solution of the Labor Problem," *Baptist Quarterly Review*, IX (1887), 924-940; D. H. MacVicar, "Social Discontent," *Presbyterian Review*, VIII (1887), 262-281; E. S. Parsons, "A Christian Critique of Socialism," *Andover Review*, XI (1889), 597-611.

[16] Batchelor, *Social Equilibrium and other Problems Ethical and Religious* (Boston, 1887), pp. 55; 16. For other Unitarian expressions of the point of view of conservative reform, see J. B. Harrison, *Certain Dangerous Tendencies in American Life* (Boston, 1880); *Notes on Industrial Conditions* (Franklin Falls, New Hampshire, 1886); *A Note on Labor Agitations* (Franklin Falls, 1887); William B. Weeden, *The Social Law of Labor* (Boston, 1882); C. F. Dole, *The Citizen and the Neighbor; or, Men's Rights and Duties as They Live together in the State and in Society* (Boston, 1884); Minot J. Savage, *Social Problems* (Boston, 1886).

[17] *Churchman*, December 4, 1886, p. 697.

of obviously conservative temperaments admitted the existence of serious unsolved problems and joined in the search for answers. Despite their defensive purpose, they helped to bring into question the certainties of the recent past. Denominational groups and other important registers of Protestant opinion often listened first to the relatively inoffensive proposals of the conservative social Christians, then moved by imperceptible degrees to the acceptance of more important innovations.

PROGRESSIVE SOCIAL CHRISTIANITY

(THE SOCIAL GOSPEL)

M ANY Protestant theorists sought for a conservative solution to the new social problems, and doubtless a still greater number insisted on ignoring them altogether. A large, growing, articulate group, however, made a definite break with the old conservatism and went well beyond the defensive modifications of Behrends and his colleagues. Most of this group, though not all, refrained from following paths sufficiently radical to separate them completely from the great mass of their Protestant contemporaries. Cautious enough to maintain contact with an essentially conservative public and yet venturesome enough to start in new directions, this moderately progressive school, often known as the Social Gospel,[1] achieved a position of great influence on the course of American social thought.

The typical middle-of-the-road proponents of the Social Gospel actually had much in common with more conservative contemporaries such as Cook or Behrends. They too were disturbed by social strife, and they called on the church to provide alternatives to socialism. The emphasis, however, was different. While their conservative colleagues were *chiefly* concerned to prove the rightness of existing institutions and to head off change, Social Gospel spokesmen were *primarily* concerned with the search for a better society. Instead of insisting on the all-sufficiency of individual regeneration as a solution for social problems, they sought, however unsuccessfully, for concrete measures of improvement and listened, however critically, to contemporary proposals for change.

As religious writers of this period frequently pointed out, the churches had become middle-class institutions. The Social Gospel, full of optimism for the American future, sacrificing only a minimum of individualism to

---

[1] This term, widely used by recent critics and historians, did not become general until about 1910. Its origin is discussed by Hopkins, in *Rise of the Social Gospel*, pp. 196-197. It is used here in the sense in which it has usually been understood in American church history, that is, as referring to the moderate progressive school of Christian social theory which developed out of the teachings of such men as Washington Gladden and became common. "Social Christianity" is used here as a more general term including all attempts to find Christian solutions to social problems, from conservative to radical.

the urgent demand for social action, was a middle-class creed. That is why it was able, for a large section of the American church public, to shatter once and for all the ironbound economic theories which had confined Protestant thought since before the Civil War. Its varied spokesmen agreed at least that social improvement was not either impossible, irrelevant or irreligious.

Washington Gladden, probably the most influential of the Social Gospel leaders, summed up in his own experience the development of the whole school.[2] He was born in 1836 and brought up in the large and struggling household of a country schoolteacher-farmer, a background which he said partly explained his "identification with the working-classes." Like many of his contemporaries, Gladden in his adolescence tortured himself with the vain effort to achieve a mystical experience, then considered indispensable as an evidence of salvation. Failing to receive assurance, he began early to abandon the old theology. Later his theological development, deeply influenced by Bushnell and Beecher, carried him to a belief in the immanence of God in the world and in society. Thus his entire experience was immediately relevant to his whole religious and social outlook.

Influenced in his youth by popular evangelists and attracted by the "ethical" antislavery teachings of the Congregational church in Owego, Massachusetts, Gladden determined early to become a minister. At Williams College he was deeply influenced by John Bascom. His first call came from a church in Brooklyn and, like many country boys of the period, he was stunned by his sudden first experience of a great city.

Gladden, like others, found his service with the Christian Commission in the Civil War lines valuable and stirring, but was saddened and disturbed by his experience of Reconstruction. In 1866 he was called to the factory town of North Adams, Massachusetts, where the importation of Chinese laborers soon provided his first experience of labor conflict. At North Adams, also, Gladden discovered his talent for clear and effective writing and started a long literary career. Four years on the staff of the *Independent* in New York deepened his knowledge of urban problems. In 1873 he resigned his position on the *Independent* staff, distressed (not surprisingly) by the paper's advertising ethics.

Leaving New York for a Springfield, Massachusetts church in 1875, Gladden arrived at the depth of the depression in a city full of angry unemployed. Requested to address meetings of jobless workers and of employers, Gladden formulated for the first time his ideas on industrial

[2] See Gladden, *Recollections.*

problems. These ideas differed little from those of his clerical contemporaries. There was nothing in Gladden's typical farm background and ministerial education to equip him to understand industrial problems. His first book on social questions, *Workingmen and their Employers* was, as he later realized, "not an important book."[3]

Gladden's ideas in 1876 were about the same as those of Behrends twenty years later. Disapproving many of the activities of labor unions, the most he could say for them was that "it does not appear to me that they are always morally wrong."[4] In time of depression, he said, laborers should take any work that offered, no matter how ill-paid. Some should return to the farm. Like his contemporaries, Gladden contrasted the rewarding life of hard work and saving with the unhappy luxury of the millionaire. He denounced all forms of radicalism and socialism in conventional terms, urging as an alternative that employers interest themselves in the physical and moral welfare of their employees. Gladden implied that a more co-operative form of society might some day replace the wage system, but to reach this goal he prescribed only the usual formula: that workingmen should save and buy shares in industry.

These ideas were, of course, the clerical commonplaces of Gladden's time and he very soon developed beyond them. His autobiography makes the reason for his changed opinions remarkably clear. In 1882 he was called to the pastorate of the First Congregational Church of Columbus, Ohio. Here he soon found himself in intimate personal contact with a great labor struggle, the Hocking Valley coal strike of 1884. Several of the principal officials of the coal company were members of Gladden's congregation and he knew that they were determined to break the union. This they finally did, forcing their men back to work under a "yellow-dog" contract against further union activity. A year later, however, another strike broke out, this time ending with success for the miners through arbitration.

This lesson in trade-unionism stirred Gladden, just as similar episodes were influencing many of his contemporaries. His utterances on labor in the middle eighties, often originally delivered to audiences of employers or striking employees, showed a considerable change of mind. Aside from their content, their tone was new; Gladden's simple, concrete language evidenced the beginning of personal, immediate understanding of labor's problems. Such realism was, and long continued to be, the outstanding lack in most clerical pronouncements on labor.

[3] *Recollections*, p. 257.

[4] *Workingmen and Their Employers* (2nd ed.; New York, 1894, [cop. 1876]), pp. 41-42.

Gladden still disliked socialism, though he agreed in part with its indictment of existing society. In 1886 his strongest blows, however, fell not on the radicals but on the conservatives, and particularly on the theory that wages should be determined by competitive forces:

The Christian moralist is, therefore, bound to admonish the Christian employer that the wage-system, when it rests on competition as its sole basis, is anti-social and anti-Christian.

The doctrine which bases all the relations of employer and employed upon self-interest is a doctrine of the pit; it has been bringing hell to earth in large instalments for a good many years.

The labor of the nation is the life of the nation; is that a commodity to be bought in the cheapest market and sold in the dearest?[5]

His actual knowledge of contemporary labor conditions had evidently forced Gladden to abandon some of the insistent optimism that had long characterized American economic thinking. Granting that the wealth of society as a whole was rising, Gladden looked far more closely than his predecessors at the workingman's share. He included in his estimates not only wages but such other concrete realities as continuous employment, demand for skilled labor, and the cost of living.[6] His startling conclusion was that labor had tripled its production in twenty-five years without materially increasing its receipts.

Gladden's most important address of this period, "Is It Peace or War?" was first delivered in 1886 to an audience mostly composed of striking employees in Cleveland and repeated at Tremont Temple before "some of the solid men of Boston."[7] This address included one of the most forthright clerical defenses of labor's right to organize that had yet appeared. Admitting that the emergence of large corporations and unions had ended the day of free individual bargains, thereby throwing overboard the assumptions of several generations, Gladden described the actual situation as one of war. "If war is the order of the day," he concluded, "we must grant labor belligerent rights." Making an admission difficult for Christians, Gladden granted that a fight could sometimes be justified: 'War is a terrible evil; but it is sometimes the lesser of two evils.

[5] *Applied Christianity*, pp. 33, 135-136, 52.
[6] *Ibid.*, p. 118-120.
[7] For the speech, see *ibid.*, pp. 102-145; for circumstances of delivery, *Recollections*, pp. 300-304.

The degradation of a large class in society would be a greater evil than a war undertaken by that class to prevent such degradation."[8]

Of course Gladden, as a nineteenth-century optimist and a Christian minister, could neither approve such social war nor grant its necessity.

> Permit me to say that I know something about this war; I have been in the thick of it for thirty years, trying to make peace, and helping to care for the sick and the wounded; and I know that the wrong is not all on one side, and that the harsh judgments and the fierce talk of both sides are inexcusable.[9]

As his principal substitute for war, Gladden urged the introduction of profit-sharing systems, under which labor would receive a fixed proportion of the total return. He also advocated, even at this early date, a reduction of hours without a corresponding decrease of wages, a proposition that had long been denounced by churchmen as sheer robbery.[10]

Gladden's realistic analysis of present society, with his firm insistence on bargaining rights for labor, remained his most distinctive contribution to Protestant social doctrine. He continued to hope for a gradual evolution toward a co-operative social order and rejected with increasing firmness the doctrines of laissez faire. Throughout his long career the list of practical reform measures which he endorsed constantly grew. In 1893 these already included state regulation of hours, factory inspection, taxation of inheritances and the strict regulation, or even confiscation, of natural monopolies. Perhaps reflecting the influence of George, Gladden insisted at the same time that property rights, especially in land, must be limited by social use.[11] He retained, however, his dislike of political socialism. In the Progressive era of the early twentieth century Gladden was to take part in almost every reform cause that arose, becoming, through his city reform activities and his acquaintance with Theodore Roosevelt, almost a national political figure.[12]

Even by the eighties and nineties, Gladden was as influential as any clergyman of his time and the central figure of the Christian social movement. He was continually called upon to represent the Social Gospel in the discussions of the major church organizations. Lay critics, friendly and hostile, often took him as the chief example of the new movement in Christianity. Early reviews of his works, both in conservative and in liberal church periodicals, were usually highly favorable. An occasional

[8] *Ibid.*, p. 114.
[9] *Ibid.*, p. 141.
[10] *Ibid.*, pp. 132-139.
[11] *Tools and the Man*, pp. 69-114; 286-302. For Gladden's other important writings, see Bibliography.
[12] See *Recollections*, pp. 328-397.

reviewer found Gladden too "sentimental" or objected to his choice of subjects. Even those who disagreed, however, usually gave him a respectful hearing. A typical conservative rebuttal, objecting particularly to his "materialistic" view of poverty as an "unalloyed evil," placed Gladden among "that considerable class of writers whose sympathy for the working people somewhat obscures their vision" but yet praised his "candor."[13]

This largely favorable reception seems surprising when one considers the difference between Gladden's views and the rigid beliefs that had long been standard. No doubt it is partly explained by personality. Gladden had the knack of speaking simply and effectively to various groups and avoided the common clerical fault of patronizing his audience. His illustrations were drawn from experience and his language was simple and clear.

The principal reason for Gladden's success, however, was that he expressed the views of a large and growing group of Protestants. His theological position undoubtedly increased his power. Discarding, like many Christians of his time, the obsession with personal sin and salvation that had tormented his youth, Gladden preached the fatherhood of God and brotherhood of man in terms that were understandable and acceptable to the untheoretical, worldly, optimistic congregations of his time. Yet he never ventured, like some of his liberal contemporaries, into the borders of sheer humanism; he retained contact with the powerful tradition in which he and his hearers had been brought up.[14]

His social opinions, similarly, were never so far in advance of his contemporaries as to lose touch. Gladden's temperament lacked entirely the taste for opposition, the capacity for sustained indignation, the loneliness that characterize the radical. Not through timidity, but through conviction, he continued to reject the arguments of the socialists. His program of gradual reform of American capitalism was essentially the same as that which was to attract millions of middle-class Americans in the early twentieth century. Though he was at times genuinely and deeply disturbed by his observations of American society, he retained a robust conviction that "if it was ever worth while to live, it is worth while to live today. No better day than this day has ever dawned on this continent."[15]

Gladden preached exactly the doctrines that the moderately progressive Protestants of his day had become willing to accept. Essentially the

[13] *Bibliotheca Sacra*, XLIV (1887), 395.
[14] For a summary of Gladden's important contribution to theology, see Buckham, *Progressive Religious Thought*, pp. 251-257.
[15] *Recollections*, p. 430.

same ideas, usually less effectively expressed, were being stated by more and more of his colleagues. It is not really surprising that Gladden could say in his autobiography that

I do not believe that there is any place of influence in the world in which a man can be as free as in the Christian pulpit. . . . A minister with a clear sense of his vocation, and with a fair amount of common sense, who can make allowances for differences of opinion, and discuss critical issues with a reasonable degree of moderation, can speak his mind more freely than most moral teachers.[16]

This conclusion reflected Gladden's experience, but it would not have been shared by his less well-adjusted contemporaries.

R. Heber Newton, a liberal New York Episcopalian, was perhaps the second most prominent figure in the early development of social Christianity. A champion of liberal, evolutionary theology, Newton reached a wide audience with his sermons and frequent periodical publications. Like Gladden, he had urged the church to turn toward social religion as early as 1876, but his concrete suggestions at that time went little beyond an appeal for honesty in business.[17]

His interest in the labor question developed even faster than Gladden's, and in 1883 he had a unique opportunity to present his views before the United States Senate Committee on Labor and Education.[18]

Newton started his testimony by presenting evidence from the census that wages had shrunk during the preceding decade. Departing somewhat less than Gladden from the traditional explanations, he blamed this decrease partly on labor's own inefficiency, lack of effort, thriftlessness and unwise use of strikes. These failings were in turn, however, partly the result of social conditions. Inefficiency was in part a physical product of slum environment, machine production inevitably caused a lessening of interest in work, and thriftlessness was partly caused by lack of education. These evils could be relieved to some extent by such measures as encouragement of education, employers' welfare work, postal savings, juster taxation and monopoly regulation. Newton warned the senators, however, that eventually some more radical change was necessary in an era of large machine production. He insisted that some day, "either directly, in great co-operative organizations, or indirectly, in the person of the state, labor shall have a share in the control of these monster forces."

[16] *Ibid.*, p. 416.
[17] Newton, *The Morals of Trade* (New York, 1876), esp. p. 79.
[18] Newton, "A Bird's Eye View of the Labor Problem," *Social Studies* (New York, 1886), pp. 3-81.

This was radical language indeed, but Newton made it plain that such a development lay in the almost unpredictable future, and that the road lay through the encouragement of the current inoffensive co-operative movement:

If such a change were made to-day, by any power under heaven, it would, in the present state of our workingmen, simply bring industry to a standstill and introduce worse evils than those now endured.

If the co-operative commonwealth ever comes, as I trust it may come, it will come as the final generalization of a long series of integrations, of which the co-operative societies, now so much neglected, form the immediate step in advance.[19]

Commenting on the end of the frontier, the increase of tenant farming, and the vogue of the single tax, Newton similarly spoke for a slow advance toward the distant goal of common soil ownership. Here, however, his immediate suggestions were more drastic, including public retention of all mineral rights not yet pre-empted.

Newton, like many of the social Christians, continued to emphasize the development of a social spirit and an eventual advance toward a co-operative society more than any particular measures. In the midst of the turmoil of 1886 he repeated substantially his opinions of 1883, denouncing many of the current practices of labor unions and calling for a gradual advance toward a co-operative society.[20] More sweeping than Gladden in his advocacy of eventual social change, Newton was somewhat less advanced in his attitude toward immediate realities. He too received a wide hearing on the platform and in the press. Perhaps because of his extreme theological liberalism, his writings attracted less favorable comment than Gladden's in church publications.

Most of the views of Newton and Gladden were echoed by a large number of less influential writers. The output of Social Gospel publications rose sharply after each of the major crises of the period. In the years immediately after the strikes of 1877, most progressive social analysis was still fragmentary and tentative.

Dudley Ward Rhodes, a Cincinnati rector, appealed in 1879 for the church to cease arguing theology and let men know her sympathy for suffering. With unusual boldness he included in his description of

[19] *Ibid.*, p. 61.
[20] See Newton, *The Present Aspect of the Labor Problem* (pamphlet, New York, 1886).

current evils a blistering attack on the Cincinnati streetcar company, which he said worked its employees a fifteen-hour day at nine cents an hour, deducting the cost of their uniforms, while its own earnings amounted to 16⅔ per cent on its investment. Such concrete attacks on flagrant examples of injustice may well have had more effect at this period than more theoretical discussions.[21]

In the same year Edward Everett Hale, long famous as a pioneer in Unitarian humanitarian and charitable movements, made a general appeal for "the life in common" as against individualism. To Hale the development of a more organic society was the task of liberal religion, working counter to Protestant individualism and Catholic authoritarianism.[22]

J. H. W. Stuckenberg, a Lutheran theologian, was one of the few leaders contributed by his church to the early social movement. Stuckenberg's *Christian Sociology* appealed to Christian love as the source of social ethics and declared that society itself was "the divinely-chosen agency for the regeneration of mankind." While taking care to maintain a spiritual emphasis in all its activities, the modern church must take account of the whole man.[23] J. H. Rylance, a New York Episcopalian, expressed in 1880 views very similar to those of Newton, calling for a gradual advance out of competition into co-operation.[24]

After a lull in the early eighties, appeals for progressive social Christianity began again to appear in some quantity in the depression year of 1885 and increased in the following year of labor conflict and anarchist "riot."[25] Perhaps the most striking Social Gospel reaction to the dramatic events of 1886 came, interestingly enough, from the son of Alonzo Potter, the most vigorous opponent of labor unions among the pre-Civil War clerical economists. Bishop Henry Codman Potter of New York had long been calling in general terms for an increase of social responsibility. Deeply disturbed by the strikes of 1877, he had insisted that "we

[21] Rhodes, *Creed and Greed* (Cincinnati, 1879), p. 89.
[22] Hale, "The Life in Common," in volume of same title (Boston, 1880), pp. 3-15.
[23] Stuckenberg, *Christian Sociology* (New York, 1880).
[24] Rylance, *Lectures on Social Questions* (New York, 1880).
[25] Progressive social-Christian analyses appearing in 1885 included Newman Smyth, "Social Problems in the Pulpit," *Andover Review*, III (1885), 297-312, 423-436, 508-519; George Washburn (president of Robert College), "Christianity and Labor," *Independent*, October 22, 1885, pp. 2-3; Edwin B. Webb, *Socialism and the Christian Church* (pamphlet, New York, 1885). Published in 1886, besides those discussed in detail below, were G. C. Lorimer, *Studies in Social Life* (Chicago); Philip S. Moxom, *The Industrial Revolution* (Boston); F. N. Zabriskie, "The Bible a Workingman's Book," beginning in the *Congregationalist*, October 28, pp. 1-2, later published in book form (New York, 1888).

shall not finally silence the heresies of the communist with the bullets of the militia."[26]

In 1886 he issued a pastoral letter concerning the current labor troubles that was one of the most influential documents of early social Christianity.[27] Potter began this official pronouncement with a standard attack on "the terrorism of unscrupulous organizations aiming to coerce workmen and wage-payers alike by such intolerable tyrannies as riot and the boycott." The bishop recognized, however, that labor's demands were for justice and that they arose from a deepening gulf between classes. The letter's most important sentence was a repudiation of the standard economic view of labor as a commodity, a theory that had been pronounced by clerical authorities consistently since the time of Potter's father.

When capitalists and employers of labor have forever dismissed the fallacy, which may be true enough in the domain of political economy, but is essentially false in the domain of religion, that labor and the laborer are alike a commodity, to be bought and sold, employed or dismissed, paid or underpaid, as the market shall decree; . . . when the principle of a joint interest in what is produced of all brains and hands that go to produce it is wisely and generously recognized; . . . then, but not till then may we hope to heal those grave social divisions, concerning which there need to be among us all, as with Israel of old, "great searchings of heart."[28]

Potter's letter, and particularly this statement, coming as it did in the midst of a period of heated social discussion, produced a widespread reaction. Many of the New York clergy responded with social sermons and the letter was widely discussed, pro and con, in the lay and clerical press.[29] Potter continued to be a leader in the moderate social movement in his church, joining the attack on slums, sweatshops and child labor, and backing with his official position the activities of many Episcopalians who were far more radical than he was.

T. Edwin Brown, the first important Baptist spokesman of the progressive social movement, also published an important work in 1886. A typical exponent of the moderate Social Gospel of his time, Brown opposed both socialism and classical economics and joined the appeal

---

[26] "The Social Indifferentist," sermon preached November 23, 1878, in *Sermons of the City* (New York, 1881), p. 79.

[27] Quoted in H. A. Keyser, *Bishop Potter, the People's Friend* (New York, 1910), pp. 21-26.

[28] *Ibid.*, p. 25.

[29] The reaction is summarized by the *Churchman*, May 29, 1886, p. 591. See also the *Nation*, XLII (1886), 419.

for a new social spirit. Like many others, he praised the ethical movement in economics and the co-operative movement as evidences of a better day coming. Rather surprisingly in view of the current tone of the religious press, Brown seemed to regard approval of labor unions as a matter of course.[30]

In this crisis year even the American Sunday-School Union, founded long before under the conservative auspices of the Benevolent Empire, offered a thousand dollars for the best book on "The Christian Obligations of Capital and Labor." The winning volume, by H. W. Cadman, was another typical specimen of this school.[31] Cadman believed that the present wage system had been beneficent, but that present inequalities should be adjusted by a series of miscellaneous reforms, of which the most radical was social insurance of the Bismarck type. He was moreover, willing to grant that if it were proved true that "the competitive system" did not fairly allocate the proceeds of production, it might be altered through the co-operative and profit-sharing movements. For the present, Cadman approved labor organizations as such, but warned them to eschew socialism, the closed shop and strikes. Commenting on this prize-winning volume, the *Independent* hoped that its readers would not be misled into the "dangerous error" of doubting the benefits of "the present wages system . . . the system under which labor is bought and sold as a commodity in the market. . . ."[32]

Between 1886 and 1891 Bishop Frederick Dan Huntington of Central New York, who had been interested in the church's social function since before the Civil War, moved into a position more and more friendly to organized labor. In 1886 he called for a Christian solution to the current labor conflicts, but stressed the faults of labor, which he said exaggerated its grievances.[33] By 1890, however, Huntington seemed far more concerned with the danger of a plutocracy in America.[34] The following year, in the course of a detailed and conscious attempt to lay down specific rules for labor relations, he seemed to question the validity of the existing social organization:

A system in which men and women of the wage-earning class are subjected to the control and caprice of their paymasters is not one that consistent

[30] Brown, *Studies in Modern Socialism.* The book was approved by the (Baptist) *Watchman*, December 23, 1886, p. 7; but strongly opposed by the ultraconservative *Baptist Quarterly Review*, VIII (1886), 571-573.
[31] Cadman, *The Christian Unity of Capital and Labor.*
[32] October 18, 1888, p. 7.
[33] Huntington, "Some Points in the Labor Question," *American Church Review*, XLVIII (1886), 1-20.
[34] Huntington, "Class Slavery," *Independent*, July 3, 1890, pp. 1-2.

Americans or intelligent Christians can contemplate with complacency or can encourage.

Still more surprisingly, Huntington seems by 1891 to have accepted a considerable part of the single-tax doctrine:

> Strikes become a struggle in the dark, each man dealing his blows blindly at his fellow, because neither sees the real oppressor, the monopoly of God's gifts, that is rapidly crushing both employer and employed in its relentless grasp.[35]

Julius H. Ward, another Episcopalian writer on social problems at the end of the decade, expressed some of the social tendencies that his church had derived from Anglo-Catholicism. Pleading for church unity for the social task, Ward made it clear that he meant unity under Episcopal leadership, going so far as to list the inadequacies of all other churches. Regretting that the church had partly abdicated its equal status with the state and the family, Ward asserted that, "Wherever pure Protestantism has prevailed, the social side of Christianity has been lost to a great extent." The opportunity of the church, he forthrightly stated, was "to tell the capitalist not less than the laboring man what he ought to do."[36] Naturally, not all of Ward's contemporaries of other denominations could accept these claims.

During the harsh years 1892-1895, Social Gospel analysis gained considerably in influence and volume, and reached a more complex and diverse development. It began to receive a more systematic formulation, for instance from Dean George Hodges of the Episcopal Theological School, who tried to develop the relation between eternal principles and necessary social deductions in a well-constructed volume.[37] The essential characteristics of the school did not, however, change during this period. All its exponents found fault with existing society, called for a new social spirit based on Christian love, approved the labor movement with more or less qualification, and endorsed such nonrevolutionary proposals for improvement as profit-sharing, co-operation and regulation of child labor. All disapproved contemporary socialist doctrine, but some believed that a less competitive society would some day come into existence.[38]

[35] Huntington, *Strikes, the Right and the Wrong* (New York, 1891), p. 14, 34. In his single-tax tendencies, Huntington may well have been influenced by his son, J. O. S. Huntington, who was, it will be recalled, George's leading clerical supporter in the mayoralty campaign.

[36] Ward, *The Church in Modern Society* (Boston, 1889), pp. 81, 43-44.

[37] Hodges, *The Heresy of Cain* (New York, 1894).

[38] Among the more important expressions of such opinions in this period were Charles Roads, *Christ Enthroned in the Industrial World. A Discussion of Christianity in Property and Labor* (New York, 1893); William Prall, *Civic Christianity* (New York, 1895); and Wilbur F. Crafts, *Practical Christian Sociology*, (lectures given at Princeton, 1895, 4th ed., New York, 1907).

THE SOCIAL GOSPEL AND THE CHURCHES

BY 1895 the doctrines of conservative and progressive social Christianity had been set forth in a large number of books and articles. It is, however, difficult to estimate the effect of these new teachings on the large, solid homogeneous mass of American Protestant opinion. Had they really displaced the frank, uncompromising, moralistic conservatism that had been the nearly unanimous creed of leading church circles for a generation?

It is easy to demonstrate, at least, that both conservative social Christianity and the more progressive Social Gospel had penetrated deeply into the major denominations and interdenominational organizations. Often the more conservative innovators had appeared first and held the door open for their liberal contemporaries; sometimes both groups had appeared at once with their separate explanations for some major crisis. It is clear, however, that it was the moderately progressive Social Gospel that had the more widespread and permanent effect.

Undoubtedly the Protestant Episcopal Church was the first major denomination to receive the new doctrines with any general welcome.[1] The General Convention, indeed, as an official body whose pronouncements committed the church, moved somewhat slowly. Perhaps the success of official Episcopalianism in avoiding a split over the Civil War was an influence in the direction of caution.

In the terrible year 1877 a Pennsylvania lay member of the Convention introduced a resolution calling for wider evangelistic and philanthropic work among wage earners. One of the reasons for such work was that laborers, having become separated from the church

have acquired habits of profanity, and have yielded to other corrupting influences, ruinous to their spiritual welfare, and through dangerous organizations are arraying themselves against the very capital that affords them employment. . . .[2]

[1] For a good account of the Episcopalian social movement, with emphasis on the later period, see Miller and Fletcher, *The Church and Industry.*
[2] General Convention, *Journal*, 1877, p. 25.

A Special Committee of the House of Bishops, reporting on this resolution, not only agreed with its recommendations of particular measures, but stated that "the work given to the Church in America, in guiding and directing the social movements of the age, is a work of permanent importance. . . ." Stressing the importance of Christian principles and examples among capitalists and employers, the bishops stated that groups of lay church workers such as those proposed "must be composed in large part of those who hold in trust the mighty forces of wealth and culture and social position." Commenting on the lesson of the late strikes, they mentioned persons in authority who had worked to imbue their employees with "Christian principle" and "were rewarded in the most intense crisis of the late social outbreak by the determination of these men to stand upon the side of law and order. . . ."[3] In this early crisis, that is, the General Convention expressed exactly the doctrines of the conservative social Christian theorists, concerned that the church assume a task of social amelioration for the purpose of preserving, rather than primarily of reforming, existing society.

In 1883 the General Convention, in a pastoral letter, commented specifically on the fact that in recent years "this Church has been awakened to increased practical sympathy with the worker and suffering classes; victims of social wrong, of unequal laws, of intemperance in drinks and an unscrupulous traffic in them, and sometimes of merciless wealth." In general the pastoral letter greeted this growing interest with approval, but it warned the clergy that: "A study of this popular philanthropy . . . discovers in its liberal opinion some ingredients of weakness —secularism, self-will, irreverence, intolerance, a bitter partisanship."[4]

In 1886 and in 1895 the General Convention included in its pronouncements brief and moderate statements reminding capital and labor of their mutual obligations and appealing in general terms for a Christian solution of industrial problems."[5]

The Church Congress, a semiofficial discussion group which had no power for action but considerable prestige, opened its discussions to remarkably progressive speakers at an early date. As early as 1879 Heber Newton read to this group a comparatively tolerant and serious study of

[3] *Ibid.*, pp. 267-268.
[4] *Journal*, 1883, pp. 466-467.
[5] *Journal*, 1886, pp. 564-565; *Journal*, 1895, p. 431. Arria Huntington Sessions, the daughter of Bishop F. D. Huntington and sister of J. O. S. Huntington, reports in her autobiography that she and Henry George made an effort in the early nineties to induce the General Convention to commit itself more concretely on industrial matters. This effort was praised by many clergymen. Sessions, *Sixty Odd. A Personal History* (Brattleboro, 1936), pp. 305-309.

"Communism."[6] Newton, like most men who used the term in this period, meant by "Communism" the general belief in common property ownership rather than the program of Marx and his followers, and he concluded that this belief was inevitably growing stronger. In 1884 the Congress called on Henry George to open a major discussion on the question "Is our Civilization Just to Workingmen."[7] George told his audience that misery and poverty had grown with civilization and that the working class was being deprived not only of material things but of the opportunity for mental and moral growth. Some of his hearers answered by citing Sumner and others in defense of existing society, but again Newton was there to support the radical indictment. Perhaps a still more significant discussion of the Church Congress was its 1891 symposium on "Socialism" in which the assembled church leaders heard a number of genuinely radical Christian socialists as well as single-taxers.[8] It is doubtful whether most of the people present would have listened to such opinions in any nonreligious gathering.

The Episcopal church gave birth to the first and most effective Social Gospel organizations. In 1887 a group of New York Episcopal clergy and laity founded the Church Association for the Advancement of the Interests of Labor.[9] Defining labor as "the exercise of body, mind and spirit in the broadening and elevating of human life," the CAIL stated that "Labor, thus defined, should be the standard of social worth." Bishop F. D. Huntington became its president shortly after its founding and it soon boasted more than forty bishops as vice-presidents.

CAIL, far more vigorously than any other major church organization, stressed action and practical solidarity with the labor movement.[10] Its early activities included campaigns against child labor, sweatshops and slums, and effective arbitration of strikes. From 1890 on it persuaded many New York Episcopalians to dedicate one Sunday a year to the cause of labor. Labor Sunday in 1891 was celebrated at Trinity Church with the participation of Knights of Labor delegates as well as clergy

[6] It is reprinted in his *Social Studies*, pp. 298-355.

[7] Church Congress, *Papers, Addresses and Debates*, 1884, pp. 135-183.

[8] *Papers, Addresses and Debates*, 1891, pp. 38-70.

[9] The most complete accounts of this much-discussed organization are those in Keyser, *Bishop Potter*, pp. 18 ff., and in Miller and Fletcher, *The Church and Industry*, pp. 52-76.

[10] It might be considered, in fact, to belong rather to the radical wing of social Christianity than to the larger moderate group. It is discussed here because it managed, despite activities that were radical for its time, to obtain official support and recognition to an extent that really radical Christian organizations and individuals, including Episcopalians, did not.

from all over the city. A red flag was borne in the procession.[11] In 1891, still more spectacularly, CAIL persuaded the Diocese of New York to resolve that henceforth it would allot church printing only to firms that paid union rates.[12] This sort of unusually practical gesture evidently attracted labor support, which CAIL long enjoyed more than any other church organization.

CAIL activities were regularly reported in the *Churchman* and in the press of other denominations. Perhaps because of its church support, outright hostility was less frequent than respectful criticism or even approval.

The Christian Social Union, founded in 1890 in imitation of the British organization of the same name, was considerably more conventional in its approach.[13] Like its British counterpart, it was intended primarily to further study and discussion of social questions within the church. Led by Bishops Potter and Huntington and for a time by Professor Ely, it included many clergymen who were members of CAIL and also others who took a more conservative position.

The most important product of the C.S.U. was its series of *Publications*, started in 1895, in which contemporary social theories and important events received more thorough study than most church writing had hitherto afforded. A Harvard professor of history, for instance, examined the Pullman strike under C.S.U. auspices in a manner unusually impartial for the period.[14] The Social Union and its publications were still more generally approved than CAIL.[15]

Contemporary and later leaders of the Christian social movement recognized the leadership of the Episcopalians. Some of them, like the *Christian Union*, found it paradoxical that "the Episcopal Church— the Church of wealth, culture, and aristocratic lineage—is leading the way."[16] Walter Rauschenbusch, the Baptist leader of later social Christianity, found Episcopalian interest in industrial problems particularly

[11] The *Churchman* explained that in such hands the red flag meant not destruction but Christian love. September 12, 1891, p. 315.

[12] Keyser, *Potter*, pp. 33-34.

[13] See Miller and Fletcher, *op. cit.*, pp. 77-89, and *What the Christian Social Union Is* (Christian Social Union, *Publications*, Series A, No. 6 [Boston, 1895]).

[14] W. J. Ashley, *The Railroad Strike of 1894* (Christian Social Union, *Publications*, Series B, No. 1 [Boston, 1895]).

[15] The conservative *Congregationalist*, for instance, hoped that the example would be followed in other denominations. April 30, 1891, p. 1. Yet the C.S.U.'s gains in Omaha were described with horror by a contemporary lay conservative. Frank B. Tracy, "Menacing Socialism in the Western States," *Forum*, XV (1893), 333-334.

[16] *Christian Union*, November 28, 1891, pp. 1024-1025. This statement is made in the course of editorial comment on the Church Congress discussion of socialism.

surprising in view of the fact that this church "failed to take any leading part in the older social conflicts with alcoholism and with slavery."[17]

Perhaps the paradox can be seen at its most striking in the career of W. S. Rainsford, the rector of New York City's exceedingly rich and aristocratic St. George's Church. Rainsford, a moderate exponent of the Social Gospel, had to combat his senior warden, J. Pierpont Morgan, on a series of points. The final showdown came over whether the vestry should include representatives of the wage earners whom Rainsford had attracted by his social preaching and welfare activities. Morgan's own attitude, as he frankly explained, was that democratizing the church was all very well, but that the process should stop short of the vestry. "I want it to remain a body of gentlemen whom I can ask to meet me in my study."[18] Surprisingly, the rector carried his point and persuaded Morgan not to resign.

Rainsford was frequently criticized, and another famous parishioner, Admiral Mahan, left St. George's because of his dislike of social preaching.[19] Rainsford's outspoken sympathy for labor continued, however, to increase. In 1892, just before the Homestead affair, he denounced the working conditions of steelworkers.[20] In 1895, speaking before the Church Club of Long Island, which one would hardly expect to be a pro-labor body, Rainsford said of contemporary labor leaders that "if our Lord and King were back on the earth, I believe from my soul that these men would be in His train."[21]

The most obvious explanation of Episcopalian social emphasis is the influence of English Christian Socialism, which all Episcopalian progressives and radicals heartily acknowledged. Perhaps a more fundamental explanation is the persistence of authoritative, disciplined, "church" tendencies in the American as well as in the English Episcopal tradition. Episcopalianism had never lost touch completely with the medieval dream of society guided and led by the church.

Significantly, many of the most outspoken Episcopalian Social Gospel leaders belonged to the High Church wing of the denomination, and thus had an especially lofty conception of their own status as priests. The fact that Bishops Huntington and Potter consistently backed the CAIL made it difficult for even the most conservative Episcopal laymen

---

[17] Rauschenbusch, *Christianizing the Social Order* (New York, 1912), p. 22.
[18] Rainsford, *Story of a Varied Life* (Garden City, 1924), p. 281.
[19] *Ibid.*, p. 314.
[20] *Ibid.*, pp. 323-324.
[21] Rainsford, *The Church's Opportunity in the City Today* (Christian Social Union, *Publications*, Series A, No. 8 [Boston, 1895]), p. 13.

to believe it altogether bad. Similarly, Morgan yielded not to Rainsford's arguments but to his priestly authority.

Congregationalists were generally conceded to be second in their participation in the early Social Gospel movement. All major schools of social opinion were discussed in the very diverse and influential Congregational press.[22] Interest in problems of capital and labor among national organizations of this church was especially stimulated by Josiah Strong's disclosures of urban evils in the middle eighties. In 1887 a speaker before the National Council, a body which passed resolutions but had no disciplinary power, recognized the existence of social maladjustment but was still skeptical of any concrete measures of improvement: "Improvement of *character* must precede permanent improvement in condition. . . . We hear much—not too much—of applied Christianity, but the swiftest and most effectual way to apply it, is to the heart.[23]

In 1892 the Council appointed a Committee on Capital and Labor, headed by Gladden. This committee's report to the next triennial meeting marked a considerable further step toward official recognition of the Social Gospel doctrines. It took a halfway position between those who thought the church concerned only with general principles and those who believed in backing specific measures. More important, it questioned, somewhat tentatively, the permanence of the existing economic system:

> If the wage system is so thoroughly identified with the pagan philosophy of life that it is difficult to attach any other meaning to it, then some modification of the wage system, which suggests and implies the action of goodwill, may assist in leading in a kindlier purpose.[24]

Also in the Homestead year the Massachusetts Congregational Association made a pioneering attempt to gather information on the industrial situation. A committee, again headed by Gladden, undertook to find out the opinions of employers and employees on the problems then so widely discussed.[25] The resulting report, which attracted considerable attention,

---

[22] By the nineties the *Christian Union*, theoretically interdenominational but under Congregational auspices, was the principal organ of the moderate social movement. The *Independent*, of similar origins, was still hostile. Though the *Congregationalist*, the denomination's official paper, did not take sides specifically, it frequently printed articles by leading Social Gospel spokesmen.

[23] Arthur Little, "The Time of Visitation," National Council of Congregational Churches, *Minutes*, 1887, p. 75.

[24] National Council, *Minutes*, 1895, p. 159.

[25] Gladden, "The Social and Industrial Situation," in *Bibliotheca Sacra*, XLIX (1892), 383-411.

found a nearly universal discontent with existing employment relations and a widely differing set of proposals for improvement. Asked about the possibility of nationalization, most employees and some employers favored it for some industries, with a minority of employees expressing completely socialist views.

Congregationalism was early penetrated by progressive doctrines partly because its organizational tradition was opposite to that of Episcopalianism. In the absence of any hierarchy either to assist or to oppose, the social movement, led by Gladden, made its way quickly through the free, separate churches and other institutions of the denomination. Yet in its different way Congregationalism too harked back to a tradition of control of worldly matters by ministerial precept, the tradition of Geneva and, more directly, of the New England beginnings. Educational leadership particularly was part of this group's proudest heritage.

Congregationalism, moreover, had been exposed more directly than any other orthodox group to the liberal impulses generated by Unitarianism in the early nineteenth century. Again, some Congregationalists saw the new proposals for social reform as successors to antislavery and other reform movements which they considered a part of their tradition. The humanitarian spirit of the new theology had deeply affected the denomination's liberal wing. Undoubtedly Congregationalist interest in labor problems was increased by concentration in industrial New England and her midwestern offshoots. All these causes combined to produce a church open, though not without a struggle, to new ideas and willing to espouse them with vigor.

The Methodists, largest of American Protestant denominations, lagged distinctly behind the two leaders in the development of the new social doctrines. This seems at first glance as surprising as the Episcopalian leadership. Methodists had always prided themselves on being a church of the poor and lowly. In America they had long taken an active part in every political movement that involved moral questions. Resolutions on Reconstruction, the Mormon question, temperance and the like were continually being passed by the General Conference and subordinate bodies.

Yet advocates of the Social Gospel received only an occasional hearing in official Methodist circles. In 1884 a memorial on justice to labor was presented to the General Conference, but buried in committee.[26] Four years later the Address of the Bishops did recognize the existence of the

[26] Garrison, *The March of Faith,* p. 163.

"labor problem," though its language was hardly that of the Social Gospel:

That millions of laborers, compactly organized under leaderships liable to become unscrupulous, chafing under real or fancied grievances, are an element of great power and no little danger is a fact too palpable to be concealed or overlooked.[27]

As remedies, the bishops recommended evangelism and emphasis on the true spiritual doctrines of the church.

At the next quadrennial meeting the Address again discussed the increase of social conflict, but this time it emphasized such causes as "the rapid accumulation of enormous wealth in the hands of a few successful speculators" and "the grinding and soulless arrogance of monopolies, working impoverishment to the masses." Despite this radical-sounding language, however, the bishops' position remained more defensive than reformist. The reason they gave for deploring these conditions was that they "are exciting hate and arousing tendencies which will be more and more difficult to repress, and which, if not arrested, will breed riot and revolution."[28] And the only remedies the bishops suggested were preaching to the rich their perils and responsibilities and to the poor the familiar doctrine of patience. The Report to the 1896 meeting was similar, except that it added concrete endorsements of arbitration and profit-sharing.[29]

Probably the fundamental reasons why the Methodists did not contribute a large share of the early leadership of the social movement lay in the church's history. The artisans and small shopkeepers that had filled the ranks of British Methodism since its patristic days had been particularly fervent in their championship of the individualist virtues of frugality and hard work. In America the church had found its greatest mass of converts among the farmers, and recently the influence of wealthy businessmen had risen sharply. Both these groups long looked askance at any departure from John Wesley's oft-repeated injunctions in favor of hard work, accumulation and charity. Industrial workers and advanced intellectuals were the first groups to feel the influence of new collectivist currents; neither group was strongly represented in Methodism. Only in the early twentieth century, when progressive social reform had become the creed of much of the American middle class, did

[27] General Conference, *Journal*, 1888, p. 58.
[28] General Conference, *Journal*, 1892, p. 56.
[29] *Ibid.*, 1896, pp. 58-60.

Methodists contribute to the Social Gospel movement in proportion to their numbers, discipline and fervency.[30]

A second obstacle was the church's conservative and individualistic theology. Filled more than any other denomination with revivalist traditions, Methodism long insisted on sin as the sufficient explanation of all social evil, and individual redemption as the only remedy. In 1882, for instance, the *Christian Advocate* pointed with fear and warning toward the growing influence of Bushnellism, citing such social Christians as Gladden and Munger as prime examples of the dangerous theological tendency.[31]

The problems of the Baptist social movement were similar in many ways. The Baptists also had a large rural membership and they too were affected by the growing influence of rich laymen, especially their great and pious benefactor, John D. Rockefeller.[32] Baptist theology inherited many conservative strains from its complex history. Traditional Baptist "separateness" and hostility to the state made the denomination tend toward suspicion of movements to control or rebuild worldly society. Yet, through the existence of a small but influential Social Gospel minority, the social movement made earlier headway than among the Methodists.

This important minority began its activities in New York City in the late eighties. From the start it was headed by Walter Rauschenbusch, who was to become the greatest leader of social Christianity thirty years later. Other early leaders, later well known, included Leighton Williams and Samuel Zane Batten. In 1889 this devoted group began to publish a paper, *For the Right.*[33] This publication, which lasted only eighteen months, called itself "Christian socialist" but was actually no more radical than Gladden and the other moderate social Christians.

In 1892 the same group organized the Brotherhood of the Kingdom, one of the most important of the early Social Gospel groups.[34] The Brotherhood played an important part in the development of social theology, emphasizing the immanence of God, the organic nature of society, and especially the realization of Christ's kingdom on earth

[30] See K. E. Barnhart, "The Evolution of Social Consciousness in Methodism" (MS Ph.D. thesis, University of Chicago, [1924]), pp. 127-141.

[31] August 17, 1882, p. 513.

[32] See R. H. Johnson, "American Baptists in the Age of Big Business," *Journal of Religion*, XI (1931), 63-85.

[33] There is a thorough account of this paper, with many quotations, in Sharpe, *Walter Rauschenbusch*, pp. 86-104. See also W. D. P. Bliss, *Encyclopedia of Social Reform* (New York, 1897), p. 141.

[34] A very complete account of this organization is C. H. Hopkins, "Rauschenbusch and the Brotherhood of the Kingdom," *Church History*, VII (1938), 138-156.

through the gradual growth of the brotherhood of man. The existence of a group with such an approach in the Baptist denomination, with its intense millennial emphasis, was particularly important.

Meeting yearly on the summer estate of Williams' father, the Brotherhood attracted liberals and progressives from outside the Baptist fold, including Henry Demarest Lloyd. Like the Christian Social Union, it emphasized study and discussion more than social action, and its early energies were principally occupied by general ethical and philosophical problems. Though it did not receive the wide contemporary publicity accorded some other organizations, it influenced the thinking of many important church leaders. Doubtless it gained strength from its almost uniquely lofty conception of its own mission: "We dare to hope that with the good favor of our God we may become a kind of organized conscience, and that as the days go by the voice of our Brotherhood may bear the accents of the Holy Ghost.[35]

Quite early, the Brotherhood and the rest of the Social Gospel minority made their voices heard in the councils of this conservative denomination, particularly in the Baptist Congress for the Discussion of Current Questions, organized in 1882. In 1885, before the Brotherhood was formed, the Congress showed little if any Social Gospel influence in a discussion of socialism. Some speakers represented the old conservatism at its most outspoken: "It seems to me that the best thing we can do is to go on as we have been going on. Let us leave the next generation to take care of itself. . . . I think there is such a thing as coddling the poor too much."[36]

In a similar discussion the following year most of the speakers expressed conservative views, but the Social Gospel position was presented by Philip Moxom, who termed the laissez faire doctrines "heartless and selfish" and insisted that, however mistaken were the methods of contemporary radicals, "Christianity is not individualistic but socialistic."[37]

In 1887 the Congress spent a large part of its session discussing the theories of Henry George and Bellamy in relation to "Natural and Artificial Monopolies."[38] Rauschenbusch expressed great admiration for the single-tax theorist, and other speakers, including Williams, treated both George and Bellamy with respect. In 1892, the year in which

[35] S. Z. Batten, "The Brotherhood of the Kingdom," *The Kingdom*, July 19, 1895, p. 3.
[36] Edward Bright, in Baptist Congress for the Discussion of Current Questions, *Proceedings*, 1885, pp. 33-34.
[37] *Proceedings*, 1886, pp. 42-43.
[38] *Ibid.*, 1887, pp. 47-71.

Rauschenbusch became secretary of the Congress, a series of speakers discussed "The Pulpit in Relation to Political and Social Reform." Most agreed with Thomas Dixon, Jr., of New York that: "If Christianity has no word social to the twentieth century, it will perish, for the twentieth century is to be the social era of the race."[39]

The 1893 discussions demonstrated in remarkably clear and dramatic terms the sharp division in the denomination. In a discussion of "The Church and the Money Power" the alternative was clearly stated by W. H. P. Faunce:

> The church must either adopt the position of Tolstoi that wealth is sin, and then take active part in the immediate reorganization of the social order; or it must recognize wealth, like knowledge, as a divine trust and develop the sense of responsibility by making its rich men responsible.

Faunce left little doubt where he personally stood:

> The man who possesses a fortune is *nolens volens* a benefactor to the community. He may be a misanthrope and atheist. But if such a man moves into a western city and begins to spend his money in the most selfish and ostentatious luxury, he is an involuntary benefactor to that city.

Twenty years before, such sentiments would have gone almost unchallenged, but Faunce, speaking in 1893, was conscious of the existence of a very different body of opinion:

> I am sorry for Christian ministers, usually of tender age, who rush into the market place with a sociological poultice for all the ills that the body politic is heir to, and thus would commit a Christianity of nineteen centuries to a philosophic theory not yet out of the cradle.

And Rauschenbusch, representing exactly the group to which Faunce referred, was on hand to answer:

> I hold that the church and money power are not friends, but enemies, opposed to each other in the same sense in which God and the world are opposed to each other. . . . The church is both a partial realization of the new society, in which God's will is done, and also the appointed instrument for the further realization of that new society in the world about it.[40]

Far less concerned in the early social movement than any other major church were the Presbyterians. Their periodicals, for the most part, held fast to the traditional social theories. Though the General Assembly fairly often discussed city evils, radicalism and strikes as menaces to

[39] *Ibid.*, 1892, p. 122.
[40] *Ibid.*, 1893, pp. 4-11.

society, it showed little effort to formulate suggestions for improvement. In 1888, Joseph T. Smith, in his Moderator's Sermon, made one of the few Social Gospel statements heard by the General Assembly in the period. Even Smith defined the church's duties in terms by no means radical:

The Church is not a divider of inheritances among men. Questions as to the equitable distribution of profits between employers and employed, questions between Capital and Labor, are beyond its jurisdiction. But it proclaims the great law of the Kingdom, which requires justice, aye, and kindness, too, from both, and forbids selfishness in either.[41]

Rather curiously, no similar statement was made in the early nineties, when the only references to social problems were appeals to evangelism to overcome the radical threat.

Presbyterian participants in the social movement were as yet scattered and isolated. In 1895, for instance, a preacher before the Presbytery of San Francisco argued that competition was fundamentally un-Christian and socialism Christian.[42] Social Christianity was to gain a hearing in the church's national councils only after the turn of the century, under the leadership of Charles Stelzle.

The reasons for the relative conservatism of this denomination are obvious. Its members, especially the influential city elements, were traditionally of the upper social and economic groups. Through the important part played by elders in Presbyterian church government, wealthy laymen had an especially influential role.

Official Presbyterianism was still defending Calvinist determinism against the inroads of humanitarian theology. Champions of the old beliefs made full use of the denomination's strict, authoritarian system of church government, which was only beginning to lose its effectiveness. Aristocratic traditions and theological conservatism were not, as in the case of the Episcopalians, balanced by an especially influential overseas radical movement.

Thus the relative strength of the Social Gospel in the various churches depended on a great many special factors, geographical, traditional and perhaps personal. In each of the major denominations, however, the new doctrines were alive and growing.

Social Gospel teachings were still more in evidence in early interdenominational organizations. One must remember that, since church unity

[41] General Assembly, *Minutes*, 1888, p. 162.
[42] J. E. Scott, *Socialism, What is It? Is it Christian? Should the Church Take any Interest in it?* (pamphlet, San Francisco, 1895).

itself was a young and controversial movement, those who participated tended to be the more liberal-minded churchmen.[43]

The American Congress of Churches, founded in 1884, devoted a major part of its second session, at Cleveland in 1886, to a discussion of "The Workingman's Distrust of the Church; Its Causes and Remedies." This topic and the arguments presented were conventional enough and did not imply any very definite tendency toward social criticism. The Congress took a new departure, however, in inviting the Knights of Labor, who happened to be meeting in Cleveland at the same time, to join the discussion. Powderly and a number of others accepted and a long account of the Congress was included in a contemporary volume of official Knights' propaganda.[44] Speakers such as Henry George and John Jarrett of the Amalgamated Iron and Steel Workers presented their views on church problems, urging the ministers to study labor's point of view.

The Interdenominational Congress, called by Josiah Strong in 1885 to discuss problems of the city, heard typical Social Gospel views presented by Strong, Gladden, Professor Ely, Lyman Abbott, and others.[45] A more important forum was the Evangelical Alliance for the U.S.A. From the time Strong became General Secretary in 1886 this powerful group became one of the principal outlets for social Christian discussion.[46] In 1893 the widely-publicized Parliament of Religions at the Chicago World's Fair gave several Social Gospel spokesmen an opportunity of speaking to a world audience as official representatives of American Christianity.[47]

One of the most concrete evidences of the spread of new doctrines was the increasing emphasis on sociology in the theological seminaries.[48]

[43] For identification and history of the earlier and more obscure interchurch organizations, see Abell, *Urban Impact,* pp. 88-100.

[44] *Labor: Its Rights and Wrongs* (Washington, D.C., 1886), pp. 230-272.

[45] A fairly full account can be found in the *Christian Union,* December 17, 1885, pp. 6-8.

[46] See for instance Evangelical Alliance for the U.S.A., *Christianity Practically Applied* (New York, 1894), II, 550-554 (Ely), 568-595 (Gladden). No new contributions to Christian social thought were developed in the Alliance's voluminous discussions.

[47] F. G. Peabody, "Christianity and the Social Question," *Neely's History of the Parliament of Religions,* etc., II, 526-535; Gladden, "Religion and Wealth," *ibid.,* II, 568-575.

[48] This subject is very thoroughly discussed in Abell, *Urban Impact,* pp. 224-245; Dombrowski, *Early Days of Christian Socialism,* pp. 60-73. A good account by a participant is found in W. J. Tucker, *My Generation* (Boston, 1919), pp. 169-177. An excellent contemporary summary, emphasizing the connection of the sociological movement in seminaries with the increasing maturity of academic social sciences in America is Graham Taylor, "Sociological Training for the Ministry," Evangelical Alliance, *Christianity Practically Applied,* pp. 396-413. Taylor included a table showing the introduction of such courses at various institutions.

Settlement work, as well as the tendency toward pulpit discussion of social problems, made some understanding of new conditions and theories an obvious necessity for young ministers. As early as 1881 when sociology was taught in very few American institutions and while college economics was still firmly controlled by the school of clerical laissez faire, Andover Seminary and Harvard Divinity School had begun to experiment in teaching social ethics. By the middle nineties some form of social study was available at most seminaries and required at a few. Men like Francis Peabody at Harvard, William Jewett Tucker at Andover, and Graham Taylor at Chicago were making sure that the social Christian movement would grow in volume in the next generation.

As the Social Gospel moved into the seminary curriculum, discussion in the pulpit and press became intellectualized. The new generation of social Christian leaders, instead of trying to formulate their own shocked reactions to critical events or disturbing conditions, began to show a firmer grasp of contemporary social and economic thought. Social Christianity also developed somewhat closer and more complex relations with modern theology, philosophy and science.

One can see the effects of the new studies of ministerial candidates particularly clearly in the books of ethics written by clerical authorities for study in church and secular institutions. In 1885 a textbook by President Noah Porter of Yale still taught theories closely akin to those of Francis Wayland and other authorities of the prewar period. Porter declared, for instance, that "to contend against the existing tenures and law of property as immoral" was to commit "the moral crime of demagoguism," which was "equally serious, whether it be committed in the political harangue, the declamatory pulpit, the journalist's editorial, or the professor's chair."[49]

Borden P. Bowne's *The Principles of Ethics* was transitional. A Methodist professor at Boston University, Bowne rejected the old doctrine that the state should be restricted to police duty. He was willing to endorse legislation for "protecting public interests from private rapacity" and "establishing a lower limit to competition, so that it shall not result in the destruction of women and children and in the abomination of the sweater's den." But Bowne warned his readers against the "current social agitation" which went beyond these purposes. Like his predecessors, he criticized socialists and other radicals for blaming on society ills that were often the fault of individuals. In the long run, the only hope was the inculcation of such traditional virtues as prudence, thrift and justice, and Bowne emphasized that "The poor need to do this quite as much as the rich. Witness the tyranny and inhumanity of labor unions toward non-unionists."[50] Bowne, that is, was in essential agreement with the most conservative, defensive wing of the new social movement.

In the same year that Bowne's book was published, however, Newman Smyth, one of the leaders of liberal theological thought, brought out a textbook of Christian ethics that clearly adhered to the new progressive doctrines. Smyth substituted evolutionary concepts for the rigid and simple dogmas of earlier moralists, declaring that "A feudal virtue might be the industrial crime of a later age," and that "Virtue, as moral health, must have some fitness to its social conditions." He discussed each of the traditional virtues in a social context, saying of justice for instance that its "whole duty" was "not fulfilled in the life of the man who, though himself just, has no will to get justice done in the world." Like Bowne, and like most Social Gospel spokesmen, Smyth rejected socialism but insisted that in this rejection "we are far from denying that there can be any change in the existing order. . . ."[51] Now such social and relativistic morality could be taught as a part of Christian ethics by a leading authority. Only a short time before the individualistic virtues had been universally proclaimed as part of an unshifting Divine Law.

Despite the considerable victories of the Social Gospel, it must not be thought that the new views had gained any easy or complete victory, in the nineties or at any other period. It would be easy to underestimate the continuing strength of Christian conservatism. Because many of the articulate, intellectual church leaders had adhered to the Social Gospel, few of the new religious books of the 1890's defended the old economic and social theories. Yet, as we have seen, a large section of the religious press with a strong circulation stuck to the old assumptions in its interpretation of events and in its reviews of current books. Obviously wealthy and conservative laymen had not lost their influence in denominational councils. Many members of all social classes, in the churches and outside, stuck to the undiluted belief in individualism that has always maintained such strength in America. Doctrines of hard work and saving that had formed part of Protestant teaching for centuries and had been most successfully acclimatized in the United States did not lose their hold in one generation of argument. By no means all conservative Protestants had even advanced to the defensive, cautious reform views of Behrends and his school; many stuck stoutly to the old insistence that all was well and no reform was necessary.

[50] Bowne, *Principles* (New York, 1885), pp. 259-266.
[51] Smyth, *Christian Ethics*, pp. 218-219, 378, 456.

One of the evidences of Social Gospel strength, in fact, was the growth of an aroused, combative conservative opposition to the movement inside leading Protestant circles. Not only did conservative critics condemn every particular proposition advanced by the Social Gospel advocates, they also frequently deplored the very existence of such a movement. Often they commenced their critiques by reasserting the old economic "laws" and then, unconscious of the contradiction, insisted that social science was no fit topic for ministers of the gospel.

As early as 1886 a writer in the *New Princeton Review* noted with alarm that clergymen were endorsing profit sharing, speaking tolerantly of socialism, and otherwise giving evidence of economic ignorance.[52] In the following year the *Independent*, commenting on the nearly simultaneous appearance of books by T. E. Brown, Gladden and Newton, stated one of the most typical arguments of conservative Christianity: ". . . the final fault and danger in books like this is that they lead people into the delusive hope that it is the machinery that is out of joint and not human nature."[53]

A torrent of objection was aroused in 1891 when the *Methodist Review* printed a piece stating that individual regeneration was not a sufficient solution of social problems. One of several articles which denounced this view overstated and then ridiculed the claims of the social Christians:

> That the "great question" for the church to-day concerns the distribution of wealth is a surprising proposition. The great question in this, as in old times, is of righteousness, temperance, and judgment to come. . . . The Gospel, in fact, shows a certain contempt for material things. . . . Fancy the religious effect upon the hearers of a minister's urging the single-tax on land to farmers, or preaching to Republicans that a protective tariff is robbery. . . .[54]

In 1894 the *Watchman*, admitting that "the Christian ideal" contemplates a "reign of brotherliness," urged social-minded Christians to remember several other religious truths. In the first place, the editors declared, Christianity taught the necessity of "rendering an equivalent" for one's daily bread. Second, the Christian society "is the outcome of a spirit, and cannot be imposed from without. . . ." Finally, the *Watchman* alleged that "the very men who are most strenuous in preaching the

[52] Henry W. Farnam, "The Clergy and the Labor Question," *New Princeton Review*, II (1886), 48-61.

[53] *Independent*, July 14, 1887, pp. 9-10.

[54] J. E. Learned, "The Church and the World," *Methodist Review*, LXXXIV (1892), 434-437. The article which aroused this criticism was C. M. Morse, "Regeneration as a force in Social Movements," *Methodist Review*, LXXXIII (1891), 923-931. Hopkins regards this article as having special importance. *Rise of the Social Gospel*, pp. 171-172.

198 *Social Christianity, 1877-1895*

Christian Society are often those who manifest the least brotherliness themselves."[55]

Such criticisms as these, ranging from sweeping denunciation to careful and tolerant disagreement, undoubtedly represented the reactions of thousands of sincere Protestants to the early Social Gospel. Most church members had, after all, been taught since childhood that America's traditions of religious, political and economic individualism were the last stage in human progress, the final working out of the Divine Plan. In many cases, these beliefs were too strong to be shaken even by the social crises of the nineties.

Not all American Protestants, of course, found it necessary to take sides either for or against the Social Gospel. A considerable number continued to be ignorant of its existence. Only rarely and slowly did it penetrate rural areas, where conservative theology was still entrenched and experience of industrial crisis was slight. In the South sectional hostility toward theories coming from the northern cities was added to all other causes for resistance.[56]

Popular evangelists continued to wield immense power. Their insistent emphasis on the all-importance of individual redemption, their emotional preaching technique, their lack of contact with modern social thought made them and their followers another stumbling block to social Christianity. In 1886 T. DeWitt Talmage, a leading revivalistic preacher who seldom mentioned social topics, contributed a sermon on "Capital and Labor" to a Knights of Labor symposium. Mystical and verbose, this oration was the exact opposite of the comparatively practical, simple discussions of Gladden or Newton. Its rapt peroration, probably without much meaning to an audience of union members, illustrates the difficulty of combining revivalism and social Christianity:

The hard hand of the wheel and the soft hand of the counting-room will clasp each other yet. They will clasp each other in congratulation. They will clasp each other on the glorious morning of the millennium. The hard hand will say: "I plowed the desert into a garden"; the soft hand will reply, "I furnished the seed." . . . Then capital and labor will lie down together, and the lion and the lamb, and the leopard and the kid, and there will be nothing to hurt or destroy in all God's holy mount, for the mouth of the Lord hath spoken it.[57]

[55] *Watchman*, July 21, 1894, p. 4.
[56] The slow and late penetration of Southern Methodism by the Social Gospel is discussed by H. D. Farish, *The Circuit Rider Dismounts. A Social History of Southern Methodism*, 1865-1900 (Richmond, 1938), pp. 332-335.
[57] *Labor: Its Rights and Wrongs*, pp. 315-321.

Millennial sects, as always, insisted that the sole duty of a Christian was to prepare for the coming cataclysm. Social and political problems could not concern the saving remnant except as an evidence of the approaching Last Days. A typical and highly successful prophet of extreme millennarianism, writing in the crisis year 1886, said of social controversy: "The Lord had no time for it; the apostles had no time for it; nor have any of the saints who are following their example."[58] Millions of American Christians who did not belong to extremist cults yet continued to be more or less preoccupied with the approach of the Judgment.

Even among those who did not confine their preaching either to personal salvation or apocalyptic warning, many resisted the slightest concession to social criticism. Russell H. Conwell, founder of Philadelphia Temple, the greatest of institutional churches and the germ of Temple University, was certainly not exclusively other-worldly in his interests. He was, however, one of the period's outstanding champions of the old attitudes toward wealth and poverty. Conwell, who left a prosperous business after a wealthy marriage to devote himself to a fabulously successful preaching career, exemplified in his own life a quality he greatly admired, "the inspired, sanctified, common sense of enterprising business men."[59]

Conwell's masterpiece, *Acres of Diamonds*, one of the most popular lectures in history, was, according to the orator's own estimate, delivered six thousand times with total earnings of eight million dollars.[60] An old-fashioned inspirational piece of the simplest sort, this phenomenal oration was based on the legend (told to Conwell by an "Arab guide") of the man who exhausted himself searching for diamonds while a rich jewel mine lay right in his back yard. In uncompromising terms, the lecturer insisted that anybody could get rich with whatever opportunities lay at hand: ". . . unless some of you get richer for what I am saying to-night my time is wasted." "I say that you ought to get rich, and it is your duty to get rich." As it had been for generations, success was linked to morality: ". . . ninety-eight out of one hundred of the rich men of America are honest. That is why they are rich."

[58] Pastor Charles Taze Russell, *The Plan of the Ages* ("Studies in the Scriptures," Series 1 [Brooklyn, 1913, cop. 1886]), p. 268. This publication of the Watch Tower Bible and Tract Society claimed by 1918 a circulation of 5 million copies. For an interesting account of the origins and present status of millennial sects, throwing considerable light on their social conservatism, see Elmer T. Clark, *The Small Sects in America* (Nashville, 1937).
[59] Quoted in A. R. Burr, *Russell H. Conwell and his Work* (Philadelphia, 1917), p. 227. For biographical information see also the biographical sketch by Robert Shackleton, in Conwell, *Acres of Diamonds* (New York, 1915), pp. 63-170.
[60] Burr, *Conwell*, p. 314.

Naturally, Conwell believed in the converse of this simple rule, the depravity of the poor:

I won't give in but what I sympathize with the poor, but the number of poor who are to be sympathized with is very small. To sympathize with a man whom God has punished for his sins, thus to help him when God would still continue a just punishment, is to do wrong, no doubt about it. . . .[61]

The continuing great popularity of this lecture and others like it demonstrates that a great many American Christians still believed that the old virtues of self-help were a sufficient solution to social problems and were sanctioned by Christian morality. Examples could be multiplied to show that a large part of American Protestantism rejected the teachings of social Christianity on religious, moral and economic grounds.

Estimates of the progress of the Social Gospel made by the movement's early leaders varied all the way from extreme optimism to deep pessimism. T. E. Brown, writing in 1886, cited denominational bodies, the church press and prominent individuals in such a way as to imply that the movement was becoming general:

Pastors of wealthy churches . . . are stirring the consciences of their parishioners with gospel ethics of trade and gospel principles for a pure social order, that but a while ago would have been dreamed most fanatical and revolutionary. The world moves, and God is in its movement.[62]

W. D. P. Bliss, the leader of the Christian socialists, answering a charge by Powderly that the clergy took no interest in labor, managed to list not only thirty-two Christian socialists but thirty-one more ministers who were actively identified either with the Knights of Labor or the Nationalists, and sixty more who were either interested in labor or members of the American Economic Association. Adding 269 members of the Christian Social Union, he concluded that there must be another 269 non-Episcopalians interested to the same degree, making a total of "662 clergymen deeply interested in the labor problem. We presume that there are several hundred more, whom we have omitted."[63] To Bliss,

---

[61] Conwell, *Acres*, pp. 18, 19, 21.

[62] Brown, *Studies in Modern Socialism*, p. 226.

[63] Bliss, *Dawn*, November 16, 1892, p. 2. A far more extravagant Christian socialist statement was that of F. M. Sprague, who deduced from similar evidence that "Probably three-fourths of all Christian ministers in the country are in sympathy with the demands of working men." Sprague, *Socialism from Genesis to Revelation* (Boston, 1893), p. 451. Vague criteria, overlapping opinions and unrepresentative selection make most contemporary attempts to "sample" clerical opinion almost equally valueless, except as examples of opinion. *Public Opinion*, for instance, found in 1886 that fourteen out of fifteen ministers queried believed in applying the principles of Christianity to the labor question from the pulpit, but their definitions of this application varied widely. *Public Opinion*, I (1886), 67-69.

always an optimist, this figure seemed to give cause for rejoicing, but if one considers it as the total of social-minded ministers known or even imagined by the most active Christian radical of the period, it hardly seems impressive.

Richard T. Ely, commenting forty years later on the movement for social Christianity in the nineties, listed a large number of pioneers and remembered that "many Protestants . . . strove mightily to bring about a better social order."[64]

Less optimistic members of the early movement included Dean George Hodges, who believed in 1894 that "Many members of the church are enthusiastically disposed towards the cause of the workingman, but not all; probably less than a majority." Hodges' analysis of the opposing majority was acute:

The church, as an organization, contains these three kinds of people,— those who thus limit the functions of the church and stand aloof from any combination between religion and economics; those who are well off themselves and do not care, preferring the present conditions for selfish reasons; and those who are not prepared to go very far in the labor movement because they see the other side, men of wealth, careful and conservative, knowing their own business sometimes better than we do. . . .[65]

Walter Rauschenbusch, looking back from 1912, described the movement in the nineties as a desperate, lonely struggle:

. . . all whose recollection runs back of 1900 will remember that as a time of lonesomeness. We were few, and we shouted in the wilderness. It was always a happy surprise when we found a new man who had seen the light. We used to form a kind of flying wedge to support a man who was preparing to attack a ministers' conference with the Social Gospel. Our older friends remonstrated with us for wrecking our careers. We ourselves saw the lions' den plainly before us, and only wondered how the beasts would act this time.[66]

Rauschenbusch's feeling of isolation might be attributed to the relative slowness of his church in entering the social movement. An Episcopalian clergyman in New York City, however, could well have considered himself in the center of a growing movement. Yet W. S. Rainsford said in his autobiography that "in the early 'nineties I was practically alone among the clergy of the Protestant Episcopal Church in attacking the social conditions among the poor—and the rich, too—in New York."[67]

[64] Ely, *Ground under Our Feet*, p. 94.
[65] Hodges, *Heresy of Cain*, p. 62.
[66] Rauschenbusch, *Christianizing the Social Order*, p. 9.
[67] Rainsford, *Story of a Varied Life*, p. 313. This statement was obviously much exaggerated.

Leonard Bacon's *History of American Christianity*, published in 1897, described the Social Gospel movement accurately and with approval, but concluded: "Thus far there is not much of history to be written under this head, but somewhat of prophecy."[68]

These differing accounts are not as surprising as they seem. Through the middle nineties the Social Gospel movement was probably numerically small. Many ministers and laymen had little contact with it; zealous progressive leaders sometimes felt isolated in their struggle against the conservative mass. Yet from a more distant view it is clear, as it was to some contemporary observers, that in a single generation the social movement in the churches had accomplished a great deal. It was a minority, but it included many of the most articulate, best educated, most zealous of American Christians. The Social Gospel was well represented already in denominational and interdenominational organizations, in the seminaries, in the press, and in some of the nation's most commanding pulpits. A very considerable body of Social Gospel literature already existed and was widely read; more was appearing yearly. Progressive social Christianity had captured much of the present, and even more of the future, church leadership.

The rigid dogmas of religious and economic individualism were still strong. Yet this set of ideas, which had dominated American Christianity for several generations, was everywhere on the defensive.

By 1895, moreover, the Social Gospel was mature. It contained variety; its doctrines were stated in different terms by different individuals. Social Gospel pronouncements were no longer couched in the timid and tentative language used by men conscious of defying well-established opinion. Believers in the new doctrines were well organized for mutual support. Younger leaders had appeared, better educated than the pioneers, ready to develop the social interpretation of Christianity on a more complex level. The movement was started, by 1895, on all the paths it was to follow in later years.

The later development of the Social Gospel is a comparatively familiar story.[69] From 1895 on through the Progressive Era of the early twentieth

---

[68] Bacon, *A History of American Christianity* ("American Church History Series," XIII), 385-386.

[69] For convenient summaries of the social movement after 1895, see Hopkins, *Rise of the Social Gospel*, pp. 245-316; Visser 'T Hooft, *Background of the Social Gospel*, pp. 24 ff.; Mathews, "Development of Social Christianity in America," in *Religious Thought in the Last Quarter-Century*, pp. 228-239; Harris, *A Century's Change*, pp. 55-267. An interesting evaluation of recent tendencies is John Coleman Bennett, "The Social Interpretation of Christianity," in *The Church Through Half a Century, Essays in Honor of William Adams Brown* (New York, 1936), pp. 113-129.

century, the doctrines developed by the generation of Gladden and New-ton increasingly dominated the most articulate sections of American Protestantism. Though their essential character remained much the same, they were elaborated, reapplied and given more thorough theological exposition by Walter Rauschenbusch and other leaders. The fullest measure of victory was achieved with the organization of the Federal Council of the Churches of Christ in America in 1908. In this federation, representing the liberal elements in all denominations, Social Gospel advocates were able to put American Protestantism officially and repeat-edly on record in comparatively concrete terms as a warm supporter of labor's cause. Though the First World War was a drastic blow to the optimistic and ordinarily pacifistic assumptions of progressive Christians, the Social Gospel retained a considerable measure of vitality during the early nineteen-twenties, when many forms of progressivism went into temporary eclipse.

Many acute observers of recent Christianity agree, however, that the Social Gospel has not proven entirely adequate to the terrifying and complex issues of the last two decades. Since the late twenties, many leaders of American Protestantism have either abandoned or drastically restated the simple social doctrines that had won such notable victories. A turn toward a more transcendent and "realistic" theology in Europe and America has cut away some of the religious basis of the Social Gospel. In the last bitter decade, religious progressivism has lost prestige and self-confidence along with all varieties of optimistic liberalism. Yet progressive social Christianity remains characteristic of a large section of American Protestantism, and some of its leaders feel that it still has a role to play, perhaps in a new, hardened more mature form.

Whatever its later fate, it is clear that the Social Gospel had acquired considerable strength in American Protestantism by the early nineties. Partly because this was a period of crisis in American social thought, this new and vigorous set of religious doctrines was able to make its influence felt far beyond the obvious bounds of official Protestantism.

THE SOCIAL GOSPEL AND AMERICAN
PROGRESSIVISM

B ASIC to any discussion of the influence of the Social Gospel or any
other religious doctrine, is the question of the hold of Protestant
teaching on the American people. Did Americans turn to the churches
for help when they found themselves suddenly confronted with the
gigantic problems of a new industrialism? Or were the hot arguments
among churchmen conducted for the sole benefit of an especially pious
group, diminishing before the advance of materialism and skepticism?

Certainly there was no statistical evidence that the churches had even
begun to lose their hold. In 1876 an optimistic clerical computer had
estimated only eight million church members; in 1880 Daniel Dorchester
put the total for "Evangelical Denominations" at over ten million.[1] The
figures of Henry K. Carroll, who compiled for the Census of 1890 more
complete religious statistics than had previously been available, indicated
that Protestant church members then numbered over fourteen million.[2]

The influence of the pulpit, however, cannot be measured by statistics
alone. As many church spokesmen admitted, other evidence indicated
some decline in church authority. The wage-earning class was generally
believed to be largely alienated. The long retreat before the new scientific
theories, though perhaps it had brought the church to more defensible
positions, had led to losses among the best-educated groups. Ministers,
once the unquestioned leaders in almost every field of thought, had to
share their place increasingly with scientists and social scientists. For the
more sophisticated portions of the American urban public in the nineties,
simple authoritative statements had lost much of their power. Many knew
that differences of opinion existed inside the church itself on every
theological, scientific and social question. Protestant publicists, insisting

---

[1] See p. 42; Dorchester, *Problem of Religious Progress*, p. 544.

[2] Henry K. Carroll, "Report on Statistics of Churches in the United States, at the
Eleventh Census: 1890," *U.S. Eleventh Census*, IX. The above result is obtained by
subtracting Carroll's computations of Catholic and Jewish bodies (xi, xii) from his
grand totals (xiii). His results were also published with comments as Carroll, *Religious Forces of the United States* ("American Church History Series," I [New
York, 1893]).

frequently that religion was *not* losing its hold, allowed a somewhat defensive, un-self-confident note to creep into their statements.

By the nineties church authority had probably begun to lessen. Whatever decline existed, however, was slow. Forces that were undermining Protestant authority were subtle; traditions that sustained it were clear and obvious. Large sections of the population still looked to the pulpit for partial guidance on many matters. While ministers no longer dominated social thinking completely, they were still among the few most influential groups. Symposia on industrial and social problems still made a point of including samples of ministerial opinion.[3] Commercial publishers still found it worthwhile to publish a large number of books by clergymen on the more controversial questions of the day. In 1891 a writer in the *Chautauquan*, doubtless representing adequately the beliefs of the churchgoing middle class, could still say that

> The greatest individual influence in social science is undoubtedly that of the preacher and pastor. He it is who most frequently arouses and informs the individual conscience, from which must come all sense of responsibility.
> Is the preacher's influence really decreasing? No—emphatically no!

The evidence cited for this assertion was probably accurate:

> If any one doubts the immense social influence of the preacher let him observe the ways of men who have any social reform in view. Be they hardheaded men of business, or even avowed infidels, they never attempt [to further a social reform] unless they first strive to enlist the sympathies of the clergy. . . . A public meeting for any but political purposes is almost unknown without preachers being, by special invitation, among its active participants. . . .[4]

The new movements of social Christianity were in a position to exert a great deal of whatever weight organized Protestantism still possessed. They represented an interesting new departure and yet were seldom so radical as to repel completely the middle-class public. Often, outside as well as inside church circles, the most conservative variety of social Christianity broke a path for the more progressive Social Gospel. The new beliefs offered a reassuring standpoint from which to examine new problems of great concern to most Americans. They commanded the

---

[3] As examples, see William E. Barnes, *The Labor Problem. Plain Questions and Practical Answers* (New York, 1886); *Labor; Its Rights and Wrongs* (Washington, D.C., 1886); George E. McNeill, *The Labor Movement, The Problem of Today* (Boston, 1887).

[4] John Habberton, "Social Science in the Pulpit," *Chautauquan*, XIV (1891-92), 175-179.

energies of many of the younger and more vigorous clergy. Thus the adherents of the new principles were able to reach large masses through various nonreligious channels.

Leading secular magazines, as well as the widely-circulated religious press, were filled with Social Gospel articles by prominent clergymen, and with discussions pro and con by editors and other lay writers. Usually the presentation was favorable to the Christian progressives; only the *Nation*, staunchly devoted to strict free enterprise, maintained a consistent opposition.[5]

Many Americans who did not read the weightier reviews were probably reached by the great cultural exchange developed at Chautauqua, New York. The original Chautauqua, founded by Bishop John H. Vincent as a Sunday school teacher-training institute, retained a moral and religious tone long after its purpose had expanded. In a letter commenting on Chautauqua's first turning toward general education, Lyman Abbott indicated that some of the institution's backers saw it, more or less according to the views of the most conservative social Christians, as a means of combating the growth of radicalism:

It seems to me if you can lay out such plans of study, particularly in the departments of practical science, as will fit our boys and young men in the mining, manufacturing, and agricultural districts to become, in a true though not ambitious sense of the term, scientific and intelligent miners, mechanics, and farmers, you will have done more to put down strikes and labor riots than an army could; and more to solve the labor problem than will be done by the Babel-builders of a hundred labor-reform conventions.[6]

The earnest, serious Chautauqua public, stoutly religious and interested

---

[5] As examples of Social Gospel articles in lay magazines, none of them with any content that differed from other presentations, see, in addition to those cited elsewhere, the following articles in the *Century*: Gladden, "Christianity and Wealth," XXVIII (1884), 903-911; Abbott, "Danger Ahead," XXXI (1885-86), 51-59. In 1889 the *Century* started a regular department of sociological discussion which was considerably affected by the religious social movement. The editors of this department included such clerics as Henry C. Potter and Theodore T. Munger as well as Professor Richard T. Ely. *Century*, XXXIX (1889-90), 26-31. In the *Forum*, see Gladden, "Socialism and Unsocialism," III (1887), 122-130; F. D. Huntington, "Causes of Social Discontent," VI (1888-89), 1-9; Abbott, "Industrial Democracy," IX (1890), 658-669; F. D. Huntington, "Social Problems and the Church," X (1890-91), 127-141; Rainsford, "What Can We Do for the Poor," XI (1891), 115-126, etc. In the *North American Review*, see J. H. Seelye, "Dynamite as a Factor in Civilization," CXXXVII (1883), 1-7; Abbott, "Christianity vs. Socialism," CXLVIII (1889), 447-453. For the *Arena*, see p. 228. An unusually objective summary of the movement in the *Nation* is "Sociology and the Church," LIII (1891), 114-115. For hostile discussions in the *Nation* and elsewhere, see pp. 213-216.

[6] Quoted, without exact citation, in J. L. Hurlbut, *The Story of Chautauqua* (New York, 1921), p. 130.

in all questions of the day was a natural audience for the Social Gospel. It is not surprising that early speakers at the great summer school included Gladden, George Hodges, Philip S. Moxom, F. G. Peabody, Lyman Abbott, Charles Stelzle, Josiah Strong, Graham Taylor and other leading exponents of progressive Christianity.[7]

A still wider public was reached by the Social Gospel's most spectacular and eventually most successful secular medium, the Christian social novel.[8] This distinct and peculiar literary form was developed over a quarter century by a series of lay and clerical authors. At first largely conservative in its viewpoint, it turned with the tide of religious opinion toward moderate progressivism.

One of the first direct ancestors of the Christian social novel was Elizabeth Stuart Phelps' *The Silent Partner*, published in 1871. More ably written than many of its successors, Miss Phelps' book presented a ghastly and detailed picture of labor conditions in a New England mill town. An attractive and frivolous society girl, inheriting a textile mill, is moved to devote herself to improving conditions. Through the influence this gains her among her employees, she persuades them not to strike against a wage cut, necessitated by hard times. In presenting unionism as an unmixed evil, Miss Phelps, a minister's daughter and a regular contributor to the religious press, was only expressing the commonplace views of American religion in the seventies.[9]

Emory J. Haynes, pastor of Tremont Temple, presented a similar viewpoint sixteen years later in his *Dollars and Duty*.[10] Helping to set a persistent pattern, Haynes made his hero, a mill-town minister, quell a vicious antiforeign strike by welfare work and sympathy. Edward Everett Hale's Utopian venture, *How They Lived at Hampton*, published 1888, marked a departure from the pattern. In Hale's model factory town a third of the profits are distributed to the employees. Once this plan is introduced, good stores, churches and places of moral entertainment spring up, management receives adequate returns, and eventually the eight-hour day is introduced. Union organizers who sullenly object receive little support.

[7] Included in Hurlbut's list of prominent speakers, *ibid.*, pp. 395-402. Abbott, Gladden, Moxom, Strong and Peabody are elsewhere mentioned as speaking before 1895.
[8] This phenomenon is discussed by Hopkins, *Rise of the Social Gospel*, pp. 140-148.
[9] Her book was warmly praised by the *Christian Advocate*, April 27, 1871, p. 131, and the *American Presbyterian Review*, III (1871), 342.
[10] New York, 1887. Later Haynes became active in the Christian social movement, undergoing attack by the Standard Oil Company and acting as president of an Anti-Tenement House League. *Dawn*, November 9, 1892, p. 1.

The influence of growing Christian progressivism was far more evident in several novels published at the end of the eighties, of which the best known was Albion W. Tourgee's *Murvale Eastman, Christian Socialist.* Actually this book was somewhat misnamed, since Tourgee's hero specifically rejects socialism in favor of gradual reform and says of Christian Socialism that

The Church has no right to permit this Christian term to be appropriated by men whose only notions of progress are either impossible changes of human nature or the overthrow of all existing social conditions.[11]

In Tourgee's melodramatic story the young pastor of a wealthy uptown church is moved by his knowledge of bad social conditions to assist in founding a "Christian Socialist League" among his congregation. The League boycotts unfair industries and persuades religious employers to institute profit-sharing systems and finance neighborhood clubs. Eastman, to find out the rights and wrongs of a streetcar strike, spends several days in disguise as a driver. By far the most real part of the book is its portrait of the rich businessman who, sincerely disliking Eastman's new activities on religious grounds, tries to get him ejected from the ministerial association. In addition to the discussion of "Christian Socialism" and labor conditions, Tourgee, an experienced popular novelist, found room in the book for two love stories, a mysterious opal and a missing heir. In general the novel was approved by the church press.[12]

Katherine P. Woods' less-known *Metzerott, Shoemaker*, published in 1889, also depicts a social Christian minister. Like his literary predecessors, Miss Woods' "Mr. Clare" preaches reform as an alternative to socialism, which he compares to the temptations of the devil. When a strike occurs, the son of the radical strike leader, converted by Clare, takes the side of the employers and is killed by mistake. Immediately the radical leader gives up his false views for Christianity.

Agnes M. Machar's *Roland Graeme, Knight*, published in Montreal in 1892, was a similar mixture of Christian social principles and melodrama. Miss Machar's hero, a social reformer of clerical antecedents, goes further than other protagonists by joining the Knights of Labor in order to influence them toward Christian reform principles. When a strike occurs, he persuades the strikers to fight a fire which breaks out in the plant, thus moving the owner to make the concessions they ask. At the

[11] Tourgee, *Murvale Eastman* (New York, 1891 [cop. 1889]), p. 124.
[12] *Churchman*, April 4, 1891, p. 535; *Watchman*, April 9, 1891, p. 4; *Congregationalist*, April 9, 1891, p. 121.

end of the book the hero receives a legacy and decides to set up a co-operative factory.

With the work of Charles M. Sheldon, the tradition established by these thin little tales reached the height of its popularity. Sheldon, after a ministry in Vermont, was called to the Central Congregational church of Topeka in 1889. Like so many other Christians suddenly confronted with urban misery, Sheldon, observing the effects of serious unemployment in his first Topeka winter, underwent a deep emotional experience.

The thing lay on me like a monstrous burden that seemed more than I could bear. I believe that at that time in my experience I felt, as I have often wished I could feel again with the same intensity, the horrible blunder and stupidity of our whole industrial system. . . . I felt the isolation of the preacher and the minister from the great world of labor.[13]

With the approval of his congregation, Sheldon spent a week disguised as an unemployed laborer looking for work. The social conditions he discovered were so shocking that he decided to continue the venture, spending a total of nine weeks living incognito the lives of each of Topeka's eight principal social groups. Sheldon gave vent to the emotions aroused by these experiences in a series of parable-novels, originally presented serially as Sunday evening talks for his congregation.

Rather surprisingly, in view of the author's unusual firsthand knowledge of social problems, Sheldon's first books differed little from the other ministerial fiction either in literary quality or social realism. All three of his books published between 1892 and 1894 depicted a sudden, revivalistic experience of social conversion, similar to Sheldon's own. In *Robert Bruce, or the Life that Now Is*, two young reformers spend great efforts helping poor boys in night school, even though the latter ungratefully maim their benefactors. Through their work and that of a helpful minister, a revival is started which results in the settling of a great railroad strike. *Robert Hardy's Seven Days* tells the story of a rich miser who suddenly realizes in a dream that he has only a week to live, and consequently hastens to put into effect in his plant a number of paternalistic reforms. In *The Crucifixion of Philip Strong*, a minister in a manufacturing town suddenly embarks on a program of social reform which includes slum visiting and preaching to workers in a union hall. In a revivalist sermon, which he has invited union leaders to hear, he denounces the selfishness of labor organizations and employers, and pleads for all churches to devote themselves henceforward to helping

[13] Sheldon, *Charles M. Sheldon, His Life Story* (New York, 1925), pp. 81-82.

the unemployed. This effort fails to convert his congregation but when, at his next sermon, the hero dramatically dies in the pulpit, many of his hearers are moved by the sacrifice to adopt his principles.

To a modern reader there seems to be little difference between these thinly-disguised tracts and Sheldon's great success, *In His Steps,* which was published in 1897 and shortly became one of the great best sellers of all time. As millions of readers learned, *In His Steps* presented the story of a town whose various leaders, under the impetus of an emotional experience, try to consider every action they take for a year on the basis of the question "What Would Jesus Do?" Many of the resulting reforms belong to the realm of morality—newspapers refuse to publish Sunday editions and reject liquor advertising; the leading citizens join in a great antisaloon campaign, etc. Economic problems are similarly solved. A manufacturer resolves to operate his business solely as a trust for the welfare of his employees; rich philanthropists buy up slum property for rebuilding. Finally the movement spreads, and at a big meeting in Chicago a socialist, a trade-unionist and a single-taxer present their rival schemes. All these are made to seem superficial and inadequate compared to the simple program of mass conversion which has already scored such successes.

According to Sheldon's autobiography, *In His Steps* eventually sold twenty-two million copies in twenty languages.[14] It has remained popular even up to the present. Perhaps the book's simple and final solution of social problems on the basis of a change of heart—a motif which it shares with the earlier and less successful specimens of the genre—explains its enormous and continuing appeal. Certainly its success, as the culminating event in the development of the social Christian parable, demonstrates the wide public interest in Christian proposals for social reform.

Somewhat less obviously but still clearly enough for definite recognition, the Social Gospel was reflected in literature of a far different order. Its influence on William Dean Howells offers perhaps a sample of the part it played, along with other manifestations of social and industrial upheaval, in forming the ideas of social-minded intellectuals in the late eighties and nineties. Howells' views were affected by several influences which church leaders largely rejected, especially the primitive communism of the Shakers and the theories of Tolstoi. He was also deeply moved, however, by the events and theories which helped to develop social Christianity. Passionately stirred by the execution of the Chicago

---

[14] Sheldon, *Charles M. Sheldon,* p. 97. This figure is persuasively challenged by F. L. Mott in his study of American best sellers, *Golden Multitudes* (New York, 1947), 193-198. Mott, however, leaves *In His Steps* on his list of twenty-one all-time best sellers.

anarchists and more outspoken in their defense than any but one or two social Christians, he was further influenced by his close interest in the strikes of the eighties and nineties. The single tax movement affected him, especially through Hamlin Garland, who was active in the Boston Anti-Poverty Society. Howells himself was much attracted by Bellamy's movement.[15] He deeply admired *Wealth Against Commonwealth* and considered Lloyd "very much my friend."[16]

Taking an interest in such causes and living in Boston and New York, Howells could hardly have avoided direct contact with some of the leaders of social Christianity. One of his frequent correspondents was Edward Everett Hale.[17] He must repeatedly have encountered W. D. P. Bliss and other leaders of the Boston Christian Socialist movement,[18] although his own views did not become as radical as theirs. Howells attended meetings of the Boston Nationalist Club, which Bliss and other Christian Socialists played a large part in, and was an occasional visitor at Bliss' Church of the Carpenter. His friend Hamlin Garland, whose own views were closer to Populism than social Christianity, allowed his name to be used as an editor of the Christian Socialist *Dawn*, and also wrote in the *Arena* which became a principal secular organ of social Christianity.[19]

Several of Howells' novels show direct and sympathetic knowledge of the activities of progressive church leaders. *Annie Kilburn*, in fact, might almost be classified with the other and far less interesting social Christian novels. Howells' heroine in this story comes home from Europe to Hatsboro, Massachusetts, full of vague determination to uplift the mill workers. Her charitable efforts, because of patronizing and ignorant methods, are as disastrous in effect as they are laudable in purpose, increasing rather than lessening Hatsboro's class gulfs. Gradually she is set right by Mr. Peck, a saintly and social-minded Congregational minister, whose working-class origin enables him to understand the needs

[15] See W. F. Taylor, "On the Origins of Howells' Interest in Economic Reform," *American Literature*, II (1930), for all these influences. The Shaker influence is obvious in Howells' *The Undiscovered Country* (Boston, 1880); both this and the Tolstoi theories are continually mentioned in *The World of Chance* (New York, 1893).

[16] Howells, *The Life in Letters of William Dean Howells*, Mildred Howells, ed. (New York, 1928), II, 13-14, 54-55.

[17] *Ibid.*, I, 416, 418-419, 424-425; II, 4.

[18] The Bliss group is discussed on pp. 241-249. Although in my opinion Christian radicalism should be sharply distinguished from the conservative and progressive schools for clearest understanding of all three, contemporary laymen often failed to make such a distinction. Howells was influenced both by the radicals and by the moderate progressives, but his own opinions were those of the latter group.

[19] For attendance at the Boston Nationalist Club, Arthur E. Morgan, *Edward Bellamy* (New York, 1944), 249; for Church of the Carpenter, W. D. P. Bliss, "The Church of the Carpenter and Thirty Years After," *The Social Preparation for the Kingdom of God*, IX (1922), 13. For Garland's editorship, *Dawn*, May 15, 1889, p. 4.

and feelings of the factory workers. In the sermon in which Mr. Peck summarizes his own views (and evidently the author's) he looks forward to the

> truly Christian state, in which there shall be no more asking and no more giving, no more gratitude and no more merit, no more charity, but only and everlastingly justice; all shall share and share alike and want and luxury and killing toil and heartless indolence shall all cease together.[20]

After this sermon, a merchant in Peck's congregation tries to get him dismissed from his charge, but fails. Finally, when Peck is on the verge of resigning his pulpit to found a co-operative boardinghouse, he is killed in an accident. Needless to say, this tragedy does not, in Howells' work, regenerate the town forthwith, as similar events had done in simpler Christian social novels.

In *A Hazard of New Fortunes*, Howells drew a masterly and complex picture of the varying elements of New York society brought into conflict by a streetcar strike. Two of the main characters, Conrad Dryfoos and Margaret Vance, are interested in labor questions chiefly through their participation in the Episcopalian social movement. Both sympathize with the strike, though both hope to persuade the workers to peace. The latter ends her life in a religious order, while the former is killed accidentally during a strike crisis. Dryfoos, a High Churchman and an active participant in social movements, reminds the reader considerably of J. O. S. Huntington, the radical son of Bishop F. D. Huntington. Whether or not such a resemblance was intended, Howells had clearly been in contact with the combination of Anglo-Catholicism and social Christianity which was fairly common in the Episcopalian church. The novel refers to Episcopalianism as "the church which seems to have found a reversion to the imposing ritual of the past the way back to the early ideals of Christian brotherhood."[21]

Howells' first Utopian novel, *A Traveller from Altruria*, describes an entirely Christian variety of socialism. The "Traveller" explains that his mythical country was founded by a castaway apostle, who established "a commonwealth of peace and goodwill" in the likeness of the "first Christian republic." When this perished, the succeeding series of revolutions resulted in monopolistic capitalism, and then in one immense monopoly called "The Accumulation." In the next stage, known as "The Evolution," a huge union of workers unsuccessfully fought "The

---

[20] *Annie Kilburn* (New York, 1889), p. 240.

[21] *Hazard of New Fortunes* (Library Edition; New York, 1911, [cop. 1889]), p. 283. J. O. S. Huntington is discussed on pp. 239-241.

Accumulation." Finally, the leaders of the working people turned away from strikes to the one weapon which the Accumulation had not dared to take away, the ballot. With this they took over one industry after another, establishing a socialist system of beauty, peace and plenty, remarkably similar to that of Bellamy.

The Traveller repeatedly makes it clear that: "In this, as in all other things, we believe ourselves the followers of Christ, whose doctrine we seek to make our life, as He made it His."[22] Like other Christian Socialists, he accuses churchgoers in America of hypocrisy:

That is what you pray for every day, but you do not believe it possible for God's will to be done on earth as it is in heaven; that is, you do not if you are like the competitive and monopolistic people we once were.[23]

Howells did not permanently adopt the proposals of Bellamy or of the Christian Socialists as a serious program. Like the Christian progressives and many other social-minded Americans, he hoped that the alarming symptoms of social disease could somehow be cured by Christian means. At times he seemed to incline toward socialism, at times toward more piecemeal measures of reform. Readers of novels on his literary plane, as well as that of Sheldon, must have become familiar at least with the existence of the Social Gospel movement. Its ideas continued to be expressed in fiction in the early twentieth century, most clearly and successfully perhaps in the religious novels of the American Winston Churchill.[24]

It is clear that a large portion of the American people were exposed to the preachments of the Social Gospel, not only in the well-attended churches, but also in leading magazines, lectures and novels. An attempt to estimate the influence of the Social Gospel cannot, however, stop with a demonstration of its wide publicity; the fact that people heard its doctrines does not prove that they were deeply influenced.

Other evidence, in fact, demonstrates that the progressive Christian movement failed to achieve several of its most cherished aims. Many of its hopeful leaders had believed, for instance, that an appeal for social reform on Christian grounds might disarm the opposition, leading conservatives to a change of heart and persuading believers in "selfish" economics to adopt more kindly principles. Such hopes proved illusory to a large extent. Not only did many ignore the Social Gospel, sticking to

[22] *A Traveller from Altruria* (New York, 1894), pp. 299-300.
[23] *Ibid.*, p. 304.
[24] *The Inside of the Cup* (New York, 1913); *A Far Country* (New York, 1915); *The Dwelling Place of Light* (New York, 1917).

the well-tried beliefs of Christian conservatism, but some who heard the call flatly rejected it. Expressions of strong opposition to the doctrines of the Christian progressives were common in lay as well as in church circles, increasing in frequency as the social movement became better known. The moderation of most progressive social Christians did not save them; their teachings were coupled, and often confused, with those of Christian radicalism in the writings of the conservative critics. In addition to making use of the ordinary anticollectivist arguments, lay opponents of the Social Gospel took progressive ministers to task for ignorance, incompetence and neglect of their true spiritual functions.

As early as 1884 an antisocialist pamphlet angrily alleged that, while most socialists were irreligious, some of them used religious arguments when others failed, making dupes of well-meaning Christians:

. . . there are some who, like Henry George, are not too conscientious to quote a mangled verse of scripture, now and then, if it seems to them that they can thereby make a point. And there are multitudes of well-meaning people, who have a decent respect for the words of the Bible, who are influenced thereby. There are, moreover, a great many teachers and preachers of Christianity, who reason loosely, and whose sympathies being with the poor, are ready to take the view of society which seems popular, and encourage the belief that somehow the laborers have been unjustly deprived by the rich of the products of their labors.[25]

Preachers of the Social Gospel were again rebuked by Edward Atkinson, an industrialist with interests in factory insurance and cotton textiles, who was a prolific publicist of the manufacturer's point of view. Atkinson, a stout believer in the classical theories, accused a clerical audience of economic ignorance:

Have you kept pace in your theological science with the progress of economic science? I sometimes think not when I read the arraignment of capital and capitalists made by some clerical gentlemen whose zeal is greater than their knowledge.[26]

Echoing clerical views of a generation earlier, this spokesman of capital especially objected to an alleged tendency on the part of liberal ministers to denounce the rich: "Now, gentlemen, every respectable business man knows better; and he may get tired of the imputation of sin, when put upon the best service which he knows how to render to his fellow-men."[27]

[25] Moses L. Scudder, Jr., *The Labor-Value Fallacy* (pamphlet, Chicago, 1884). pp. 48-49.
[26] Atkinson, *Addresses Upon the Labor Question* (Boston, 1886), p. 4.
[27] *Ibid.*, p. 8.

In 1893 the *Nation* used Gladden, despite his moderation, as its main target in an editorial on "Christian Socialism" in which it urged a return to the old-fashioned heart-religion:

> . . . every attempt to prescribe modes of action as essentially "Christian" is an attempt to substitute a code of external observances for a religion of the heart—the very evil against which Jesus uttered his most terrible denunciations.[28]

Such an argument was, perhaps, rather surprising in a magazine which ordinarily expressed sophisticated and highly secular points of view. In 1894 the *Evening Post*, a sister publication, coupled Professor Ely, a consistent exponent of moderate Social Gospel views, with the far more radical George D. Herron in a fiery denunciation.[29]

Not only militant conservatives, but some writers who at least considered themselves liberals rejected much of the Social Gospel appeal. Nicholas Paine Gilman, the principal advocate of profit-sharing, warned ministers against not only socialism but also co-operation, perhaps the most common proposal of Social Gospel spokesmen:

> . . . if I am not mistaken, the ideas denoted by these two names [socialism and co-operation] have had more influence on the ministerial mind than their successes in practice have warranted.[30]

R. E. Thompson, the nationalist sociologist and economist who had been one of the earliest academic authorities to object to the rigid classical doctrines on ethical grounds, approved the Social Gospel only with serious qualifications. Commenting on new trends in seminary teaching, Thompson said that students were "invited on Christian principles to repudiate the whole structure of society and to aid in its overthrow."[31] Accepting an increase of clerical interest in science and economics as desirable, Thompson feared that

> . . . there is danger—nay, there is certainty—of exaggeration. We see that all around us already. We see it in the weaker brethren, who are carried most easily off their balance by popular tendencies of any kind, and who talk sometimes as though men were to be regenerated by clean homes and fresh air, or as if the gospel had been superseded by political economy.[32]

[28] *Nation*, LVI (1893), 381-382.
[29] Quoted by George A. Gates, "The Real Anarchist," *Kingdom*, September 7, 1894, p. 1. Herron is discussed on pp. 249-253.
[30] Gilman, *Profit-Sharing between Employer and Employee* (Boston, 1889), pp. 443-444.
[31] Thompson, *De Civitate Dei; The Divine Order of Human Society* (Philadelphia, 1891), p. 1.
[32] *Ibid.*, p. 10.

Thompson urged that the church should be careful to avoid "direct discussion and attack of social evils," confining itself to "the great principles of right action," leaving these "to work themselves into better social methods."[33] In his history of Presbyterianism the same critic expressed similar views in his brief discussion of the social movement, insisting that the reaction against individualistic religion had gone too far and that the church was not a "divider between rich and poor or between labor and capital."[34]

In 1894 a sociology textbook by Albion W. Small and George R. Vincent criticized not only Christian Socialists but also "certain men who prefer to call themselves Christian Sociologists." Small and Vincent gave these men credit for causing "the lively interest which religious leaders of all denominations are beginning to manifest in the investigation of social problems" and agreed with their belief that "the ultimate Sociology must be essentially Christian." These professionals disliked, however, what they considered a clerical tendency "to quarrel with economic facts rather than to discover the real meaning of the facts."[35]

The Social Gospel's warm appeal for a Christian solution of current ills was forcefully rejected by conservative businessmen and sharply criticized by some representatives of middle-of-the-road academic opinion. Even this, however, was not the most serious failure of Christian progressivism. The most fervent hope of many of its spokesmen was for the conversion of the labor movement. Purged of evil passions and filled with visions of a Christian society, labor would, they hoped, march under the banners of the church in its peaceful quest for a better world.

The radical, political minded minority of labor leaders naturally ignored the mild proposals of progressive Christians. Representatives of the major strain in American labor history, pure-and-simple, nonpolitical unionists of the Gompers tradition, were equally distrustful of the churches. The Social Gospel did not succeed in abating the anti-clericalism developed in the American labor movement by several generations of church opposition. Nor did it draw back into the churches the largely non-Protestant urban working class.

Perhaps the clearest example of labor's persistent hostility was Terence

[33] *Ibid.*, p. 253. *De Civitate Dei* received highly favorable reviews in the church press. *Churchman*, September 26, 1891, pp. 391-392; *Watchman*, October 8, 1891, p. 3; *Congregationalist*, October 1, 1891, p. 3.

[34] Thompson, *A History of Presbyterian Churches in the United States of America* ("American Church History Series," VI [New York, 1895]), 239-240; 304-305. Quotation, 240.

[35] Small and Vincent, *An Introduction to the Study of Society* (New York, 1894), p. 38.

V. Powderly. Hailed for a time by the religious press as an unusually acceptable labor leader, Powderly, of all union men, might have been expected to respond in a friendly way to Protestant cordiality. Deeply religious, he had left the Catholic church because of his disillusion with the views and practices of its hierarchy.[36] Yet he always kept above his desk a picture of Christ, "the world's greatest agitator."[37] Repeatedly Powderly expressed sentiments very close to the humanitarian religion of the Social Gospel: ". . . until men and women realize that He lived, worked and died for all, . . . and that He meant just what He said when He told the men of His day to love their neighbors, they will continue to walk in the wrong path."[38] The first question asked a candidate in an initiation to the Knights of Labor was whether he believed in God.

Nothing in Powderly's social beliefs was too radical for the moderate Social Gospel leaders to have approved. Denouncing advocates of force, he pinned his hopes to the favorite clerical devices of profit-sharing and co-operation. He disliked union political action and opposed the closed shop.

Yet this model leader showed in his two books of reminiscences little knowledge that some ministers were saying a good word for him and that a few, like W. D. P. Bliss and J. O. S. Huntington, had even joined his Order. On the contrary, he told a story of repeated and active hostility on the part of Protestant as well as Catholic clerics. Ministers had opened with prayer citizens' meetings called to denounce his activities.[39] They had spoken in favor of the Reading Railroad during a strike (he alleged in return for passes).[40] Powderly himself had been accused from the pulpit of seeking, with the help of the pope, to overthrow the country.[41]

Repeatedly and angrily, Powderly denounced organized religion in general, echoing the charges of partisans of labor before and after his day. The "masters" were able to use "the powers of press and pulpit to convince the laborer that he should not aspire to the good things of earth, but should be content to live in that sphere to which it had pleased his God to call him." Powderly charged, as had many of the social Christians, that the churches treated the laboring man with cold neglect:

[36] See Powderly, *The Path I Trod*, Harry J. Carman, Henry David and Paul N. Guthrie, eds. (New York, 1940), pp. 370-371.
[37] *Ibid.*, pp. 38-39.
[38] *Ibid.*, p. 284.
[39] *Ibid.*, p. 76.
[40] *Ibid.*, pp. 236, 251.
[41] *Ibid.*, pp. 392, 396-400.

He saw that the minister of the religion which he professed never made calls of a friendly nature on him; his neighbors, who worked where he did, never received a visit from the clergyman, but he saw that the man who could not get into heaven until the camel passed through the eye of a needle was often favored with a visit from the minister who preached poverty and humility as a means of acquiring grace on earth and happiness in heaven. . . .[42]

Powderly knew, of course, that religious-minded reformers and philanthropists were active in various movements for the relief of the poor, but like many other labor spokesmen and particularly those of Catholic background, he was somewhat suspicious of organized reformers, particularly those interested in questions of personal morality. He accused such people of hypocrisy, puritanism and of ignoring or even contributing to the causes of poverty:

The self-appointed, personally appointed censors of our morals who are now devoting time, talk, and other people's dollars to scavenger work in the slums, alleged social betterment, community welfare with an occasional excursion into the realms of the latest outlet for virtuous strenuosity, white slavery, weren't agitating the atmosphere then in vociferating against the practices in the train of which many modern evils follow. I can name the fathers of some present-day reformers who were engaged in exploiting the workers and contributing the money so acquired to the building and upkeep of churches without giving a thought to those whose labor provided the funds they were expending and whose homes they may have been pauperizing.[43]

Finally, of course, Powderly denounced with still greater passion the widespread pulpit opposition to strikes:

The deep-toned voice of many a minister of God rang out in denunciation of the workingman, who, in his poverty, in his agony, in his very despair often struck against the systems which crushed him to earth. . . .[44]

Though Powderly himself was not alienated from religion as such, he believed that many working people had been, and sympathized with their reasons:

. . . it cannot be wondered at that many who strove to better the condition of the toiler lost all respect for religion when they saw that those who affected to be the most devout worshipers at the foot of the heavenly throne, were the most tyrannical of task-masters when dealing with the poor and the lowly . . .

[42] Powderly, *Thirty Years of Labor* (Columbus, 1890), pp. 262-264.
[43] *Path I Trod*, pp. 88-89.
[44] *Thirty Years*, p. 264.

it could not be wondered at that some of them

REBELLED AGAINST THE DECREE

which had rung in their ears for centuries: "servants, obey your masters"; we are the children of the one father, and that father has given to one brother all the good things of earth, while to us he has given nothing.[45]

Plenty of evidence showed that Powderly was representative of labor's continuing attitude. In 1885 a labor spokesman expressed, in a letter to the *Christian Union*, his strong and typical dislike of two recent articles by Gladden. Gladden, urging that both sides of the capital-labor controversy mend their ways, had exhorted the workers to be moral, patient and abstemious. The indignant rebuttal rejected the implied criticism, insisting that working people were already far more moral and abstemious than the upper classes and excessively patient. Ministers who, the writer alleged, had been conducting a discussion whether a laborer's family could live on a thousand dollars a year were insultingly ignorant; the average working family of five in America did not average three hundred dollars.[46]

In the same year John Swinton, the radical union journalist who was one of religion's most consistent critics, commented sarcastically on clerical approaches to labor:

The preachers all over the country are now pounding away at the labor question in their pulpits. We have been picking up their sermons for the past three months, but now the pile has grown so high that we are unable to handle them. These preachers have somehow heard that the labor question is up; but, we regret to say, few of them appear to know anything about it.[47]

At the 1886 meeting of the American Congress of Churches, when that organization invited labor spokesmen to address it, John Jarrett of the Amalgamated Iron and Steel Workers, an unusually religious labor spokesman, expressed a common complaint:

We are told, and I hope that my dear friends of the ministry will not be offended if I say that we are told principally by them, that the Saviour came here simply that we might have heaven after leaving this world. The workingmen want to get a little of that heaven here, if they can.[48]

[45] *Ibid.*, pp. 260-261.
[46] J. Willet, "A Letter from a Workingman," *Christian Union*, October 29, 1885, pp. 7-8.
[47] *John Swinton's Paper*, April 5, 1885, quoted in *Independent*, August 27, 1885, p. 4.
[48] *Labor: Its Rights and Wrongs* (Washington, 1886), pp. 253-254.

At the same Congress Henry George, who did not share organized labor's hostility to the churches, told his clerical friends that such hostility must be recognized as a fact, at least among the foremost union leaders:

It may be an open question . . . whether the workingmen do or do not distrust the church; but this is certain; that the active, ardent spirits among the workingmen, not in this country alone, but all over the world—the men who are stretching forward, and hoping and struggling for some improvement in the material condition of the hard-worked masses—almost without exception distrust the church. Any man who mingles with them may hear it day after day.[49]

George, like other critics, blamed this distrust on the shortcomings of the churches' social outlook:

Social questions are now beginning to attract attention among the clergy of all denominations, and it is one of the most hopeful signs. But what is the tenor of the great majority of the sermons that are preached. . . . it is temperance, and such virtues for the poor, and the gospel for the poor and the rich. It is: be kind, be generous, let the workman serve his master diligently, and let the master be generous to the workman. Kindness, generosity, none of these amiable virtues can narrow that widening gulf between the rich and the poor. What is needed is something higher, and something that must come first. What is needed is justice.[50]

Charles Sotheran, in a socialist pamphlet of 1892, was less sweeping in his indictment. Sotheran approved such evidences of Christian sympathy with the working class as Bishop Potter's letter and the acts of Father J. O. S. Huntington. But Washington Gladden, the most prominent spokesman of the Social Gospel, was condemned by Sotheran as a leading apologist of the present system of society, whose superficial and ignorant account of socialism and social problems resulted only in confusion.[51] Another socialist and active labor organizer, Taral T. Frickstad of Oakland, California, attacked the ministry in a pamphlet of 1894 for lack of sympathy with the poor, commercial-mindedness, and preaching a theology too complex for working-class audiences.[52]

Though the leader of the A. F. of L. seldom agreed with socialists on any question, Samuel Gompers indicated in reply to a questionnaire sent

---

[49] *Ibid.*, pp. 262-263.
[50] *Ibid.*, p. 266.
[51] Sotheran, *Horace Greeley and other Pioneers of American Socialism*, pp. 247-256, 332-333.
[52] Frickstad, *From Behind the Scenes: The Church and the Masses; or, the Social and Religious Problem* (pamphlet, Oakland, 1894).

him by Professor Commons that his estimate of churchmen was equally low. Asked to range various categories in the order of their usefulness to labor, Gompers placed them as follows:

1. Members of Ethical Societies
2. Unitarians
3. Non-Believers
4. Catholics
5. Protestants
6. Jews
7. Ministers
8. Physicians
9. Lawyers[53]

Commenting on the same questionnaire, W. B. Prescott, President of the International Typographers' Society, most unusually granted an exceptional status to "such men as Father Huntington, Reverend Heber Newton, etc., whose names are enshrined in the hearts of the struggling wage-earner." Prescott had, however, a very low opinion of most clerical utterances on labor:

It is true the profession contains many who refer to the subject frequently, but their utterances indicate a scant knowledge of the wants of the people, and as a result their remedies and suggestions are often superficial and insulting. They seldom come to the front in times of stress, such as during strikes or political movements. When action is necessary they are missing. It is becoming quite a fad to 'preach at' instead of to the working man, and he does not relish it.[54]

The two polls taken by Congregationalist organizations in 1892 gave the same impression as these various statements. Gladden's committee which investigated, for the Congregational Association of Ohio, the economic opinions of employers and employees included the following question:

Do laboring-men, as a class, complain of the churches; if so, what are their complaints?

Answers from the employee group said that they found the churches inhospitable to working-class visitors and indifferent or hostile to labor's cause.[55] A similar investigation carried on by the Congregational Associa-

[53] John R. Commons, "Christianity and Social Reform," *Kingdom*, June 22, 1894, pp. 157-158. Gompers evidently felt especially bitter toward lawyers, saying "If there were any others you had enumerated, I should still have placed the latter last."
[54] *Ibid.*, p. 158.
[55] Gladden, "The Social and Industrial Situation," *Bibliotheca Sacra*, XLIX (1892), 408-410.

tion of Massachusetts asked a group of labor leaders whether "industrial discontent had produced any effect upon the attitude of the workingmen of Massachusetts toward the churches." Thirty out of the thirty-three who answered believed that labor had been alienated from the churches, giving as their reasons oppression by employers who were church members, the tendency of the churches to side with employers in strikes, and the prevalent preaching of charity instead of justice.[56]

Instances of labor leaders reporting positive help from clergymen are very few. J. R. Buchanan, a radical Knights of Labor organizer who worked among the Colorado miners, mentioned with much gratitude the active sympathy of two Denver ministers, Gilbert De La Matyr and Myron W. Reed, both of whom became members of the Denver Assembly of the Knights in 1892. According to Buchanan, De La Matyr's pro-labor activities cost him his church and Reed was "blacklisted through the Western railway world."[57] In 1889 the Franklin Club, a Cleveland organization supporting the United Labor party, passed a resolution praising the *Christian Union* for its friendship to labor and stating that "that paper alone of all the orthodox papers in this country places a higher value upon principle than party, upon character than wealth, upon men than property." The rareness of such recognition, even for this Social Gospel organ, is demonstrated by the enthusiastic statement of the editors that "No expression we have ever received . . . has ever given us keener pleasure. . . ."[58]

The overwhelming evidence demonstrates that the wage earners, whose recognized lack of interest in the churches was one of the contributing causes to the Christian social movement, were not won back by the increasing friendliness of large numbers of churchmen. Labor comments suggest two main reasons for this failure. First, the tradition of clerical hostility was too consistent and too old to be easily broken down. All union members must have known that official organs of the churches, prominent ministers and clerical professors had long made the labor organizations targets of hostile criticism. The new movements of sympathy had to break through a solid wall of hostility which had been built up by churchmen ever since the crusade against the New York workingmen in Jacksonian times. It seems evident that many leaders of labor,

[56] John P. Coyle, "The Churches and Labor Unions," *Forum*, XIII (1892), 766-768.

[57] Buchanan, *Story of a Labor Agitator* (New York, 1903), pp. 48, 137-139, 212-213, 239.

[58] *Christian Union*, June 13, 1889, pp. 747-748.

long out of touch with church opinion, did not know that they had new friends.

Second, even those ministers who sincerely professed friendship for organized labor often displayed an extreme lack of understanding of its problems. The American labor movement, and indeed almost all the long tradition of American protest, had stressed certain definite, concrete aims. Its participants were activated by immediate and often desperate needs. The clerical progressives, often lacking firsthand experience of labor conditions, did not understand this immediacy. Rejecting the large-scale reconstruction demanded by socialists as too radical, they tended to ignore wages-and-hours proposals as too materialistic. Often they deplored strikes without suggesting practical alternatives. Labor leaders of all types usually had little confidence in the hope of religious progressives that industrial conflicts could be solved by an appeal to the better natures of the contending parties. The concrete suggestion most often brought forward by moderate social Christians, that workers save their wages to buy industrial shares, thereby eventually building co-operative industry, could hardly be expected to appeal to men who found their wages too low for their immediate needs.

Third, the manner of the clerical approach to union men, regardless of its content, was often extremely unfortunate. Too often ministers urged working people to free themselves of their assumed "vices" or offered to explain to "the ignorant classes" problems with which their hearers had long been all too familiar.

A few spokesmen of social Christianity understood these shortcomings and warned their colleagues concerning them. Amory H. Bradford, a Congregational minister who commented on John Swinton's attack, found some truth in it:

> Those who study pages written in blood . . . not unnaturally feel that they know some elements in the problem that never reach pulpits and professor's chairs. They are right. . . . These men are not all dreamers or imposters. They have a cause.[59]

In 1893 Charles Worcester Clark, writing in the *Andover Review*, summed up with amazing clarity and understanding the defects of the social preachers. Clark sharply criticized the approach from above:

> . . . one more disposed than the present writer to be cynical might remark that it certainly is a very pleasing idea to Christianize the working-classes,

---

[59] Bradford, "Socialism from the Socialistic Standpoint," *Independent*, August 27, 1885, pp. 4-5.

and thereby teach them to bear with patience the burdens we impose; but it were better to Christianize ourselves and cease to impose the burdens.

Ministers, Clark believed, had failed really to rid themselves of their laissez faire indoctrination or to recognize the reality of changes that had come over American society:

The fair field for individual merit to prove itself and win its due reward has been our pride so long that it is hard to believe it gone. But it is gone. . . .

We are still blinding ourselves to the change, and insisting that the social system best suited to a condition when equality of opportunity for all men was the rule is best now that equality is no more.

The lack of concrete, vital understanding of labor's point of view was clearly pointed out by Clark:

. . . nearly all our talk about the "masses," the working-classes, and their aims and rights, is ignorant and condescending. About strikes in particular, we lay down the law, and make sweeping misstatements with the utmost complacency. The baseless assertion that "in nine cases out of ten strikes are a failure" seems to be an especial favorite with the religious press.

Criticizing a type of preaching which even some of his most progressive colleagues recognized as at least a part of their duty, Clark found "the very irony of heartlessness in our telling the poor that the remedy for their troubles lies in personal Christianity. . . ."[60]

The appearance of such acute self-criticism demonstrates the remarkable maturity which some leaders had attained in one generation of the Social Gospel movement. But men who can realize the defects of their own class or profession are rare in any age or group. The evidence indicates that in Clark's time, and indeed long afterward, few clergymen acted on his criticisms and few labor representatives realized the existence of such thoroughly sympathetic points of view within the church.

Progressive social Christianity failed, in general, either to convert conservatives or to attract labor support. Its considerable importance in the development of American thought came from its influence on another group, a group of crucial importance at the end of the century. On the ideas of the progressive middle class the Social Gospel made its deepest impression.

The new Christian theories were not, of course, the only source of the middle-class progressivism that arose in this period and dominated the

[60] Clark, "Applied Christianity: Who Shall Apply it First," *Andover Review*, XIX (1893), 18-33.

next decades. Not only liberal clergymen, but also liberal educators,[61] editors, social workers and other groups were learning the same lessons. The spectacular crises of the period—the drastic depressions and grim labor conflicts—were suggesting to many types of Americans that all was not well with their institutions. The challenge of European radical thought operated, directly and indirectly, on many levels. And then, as in every crisis of American history, the old Jeffersonian and Jacksonian traditions were available for new adaptation. But churchmen reacted to this particular crisis as early as any of the other groups,[62] and their reaction had, still, a special authority. The progressivism of the late nineteenth century had a religious sanction which had been notably withheld from the Jeffersonian and Jacksonian "revolutions."

Clergymen co-operated with other middle-class groups in various aspects of a widespread social awakening. Some of them, for instance, were active in the movement of civic reform, an idealistic upsurge which had much in common with the Social Gospel. Sometimes clerical participation in civic uplift had little direct connection with the Social Gospel's fundamental criticisms of American society. Dr. Charles H. Parkhurst, for instance, in his spectacular personal crusade to clean up New York, was almost entirely concerned with an attack on protected vice, an object which would not have seemed strange to the conservative clerical reformers of the 1820's.[63]

More often, however, churchmen who took part in the new civic reforms were motivated by definite Social Gospel beliefs. The closeness in spirit of the two movements is demonstrated by a manual of city reform, published in 1895, which listed among "Movements for Civic Betterment" both the American Institute of Christian Sociology and the Brotherhood of the Kingdom.[64] Heber Newton was criticized by conservative clerics for his part in New York reform politics, but defended

[61] For the currents of thought among educators in this period, see M. E. Curti, *The Social Ideas of American Educators* (Report of the Commission on the Social Studies of the American Historical Association. Part X. [New York, 1935]). The opinions of educators ran amazingly parallel to those of the ministry as presented above, even though by the nineties the two groups no longer coincided.

[62] John Chamberlain, in his *Farewell to Reform* (New York, 1932), says that even in the early twentieth century "we find the church on the defensive, giving ground here and there, probably a force making for a genteel liberalism, but certainly not a generating force. Clergymen like Dr. Washington Gladden, who denounced Rockefeller, had a following, but they took their cue from the muckrakers." P. 150. Actually Gladden and others of the same opinions were writing twenty years before the muckrakers.

[63] See C. H. Parkhurst, *Our Fight with Tammany* (New York, 1895).

[64] W. H. Tolman, *Municipal Reform Movements in the United States* (New York, 1895), pp. 139-140, 142-145. Tolman was later an associate of Josiah Strong. See Hopkins, *Rise of the Social Gospel*, p. 260.

by Bishops Huntington and Potter.[65] Washington Gladden, impressed by his observation of the overthrow of Boss Tweed in 1871, was elected to the Columbus City Council in 1900 and active in city affairs for several years thereafter.[66] In 1894 Walter Rauschenbusch and Samuel Zane Batten spoke before a Detroit group which wanted to imitate the movement which had succeeded in New York.[67]

Two of the most famous turn-of-the-century leaders of city reform showed definite Social Gospel backgrounds. Tom L. Johnson, the reform mayor of Cleveland, began his career as a wealthy manufacturer. Struck by the teachings of Henry George, he underwent a conversion reminiscent of Sheldon's novels, a change of heart compared by one of Johnson's admirers to "Paul's vision on the road to Damascus."[68] Johnson was directly influenced by social Christianity through his friend and close collaborator, Harrison R. Cooley of the Cedar Avenue Church, whom he described in typical Social Gospel terms: "Cooley was an idealist, the gentlest of men, the son of a minister, himself a minister, who believed in applied Christianity. To him the teachings of the Sermon on the Mount were personal commands."[69] When Johnson became mayor in 1901 Cooley, as his Director of Charities, played an important part in his administration of humanitarian reform.[70]

Samuel L. ("Golden Rule") Jones, the remarkably similar Toledo reform mayor, was also a devout believer in social Christianity. Fighting inhumane prisons and capital punishment, befriending victims of society, he continually quoted the Bible and announced that his model was Christ.[71]

Jane Addams, perhaps the period's greatest pioneer in charitable reform, and a major contributor to the new environmental emphasis, maintained a friendly though not uncritical relation with the Social Gospel pioneers. Hull House itself, indeed, received little clerical support and even underwent serious attacks by ministers in its early years because of its lack of religious education and Miss Addams' failure to show interest in the temperance movement.[72]

[65] *Arena*, II (1890), 381-383.
[66] Gladden, *Recollections*, pp. 197-208, 337-351.
[67] Sharpe, *Rauschenbusch*, p. 77.
[68] F. C. Howe, *The Confessions of a Reformer* (New York, 1925), p. 129. See also L. F. Post, *The Prophet of San Francisco* (New York, 1930), pp. 130-135.
[69] Tom L. Johnson, *My Story* (New York, 1911), p. 183.
[70] *Ibid.*, pp. 173-179.
[71] Howe, *op. cit.*, pp. 185-186.
[72] Jane Addams, *Twenty Years at Hull House* (New York, 1930), pp. 141, 204-205.

Yet social Christianity of various types made up a large part of the progressive ferment that filled the Chicago of Jane Addams, Florence Kelley and John Peter Altgeld. In Miss Addams' autobiography she mentions with respect the activities of George D. Herron, J. O. S. Huntington, Graham Taylor, and Washington Gladden.[73] She was an associate editor of the *Kingdom*, an organ of mixed radical and progressive Christian opinion, and visited the Christian Commonwealth Colony, the belated communal attempt in Georgia, an experiment which she admired, though she doubted its practicability.[74] During the nineties, she realized, "clergymen were making heroic efforts to induce their churches to formally consider the labor movement."[75] Yet Miss Addams, a consistent partisan of the concrete and immediate type of reform, retained a somewhat skeptical attitude toward the wider hopes of some of her clerical friends. When a group of Christian Socialists met at Hull House, she seems to have found their fervent but "literary" expressions typical of church comment in general, a "striking portrayal of that 'between-age mood' in which so many of our religious contemporaries are forced to live."[76]

One of the more successful attempts made in the nineties to unite Social Gospel leaders with other advocates of reform was the Union for Practical Progress.[77] B. O. Flower, the Union's founder, had been educated for the ministry of the Disciples of Christ. Moving toward extreme theological liberalism, he devoted his efforts to reform agitation of a proto-religious character. The purpose of the U.P.P., as stated by its national organizer, the Reverend Walter Vrooman, was "to make possible simultaneous action on the part of all the religious and moral forces of society." Circular letters were to be sent to clergymen and labor leaders of a given town, urging them to speak out, within a set time, regarding some designated problem such as sweatshops, child labor or municipal government. The names of those who complied and those who did not were to be published, so that "the line will be drawn between that part of the church which still worships God spelled in the old-fashioned way, and that part to whose God a new letter has been added, making it G-o-l-d."[78] Ministers were active in several of the Union's branches,

---

[73] *Ibid.*, pp. 189, 304, 141.
[74] Dombrowski, *Early Days*, pp. 111, 145; Addams, *Twenty Years*, pp. 277-279.
[75] *Twenty Years*, p. 190.
[76] *Ibid.*, pp. 190-191.
[77] This is made clear by the account in Abell, *Urban Impact*, pp. 103-106.
[78] *Kingdom*, April 27, 1894, p. 30.

though in at least one instance some of them withdrew when U.P.P. activities clashed too sharply with entrenched interests.[79]

The *Arena*, Flower's lively organ, continually exhorted the clergy toward more daring social-reform activities.[80] It also furnished one of the chief vehicles for the publication of the general doctrines of the Social Gospel, many of whose leaders contributed to it at one time or another.[81]

The political progressivism that developed in the nineties and dominated the national scene in the succeeding decades showed clear traces of the influence of the early Social Gospel. Robert LaFollette, in his college days, was deeply affected by the teachings of John Bascom, then beginning to turn toward the new social spirit. Later, when LaFollette was governor and sought Bascom's advice he received an injunction that typified much of the older, as well as the newer, religious spirit: "Robert," he said, "you will doubtless make mistakes of judgment as governor, but never mind the political mistakes so long as you make no ethical mistakes."[82]

Theodore Roosevelt was directly in contact with several Social Gospel leaders. According to Rauschenbusch's enthusiastic biographer, both he and Wilson consulted that important religious leader regarding their general social programs.[83] Roosevelt praised W. S. Rainsford as an example of those clergymen who obey the law of service.[84] He was a friend of Gladden's from his early Police Commission days on into his presidency, speaking in Columbus on Gladden's invitation. (Gladden said, however, that he had "never belonged to the inner circle" of "Roosevelt's intimate advisers," and was himself not an uncritical admirer of the Rough Rider.[85])

Roosevelt himself not only endorsed but promoted the Social Gospel:

The church must fit itself for the practical betterment of mankind if it is to attract and retain the fealty of the men best worth holding and using. . . .

Under the tense activity of modern social and industrial conditions the church, if it is to give real leadership, must grapple, zealously, fearlessly and cool-headedly with the problems of social and industrial justice. Unless it is the poor man's church it is not a Christian church at all in any real sense.[86]

[79] See Abell, *Urban Impact*, p. 105.
[80] E.g. *Arena*, IV (1891), 767-768.
[81] Early social Christian articles in the *Arena* included the Reverend Francis Bellamy, "The Tyrany of All the People," IV (1891), 180-191; M. J. Savage, "The Present Conflict for a Larger Life," X (1894), 297-306; the Reverend C. H. Zimmerman, "The Church and Economic Reforms," X (1894), 694-700.
[82] R. M. LaFollette, *LaFollette's Autobiography* (Madison, 1913), pp. 26-28.
[83] Sharpe, *Rauschenbusch*, pp. 413-414.
[84] Roosevelt, *The Foes of Our Own Household* (New York, 1917), p. 226.
[85] Gladden, *Recollections*, pp. 389-390.
[86] Roosevelt, *The Foes*, pp. 224-225.

A suggestion of Roosevelt's for the settlement of labor disputes echoed that so frequently put forth by the more conservative social Christians:

> Surely half our labor troubles would disappear if a sufficient number of the leaders on both sides had worked for common ends in the same churches and religious organizations, and approached one another's positions with an earnest desire to understand and respect them.[87]

The Colonel, unlike some of his contemporaries, distinguished sharply between the Gladden type of progressivism and more radical Christian movements. In a typical diatribe against socialism he addressed a special word to "the so-called 'Christian Socialists' ":

> . . . that men who pretend to speak with culture of mind and authority to teach, men who are or have been preachers of the Gospel or professors in universities, should affiliate themselves with the preachers of criminal nonsense is a sign of grave mental or moral shortcomings.[88]

Even later in the development of American political liberalism, when direct contact with the early Social Gospel is not provable, its influence is still apparent. The moral, ethical, optimistic and fundamentally religious strain that runs through a great deal of twentieth-century progressivism could hardly have been developed without the change in religious opinion which we have studied. Few of the later progressive leaders were uninfluenced by George, Bellamy or Lloyd, three pioneers who were so close to the Social Gospel movement as to be almost a part of it. Typical statements of many major leaders of later decades have, to any student of early social Christianity, an unmistakable ring.

William Allen White, discussing his own departure from straight plutocratic politics, describes a conversion that can hardly have been entirely independent:

> . . . it was not until the turn of the century that I began to understand the New Testament.
> I have no recollection that I ever travelled on the road to Damascus. But Theodore Roosevelt and his attitude toward the powers that be, the status quo, the economic, social and political order, certainly did begin to penetrate my heart. And when I came to the New Testament and saw Jesus, not as a figure in theology—the only begotten son who saved by his blood a sinful world—but as a statesman and philosopher who dramatized his creed by giving his life for it, then gradually the underpinning of my Pharisaic philosophy was knocked out. Slowly as the new century came into its first decade, I saw the Great Light. Around me in that day scores of young

[87] *Ibid.*, p. 227.
[88] *Ibid.*, p. 171.

leaders in American politics and public affairs were seeing what I saw, feeling what I felt.[89]

For all his Fundamentalist theology, William Jennings Bryan could echo the demands of the Christian social movement:

The social ideal towards which the world is moving requires that human institutions shall approximate towards the Divine measure of rewards and this can only be realized when each individual is able to draw from society a reward proportionate to his contribution to society.[90]

Woodrow Wilson, in the years of his sudden turn toward progressivism, altered his religious opinions as well as some of his social views. In 1909 he had expressed his specific opposition to social Christianity:

For my part, I do not see any promise of vitality either in the church or in society except upon the true basis of individualism. . . . He [the minister] must preach Christianity to men, not to society. He must preach salvation to the individual, for it is only one by one that we can love, and love is the law of life.[91]

By 1914, however, Wilson had completely changed his mind:

For one, I am not fond of thinking of Christianity as the means of saving *individual* souls. . . . Christ came into the world to save others, not to save himself, and no man is a true Christian who does not think constantly of how he can lift his brother, how he can enlighten mankind, how he can make virtue the rule of conduct in the circle in which he lives.[92]

It would not be hard to find in the statements of still later progressive leaders, not least Franklin Roosevelt, a tendency to state humanitarian social objectives in religious terms. This would hardly have been possible had not the early Social Gospel leaders shattered the hold of the old, confining doctrines. Before the work of Gladden's generation Protestant religion had been riveted fast to the theories of Divinely-sanctioned laws, the depravity of the poor, the futility of collective action, and the other dogmas of clerical laissez faire.

[89] White, *Autobiography* (New York, 1946), p. 325.

[90] W. J. and Mary Baird Bryan, *The Memoirs of William Jennings Bryan* (Chicago, 1925), p. 305.

[91] Wilson, "The Ministry and the Individual," Address before the McCormick Theological Seminary at Chicago, November 2, 1909, in *The Public Papers of Woodrow Wilson*, Ray Stannard Baker and William E. Dodd, eds. (authorized ed.; New York, 1925-27), I, 186-187.

[92] Wilson, "Militant Christianity," Address at Y.M.C.A. Celebration, Pittsburgh, October 24, 1914, *ibid.*, I, 200.

Undoubtedly the ability to justify social change in terms of Christian doctrine has given American progressivism authority, power and a link with tradition. These gifts were particularly valuable during the difficult first adjustment of the American liberal tradition to the age of giant industry. More recently, it has become evident that American progressivism may owe partly to the Social Gospel also some of its less happy attributes, its tendencies toward facile optimism, neglect of machinery, and sporadic, revivalist techniques.

Much of the permanent effect of the Social Gospel on American thinking can be better understood if one examines some of its original traits. For the central doctrines of this school, though amplified and elaborated, changed little in essence at least until after the First World War.

First, one must remember the complete break with the past which the Social Gospel once implied. The simple teachings of the movement's early phase have now become so commonplace and are so much taken for granted that it is hard to imagine them as daring innovations. Yet to challenge the adequacy of laissez faire, to admit that fundamental deficiencies might exist in American society, was to challenge the basis of America's colossal growth. To plead for the recognition of human solidarity as a part of Christian teaching, to talk about social sin and social salvation, was to break with fundamental tenets cherished by Protestantism since the Reformation. Finally, the proposal that the church's responsibility should cover not only moral issues but also questions of material welfare seemed to involve a change in basic spiritual values.

At their best, the first statements of the Social Gospel were vigorous and effective. Gladden's simple deductions from his experience of depression and labor conflict stated beliefs toward which many of his contemporaries had been unconsciously working. The sudden and widespread acceptance of drastically changed opinions by large numbers of forward-looking American Christians was possible only because of the obvious, unquestionable honesty and timeliness of the new views.

The most obvious and pervasive weakness of the Social Gospel, its tendency toward facile optimism, was partly an inevitable consequence of its position in the history of Christian thought. The ideas of the Enlightenment, with their exalted view of the nature and possibilities of man, had long since dominated American political thought and finally, having penetrated religion through the Unitarian salient, were overcoming their last adversary in Protestant theology. It was the new hope and confidence of humanistic religion that enabled the Social Gospel leaders to defy the traditional assertions that poverty, oppression and class differences were part of the nature of things.

Yet many later Protestants have thought that the new theology, often (though by no means always) identified with social Christianity, made essential sacrifices that religion could ill afford. Advancing from the humanistic doctrines of the Bushnell school, social theologians reinterpreted all the major Christian beliefs in terms of an Immanent God, working not only through man but through society. In the more extreme statements of the school, the Atonement seemed to become little more than a symbol of suffering for the good of others, sin was selfishness and could be overcome by education, the church was a school of social service and the Kingdom of God (a concept greatly emphasized by social Christians) was merely the working out of the Divine Will through gradual social improvement.[93]

Critics of the "new theology" of which this "social theology" was one manifestation, have deplored the loss of the transcendent goal and transcendent perils which stimulated past Christians to great moral efforts. Some have questioned whether a belief in the universal efficacy of education reflects the reality of human emotions as well as a recognition of the possibility and validity of sudden conversion. Still more have regretted the steady de-emphasis on sin, the complete substitution of love for justice. Certainly it is possible even for the least theologically-minded historian to recognize the effectiveness of the great metaphors in which, for two thousand years, Christians had expressed human experience of evil and hope, and to realize the difficulty of replacing them.

Whether primarily because of its theological inheritance or because of its relation to secular currents of American thought, the Social Gospel displayed from its beginnings a tendency toward optimism on all levels of its teaching, with regard to particular problems as well as fundamental beliefs.

It seemed to many of us who were studying theology and beginning our ministry in the eighties and nineties as if humanity were on the eve of the golden age. . . . The Kingdom of God appeared to be at hand. . . . As the

[93] For good statements of "social theology," see W. DeW. Hyde, *Outlines of Social Theology* (New York, 1895); D. N. Beach, *The Newer Religious Thinking* (New York, 1893); Gladden, *Ruling Ideas of the Present Age* (Boston, 1895). A valuable secondary account is the chapter on Gladden in Buckham, *Progressive Religious Thought*, pp. 217-257.

dawn of the twentieth century approached we felt sure that it meant the ushering in of the reign of universal brotherhood. . . . It has been a harsh awakening.[94]

No doubt social Christian leaders drew confidence and courage from their rosy dreams of the future. They also developed, however, the faults of the social dreamer, including a fatal tendency to underestimate difficulties and to neglect mechanisms. It is of course, possible to argue, and some of the recent and more sophisticated spokesmen of social Christianity have argued that the concern of religion is with motive and not with method. But too often the early Social Gospel leaders seemed to imply that mechanisms were not necessary on any level, to neglect completely the complicated problem of ends and means in a surge of revivalistic confidence. Strikes, legislation, reform proposals were at most proposals to hasten the working out of inevitable tendencies toward the elevation of humanity. Opponents never needed, even temporarily, to be overcome but rather to be given the opportunity of enlightenment.

Some of the most acute of the early leaders realized that to certain groups faced with immediate and pressing problems questions of mechanism and power were urgent. Occasionally, well-meaning Christians did their utmost at least to investigate the demands of the dissatisfied. But their fundamental certain reliance on the social spirit of the new Christianity tended to separate them from potential allies. Few of them managed to achieve a successful working relation between their ultimate confidence in the new social spirit and the drab realities of day-to-day struggle.

Their deep confidence in the power of religion sometimes led the social Christians into an exaggerated belief in their own strength and in the ability of the church to accomplish quickly and alone the necessary reform of society. Josiah Strong, whose experience of contemporary evils was fuller than that of most of his colleagues, could say in 1893 that

. . . such is my confidence in the saving power of the complete Gospel, that in my very soul I believe a single generation will suffice to solve the problem of pauperism, to wipe out the saloon, to inaugurate a thousand needed reforms, and really change the face of society, provided only the churches generally enter into this movement.[95]

Because they were constantly in the role of expounding doctrines which to them seemed obvious, sufficient and unquestionable, some

[94] Buckham, *op. cit.*, pp. 316-317.
[95] Strong, *The New Era*, p. 270.

Social Gospel leaders tended to lose touch with their hearers. To labor audiences they were sometimes patronizing; in their middle-class congregations they may well have failed to realize the strength and depth of the prejudices and opinions they were attacking.[96]

Again because Christian social leaders were confident of the sufficiency of their simple appeals to the teachings of the New Testament, many of them, especially in the early generations, neglected to familiarize themselves with contemporary secular thought. The more complex currents of economics, sociology and psychology usually passed them by. Historical studies of earlier attempts to carry into practice Christ's social teachings were often unknown to them. And their reconciliation of religion with science was—as was later proved—almost disastrously facile. During the years when the anthropocentric conception of the universe was finally being blasted, social religion was preaching a doctrine essentially more anthropocentric than that of Calvin.

The strengths and weaknesses of the Social Gospel fitted it exactly for the role it had to play. Its optimism and simplicity enabled it to appeal to the widest possible group of middle-class American Protestants. Its elementary plea for social solidarity involved a large enough break with the past. Had it subjected existing social beliefs to any more destructive analysis, it could not have penetrated the great denominations; it would have remained forever on the fringes of organized religion. Yet two great deficiencies soon became apparent. First, the Social Gospel's somewhat shallow theological and emotional content made it unable to provide the great mass of Christians with the spiritual sustenance they demanded, and eventually it was demonstrated that vast areas of American religion had never been penetrated by the social interpretation. Second, the simplicity and optimism of its social analysis did not fit it to lead the way through the deep jungles and morasses of the twentieth century.

[96] It seems significant that recent opinion surveys have found ministers more progressive in their social views than church laymen. J. M. Yinger, *Religion in the Struggle for Power* (Durham, 1946), pp. 155-159.

RADICAL SOCIAL CHRISTIANITY

MOST of the limitations of the moderately progressive and widespread form of social Christianity are implied by comparing it to earlier outbreaks of Christian social protest. As Richard Niebuhr has pointed out, the secular-minded nineteenth century did not produce any major religious movement of the "disinherited," as had most previous Christian centuries.[1] The Anabaptists of the sixteenth century, the more revolutionary forms of English dissent in the seventeenth century and many other movements throughout Christian history had given vent, in religious terms, to bitter complaints against oppression. The Social Gospel of the American nineteenth century, on the other hand, did not grow out of actual suffering but rather out of moral and intellectual dissatisfaction with the sufferings of others. It originated not with the "disinherited" but rather with the educated and pious middle class. It grew through argument, not through agitation; it pleaded for conversion, not revolt or withdrawal.

Even in this period, however, various smaller groups of earnest Christians were trying to formulate more radical complaints against society, and even to join forces with nonreligious radical movements. Some individuals, resembling come-outers of other periods, followed their consciences far beyond the paths of conventional, acceptable reform.

Genuine radicalism can easily be distinguished from the reform appeal of the moderate Social Gospel, though some contemporaries, and particularly conservative critics of both movements, failed to make the distinction. The radical Christians, though in this period even they were by no means drawn from the bottom layers of society, rejected the basic existing social and economic organization. They did not confine themselves to demanding a "new social spirit" or a few limited reforms. They did not believe that everything was basically all right. The remedies they proposed, though they were Christian, nonviolent, and often unrealistic, were sweeping.

[1] H. Richard Niebuhr, *The Social Sources of Denominationalism* (New York, 1929), pp. 72-76 and *passim*.

The Christian radical leaders differed in temperament and manner from the moderate Social Gospel spokesmen, as radicals always differ from liberals. They spoke in terms of crisis and crusade, instead of continually appealing for patience and conciliation. They were, necessarily, willing to leave the mass of church opinion far behind and to accept rebuke, ridicule and loneliness. Yet in this period of social doubt, a few of them won a remarkably wide hearing.

Some of the religious radicals, of course, remained isolated by their own eccentricity or by their tendency to shock religious as well as social opinion. In 1882, for instance, Henry Cherouny published a pamphlet full of pretentious learning and biblical verbiage, demanding the organization of capital and labor into one "National Council of the Toilers" with power to regulate wages and prices. If this institution and a parallel Council of State to manage highways, railways and other "necessary dependencies of industry" were formed, neither the form of government nor the question of socialism would be a problem and poverty would cease to exist.[2] Another obscure pamphlet, written by Theodore Bourne and published in 1884, appealed, as Christian radicals had appealed in all periods, for a solution of current problems along the lines of the Christian communism of the apostles.[3]

Charles Richardson, writing in 1888, echoed the single-taxers and socialists in his angry charge that the miseries of the poor were caused by predatory appropriation of the means of production. His panacea was for the church to commence teaching that Christianity flatly prohibited the acquisition of wealth.[4] In the following year C. Osborne Ward, a less specifically Christian writer, published a learned interpretation of ancient history in terms of "strikes" and slave revolts. According to Ward, tradeunionism had been taught by Solon and greatly furthered by Christ, only to be destroyed by Constantine. Present-day unions were thus following the true Christian tradition.[5]

Possibly the author who most deeply shocked prevailing Christian modes of thought was Austin Bierbower. In a book published in 1885 Bierbower declared, in comparatively conventional Social Gospel terms, that Christ had throughout his life increased the social and democratic

[2] Cherouny, *Socialism and Christianity* (New York, 1882), esp. pp. 40-41.
[3] Bourne, *Money and Labor. Corporation and Co-operation.*
[4] Richardson, *Large Fortunes; or, Christianity and the Labor Problem* (Philadelphia, 1888).
[5] Ward, *A History of the Ancient Working People* (Washington, 1889). This volume is subtitled *The Ancient Lowly* and the subtitle forms the title of a second volume (published Washington, 1900).

emphasis of his teachings.[6] In a book published five years later, however, Bierbower set forth the amazing theory that Christ, originally promising a revolution which would produce government by the poor and distribution according to need, had gradually abandoned this promise and increased the monarchical and autocratic emphasis in His teaching. This reactionary tendency had been increased by the apostles, who neglected half the content of Christianity for an exclusive emphasis on its individual and spiritual meaning.[7] Naturally, clerical reviews of Bierbower's second book strongly disagreed with the author.[8]

Morrison I. Swift, a spokesman for New Thought, should perhaps hardly be considered within the Protestant fold. He combined social radicalism of a confused sort with his extreme theological unorthodoxy. In one pamphlet Swift called for the founding of a "social university to educate workingmen," and in another, described with evident approval an imaginary revolution started by a band of devoted clerks who stole their employers' funds in order to finance unions and co-operatives.[9]

None of these isolated radicals achieved any influence in a large denomination and none even became very well known to more orthodox contemporaries. Hugh O. Pentecost, the Christian anarchist, was perhaps the first religious radical of the period to receive widespread notice. Pentecost, almost alone among Christian ministers, denounced the hanging of the Chicago anarchists as murder.[10] He had been a labor candidate for mayor of Newark and was known as one of the foremost clerical proponents of the single tax.[11]

In 1887-1888 Pentecost finally resigned his Congregational pulpit, explaining his action in a long letter to the *Christian Union* in which he stated his conclusion that Jesus was a natural man with an "extraordinary spiritual nature" and the Bible a natural book of legend and history. In angry denunciation Pentecost contrasted the teachings of Jesus with the preachments of the church:

[6] Bierbower, *The Morals of Christ* (Chicago, 1885).

[7] *Ibid. The Socialism of Christ* (Chicago, 1890).

[8] *Watchman*, March 12, 1891, p. 7; *Congregationalist*, March 12, 1891, p. 3.

[9] Morrison I. Swift, *Plan of a Social University* (Ashtabula, 1890); *A League of Justice or Is it Right to Rob Robbers?* (Boston, 1893).

[10] His sermon on this subject is quoted, with extreme condemnation, by the *Watchman*, November 17, 1887, p. 1.

[11] See Post, *The Prophet of San Francisco*, p. 91. Pentecost carried on a controversy with M. M. Trumbull in the magazine, *The Open Court*, in defense of the single tax. Part of this controversy is reprinted in Trumbull ("Wheelbarrow," *pseud.*), *Articles and Discussions on the Labor Question* (Chicago, 1890), pp. 262-273. Trumbull says "If Mr. George left the key to his problem in the hands of any man, he left it in the hands of Mr. Pentecost." *Ibid.*, p. 263.

Jesus said "Do unto others as you would have others do unto you"—the gospel of transparent rightness. The commercial laity of the church say "If you do, you will fail in business"—the gospel of getting on in the world. . . . The church opens a wide door for the entrance of the rich, and makes it harder for the poor man to enter than for a camel to go through a needle's eye.[12]

A rejoinder by the editors provided a clear definition of the differences between the Social Gospel and Christian radicalism. Admitting that some Christians neglected the social part of Christ's teaching, this rebuttal charged that Pentecost neglected the far more important spiritual side. He also forgot, they said, that social reform and even "the modern socialistic movement" owed their existence to Christianity. As proof of this origin, the *Christian Union* pointed to the work of Ely, Gladden and Bishop Potter, concluding somewhat dogmatically that "As to men who have no Christian faith, it is difficult to name one who has done or suffered aught for the moral, political or social elevation of the overworked and the underpaid." Finally, the editors insisted that Pentecost misunderstood the duty of the clergy, which was to provide the spirit for social reform, leaving particular applications and concrete proposals to others.[13]

Like many basically religious-minded radicals, Pentecost developed more and more bizarre social theories when he left behind the restraining influence of the church. After 1888 he preached his naturalistic gospel to a "Unity Congregation" meeting in a Masonic temple and a theater, and edited the *Twentieth Century*, an organ of religious and political radicalism. This come-outer journal was intended to fill the gap between certain liberal Unitarian papers which neglected social problems and the socialist, anarchist, and single-tax press which seldom dealt with religious problems.[14] At first the *Twentieth Century* supported such concrete objectives as single tax, paper money, national ownership of communications, and so forth. It was consistently friendly to labor's struggles, though it believed little would be accomplished by strikes without a concurrent effort for sweeping social change. By the middle of 1890, however, the paper had veered sharply toward a more dogmatic espousal of philosophic anarchism, condemning the single tax, socialism, and Nationalism and urging instead the primacy of individualist reform.

[12] Pentecost, "Mr. Pentecost's Views," *Christian Union*, February 9, 1888, pp. 167-168.

[13] *Christian Union*, February 9, 1888, pp. 163-164.

[14] See its statement of principles, February 23, 1889, p. 1. Descriptive information in this paragraph is drawn from the paper's files.

Until Pentecost left the paper in 1892, it centered its attention increasingly on such measures as a complete freedom from taxation, the right of individuals to issue money, and the end of the patent system.

Pentecost's lectures during this period of growing eccentricity seem to have attracted considerable attention. When, after preaching on the topic "The Single Tax No Remedy," he announced an address called "Trade Unions No Remedy," Samuel Gompers thought it well to go. According to that trade-union leader, the lecture was "the worst I ever heard!" Gompers, always slightly inclined to overrate his own influence, says in his autobiography that he later convinced Pentecost of his error and led him back toward a position friendly to unionism and that later Pentecost so far deserted his anarchism as to become a member of Tammany Hall![15]

A more effective and less eccentric figure was J. O. S. Huntington, the radical son of Bishop F. D. Huntington.[16] Huntington was one of the founders of CAIL, and remained in close touch with the strong Episcopalian social movement. In temperament and in some of his actions, however, he was closer to the come-outer radicals than to the organized progressives of his church.

Like some other social radicals of Episcopalian faith, Huntington was deeply influenced by the Oxford Movement, and founded in 1881 the Order of the Holy Cross, a semimonastic organization which engaged in mission work on New York's East Side. Huntington's experience of slums and poverty stirred him into a career of fervent, mystical agitation for social improvement. With the other members of CAIL, he worked hard for the eight-hour day, child-labor reform, tenement improvement, and consumer boycott of sweated industry, but he did not stop with this program.

Like Pentecost, this bold priest protested the execution of the Chicago anarchists.[17] He became second only to McGlynn among all-out clerical supporters of Henry George, taking part in the 1886 campaign in a manner that George's biographer vividly recalls:

One of the sensations I experienced in that campaign was caused by the sight, as I approached a large street meeting near Cooper Union, of a speaker in priestly robes addressing the crowd from a truck and raising it to a high

---

[15] Gompers, *Seventy Years*, pp. 324-326.

[16] Vida D. Scudder, *Father Huntington* (New York, 1940), is one of the most informative biographies of clerical leaders in this period. For the philanthropic and institutional side of Huntington's career, see Miller and Fletcher, *The Church and Industry*, pp. 90-91; Abell, *Urban Impact*, p. 216.

[17] Scudder, *Huntington*, p. 180.

pitch of enthusiasm by his advocacy of Henry George's election. He was the Reverend J. O. S. Huntington. . . . More than one such street meeting was addressed by Father Huntington in that campaign in support of Henry George's candidacy.[18]

Convinced that the single tax was the fundamental cure for misery and injustice, Huntington spoke warmly in its favor before the Church Congress in 1891.[19] He contrasted this basic and sufficient reform with the piecemeal methods of church philanthropy in which he had formerly believed but which he came to consider ineffective, patronizing and actually harmful.[20]

Huntington developed a passionate and sometimes mystical belief in the labor movement, arguing that, although many strikes were unjustifiable, yet "there is about every strike a great deal that is heroic, unselfish and, therefore, highly moral" and asking, with regard to sympathetic strikes, "How many rich men would do as much for their dearest friends?"[21] He became a member of the Knights and reported their meetings enthusiastically for the Episcopalian press. With Henry D. Lloyd, he was particularly active in support of the Spring Valley miners in 1889-90.[22]

This bishop's son was no socialist.[23] He was in fact, like some other Episcopalian progressives, an aristocrat; according to his biographer he was particularly proud of his Harvard background. Yet he clearly belonged to the come-outer radical tradition, both by virtue of his militant activity and his passionate, prophetic language. He was capable of calling the Exodus a strike and Palm Sunday a political demonstration, and of issuing a warning that "Unless we repent, Christ will come even as He came in France, in the blood and fire and vapor of smoke of the First Revolution."[24] People who patronized sweat shops he accused of "Bloodguiltiness."[25]

---

[18] Post, *Prophet of San Francisco*, p. 76.

[19] Protestant Episcopal Church, Church Congress, *Papers, Addresses and Debates*, 1891, pp. 69-70.

[20] Huntington, "Philanthropy—its Success and Failure" and "Philanthropy and Morality," *Philanthropy and Social Progress* (various authors, "Delivered before the School of Applied Ethics, Plymouth, Massachusetts, during the Session of 1892," [New York, 1893]), pp. 57-204.

[21] "Philanthropy, etc.," p. 194.

[22] E.g. Huntington, "Congress of the Knights of Labor," *Churchman*, February 13, 1892, p. 190; Scudder, *op. cit.*, pp. 117-118.

[23] He repudiated socialism particularly and repeatedly, e.g. in the speech before the Church Congress cited above.

[24] Quoted by Scudder, *op. cit.*, pp. 156-157.

[25] Huntington, "Blood-guiltiness," *Christian Union*, December 19, 1889, pp. 795-796.

Supported, though not with complete agreement, by his father and Bishop Potter, Huntington retained more influence in regular denominational circles than most of his radical contemporaries. Yet his typically High Church combination of social reform and mysticism, not uncommon in England, was an exotic in America, far less suited to the tastes of the American Protestant public than Gladden's calm reasonableness. Its weakness was demonstrated dramatically when, in 1892, Huntington suddenly abandoned all social causes to concentrate on the monastic life. According to his biographer, this action was motivated partly by a lifelong preoccupation with monasticism and partly by a feeling of frustration in his social work. Huntington had come to feel that he did not really understand the working people for whom he labored, and was perturbed that the social-monastic Order of the Holy Cross had only three members at the end of its first decade. This withdrawal was a serious blow to the Episcopalian social movement and was deplored by Bishop Potter and Dean Hodges.[26]

Huntington's far less radical pupil, Vida D. Scudder, became a believer in Christian Socialism, which she defended in a number of publications whose mystical nature and ethical emphasis show the Huntington influence.[27] A contemporary whose life somewhat resembled Huntington's was B. F. DeCosta, who held the presidency of CAIL for a brief turn. DeCosta was widely attacked in the press in 1890 for stating that Jesus, if he returned to earth, would be called an anarchist.[28] As in the case of Huntington, DeCosta's High Anglican tendencies finally proved more important than his social reform preoccupations and in 1899 he became a Roman Catholic.[29]

The most tireless of Christian radicals, and the most successful organizer, was the Reverend William Dwight Porter Bliss.[30] Having begun his career as a Congregationalist clergyman, Bliss became convinced by 1885 that the social application of Christianity was religion's most important task and that this could best be carried out through the Episcopal church. Called to the Episcopalian Mission of Grace Church in

[26] This incident is discussed in some detail by Scudder, *op. cit.*, pp. 169-174.

[27] See Scudder, *Socialism and Spiritual Progress* ("An Address delivered before the Society of Christian Socialists, Boston, March, 1891,") pamphlet, n.p., n.d., reprinted as Christian Social Union, *Publications*, Series A, No. 10 (Boston, 1896).

[28] DeCosta's statement and its upshot are described in the *Christian Union*, March 19, 1890, p. 418.

[29] DeCosta, *Letter to a Layman* (pamphlet, New York, 1899).

[30] Bliss has been much discussed by recent historians. The fullest account is in Hopkins, *Rise of the Social Gospel*, pp. 171-183. See also Dombrowski, *Early Days*, pp. 96-106; Abell, *Urban Impact*, pp. 75-78. Bliss gives a brief account of his own life in his *A Handbook of Socialism*, p. 214.

South Boston in 1887, Bliss was further influenced by his experience of city conditions. His thought owed much to British Christian Socialism, George and particularly Bellamy.

The Society of Christian Socialists, organized by Bliss in 1889, was by far the most effective of radical Christian organizations. Dedicated to the task of showing socialists and church members that socialism was a necessary result of Christianity,[31] it held frequent meetings, discussions and lectures, published a newspaper and many tracts, and eventually developed branches in several western cities. Though the Society's methods were principally educational, it sometimes took an active part in local labor struggles. In 1890, for instance, it sent a letter signed by several Boston clergymen to the locked-out shoe workers of Haverhill, urging them to stand firm.[32]

Other organizations constantly developed out of the nucleus provided by the Boston Christian Socialists. The membership of the Nationalist Club of Boston largely overlapped.[33] In 1890 Bliss found it necessary to give up his Grace Church charge because of the pressure of his organizing work and founded instead the Mission of the Carpenter, a Christian Socialist congregation. This in turn became the headquarters of the Brotherhood of the Carpenter, another propaganda group with purposes very similar to those of the Christian Socialists. The following year the Brotherhood acquired a house which became the Wendell Phillips Union, headquarters of the Anti-Tenement House League, the Wendell Phillips Purchasers League and other proliferating societies.[34]

Beside providing the initial impetus and much of the sustaining vigor for all these interlocking Christian Socialist activities and editing the newspaper the *Dawn*, Bliss took a leading part in all the work of the regular Episcopalian reform organizations such as CAIL and the C.S.U., was a member of the Knights of Labor and an organizer of the American Fabian League and the Union Reform League. He lectured, traveled and wrote ceaselessly under varying auspices. In his *Encyclopedia of Social Reform*[35] he made an important contribution to American social science.

[31] The Society's "Declaration of Principles" is published in Philo W. Sprague, *Christian Socialism, What and Why?* (New York, 1891), pp. 144-145.

[32] See *Dawn*, January 17, 1890.

[33] The Declaration of Principles of this organization, specifically religious in language and very similar to that of the Christian Socialists, is published in Sprague, *op. cit.*, pp. 145-146.

[34] See *Dawn*, for the best accounts of these organizations, especially December 4, 1890, p. 9; May 1, 1891, p. 9; September 1891, p. 3; October 26, 1892, pp. 3-4; May 1892, rear cover.

[35] New York, 1897.

Earnest to the point of fanaticism, incredibly energetic, persistently optimistic, forceful in print and far better informed than most clerical leaders, Bliss was an appropriate spearhead for the left of the social movement. His Christian Socialism was actually socialism and not just reform, but it was gradualist and political in its methods.[36]

We are not to be in haste to turn everything over to Uncle Sam, trusting to Uncle Sam to realize God's Kingdom in the United States. With every respect for Uncle Sam we still believe in the necessity of the development of the individual. We are to be eternally democratic. . . . Christian Socialists are to make their main stand for the divine conception of the State, and the necessity of a true environment as one of the elements, though by no means the only element, in the development of perfect character. Hence **we** are, in this sense, first and foremost, State Socialists.[37]

Bliss made it particularly clear that piecemeal philanthropy of the character widely acclaimed by religious reformers was not to be confused with the purpose of his organizations:

. . . we are not to work to establish a Christian co-operative colony, no system of profit-sharing, no individualistic scheme, no *ignis fatuus* of associated charities and model houses and aristocratic patronage. We are to work for the development of the Christian *State*, and so for the conversion of people to our ideas.[38]

However, since "people desire the concrete," Bliss urged his followers to include among their immediate aims municipal ownership of utilities, a new political party, and the encouragement of the co-operative movement "to prepare people for the Co-operative Commonwealth."[39]

The actual methods upon which Bliss and his followers relied to achieve both their immediate and their long-run goals were essentially educational. Like other radicals in other periods, Bliss believed that events would work into his hands:

Men will say we are doing nothing practical; they will ask us to point to our results. But, bye-and-bye, there will come a sudden birth of the new life; a bad crop, a financial panic, a widespread strike will precipitate the crisis, and the work that Socialists and Nationalists and Christian Socialists have long been doing will become suddenly manifest.[40]

Despite his constant criticism of present religious as well as economic

[36] For important statements of Bliss' general beliefs see *Dawn*, May 15, 1889, p. 1; January 15, 1890, pp. 1-2; February 1890, pp. 1-2; July-August 1890, pp. 109-114.
[37] *Dawn*, July-August 1890, pp. 110-111.
[38] *Loc. cit.*, p. 111.
[39] *Loc. cit.*, pp. 112-114.
[40] *Loc. cit.*, pp. 112-113.

institutions, Bliss remained within the Episcopal church, insisting that "we think of the Church as a lover does, who sees wrong in one he loves."[41]

Bliss' organizing talent and his crusading zeal attracted the assistance of several other articulate and convinced Christian Socialist clergymen. F. E. Tower contributed several tracts to the Society's publications. His What's The Trouble? presented a thoroughly socialist indictment of existing society and demanded that capital "be peacefully changed to public ownership by law." He offered Nationalism, which he identified with Christian Socialism, as an alternative to "violent" socialism or anarchism and appealed to the middle class of America to come to its support.[42] His The Advancing Kingdom offered a complicated and marvelous interpretation of history in terms of revelation, leading to the conclusion that it was America's destiny to overcome Romanism and usher in Christian Socialism.[43]

The Reverend Philo W. Sprague, another pillar of the Society of Christian Socialists, also believed the existing economic system entirely incompatible with Christianity. He denied that Man was naturally selfish and believed that existing social arrangements were forcing him to deny the best sides of his nature. With the advance of socialism humanity would develop its better instincts. Calling for social ownership of all means of production as the final goal, he insisted on peaceful and gradual means of advance, believing that the spread and success of municipal ownership would convince the nation of the superiority of collectivism.[44]

One of the most authoritative and revealing statements of Christian Socialism was F. M. Sprague's Socialism from Genesis to Revelation.[45] Sprague knew contemporary socialist theory better than most of his colleagues, expressing his debt to Christian Socialism but also emphasizing the classical and Marxist labor theory of value. Like the other Christian Socialists, he dismissed piecemeal reform, insisting that "You cannot Christianize exploitation. . . ." More specifically than any other Christian socialist, he attacked the beliefs of the conservative and moderate Christian social movements, making Behrends his special target, disapproving statements of Joseph Cook, and condemning Gladden's tendency to accept the essentials of capitalism.[46]

[41] Dawn, January 1895, p. 1.
[42] Pamphlet, Boston, 1891.
[43] Hartford, 1892.
[44] Sprague, Christian Socialism, What and Why?
[45] Boston, 1893.
[46] Ibid., pp. 65-66, 72-73, 66-89, 105, 230-231 (Behrends); pp. 75, 79 (Cook); pp. 236-237 (Gladden).

Yet, like his fellows, Sprague was essentially an idealist. He said almost nothing about the American labor movement or about non-Christian socialist programs in his own time and country. The chief necessity for social change was the conversion of the church. Present owners of capital would be little disturbed:

They [the Christian Socialists] believe that private capital may become public so gradually, with so little friction, that vested interests will realize no interference, and that capitalists as well as laborers will rejoice in the change.[47]

It is interesting to remember that this was written the year after the battle at Homestead.

Despite their hopes for a social millennium the Christian Socialists expressed consistent and militant views on immediate problems in the *Dawn*. This struggling little sheet, which started publication in 1889, became the official organ of the Society on June 15, 1890. In December Bliss announced that it had proved too much of a drain on the Society and that he was assuming its burdens himself.[48] Appearing irregularly and in many forms, it remained essentially his own organ. Yet it served as the principal outlet for the views of the radical Christian social movement, and its associate editors included many of the leading moderates as well as radicals in the churches.[49]

Besides continually setting forth the broad principles of the Society the *Dawn* backed such concrete measures as the Australian ballot, public works to relieve unemployment, tax reform, woman suffrage and many others. Though it always maintained that strikes could never achieve labor's aims by themselves, it heartily supported most of the principal strikes of its day, including those at Homestead and Pullman. In discussing the latter struggle, it hoped that peaceable strikes would increase until the government was forced to take action in such directions as railroad nationalization, tax reform, hours limitation, and employment of the unemployed.[50] It vigorously supported the nascent Peoples' Party.[51]

Considering the distance between Christian Socialism and the views being expressed by the church press and other organs of dominant clerical opinion, Bliss and his followers were surprisingly successful in

[47] *Ibid.*, p. 339.
[48] *Dawn*, December 4, 1890, p. 7.
[49] A list was published May 15, 1889, including Bellamy, the Reverend H. C. Vrooman of the Union for Practical Progress, and Heber Newton as well as the Christian Socialist leaders.
[50] July-August 1894, pp. 97-98.
[51] December 4, 1890, pp. 2-3; January 15, 1891, p. 11; June 1891, pp. 3-4.

their efforts to get a hearing. P. W. Sprague expressed the views of the Society in the Church Congress discussion of socialism in 1891, and his *Christian Socialism* was reviewed with tolerance and qualified approval by the *Watchman*.[52] Richard T. Ely, in an address before the large and powerful Evangelical Alliance, welcomed the movement in the name of the moderate Christian progressives:

> . . . I rejoice in the growth here in Boston—I may say frankly—of nationalism and Christian socialism. It is not that I accept all the principles of those who support these movements. . . . I do think, however, and I do not hesitate to say that I think that to-day they are the leaven which is needed in American society, and as I fear nothing from those doctrines of theirs which strike me as extreme, I rejoice in their activity.[53]

When the Church of the Carpenter ended in 1896, and with it Bliss' efforts at strictly Christian Socialist organization in Boston, the Christian Social Union employed him as its traveling secretary, and he spent the rest of his life lecturing on the broad principles of Christian Socialism under these and other auspices.[54]

During the period of his Boston activity, however, many Christians responded in kind to the Christian Socialist denunciation of conservative churches. The *Churchman* disliked the Society's "use of Christ's name as the badge of what is after all, an economic or political faction or party." It considered the Christian Socialist advocacy of "nationalization of capital" dangerous, and reminded the group in Spencerian terms that, "While natural and orderly evolution can be hindered or prevented by adventitious interference, it needs no adventitious assistance to produce precisely what is best."[55] The *Methodist Review* condemned Bliss and his group by name in a general editorial diatribe against socialism. Even Bishop Potter, deciding that Bliss' group went beyond the reform views which he considered proper, warned the clergy of his diocese against the "erroneous teaching" of Christian Socialism.[56]

The Christian Socialist movement of the nineties was far more ably led than any radical Christian movement since the Civil War. Because it grew at a time of widespread social discussion in the churches, it re-

[52] Protestant Episcopal Church, Church Congress, *Papers, Addresses and Debates*, 1891, pp. 57-60; *Watchman*, February 26, 1891, p. 3.
[53] Evangelical Alliance for the U.S.A., *National Needs and Remedies*, p. 48.
[54] See Hopkins, *Rise of the Social Gospel*, pp. 179-180.
[55] *Churchman*, February 22, 1890, p. 194; May 3, 1890, pp. 552-553.
[56] *Methodist Review*, LXXIII (1891), 120-126. Potter's statement was quoted in the *Dawn*, November 1894, pp. 162-163. The *Dawn* stated that Potter must have been misled, since he was himself close to the Christian Socialist position.

ceived much more attention than its predecessor, the Christian Labor Union of the seventies. Yet in view of the great hopes of its founder it can hardly be called successful. Its membership remained small and its branches outside Boston never approached the activity of the parent organization. Its members, interpreting the events of their day as signs of the birth of a new order, greatly overestimated the radicalism of American Protestants. The Society's demand for collective ownership was far too radical to draw any large following from the middle-class church public. Yet its idealism and its lack of emphasis on immediate problems prevented it from appealing successfully to discontented labor groups or from coalescing with the infant socialist movement outside the church.

Despite his usual optimism, his courage, his unflagging zeal, Bliss realized that the movement was not popular. In explaining one of the frequent alterations in publication plans for the *Dawn*, he gave an excellent picture of his group's heroic, discouraging struggle:

Without entering into details, we may say that editing and attending to the business of THE DAWN, for nothing, and sitting up nights to earn a living with our pen, besides taking the care and labor of three preaching services on the Sabbath, is a pace we cannot continue. Money sufficient for THE DAWN and an assistant has not come in. While the few who believe in THE DAWN have risen manfully to its support, the large majority of radical social reformers do not believe in our position on Christianity, and the large large [sic] majority of Christians only believe in a very mild and cautious Social reform. We are not willing, in order to gain support, to make the slightest compromise of our principles and therefore prefer a less frequent issue. Christianity without Socialism we believe to be a lie; Socialism without Christianity we consider a fatal mistake.[57]

A still more uncompromising movement was Herbert N. Casson's Labor Church of Lynn, Massachusetts, founded in 1894.[58] Casson had left the Methodist clergy because of his conviction that all existing denominations were unable to reach the working class. His movement was organized as a branch of the Labor Church founded in England in 1891 by John Trevor, a British Socialist and Unitarian.[59] Perhaps because of this connection, the American movement's theology was radically humanistic:

[57] *Dawn*, March 26, 1891, p. 2.
[58] For accounts see Hopkins, *Rise of the Social Gospel*, pp. 86-87; Bliss, *Handbook of Socialism*, pp. 217-218.
[59] For an account of the British Labor Church and comments on Casson's organization see John Trevor, "The Labor Church: Religion of the Labor Movement," *Forum*, XVIII (1894-95), 597-601.

We are not to look back two thousand years to a foreign community for our God or our inspiration. If we can not find God in the activities of our own time we shall not find Him anywhere. . . .

To the Labor Church Christ is not a fetish, nor a name to pray by, nor an idol, but a comrade, and a noble hero whose memory cheers and guides us on.[60]

Instead of merely approving the labor movement, Casson's group identified it with religion. The Labor Church's first two articles of faith were:

1. God is the cause and strength of the Labor Movement, and whatever institution or individual opposes the Labor Movement opposes him.
2. All who are working for the abolition of wage-slavery are, consciously. working together with Him, and are therefore members of the real Church.[61]

With the zeal of the true come-outer Casson condemned existing institutions:

The present Church and State are both cut out of the same piece of cloth. . . . The Labor Church teaches therefore that it is impossible to destroy capitalism and leave the Church untouched. The axe must be laid at the ROOT of both.[62]

Many a church is nothing but a spiritual opium joint.[63]

Casson had nothing but contempt for the mildly progressive churchmen of his day, and his indictment of their timidity was not without truth:

Even those preachers who are called practical and modern, seldom go farther in applying Christian principles than to pick out a few personal frailties whose evil influence is slight and limited. Many think they are very bold and radical if they denounce dancing and cards, and prohibition is the high-water mark. If they are especially advanced and ambitious, and dare to touch social questions, they speak in a "yes, I mean no" style that does not commit them to anything, and qualify any strong statement of truth with so many pious or apologetic phrases that its force is lost.[64]

Christian Socialism of the Bliss variety was likewise rejected because of its Episcopalian orthodoxy:

[60] Casson, *What We Believe* (Lynn, 189-?), pp. 4, 9-10.
[61] *Ibid.*, back cover.
[62] *Ibid.*, p. 3.
[63] *Ibid.*, p. 6.
[64] *Ibid.*, pp. 8-9.

Christian Socialism takes its stand in the Church as a divinely-sanctioned institution, while the Labor Church places itself in the centre of the Labor Movement, and says "God is here." Christian Socialism . . . still believes in the sacredness of mould and cobwebs.[65]

Casson, even more vigorously than Bliss, rejected lesser reform measures and called for common ownership of industry. Instead of relying, with the Christian Socialists, on political methods for accomplishing this objective, he centered his hopes in the labor movement. The task he foresaw for the Labor Church was that of providing unity and solidarity through its teaching of Christian love, evidently leaving methods to be worked out by other labor organizations.[66] Casson's wholehearted offer of spiritual help was evidently accepted only sporadically. When he was forced to leave Lynn for reasons of health in 1900, the movement collapsed.[67]

Of all Christian radicals the most influential leader, the most controversial figure, and to many contemporaries and later students the most compelling personality, was the western social messiah, George D. Herron.[68] His first social sermon, delivered before the Congregational ministers of Minneapolis in 1890, attracted nationwide attention and resulted in a call to Burlington, Iowa. In 1893 Mrs. E. D. Rand of Burlington founded for him a chair of Applied Christianity at Iowa College (later Grinnell). Through his teaching there and through his constant and forceful preaching to college and church audiences throughout the Middle West, Herron became for a few years the center of considerable national controversy, attracting both denunciation and fervent defense. By 1898 his increasingly outspoken socialism necessitated his resignation from the college.

Herron's influence in church circles came to an abrupt end in 1901 when he was divorced by his wife and promptly married the daughter of Mrs. Rand in a ceremony designed and consecrated (with unquestioned sincerity) only by himself.[69] By this time, also, he had abandoned much of the Christian content of his social philosophy and had become active in the Socialist party. His later political and diplomatic activities, mostly carried on from abroad, are of great interest, but have little to do

[65] *Ibid.*, p. 3.
[66] *Ibid.*, p. 7.
[67] Hopkins, *Rise of the Social Gospel*, p. 87.
[68] Herron's career and opinions are discussed in some detail in Dombrowski, *Early Days*, pp. 171-193, and Hopkins, *op. cit.*, pp. 184-200. Both these authors express deep admiration for Herron. See also Abell, *Urban Impact*, pp. 78-81, 110-111.
[69] Dombrowski's account of Herron's life is seriously distorted by his placing this event ten years too early. *Op. cit.*, p. 172.

with the story of social Christianity. His contribution to church opinion must be assessed on the basis of his statements and activities in the middle nineties.

The personality of this powerful preacher was admitted by all who knew him to be of central importance for the understanding of his effectiveness. His passionate sincerity, courage and fervency were coupled with an exalted view of his own mission and with a complete confidence in his own rightness that alienated some contemporaries.[70] Emotional and prophetic, he attached little value to consistent analysis: "Great spiritual facts and principles are not apprehended, but generally distorted, by the intellect. Not the clear in head, but the pure in heart, shall see God."[71] His enemies accused him of having a far too messianic conception of his own role, and there is no doubt that at times he did seem to take for granted some degree of personal inspiration. He had no hesitation in comparing the task of modern social preachers to the work of Jesus:

Through great tribulations will the new redemption come, bringing crowns of thorns and crosses for its prophets. The early workers upon the foundation which Jesus is laying for a divine society will accomplish the fall of this hideous, colossean materialism which we call civilization; but they themselves will be crushed in the fall and buried beneath the ruins.[72]

This supreme redemptive role, however, was no more than Herron offered to all men. Carrying the social theology to a passionate extreme, he centered his religion in the Cross. All men were to aid in the redemption through suffering of humanity, in the overcoming of sin, and in the achievement of that inner change which constituted salvation. The Atonement was an example which could be followed and a continuing task:

If there was that in the character of Christ impossible to us; if he, as a human being, was what we cannot be; if he was not tried by everything that tries us, and had spiritual resources which we have not; if we cannot overcome in what he overcame; then he was not a perfect Redeemer, and we are not redeemed.[73]

Herron's interpretation of the doctrine of the Immanent God broke

[70] William Allen White, who shared with Herron a mission to discuss a treaty with the Soviet government immediately after the First World War, gave a respectful but not over-sympathetic account of his ill-matched colleague. White, *Autobiography*, pp. 560-561.
[71] Herron, *The Larger Christ* (New York, 1891), p. 45.
[72] Herron, *The New Redemption* (New York, 1893), p. 98.
[73] *The Larger Christ*, p. 28.

completely the boundary between the spiritual and the material world and brought him to a definition which had been expounded by another radical Christian a half century before:

Man is spirit as God is spirit, and the use of the material is the fellowship of the spiritual. This conception is the inspiration of Dr. Brownson's definition of property as "communion with God in the material world."[74]

Like Pentecost and Casson, Herron roundly condemned the existing church, urging it to adopt a completely new view of its function:

There is nothing which the vested interests of conservative Protestantism resent so much as the Kingdom of God, which is the brotherhood of man. The world knows the church is failing; that it has become a secular more than a Christian institution.[75]

He heaped Old-Testament anathemas on the Protestant rich and castigated the churches for their sycophancy:

The adulation which the religious press lavishes upon the benevolence of mammon, the adoration which it receives from the pulpit, converts the church into an apostle of atheism to the people. The priests who accompanied the pirate ships of the sixteenth century, to say mass and pray for the souls of the dead pirates for a share of the spoil, were not a whit more superstitious or guilty of human blood, according to the light of their teaching, than Protestant leaders who flatter the ghastly philanthropy of men who have heaped their colossal fortunes upon the bodies of their brothers.[76]

Herron, more drastically than any of his contemporaries, broke with the tradition of classical economics and individualist sociology, insisting that, "Unless it be primarily a science of righteousness, sociology cannot be a science of society," and that "Economic science is thus an ethical science; it is a science of righteousness; it is a science of the communism of justice. . . ."[77] He repudiated the wage system, insisting that its "inevitable result" must be "to increase social inequalities, to increase the wealth of the few and the poverty of the many. . . ."[78]

Herron, like so many of his contemporaries, was deeply moved by the crisis of the early nineties, calling it "the first real test of the worth of our American civilization."[79] He refused to join in the prevalent ridicule of

[74] *New Redemption*, p. 52.
[75] Herron, *A Plea for the Gospel* (New York, 1892), p. 23.
[76] *New Redemption*, p. 60.
[77] *Christian Society*, pp. 18, 125.
[78] *New Redemption*, p. 27.
[79] *Christian Society*, p. 15.

Coxey's army and its proposal for state work relief financed by a bond issue:

> . . . when the divine judgment of history passes between the national legislature of 1894, and the vagabond citizens who were mobbed by the police for bearing this proposition to the Capitol steps, I pray to be judged among the vagabonds.[80]

He had little confidence, however, in political remedies, believing that "the power of immoral wealth" was in complete control of state and national legislatures.[81]

Herron has been described by some disciples and others as the first revolutionary socialist produced by the Christian social movement. It is true that his speeches, even before he left the church, contained many tocsin sounds. In 1893 he stated that "Any wealth that is not the creation of labor is fictitious" and that any claim to manage property for the purpose of self-interest was "morally unlawful."[82] As early as 1895 he had concluded that: "Unless democracy retreat from the field of progress, it must take possession of the industrial world. . . . the people must finally own and distribute the products of their own labor. . . ."[83] He has been quoted as approving "Revolutions, even in their wildest forms" as the "impulses of God."[84]

Actually, however, Herron was both vague and contradictory about the means by which the co-operative commonwealth would be achieved. In a more specific passage than the above, as in many others, he repudiated social violence:

> Revolutions that come through enforced separation and war, notwithstanding their historical gains, always carry with them elements that react and curse, degrade and corrupt. The nation, the cause, that triumphs by the sword, takes death into its moral life quite as much as perished armies have taken death into the bodies of their soldiers.[85]

Again and again, as long as he remained in the church, Herron showed that his essential reliance, like that of all the other religious radicals of the period, was in social conversion:

> The simple fact of our industrial situation is that the men of wealth in

[80] *The Christian State* (New York, 1895), p. 98.
[81] *Ibid.*, pp. 77-78.
[82] *New Redemption*, p. 23.
[83] *Christian State*, pp. 86-87.
[84] *New Redemption*, p. 15, quoted by Dombrowski, *op. cit.*, p. 193.
[85] *Christian State*, p. 22.

our American churches can begin to solve our pressing social problems any time they choose, by simply being disciples of the Lord Christ. . . .[86]

Many run to and fro with panaceas, which they think will adjust the inequalities of society and hush the cries of discontent. While many of the proposals are wise and needful . . . yet no political legislation has power, or ever can have power, to make men unselfish.[87]

More fundamentally than he was ever a socialist, Herron was a social revivalist, the first preacher in America who was able to combine the method of Moody or Talmage with the doctrines of Christian radicalism. His strongest sermons were preached in an effort to bring society to the mourner's bench:

Christ is disappointed in this nation. We are a fallen nation, an apostate people. We have done those material and political things we ought not to have done, and left undone the social and righteous things we ought to have done. . . .[88]

I see no other hope for our nation, no other redemption for society, than a religious revival such as the world has never known, that shall enthrone Christ in our national ideals, and give men the common will and the power to put the Christ life into social practice.[89]

It was partly because of his masterly use of this familiar American style that Herron, in the period of his Iowa professorship, 1893-98, achieved such a wide influence on individuals and institutions who did not share his radical views. Until he became too much of a storm center, he had the cordial and valuable support of Iowa's President George A. Gates, himself a Congregationalist minister of moderate Social Gospel views.[90] Together Gates and Herron attained for a few years a position of considerable regional leadership.

In 1893 Herron's influence was partly responsible for the founding of the American Institute of Christian Sociology.[91] This organization, founded at Chautauqua under the presidency of Professor Ely, adopted the principles of the Christian Social Union. Like the Episcopalian organization, the Institute was dedicated mainly to propaganda for the

[86] *Christian Society*, p. 114.
[87] *Plea for the Gospel*, pp. 145-146.
[88] *Christian State*, p. 179.
[89] *Ibid.*, p. 183.
[90] Considerable material on Gates' association with Herron can be found in Isabel Smith Gates, *The Life of George Augustus Gates* (Boston, 1915).
[91] See Abell, *Urban Impact*, pp. 110-111; Bliss, *Encyclopedia*, pp. 45-46; W. H. Tolman and W. I. Hull, *Bibliography of the American Institute of Christian Sociology* (2nd ed.; New York, 1893), pp. 135-137.

Social Gospel, and its members included many of the most influential of the mildly progressive leaders. It sponsored a Summer School of Applied Christianity which Herron had already organized at Iowa College. In 1894 Ely, Josiah Strong, John R. Commons and others took part in this school's sessions and the following year a similar institute was held at Oberlin with Gladden as president.[92]

In 1894 a group of social Christians led by Gates and Herron took over the *Northeastern Congregationalist* as the *Kingdom*. This journal, published in Minneapolis, became an important regional organ of the Social Gospel. Though Herron and Gates were frequent contributors, much of the paper's content was far less radical than Herron's views. It was, in fact, more like the *Christian Union* than the *Dawn*. Occasional writers in the *Kingdom* included such leaders as Josiah Strong and Washington Gladden. John R. Commons, one of the leaders of the ethical movement in economics, contributed regular articles on economic questions.[93]

Like most social Christians, the *Kingdom's* editors were deeply puzzled by the problem of strikes, and especially by the status of the nonunion worker, the point which, as much as any other, separated the Social Gospel from the labor movement. John P. Coyle was in advance of many writers in the *Kingdom* when he said that most men "will be glad if a step can be taken by which the liberty to work may come to mean something nobler than the liberty to grab another poor creature's job under guard of a squad of deputies." Yet even Coyle insisted that for the present "until the new step is taken, and taken constitutionally, we must all stand by the present system though we have to bear arms to protect the non-union laborer."[94] And an editorial note, commenting on the Northwestern Pacific Railroad strike, took it for granted that "the strike, as usually conducted, is condemned both by the civil and moral law."[95] The paper took a much less definite stand on the Pullman strike than the *Dawn*, blaming both sides for the crisis.[96] Though the western Christian social movement has sometimes been linked to the growth of Populism, the *Kingdom* printed both sides of the silver question. In 1899, following a lawsuit provoked by its attack on a textbook monopoly, the paper ceased to exist.[97]

[92] *Kingdom*, April 20, 1894, p. 9; June 7, 1895, p. 12.
[93] For an account of the paper, see Dombrowski, *Early Days*, pp. 110-120.
[94] Coyle, "My Neighbor's Job," *Kingdom*, September 14, 1894, p. 1.
[95] October 12, 1894, p. 10.
[96] E.g. July 6, 1894, pp. 8-9.
[97] Gates, *Gates*, pp. 18 ff.

The *Kingdom's* dominant note of reform, and its broad representation of moderate Social Gospel leaders, makes all the more striking its repeated and fervent defense of Herron when he was attacked for his genuinely radical views. Yet relations between this fiery crusader and the moderate Social Gospel were not as smooth and simple as this might indicate. Josiah Strong wrote an introduction to one of Herron's books, and in 1893 Herron was given an opportunity to set forth his views before the Evangelical Alliance, of which Strong was general secretary.[98] Yet the following year the executive committee of the Evangelical Alliance induced Strong to resign as an editor of the *Kingdom* because they objected to any link with Herron's increasing radicalism.[99] The *Christian Union* announced its "hearty approval" of Herron's first social-Christian utterance in 1890 but by 1894 found him "too passionate," regretting that his work, in some ways "admirable," was "robbed of its power by these fatal defects."[100]

Of course the conservatives in the church attacked Herron bitterly. Perhaps the strongest denunciation was produced by his 1895 speech in San Francisco, then as now a center of labor controversy and strong political opinion. The Reverend C. O. Brown, pastor of the First Congregational Church of Oakland, previously a well-known opponent of radicalism in the Middle West, led the offensive. Though Brown admitted Herron's sincerity he accused him of inciting anarchy and plunder, attacking American institutions "which are the unfolding of God's thought," teaching false economics, giving aid and encouragment to the pope through his call for church unity, and expressing an un-Christian spirit of class conflict.[101] The trustees of Brown's church added a circular, distributed with the pamphlet, in which they expressed great alarm that evangelical pastors were actually welcoming Herron's teachings, thereby evidencing the progress made in religious circles by "socialistic propaganda," from which their city and state had "suffered enough."[102]

Herron, of course, denied that he was an anarchist, striking back in characteristic fashion by accusing those who used the law as "the instrument of social injustice and industrial lawlessness," particularly railroads,

[98] Strong, "Introduction," Herron, *The Larger Christ*, pp. 7-10. Herron, "The Christian Basis of Social Reform," Evangelical Alliance for the U.S.A., *Christianity Practically Applied*, II, 457-463.

[99] This incident is discussed in some detail in E. and M. Strong, MS. biography of Josiah Strong, chap. 12.

[100] *Christian Union*, December 11, 1890, p. 799; May 12, 1894, p. 837.

[101] C. O. Brown, *Professor Herron's Teachings Reviewed, Ought the Church of Christ to Join the Propaganda of Socialism* (pamphlet, San Francisco, 1895), pp. 1-4.

[102] Circular distributed with above pamphlet, no separate title.

of being the real anarchists.[103] The *Kingdom* published a special edition entirely devoted to a refutation of Brown.[104] More surprisingly, the *Arena* in a sympathetic symposium was able to quote nine leading Protestant ministers of California who were to some extent sympathetic to Herron and critical of Brown's exaggerated attack.[105]

Despite Herron's increasing radicalism, his passionate sincerity and his compelling evangelistic preaching won him a surprisingly wide following in church circles during this period of social crisis. More than any other radical he retained the fellowship and support of the moderate social Christians. It is an interesting speculation whether his entrance into the Socialist party would have ended or greatly diminished his influence in church circles in 1900, had not his standing already been destroyed by the disastrous personal scandal.

The Christian radicalism of this period represents, to some extent, the survival of the come-outer spirit in Christianity. Small radical Christian groups have always existed in America as in other countries, and the extent of their influence has been determined by the social situation. In the prewar period, when vigorous currents of reform were flowing through the land, radicals like Brownson and Parker were strongly opposed by dominant church opinion, but their names were known, their works read. In the complacent postwar decade, Jesse H. Jones and his devoted little group remained frustrated and unknown. In the eighties and particularly in the nineties, when social crises had shaken the confidence of many Americans in some of their institutions, Christian radicals again achieved a certain limited hearing.

The most eccentric or defiant of these prophets, men like Bierbower, Pentecost or even Casson, remained largely isolated. Yet even these men attracted more attention than the similarly uncompromising members of the Christian Labor Union of the previous generation. Significantly, the new interest in social problems now provided church audiences even for the leaders of this long-dead movement on at least two occasions.[106]

---

[103] Herron, *Christian Society*, p. 119.

[104] June 7, 1895.

[105] *Arena*, XIV (1895), 110-128.

[106] In 1887 E. H. Rogers (see p. 78) contributed a paper on "The Relation of the Church to Capital and Labor," to the discussions of the Evangelical Alliance. Evangelical Alliance for the U.S.A., *National Perils and Opportunities*, pp. 234-246. Jesse H. Jones, the former leader of the Christian Labor Union, contributed two articles defending the Pullman strike to the *Kingdom*, July 13, 1894, p. 5; July 27, 1894, p. 4.

The two radical leaders who attained the widest effect did so through their contact with the moderate progressive Christian forces. Bliss kept in touch with CAIL and the left wing of the Episcopalian Social Gospel, though few Episcopalians agreed with the Christian Socialist platform. Herron, in his most effective years, won the partial co-operation of a large group of midwestern clerical progressives.

These courageous and convinced prophets of a new order managed to persuade very few Protestants to agree with their outright rejection of existing society. Some church members were very likely repelled from all social Christianity by the doctrines of the movement's extreme left. The Christian radicals were probably most effective in church circles as stimuli or irritants to their more hesitant, but essentially progressive brethren.

Leading Protestant circles in America still expressed the viewpoint of the middle class, and this immense group, though its conscience had become sensitive to some of the obvious defects of capitalism, was by no means disposed to consider seriously the socialist program. Bliss, Herron or Casson, calling on the American church to lead the way toward a collectivist world, showed they seriously misinterpreted their own powers, the nature of their potential following, and the contemporary social situation.

In later years, and particularly in the periods of widespread social criticism that immediately preceded the two world wars of the twentieth century, Christian radicals were to play a similar but increasing role, stimulating the conscience of church liberals and drawing down the denunciations of conservatives. In the later periods the lines between the moderate Social Gospel and the doctrines of Christian radicalism sometimes became less sharp, partly because some of the leading church liberals moved leftward and partly because all Protestant social critics tended at times to draw together in opposition to Marxist movements, with which very few of them ever maintained close relations.

Outside church circles, the Christian radicals of the nineties received public attention somewhat disproportionate to their numbers. Conservative and moderately progressive church statements on social questions were both commonplace, but every utterance of Christian radicalism had the interest of novelty. Much of the publicity accorded the radicals came from their critics. To many conservatives, it was and is particularly shocking that radical doctrine should be presented in Christian terms. Some defenders of the existing order lumped together Christian radicalism and the moderate Social Gospel, as we have seen. In addition, leading church radicals received a good deal of unfavorable comment directed at them in particular, and ranging from calm analysis to fervid denunciation.

In 1893 Nicholas Paine Gilman, in a book whose main purpose was to uphold moderate reform, especially profit-sharing schemes, as a superior substitute for all varieties of socialism, included a specific attack on Bliss' Boston Society of Christian Socialists. His principal criticism was that this little group insisted on taking some of the admittedly socialistic teachings of the New Testament too literally, when these doctrines were only intended to impart a general social spirit.[107] Two years later Professor Paul Monroe of the University of Chicago, in a much more sympathetic discussion of Christian Socialism, made the opposite criticism, alleging that Bliss and others, though admirable for their social spirit, were far too vague about their precise goals.[108] As the most widely publicized of the Christian radicals, Professor Herron became a favorite target of lay as well as clerical conservatives. When he said, in a commencement speech at Lincoln in 1894, that the United States was falling under the domination of capitalists and that such conditions sometimes had been known to lead to revolution, the bold preacher was attacked as an anarchist first by the Governor of Nebraska in an angry speech immediately following, and then by the Chicago press.[109] The *Nation*, always opposed to any socialistic doctrines, contributed a bitter attack on Herron and other preachers of "inflammatory" doctrines.[110]

Not all who heard the bold statements of the Christian radicals, however, were shocked into a completely hostile reaction. Some who disagreed with many of their tenets yet admired the courage and steadfastness of the little groups and were influenced by them in some degree. As we have seen, William Dean Howells, a typical representative of the liberal conscience at its best, was influenced by Bliss as well as by more moderate spokesmen of Christian reform. The effect of radicals on liberal opinion is often important and always hard to measure.

[107] Gilman, *Socialism and the American Spirit* (Boston, 1893), pp. 229-251. This book was highly praised by the *Churchman*, May 18, 1893, p. 622 and the *Andover Review*, XIX (1893), 477-480. The *Christian Union*, however, disagreed with Gilman's opinions. July 8, 1893, p. 83.

[108] Monroe, "English and American Christian Socialism: an Estimate," *American Journal of Sociology*, I (1895-96), 50-68.

[109] The incident is described, with considerable quotation, in the *Kingdom*, June 29, 1894, p. 171.

[110] XVIII (1894), 323-324.

On the tradition of American radicalism, and especially on the nascent American socialist movement, the religious radicals left certain more obvious effects. One of the first lay leftists to show this influence was Lawrence Gronlund. As early as 1884 Gronlund's socialist writing had emphasized ethical values, though it had not been specifically Christian.[111] In 1891, stating his debt to the recent Nationalist and (American) Christian Socialist movements, he moved toward a definitely religious emphasis:

> I more and more have become convinced that Karl Marx's doctrine, that the bread-and-butter question is the motive force of progress, is not tenable, but that we must grasp the very highest moral and religious truths.[112]

Addressing his socialist appeal primarily to religious readers, Gronlund said that the existing system fostered immorality, while the coming order would make goodness natural and easy. The dawn of socialism would bring with it a great religious revival, making God's purpose simpler to understand and bringing out the Divine element in humanity. Even belief in immortality would become easier, since people would insist less on personal identity and would accept the idea of the survival only of man's highest part.[113]

Through Henry Demarest Lloyd, Christian radicalism played a considerable part in American socialist organization.[114] An important influence on the development of Christian social thought, Lloyd was affected in turn by church leaders, remaining in close touch especially with the left wing of the Christian social movement.[115] After the Pullman debacle in 1894, Lloyd and many other religious-minded radicals, including ministers, turned once more toward the organization of Christian communist communities.[116] Partly because he did not share the optimistic opinion of some of his colleagues that socialism could be brought into being by the community movement alone, Lloyd agreed to sign a call for a national socialist convention at St. Louis in 1896. This meeting resulted in the organization of the Brotherhood of the Co-operative Commonwealth, a socialist organization with a distinct religious tinge.

---

[111] Gronlund, *The Cooperative Commonwealth* (Boston, 1884).

[112] Gronlund, *Our Destiny. The Influence of Socialism on Morals and Religion* (London, 1891), p. vii. This book was serialized in the *Nationalist*, beginning March 4, 1890, pp. 1-12.

[113] *Ibid.*, pp. 128-170.

[114] For a brief account of this episode, see Dombrowski, *Early Days*, pp. 74-75.

[115] See pp. 158-159.

[116] See Lloyd, *Henry Demarest Lloyd*, II, 45, 59-60. For an account of one of the more important colonies, see Dombrowski, *op. cit.*, pp. 132-170.

When Lloyd refused the presidency of this organization, the Reverend Myron W. Reed was elected, and Eugene Debs became national organizer. Out of the Brotherhood, together with the American Railway Union, developed the Social Democracy of America. When the S.D.A. split in 1898, over the perennially significant issue of politics vs. community organization, one wing of it became the Social Democratic party of America, the immediate ancestor of the Socialist party.[117] Probably a large proportion of the specifically religious members whom the S.D.A. had inherited from the Brotherhood of the Co-operative Commonwealth went with the antipolitical wing. Nonetheless, certain sections of the Socialist party, from the time of its founding in 1901, advocated a distinctly religious and ethical variety of socialism.

One of the important individuals contributed by religious radicalism to the Socialist party was George D. Herron. During his last years in the church, Herron had leaned increasingly toward political socialism, and in the years following the marriage scandal he played an important part in Socialist party affairs. In 1904 Herron gave the nominating speech for Eugene V. Debs at the party's Chicago convention.[118]

The part played in American socialist development by the Christian radicals of the nineties was, of course, limited by their small numbers. The official historian of the Socialist party, after describing with respect the activities of Bliss, Herron and others, concluded that ". . . the movement as a whole never reached considerable proportions, and disappeared within a few years."[119] Yet even this degree of attention is, in view of the novelty and minuteness of the religious groups, a tribute to their energy. Moreover, whether or not this early movement ever completely "disappeared," church socialism revived in a far stronger form in the early twentieth century. The Christian Socialist Fellowship, founded in 1906, published a paper that reached a circulation of twenty thousand before the eclipse of the American Socialist party following the First World War. Though its emphasis was ethical, its socialism was officially orthodox and it was an affiliate of the Socialist party.[120] Among the later

[117] This sequence of events is described by Lloyd, *Lloyd*, II, p. 61. An interpretation which deprecates the contribution of the religious elements, describing the controversy as one between Utopianism and practicality, is in McAlister Coleman, *Eugene V. Debs* (New York, 1930), pp. 195-197.

[118] Coleman, *Debs*, p. 222.

[119] Morris Hillquit, *History of Socialism in the United States* (5th ed.; New York, 1910), pp. 291-293; quotation from p. 293.

[120] For accounts of this phase of Christian Socialism see John Spargo, "Christian Socialism in America," *American Journal of Sociology*, XV (1909-10), 16-20; Hopkins, *Rise of the Social Gospel*, pp. 233-244; Hillquit, *op. cit.*, pp. 356-357.

socialist leaders strongly affected by Christian liberal and radical thought were John Spargo, J. Stitt Wilson, and Norman Thomas.[121]

The American church radicals of the nineties, few in number though they were, made a distinct contribution to the ethical, idealistic wing of developing American radicalism. This wing has not been without importance. It has, indeed, failed to affect the nation's intellectual and political history as strongly as has the corresponding tradition of religiously motivated radicalism in England. There are many reasons for the difference, including the more authoritative and universal character of the English church and the older and more persistent tradition of English Christian Socialism.

So far, religious radicals in the United States have been able only temporarily and on a small scale to bridge the gap which separates them from other radical groups. A more solid coalition is partly prevented by the old anticlericalism of the American left, dating at least back to Jeffersonian times, and partly by the nature of religious radical doctrine. The sincere, fervent, somewhat unimplemented hope for a new social order developed under Christian influences does not combine easily with the hard-bitten realism produced by the violent history of left-wing labor. Only an occasional radical leader like Eugene Debs has been able to work with both groups, combining in himself the bitter experience of the left-wing rank and file with strong ethical, semireligious motivation.[122] Such organizations as the Western Federation of Miners or the I.W.W. have stressed a bitter suspicion of religion, a hatred of "pie in the sky." More recent syndicalist or Marxist groups have manifested equally strong antireligious or nonreligious tendencies.

Radicals of strong Christian and ethical beliefs have, therefore, been able to co-operate with other leftists only sporadically, as in the turn-of-the-century Socialist party.[123] More often, they have been limited to their own small circles or to the fellowship of moderate progressives who have shared their philosophic orientation more fully than their social analysis. The lone clergyman, opening left-wing meetings with prayer and maintaining a somewhat uneasy relation with nonreligious radicals, is a fairly

[121] For Spargo, in addition to the article cited above, see Sharpe, *Rauschenbusch*, p. 158; for Wilson, his *How I Became a Socialist* (Berkeley, 1912); for Thomas, the letter quoted in Sharpe, *Rauschenbusch*, pp. 414-415.
[122] According to Debs' biographer, he believed strongly in the basic doctrines of the New Testament. Coleman, *Debs*, p. 320.
[123] Another attempt is the present Progressive Party, formed under the leadership of a man who has often expressed typically social-Christian views. See, for instance, Henry A. Wallace, *Statesmanship and Religion* (New York, 1934).

familiar figure in all periods of American dissent. Still more familiar in recent times is the church organization or publication which expresses genuinely radical sentiments despite the lack of any contact whatever with nonreligious radical groups.

CHRISTIAN SOCIAL TEACHING AND
AMERICAN THOUGHT

FOR American churchmen to take a stand on major social problems was nothing new. At least since the days of Jefferson the churches had insisted on their right to comment on any subject that had moral bearings. Clergymen had interpreted and used this right broadly and vigorously throughout the nineteenth century.

As de Tocqueville sensed, religion in America has owed part of its power to the tradition of separatism. Lacking any single, central interpretive authority, yet accepted in some form or other by the overwhelming majority of the population, Christian doctrine has been construed by various groups in terms of their own needs and purposes. In the dominant circles of major Protestant churches, a social consensus has existed, but it has been able to change with the times. This consensus has reflected current doctrines and events, and it has in turn constituted a major influence on American thought.

At least from the time of the battle with the Enlightenment, religious social doctrine offered a powerful and uncompromising support to the status quo. This support was hardened in the fiercer struggle with the anticlerical radicalism of Jacksonian times. The clerical economists and their contemporaries preached with force and conviction that riches and poverty were Divine ordinances, that unrestricted individualism was a Divine method, and that collective action for human betterment was both unnatural and impious. Outside the transcendentalist fringe of religious opinion, few quarreled with these doctrines. The participation of the churches, to various limited degrees, in certain movements of social reform did not shake their basic satisfaction with the status quo.

In the patriotic exaltation of the postwar years, the standard economic doctrines of American Protestantism seemed to be vindicated for all time. In this period when great industrialists were performing gigantic tasks and pouring out their bounty for religious and charitable work, the doctrines of clerical laissez faire were stated with new rigidity and unanimity in classroom, pulpit and press. The few radicals who revolted against contemporary selfishness and materialism and called for a new order were ignored or dismissed.

In the century's last two decades, traditional religious conservatism was severely shaken by social crisis and the development of rival doctrines. Yet the old ideas by no means lost their hold completely. Some religionists continued to preach the theories of clerical laissez faire in their stark original forms, others palliated their severity with appeals to individual benevolence in the manner of Cook, Behrends and the conservative social Christians. Down to the present, leading conservatives frequently appeal to religious principles, insisting, with a long tradition to back them up, on the sanctity of the status quo, the moral rightness of unrestricted individualism, the immorality of "encouraging idleness" or "discouraging hard work" or "interfering with the law of supply and demand."

From the time of the late seventies onward, however, these familiar teachings have been seriously challenged from within the church. The new doctrines of social Christianity arose partly in response to collectivist currents in sociology, economics and nonacademic radical thought, at home and abroad. They were affected indirectly but considerably by theological change. Primarily, however, social Christianity, like the new social criticism that arose in many different contexts at this time, was a response to a series of shocking crises. From 1877 through the middle nineties, it became more and more difficult to believe that strikes, depressions, unemployment and bankruptcies were part of a Divinely-regulated and unchangeable social order.

Social Christianity, widely expressed in sermons, editorials, official gatherings and even novels, was divided into three wings, conservative, moderately progressive and radical. Of these the middle group exerted the most powerful effect. Conservative social Christianity, primarily apologetic and defensive in its emphasis, was important chiefly as a bridge to more critical doctrines. Radical social Christianity, though growing in volume in this period, was limited by its own eccentricities and the apathy of its audiences to the important, but secondary role of the gadfly.

The doctrines of moderate social Christianity or the Social Gospel, which became very widely characteristic of the American Protestant leadership, had many shortcomings. The progressive writers in the early period were over-optimistic, facile and vague. They were uncertain as to their precise social role and unable to solve the problem of ends and means. They failed to achieve their hope of overcoming the hostility that had long existed between Protestantism and organized labor. These shortcomings persisted into the twentieth century at least sufficiently to produce a reaction away from the Social Gospel in recent times. From its religious background, middle-class American progressivism may have inherited some of its weaknesses: its lack of thoroughness, its substitution of enthusiasm for economic analysis, its tendency to underestimate its opponents, to believe with every victory that the war is over.

Yet to overemphasize these shortcomings is to lack historical perspective. At a crucial time, the social Christian movement gave encouragement to developing American progressivism. To attack the undiluted individualism which had, in America, the prestige of historical success, social critics of the late nineteenth century had to call to their aid the equally powerful tradition of equality. Yet in the tradition of the Enlightenment, individualism and equality were almost inseparably linked. Only in the Christian doctrine of brotherhood could men of this period find a belief universally recognized which at once proclaimed equality and condemned selfish individualism in telling terms. Without the support of religious argument, bringing to bear the most deeply-rooted beliefs and appealing to the most powerful human motives, the uphill fight of the progressives might have been far more difficult.

The Social Gospel thus played a part in developing and encouraging the progressivism which has, in the broadest perspective and with many interruptions and failures, dominated American history increasingly since its appearance. Whether Christian social doctrine has an important role in the present confused and desperate period of American social thought remains an open question. It seems likely however that whatever group prevails will make use, in some form or another, of the goals and motives which religion has always provided.

BIBLIOGRAPHY

SOURCES

A. BIBLIOGRAPHIES

(The most important bibliographical source was the church press, which reviewed most books of current religious-social interest. Some of the Social Gospel volumes contain brief bibliographies. C. H. Hopkins has permitted consultation of his notes for his forthcoming bibliography of the Social Gospel.)

BOWERMAN, G. F. *A Selected Bibliography of the Religious Denominations of the United States.* New York, 1896.

BROWN, T. E. *Socialism and Labor Problems.* New York, 1886. (See "Bibliography of Subjects," pp. 234-268.)

CASE, S. J., ed. *A Bibliographical Guide to the History of Christianity.* Chicago, 1931.

COMMONS, JOHN R. *A Popular Bibliography of Sociology* (Oberlin College Library Bulletin, I, 1). Oberlin, 1892. (Useful.)

JACKSON, S. M. "A Bibliography of American Church History, 1820-1893." PHILIP SCHAFF AND OTHERS, eds. "American Church History Series," XII. New York, 1894, pp. 441-513.

McINTYRE, W. E. *Baptist Authors—A Manual of Bibliography, 1500-1914.* Montreal, 1914.

MODE, P. G. *Source Book and Bibliographical Guide for American Church History.* Menasha, Wisconsin, 1921. (Very valuable, esp. pp. 626-641.)

NEW YORK PUBLIC LIBRARY. *List of Periodicals in the New York Public Library, General Theological Seminary, and Union Theological Seminary Relating to Religion, Theology and Church History.* New York, 1905.

PEABODY, F. G. *Jesus Christ and the Social Question.* New York, 1901. (Bibliography, pp. 67-69.)

RICHARDSON, E. C. *An Alphabetical Subject Index Encyclopaedia to Periodical Articles on Religion, 1890-1899.* New York, 1907.

———. *Periodical Articles on Religion, 1890-1899. Author Index.* New York, 1911.

STRONG, JOSIAH. *The Challenge of the City.* New York, 1921. (Bibliographies on various social reform subjects, pp. 38, 127-128, 166, 236-237, 312-317.)

TOLMAN, W. H., AND WILLIAM I. HULL. *Bibliography of the American Institute of Christian Sociology.* 2nd ed. New York, 1893. (Very valuable for short descriptions and bibliographies of principal religious reform organizations.)

B. DICTIONARIES AND ENCYCLOPEDIAS

BLISS, W. D. P. *Encyclopedia of Social Reform.* New York, 1897. (Very valuable for liberal and radical movements of period.)

——. *A Handbook of Socialism.* New York, 1895. (Valuable for brief biographies of socialist and near-socialist leaders.)

JOHNSON, ALLEN, AND DUMAS MALONE, eds. *Dictionary of American Biog raphy.* 20 vols. New York, 1928-1937.

MATHEWS, SHAILER, AND G. B. SMITH, eds. *Dictionary of Religion and Ethics.* New York, 1921.

SCHAFF, PHILIP. *A Religious Encyclopaedia: or Dictionary of Biblical, Historical, Doctrinal, and Practical Theology. Based on the Real-Encyklopädie of Herzog, Plitt and Hauck. Together with an Encyclopaedia of Living Divines and Christian Workers of all Denominations in Europe and America.* Edited by Philip Schaff and Samuel Macaulay Jackson. 3rd ed. 4 vols. New York, 1891. (Useful for biographical information only.)

SELIGMAN, EDWIN R. A., ed.-in-chief. *Encyclopedia of the Social Sciences.* 15 vols., 3rd ed. New York, 1935.

SPRAGUE, WILLIAM B. *Annals of the American Pulpit.* 7 vols., New York, 1857-61. (Useful for biographical information.)

C. RECORDS OF OFFICIAL DENOMINATIONAL ORGANIZATIONS

(Consulted for 1865-1895 unless otherwise noted.)

BAPTIST CONGRESS FOR THE DISCUSSION OF CURRENT QUESTIONS. *Proceedings.* Various places, from 1882.

METHODIST EPISCOPAL CHURCH, GENERAL CONFERENCE. *Journal.* New York.

NATIONAL COUNCIL OF CONGREGATIONAL CHURCHES. *Debates and Proceedings.* Boston. (From 1872, title changes to *Minutes.*)

PRESBYTERIAN CHURCH IN THE U. S. A., GENERAL ASSEMBLY. *Minutes.* Philadelphia.

PROTESTANT EPISCOPAL CHURCH, CHURCH CONGRESS. *Papers, Addresses, and Debates.* New York (From 1874.)

——, GENERAL CONVENTION. *Journal.* (Title and place of publication vary.)

D. OTHER ORGANIZATIONS

(For principal sources for the Brotherhood of the Kingdom, see under Hopkins, in list of secondary material on church history. For newspapers published by organizations, see under periodicals.)

AMERICAN CONGRESS OF CHURCHES. *Proceedings.* Hartford, 1885.

THE AMERICAN TRACT SOCIETY. *Tracts of the American Tract Society. General Series.* New York [18–].

ANONYMOUS. *The American Home Missionary Society and Slavery.* Pamphlet. n.p., 1885.

CHRISTIAN SOCIAL UNION. *Publications.* Boston, 1893-1900.

——. *A Short History of the Christian Social Union in This Country and England.* Boston, 1908.

EVANGELICAL ALLIANCE. *History, Essays, Orations and other Documents of the Sixth General Conference.* . . . (1873). New York, 1874.

——. *Proceedings of the General Conference of the Evangelical Alliance.* . . . (1861). London, 1862.

——. *The Religious Good of Christendom Described in a Series of Papers Presented to the . . . General Conference of the Evangelical Alliance.* . . . London, 1880, 1884, 1885.

EVANGELICAL ALLIANCE FOR THE U. S. A. *Annual Report.* New York, from 1867.

——. *Christianity Practically Applied.* 2 vols. New York, 1894. (Records of meeting of 1893.)

——. *Documents.* New York, from 1867.

——. *National Needs and Remedies.* New York, 1890. (Records of meeting of 1889.)

——. *National Perils and Opportunities.* New York, 1887. (Records of meeting of 1887.)

HOUGHTON, WALTER R., ed.-in-chief. *Neely's History of the Parliament of Religions and Religious Congresses at the World's Columbian Exposition.* 2 vols. Chicago, 1894.

KNIGHTS OF LABOR. *Labor: Its Rights and Wrongs.* Washington, D. C., 1886. (Contains records of 1886 meeting of the American Congress of Churches, pp. 230-272.)

NATIONAL REFORM CONVENTION. *Proceedings.* . . . 1874. Philadelphia, 1874.

E. PERIODICALS

(Periodicals listed below are those which were systematically read for the period 1865-1895 or the years noted. The religious magazines and newspapers were selected to represent adequately the churches covered. Many other periodicals, lay and religious, were consulted for particular subjects and particular dates. The weeklies are the most important sources for social opinion.)

American Church Review. New York, to 1891. (Title varies, quarterly, Episcopalian.)

American Presbyterian and Theological Review. New York, to 1871. (Quarterly.)

Andover Review. Boston, 1884-1893. (Monthly until 1892, bimonthly in 1893. Congregational.)

Baptist Quarterly. Philadelphia, 1867-1877. (Title varies.)

Baptist Quarterly Review. Cincinnati, 1879-1892.

Biblical Repertory and Princeton Review. New York, Princeton, and various places to 1888. (Title varies.)

Bibliotheca Sacra. Boston. (Quarterly, Congregationalist.)

Christian Advocate. New York. (Weekly, Methodist.)

Christian Union. New York. (Weekly, nondenominational.)

Christian Watchman. New York, Boston. (Weekly, Baptist.)

Churchman. New York. (Weekly, Episcopalian.)

Congregationalist. Boston. (Weekly.)

Congregational Quarterly. Boston, to 1876.

Dawn, The. Boston, from 1889. (Irregularly published, organ of the Society of Christian Socialists.)

Equity. Boston, April, 1874-December, 1875. (Irregularly published, organ of the Christian Labor Union.)

Independent. New York, from 1870. (Weekly, nondenominational.)

Labor Balance. North Abington. October, 1877-December, 1878. (Irregularly published, organ of the Christian Labor Union.)

Kingdom, The. Minneapolis, from 1889. (Weekly, originally Congregationalist, Social Gospel.)

Methodist Review. New York. (Quarterly to 1884, then bimonthly. Title varies.)

New Princeton Review. New York, 1886-1880. (Bimonthly.)

New World. Boston and New York, from 1892. (Quarterly, Unitarian.)

Presbyterian Quarterly and Princeton Review. New York, Princeton, 1872-1877.

Presbyterian and Reformed Review. New York, from 1890. (Quarterly.)

Presbyterian Review. New York, 1880-1889. (Quarterly.)

Princeton Review. New York, Princeton, 1878-1884. (Quarterly.)

Radical. Boston, to 1873. (Quarterly, transcendentalist.)

Twentieth Century. Newark and New York, from 1883. (Christian anarchist.)

Unitarian Review. Boston, from 1874. (Monthly.)

F. CHRISTIAN SOCIAL THEORY TO 1895

(This section includes books written by ministers which shed light on religious-social opinion whether or not social theory is their main subject. Books by laymen are included only when the interpretation is primarily religious. Since the more important of the books in this section are fully discussed in the text, comment is largely omitted here. The most influential books are starred.)

ABBOTT, LYMAN. *Christianity and Social Problems.* Boston, 1896.

———. *The Evolution of Christianity.* Boston, 1892.

ALDEN, JOSEPH. *First Principles of Political Economy.* Syracuse, 1879.

ALGER, WILLIAM ROUNSEVILLE. *The Genius and Posture of America.* Pamphlet. Boston, 1857.

[ALLIBONE, S. A.] *New Themes Condemned: or, Thirty Opinions upon "New Themes," and its "Reviewer,"* etc. Philadelphia, 1853.

———. *A Review by a Layman, of a Work Entitled, "New Themes for the Protestant Clergy, etc."* Philadelphia, 1852.

BAIRD, ROBERT. *Religion in America.* New York, 1844.

BALLOU, ADIN. *Practical Christian Socialism.* Hopedale, 1854.

BASCOM, JOHN. *Political Economy.* Andover, 1859.

———. *Social Theory.* New York, 1895.

*———. *Sociology.* New York, 1887.

BATCHELOR, GEORGE. *Social Equilibrium and other Problems Ethical and Religious.* Boston, 1887.

BEACH, DAVID NELSON. *The Newer Religious Thinking.* New York, 1893.

*BEECHER, LYMAN. *Lectures on Political Atheism and Kindred Subjects Together with Six Lectures on Intemperance.* (Works, vol. 1.) Boston, 1852.

BEECHER, HENRY WARD. *Eyes and Ears.* Boston, 1863.

———. *Freedom and War. Discourses on Topics Suggested by the Times.* Boston, 1863.

———. *Henry Ward Beecher on Free Trade and Congressional Elections.* Pamphlet. New York, 1883.

———. *New Star Papers; or, Views and Experiences of Religious Subjects.* New York, 1859.

———. *Patriotic Addresses.* J. R. Howard, ed. New York, 1881.

* ———. *Plymouth Pulpit.* A Weekly Publication of Sermons preached by Henry Ward Beecher. N.Y. 1868—(This publication, of which copies in the original weekly form are hard to locate, is bound in the following two series, which together give an excellent sample of Beecher's preaching.)

———. *The Sermons of Henry Ward Beecher in Plymouth Church, Brooklyn.* "From verbatim reports by T. J. Ellinwood." 9 vols., New York, 1868-1873. (Volumes of this series are separately titled *Plymouth Pulpit*, First-Ninth Series, and are so cited in the text.)

———. *Plymouth Pulpit, New Series.* 4 vols., New York, 1874-1875.

———. *Sermons. Selected from Published and Unpublished Discourses and Revised by their Author.* 2 vols. New York, 1868-1869.

———. *Statement before the Congregational Association of New York and Brooklyn, etc.* Pamphlet. New York, 1882.

———. *Universal Suffrage.* Pamphlet. New York, 1865.

* BEHRENDS, A. J. F. *Socialism and Christianity*. New York, 1886.

BEMIS, EDWARD W. *The Relation of the Church to Social Problems*. "*Dawn* Library," Tract No. 2. Pamphlet. Boston, 1890.

BIERBOWER, AUSTIN. *The Morals of Christ*. Chicago, 1885.

———. *The Socialism of Christ, or Attitude of Early Christians toward Modern Problems*. Chicago, 1890.

BLISS, W. D. P. *American Trade Unions*. Pamphlets. Boston, 1886.

———. *Objections to Christian Socialism*. Pamphlet. Boston, 1894. (This author's opinions are best studied in the *Dawn*.)

———. *What Christian Socialism Is*. Pamphlet. Boston, 1894.

———. *What Is Christian Socialism*. Pamphlet. Boston, 1890.

BONNEY, C. C. *The Present Conflict of Labor and Capital*. Chicago, 1886.

BOURNE, THEODORE. *Money and Labor. Corporation and Co-operation*. Pamphlet. New York, 1884.

BOWEN, FRANCIS. *The Principles of Political Economy*. Boston, 1856. (Belongs with clerical school of economists, though Bowen was not a minister.)

BOWNE, BORDEN P. *The Principles of Ethics*. New York, 1892.

* BRACE, CHARLES LORING. *The Dangerous Classes of New York and Twenty Years Work Among Them*. New York, 1872.

———. *Gesta Christi: or A History of Humane Progress under Christianity*. New York, 1882.

BRADFORD, AMORY H. *Spirit and Life*. New York, 1888.

* BROOKS, PHILLIPS. *Essays and Addresses Religious Literary and Social*. J. C. BROOKS, ed. New York, 1895. (Brooks' social opinions are scattered through his work.)

———. *The Influence of Jesus*. New York, 1879.

———. *The Law of Growth and other Sermons*. "Sermons, Ninth Series." New York, 1902.

———. *Lectures on Preaching*. New York, 1877.

———. *The Light of the World and other Sermons*. "Sermons, Fifth Series." New York, 1891.

———. *New Starts in Life and other Sermons*. "Sermons, Eighth Series." New York, 1897. (Collections of sermons after 1895 contain some sermons of before that date).

———. *Phillips Brooks' Addresses*. Boston, 1893.

———. *Seeking Life and other Sermons*. "Sermons, Tenth Series." New York, 1904.

———. *Sermons*, "Sixth Series." New York, 1893.

———. *Twenty Sermons*. "Sermons, Fourth Series." New York, 1887.

BROWN, C. O. *The Kingdom's Extra Edition—a Rejoinder*. Pamphlet n.p., n.d.

———. *Professor Herron's Teachings Reviewed, Ought the Church of Christ to Join the Propaganda of Socialism?* Pamphlet. San Francisco, 1895.

Bibliography

BROWN, C. O. *Talks on Labor Troubles.* Chicago, 1886.

*BROWN, T. EDWIN. *Studies in Modern Socialism and Labor Problems.* New York, 1886.

BRUCE, ALEXANDER B. *The Kingdom of God.* 4th ed. New York, 1891.

*BUSHNELL, HORACE. *Building Eras in Religion.* "Literary Varieties," III. New York, 1881. (Bushnell's theological works contain certain direct statements of the author's own social opinions and are indispensable for an understanding of the theological outlook of his Social Gospel successors).

———. *A Discourse on the Slavery Question.* Pamphlet. Hartford, 1839.

———. *Nature and the Supernatural.* New York, 1858.

———. *The Northern Iron.* Pamphlet. Hartford, 1854.

———. *Sermons on Living Subjects.* New York, 1873.

———. *Society and Religion: A Sermon for California.* Pamphlet. Hartford, 1856.

———. *Women's Suffrage: the Reform against Nature.* New York, 1869.

———. *Work and Play, or Literary Varieties.* New York, 1866.

*CADMAN, H. W. *The Christian Unity of Capital and Labor.* Philadelphia, 1888.

CARWARDINE, W. H. *The Pullman Strike.* 4th ed. Chicago, 1894.

CASSON, HERBERT N. *God Wills It.* Pamphlet. Lynn, 189–.

———. *The Socialism of Nature.* Pamphlet. Lynn, 1895.

———. *What We Believe.* Lynn, 189–.

CHANNING, WILLIAM ELLERY. *Works.* 17th ed. 6 vols. Boston, 1866.

CHANNING, WILLIAM HENRY. *The Christian Church and Social Reform.* Pamphlet. Boston, 1848.

———. *Real Christianity for To-day.* Boston, n.d.

CHAPIN, AARON L. *First Principles of Political Economy.* New York, 1880.

CHAPIN, E. H. *The American Idea, and What Grows Out of It.* Pamphlet. Boston, 1854.

*———. *Humanity in the City.* New York, 1854.

*———. *Moral Aspects of City Life.* New York, 1853.

———. *The Relation of the Individual to the Republic.* Pamphlet. Boston, 1844.

———. *The Responsibilities of a Republican Government.* Pamphlet. Boston, 1841.

CHEROUNY, HENRY. *Labor and Liberty.* New York, 1885.

———. *Socialism and Christianity.* Pamphlet. New York, 1882.

COLLENS, T. WHARTON. *The Eden of Labor; or the Christian Utopia.* Philadelphia, 1876.

COLTON, CALVIN. *Public Economy for the United States.* New York, 1848.

*COLWELL, STEPHEN. *New Themes for the Protestant Clergy; Creeds without Charity; Theology without Humanity; and Protestantism without Christianity.* 2nd ed. Philadelphia, 1852.

COLWELL, STEPHEN. *Politics for American Christians: A word upon our Example as a Nation, our Labor, our Trade, Elections, Education, and Congressional Legislation.* Philadelphia, 1852.

——. *The Position of Christianity in the United States.* Philadelphia, 1854.

——. "Preface," WILLIAM ARNOT. *The Race for Riches.* Boston, 1853.

*COMMONS, J. R. *Social Reform and the Church.* New York, 1894.

CONWELL, RUSSELL H. *Acres of Diamonds.* New York, 1915. (Late edition of sermon first delivered much earlier. Includes biography of author by ROBERT SHACKLETON, 63-181.)

COOK, JOSEPH. *Conscience, with Preludes on Current Events.* "Boston Monday Lectures," IV. Boston, 1878.

*——. *Outlines of Music Hall Lectures, Embracing Five Addresses on Factory Reform in the Largest Trade of the United States.* Boston, 1871.

——. *Socialism, with Preludes on Current Events.* "Boston Monday Lectures," VIII. Boston, 1880.

CRAFTS, WILBUR F. *Practical Christian Sociology.* New York, 1895.

——. *Successful Men of To-day and What They Say of Success.* New York, 1905 (cop. 1883).

DEWEY, ORVILLE. *Moral Views of Commerce, Society and Politics, in Twelve Discourses.* New York, 1838.

DIXON, THOMAS, JR. *The Failure of Protestantism in New York.* New York, 1895.

DOLE, CHARLES FLETCHER. *The Citizen and the Neighbor; or, Men's Rights and Duties as They Live Together in the State and in Society.* Boston, 1884.

EGGLESTON, N. H. *God Among the Nations.* Pamphlet. Hartford, 1845.

*ELY, RICHARD T. *Social Aspects of Christianity.* Rev. Ed. New York, 1889.

FINNEY, CHARLES G. *Lectures on Revivals of Religion.* Oberlin, 1868.

——. *Sermons on Gospel Themes.* Oberlin, N. Y., 1876.

FREDERICK, HAROLD. *The Damnation of Theron Ware.* New York, 1896. (Essentially concerned with theology, but casts some light on the relation of a small-town minister to businessmen who are trustees.)

FRICKSTAD, TARAL T. *From Behind the Scenes: The Church and the Masses; or, the Social and Religious Problem.* Pamphlet. Oakland, 1894.

FROTHINGHAM, OCTAVIUS B. *The Religion of Humanity.* New York, 1873.

GIFFORD, O. P. *In Memoriam and Other Sermons.* Boston, 1881.

*GLADDEN, WASHINGTON. *Applied Christianity. The Moral Aspects of Social Questions.* Boston, 1886. (One of the most important documents of social Christianity.)

——. *Ruling Ideas of the Present Age.* Boston, 1895.

*——. *Tools and the Man. Property and Industry under the Christian Law.* Boston, 1893.

Bibliography 275

GLADDEN, WASHINGTON. *Working People and their Employers*. 2nd ed. New York, 1894 (1st ed. Boston, 1876).

GRONLUND, LAWRENCE. *Our Destiny. The Influence of Socialism on Morals and Religion*. London, 1891.

HAGUE, WILLIAM. *Christianity and Statesmanship with Kindred Topics*. Boston, 1865.

HALE, EDWARD EVERETT. *How They Lived in Hampton*. Boston, 1888.

———. *If Jesus Came to Boston*. Boston, 1894.

———. *The Life in Common and Twenty Other Sermons*. Boston, 1880.

———. *Workingmen's Houses*. Boston, 1875.

HALEY, WILLIAM D. *Words for the Workers; in a Series of Lectures to Workingmen, Mechanics, and Apprentices*. Boston, 1855.

HARRIS, S. S. *The Kingdom of Christ on Earth*. Andover, 1883.

———. *The Relation of Christianity to Civil Society*. New York, 1883.

HARRISON, J. B. *Certain Dangerous Tendencies in American Life, and Other Papers*. Boston, 1880.

———. *A Note on Labor Agitations*. Franklin Falls, N. H., 1887.

———. *Notes on Industrial Conditions*. Franklin Falls, N. H., 1886.

HAVEN, JOSEPH. *Moral Philosophy*. New York, 1880 (cop. 1859).

HAVEN, WILLIAM I. *My Brother and I*. Cambridge, 1895.

HAYNE, EMORY J. *Dollars and Duty*. New York, 1887.

HENRY, CALEB SPRAGUE. *Considerations on Some of the Elements and Conditions of Social Welfare and Human Progress*. New York, 1861.

HEPWORTH, GEORGE H. *Hiram Golf's Religion or the "Shoemaker by the Grace of God."* New York, 1893.

———. *They Met in Heaven*. New York, 1894. (Religion in stories, only incidentally expressing social opinions.)

HERRON, GEORGE D. *The Call of the Cross*. New York, 1892.

*———. *The Christian Society*. Chicago, 1894.

———. *The Christian State*. New York, 1895.

———. *The Larger Christ*. New York, 1891.

———. *The New Redemption*. New York, 1893.

———. *A Plea for the Gospel*. New York, 1892.

HILL, DAVID JAYNE. *The Social Influence of Christianity with Special Reference to Contemporary Problems*. Boston, 1888.

*HITCHCOCK, ROSWELL D. *Socialism*. 2nd ed. New York, 1879.

HODGES, GEORGE. *The Heresy of Cain*. New York, 1894.

HOLBROOK, Z. S. *The American Republic and the Debs Insurrection*. Oberlin, 1895.

HUNTINGTON, F. D. *Human Society: Its Providential Structure, Relations, and Offices*. New York, 1860. (This title appears on title page; outside cover is titled *Divine Aspects of Human Society*.)

———. *Sermons for the People*. Boston, 1856.

276   *Bibliography*

HUNTINGTON, F. D.   *Strikes, the Right and the Wrong.* New York, 1891.

HUNTINGTON, WILLIAM REED.   *The Religious Use of Wealth.* Pamphlet. New York, 1887.

*HYDE, W. DEW.   *Outlines of Social Theology.* New York, 1895.

Institute Essays. Boston, 1880. (Essays read before the Ministers Institute, Providence, R. I., October, 1879. Includes social sermons by several leading Unitarians.)

JAMES, HENRY [SR.]   *Moralism and Christianity or Man's Experience and Destiny.* New York, 1850.

———.   *The Social Significance of Our Institutions.* Boston, 1861.

JONES, JENKIN LLOYD.   *The Word of the Spirit to the Nation, Church, City, Home and Individual.* Chicago, 1894.

JONES, JESSE H.   *The Bible Plan for the Abolition of Poverty, and the New Political Economy Involved Therein.* Boston, 1873.

———.   *Joshua Davidson, Christian.* New York, 1907. (This posthumous novel, written 1897-1903, expresses the author's ideas. It is valuable for the biographical sketch of Jones by HALAH H. LOUD.)

———.   *The Kingdom of Heaven.* Boston, 1871.

JUDD, SYLVESTER.   *Margaret: A Tale of the Real and The Ideal.* Rev. ed. Boston, 1857 (cop. 1851).

———.   *Philo: An Evangeliad.* Boston, 1850.

———.   *Richard Edney and the Governor's Family.* Boston, 1850.

KING, T. STARR.   *The Relation of This Life to the Next.* Pamphlet. Albany, 1859.

LATHAM, J. H.   *God in Business.* New York, 1887.

*LOOMIS, W. L.   *Modern Cities and Their Religious Problems.* New York, 1887.

LORIMER, G. C.   *Isms, Old and New.* Chicago, 1881.

———.   *Studies in Social Life.* London, 1886.

MACHAR, AGNES MAULE.   *Roland Graeme, Knight.* Montreal, 1892.

McCOSH, JAMES.   *Christianity and Positivism.* London, 1875.

McVICKAR, JOHN.   *Outlines of Political Economy.* New York, 1825.

MEARS, JOHN W.   *The Bible in the Workshop; or, Christianity the Friend of Labor.* New York, 1857.

MUHLENBERG, WILLIAM AUGUSTUS.   *St. John-land: A Retro-Prospectus.* New York, 1864.

MUNGER, T. T.   *The Appeal to Life.* Boston, 1887.

———.   *Freedom of Faith.* Boston, 1883.

MURRAY, W. H. H.   *Music Hall Sermons.* Boston, 1870. (Little of social interest.)

NASH, JOSEPH.   *The Relations Between Capital and Labor in the United States.* Boston, 1878.

NEWTON, R. HEBER.   *The Morals of Trade.* New York, 1876.

NEWTON, R. HEBER. *The Present Aspect of the Labor Problem.* New York, 1886.

*———. *Social Studies.* New York, 1886.

PARKER, THEODORE. *Collected Works.* F. P. COBBE, ed. 14 vols. London, 1863-1872.

PERRY, ARTHUR LATHAM. *Elements of Political Economy.* New York, 1866.

PORTER, NOAH. *The Elements of Moral Science.* New York, 1885.

POTTER, ALONZO. *Political Economy.* New York, 1840.

POTTER, HENRY C. *Individual Responsibility to the Nation.* Pamphlet. Boston, 1867.

———. *Sermons of the City.* New York, 1881.

PRALL, WILLIAM. *Civic Christianity.* New York, 1895.

RICHARDSON, CHARLES. *Large Fortunes; or, Christianity and the Labor Problem.* Philadelphia, 1888.

RHODES, D. W. *Creed and Greed.* Cincinnati, 1879.

ROADS, CHARLES. *Christ Enthroned in the Industrial World.* New York, 1893.

ROBINS, JOHN B. *Christ and Our Country; or, a Hopeful View of Christianity in the Present Day.* Nashville, 1889.

ROGERS, E. H. *The Hope of the Republic.* Pamphlet. Boston, 1881.

———. *Like Unto Me.* Pamphlet. Boston, 1876.

———. *National Life in the Spirit World.* Boston, 1891.

[RUFFNER, W. H.] *Charity and the Clergy: being a Review, by a Clergyman, of the "New Themes" Controversy, etc.* Philadelphia, 1853.

[RUSSELL, PASTOR] *The Plan of the Ages.* "Studies in the Scriptures," Series 1. Brooklyn, 1918 (cop. 1886). (Early editions were entitled *Millennial Dawn.*)

*RYLANCE, J. H. *Lectures on Social Questions.* New York, 1880.

SALTER, WILLIAM M. *Anarchy or Government? An Inquiry into Fundamental Politics.* New York, 1895.

———. *The Social Ideal.* Pamphlet. Chicago, 1883.

*SAVAGE, M. J. *Social Problems.* Boston, 1886.

*SCHAFF, PHILIP. *America.* New York, 1855.

———. *Church and State in the United States.* "Papers of the American Historical Association," II, 4. New York, 1888.

SCOTT, J. E. *Socialism What Is it? Is it Christian? Should the Church Take any Interest in it?* Pamphlet. San Francisco, 1895.

SCUDDER, VIDA D. *Socialism and Spiritual Progress.* Pamphlet. N.p., 189[1?].

SHELDON, CHARLES M. *The Crucifixion of Philip Strong.* Chicago, 1898. (cop. 1894).

*———. *In His Steps.* New York, 1897.

———. *Richard Bruce or the Life that Now Is.* Boston, 1892.

———. *Robert Hardy's Seven Days.* Boston, 1893.

SMYTH, NEWMAN.   *Christian Ethics.* International Theological Library Edition. New York, 1914, (cop. 1892).

――――.   *Social Problems. Sermons to Workingmen.* Boston, 1885.

"SOCIALIST, by a."   *A Reply to Roswell D. Hitchcock, D.D. on Socialism.* Pamphlet. New York, 1879.

*SPRAGUE, F. M.   *Socialism from Genesis to Revelation.* Boston, 1893.

SPRAGUE, PHILO W.   *Christian Socialism. What and Why.* New York, 1891.

――――.   *The Slums of Great Cities.* Boston, 1895.

STEELE, GEORGE M.   *Outline Study of Political Economy.* New York, 1889.

STORRS, RICHARD S.   *The Divine Origins of Christianity as Seen in its Historical Results.* Boston, 1884.

STRONG, A. H.   *Philosophy and Religion.* New York, 1888.

STRONG, JOSIAH.   *My Religion in Everyday Life.* New York, 1910. (Later than period of thesis but casts important light on Strong's opinions).

*――――.   *The New Era or the Coming Kingdom.* New York, 1893.

*――――.   *Our Country, its Possible Future and its Present Crisis.* New York, 1885.

――――.   *The United States and the Future of the Anglo-Saxon Race.* Pamphlet. London, 1889. (Extracts from *Our Country*).

STUCKENBERG, J. H. W.   *The Age and the Church.* Hartford, 1893.

*――――.   *Christian Sociology.* New York, 1880.

SWIFT, MORRISON I.   *A League of Justice or Is it Right to Rob Robbers?* Pamphlet. Boston, 1893.

――――.   *The Plan of a Social University.* "Social University Monographs," No. 1. Pamphlet. Ashtabula, 1890.

――――.   *Problems of the New Life.* Ashtabula, 1891.

――――.   *Vicarious Philanthropy.* Pamphlet. N.p., n.d.

[SWING, DAVID].   *The Great Presbyterian Conflict. Patton vs. Swing. Both Sides of the Question.* Chicago, 1874.

SWING, DAVID.   *Truths for To-day.* Series 1-2. Chicago, 1874-1876.

THOMPSON, JOSEPH P.   *Church and State in the United States.* Boston, 1873.

――――.   *The Duties of the Christian Citizen.* New York, 1848.

――――.   *The Workman: His False Friends and His True Friends.* New York, 1879.

*THOMPSON, R. E.   *De Civitate Dei; The Divine Order of Human Society.* Philadelphia, 1891.

TOURGEE, ALBION W.   *Murvale Eastman: Christian Socialist.* New York, 1891 (cop. 1889).

TOWER, F. E.   *The Advancing Kingdom or the Wonders of Foretold History.* Hartford, 1892.

――――.   *What's The Trouble?* Pamphlet. Boston, 1891.

TUCKER, WILLIAM JEWETT.   *The New Movement in Humanity.* Boston, 1892.

Tuckerman, Joseph. *An Essay on the Wages Paid to Females for their Labour.* Pamphlet. Philadelphia, 1830.
————. *On the Elevation of the Poor.* Boston, 1874
————. *The Principles and Results of the Ministry at Large, in Boston.* Boston, 1838.
Tyler, R. H. *The Bible and Social Reform or the Scriptures as a Means of Civilization.* Philadelphia, 1860.
Van Amringe, H. H. *Association and Christianity.* Pamphlet. Pittsburg, 1845.
Vethake, Henry. *Principles of Political Economy.* Philadelphia, 1838.
Walker, Amasa. *The Science of Wealth.* 5th ed. Boston, 1869 (cop. 1866).
Ward, Julius H. *The Church in Modern Society.* Boston, 1889.
Washburn, Edward. *The Social Law of God: Sermons on the Ten Commandments.* New York, 1875.
Wayland, Francis. *Elements of Moral Science.* 5th ed. Boston, 1841 (cop. 1835).
*————. *The Elements of Political Economy.* 4th ed. Boston, 1852. (According to the author's preface, "No material alteration" had been made since the first edition, 1837.)
Webb, Edwin B. *Socialism and the Christian Church.* Pamphlet. New York, 1885.
Weeden, W. B. *The New Socialism and Economics.* N.p. 1893.
————. *The Social Law of Labor.* Boston, 1882.
Williams, Leighton. *The Established Tendencies toward Social Reform.* Pamphlet. New York, 1888.
Winslow, Hubbard. *Christianity Applied to our Civil and Social Relations.* Boston, 1835.
Woods, Katherine Pearson. *Metzerott, Shoemaker.* New York, 1890.
Woolsey, Theodore. *Communism and Socialism in their History and Theory.* New York, 1880.
Wright, Robert J. *Principia: or the Basis of Social Science.* Philadelphia 1875.
Wyckoff, J. F. *The Christian Use of Money: Especially in Relation to Personal Expenditure.* Pamphlet. New York, 1872.
Zabriskie, F. N. *Landmarks of my Ministry. A Farewell Sermon.* Pamphlet. New York, 1859.

G. related opinion

Addams, Jane, and others. *Philanthropy and Social Progress.* New York, 1893. ("Seven essays by Miss Jane Addams, Robert A. Woods, Father J. O. S. Huntington, Professor Franklin H. Giddings, and Bernard

Bosanquet. Delivered before the School of Applied Ethics at Plymouth, Mass., during the Session of 1892.")

ANDREWS, E. BENJAMIN. "The Duty of a Public Spirit," Brooklyn Ethical Association, *Man and the State* (New York, 1892), pp. 3-19.

——. *Wealth and the Moral Law.* Hartford, 1894.

ATKINSON, EDWARD. *Addresses upon the Labor Question.* Boston, 1886. (Anti-Social Gospel address given to alumni of Andover Seminary.)

BARNS, WILLIAM E. *The Labor Problem. Plain Questions and Practical Answers.* New York, 1886. (Contains sample opinions of manufacturers, industrial workers, journalists, clergymen and others.)

BELLAMY, EDWARD. *Looking Backward, 2000-1887.* Boston, 1888.

BIRNEY, JAMES GILLESPIE. *American Churches the Bulwarks of American Slavery.* Pamphlet. 3rd ed. Newburyport, 1842.

CAMPBELL, HELEN. *Women Wage-Workers, Their Trades and Their Lives.* Boston, 1900 (cop. 1887).

CAREY, HENRY C. *Principles of Social Science.* 3 vols. Philadelphia, 1858-1859.

CARNEGIE, ANDREW. *The Gospel of Wealth and other Essays.* New York, 1933.

CLARK, J. B. *The Philosophy of Wealth.* Boston, 1887 (cop. 1885).

CUSHING, CALEB. *A Discourse on the Social Influence of Christianity.* Pamphlet. Andover, 1839.

ELY, RICHARD T. *French and German Socialism in Modern Times.* New York, 1883.

——. *An Introduction to Political Economy.* New York, 1889.

——. *The Labor Movement in America.* New York, 1886.

——. *Outlines of Economics.* New York, 1893.

——. *The Past and the Present of Political Economy.* "Johns Hopkins University Studies," III. Baltimore, 1884.

——. *Problems of To-day.* New York, 1888.

——. *Socialism; an Examination of its Nature, its Strength, and its Weakness, with Suggestions for Social Reform.* New York, 1894.

——. *The Social Law of Service.* New York, 1896.

"FOREMAN, by a." *Big Wages, and How to Earn Them.* New York, 1888. (States the conservative Christian point of view, not identifiable as to author.)

GEORGE, HENRY. *Progress and Poverty.* New York, 1879.

GILMAN, N. P. "'Nationalism' in the United States," *Quarterly Journal of Economics,* IV (1890), 50-76. (A hostile review.)

——. *Profit-Sharing Between Employer and Employee.* Boston, 1889.

——. *Socialism and the American Spirit.* Boston, 1893. (Includes attack on Christian socialism.)

GREENE, WILLIAM B. *Socialistic, Communistic, Mutualistic, and Financial*

Fragments. Boston, 1875. (Eccentric proposals for reform similar to those of the J. H. Jones school.)

GRONLUND, LAWRENCE. *The Cooperative Commonwealth*. Boston, 1884.

HOWELLS, W. D. *Annie Kilburn*. New York, 1889. (The Howells novel which most clearly shows the influence of Social Christianity.)

———. *A Hazard of New Fortunes*. Library ed. New York, 1911 (cop. 1889).

———. *A Traveller from Altruria*. New York, 1894.

———. *The World of Chance*. New York, 1893.

KIRKUP, THOMAS. *An Inquiry into Socialism*. London, 1887.

KNIGHTS OF LABOR. *Labor: Its Rights and Wrongs*. Washington, D. C., 1886. (Symposium, including considerable clerical opinion.)

LAUGHLIN, J. LAWRENCE. *Elements of Political Economy*. Rev. ed. New York, 1902. (One of the late survivals of the influence of the clerical school.)

LAVELEYE, EMILE, BARON DE. *The Socialism of To-day*. G. H. ORPEN, trans. London, 1885.

LLOYD, HENRY D. *A Strike of Millionaires against Miners or the Story of Spring Valley*. Chicago, 1890.

———. *Wealth against Commonwealth*. New York, 1894.

McNEILL, GEORGE E. *The Labor Movement, the Problem of To-day*. Boston, 1887. (Pro-labor symposium.)

NEWCOMB, SIMON. *Principles of Political Economy*. New York, 1885.

PHELPS, ELIZABETH STUART. *The Silent Partner*. Boston, 1871. (The ancestor of the Christian social novel.)

PHILLIPS, WENDELL. *The Labor Question*. Pamphlet. Boston, 1884.

RAE, JOHN. *Contemporary Socialism*. London, 1884. (Introduced many clergymen to the subject.)

ROGERS, JAMES E. THOROLD. *Six Centuries of Work and Wages*. New York, 1884.

SCUDDER, MOSES L., JR. *The Labor-Value Fallacy*. Pamphlet. Chicago, 1884.

SOTHERAN, CHARLES. *Horace Greeley and other Pioneers of American Socialism*. New York, 1892. (A tract rather than a biography.)

STEAD, WILLIAM T. *If Christ Came to Chicago! A Plea for the Union of All Who Love in the Service of All Who Suffer*. Chicago, 1894.

The Poor in Great Cities. Their Problems and What is Doing to Solve Them. New York, 1895. (Symposium, includes clerical opinion.)

THOMPSON, R. E. *Elements of Political Economy*. Philadelphia, 1882. (Originally published with title *Social Science and National Economy*, Philadelphia, 1875.)

———. *Hard Times and What to Learn from them. A Plain Talk with Working People*. Pamphlet. Philadelphia, 1877.

TREVOR, JOHN. *My Quest for God*. London, 1897. (By the founder of the British Labor Church.)

TRUMBULL, M. M. ("Wheelbarrow," *pseud.*) *Articles and Discussions on the Labor Question*. Chicago, 1890. (Anti-single tax; includes controversy with H. O. Pentecost.)

WALKER, FRANCIS A. *Political Economy*. Rev. ed. New York, 1887.

WRIGHT, CARROLL D. *The Relation of Political Economy to the Labor Question*. Pamphlet. Boston, 1882.

H. BIOGRAPHIES AND AUTOBIOGRAPHIES

ABBOTT, LYMAN. *Henry Ward Beecher*. Boston, 1903. (Admiring.)
———. *Reminiscences*. Boston, 1915.

ADDAMS, JANE. *Twenty Years at Hull House*. New York, 1930.

ALLEN, ALEXANDER V. G. *Life and Letters of Phillips Brooks*. 2 vols. New York, 1900.

ARCHIBALD, WARREN SEYMOUR. *Horace Bushnell*. Hartford, 1930.

AYRES, ANNIE. *William Augustus Muhlenberg*. 5th ed. New York, 1894.

AYRES, M. C. *Phillips Brooks in Boston*. Boston, 1893.

BAILLIE, WILLIAM. *Josiah Warren, the First American Anarchist, a Sociological Study*. Boston, 1906.

BALLOU, ADIN. *Autobiography*. W. S. HEYWOOD, ed. Lowell, 1896.

BARNARD, HARRY. *"Eagle Forgotten," The Life of John Peter Altgeld*. Indianapolis, 1938.

BRACE, EMMA. *The Life of Charles Loring Brace*. New York, 1894.

BRADFORD, GAMALIEL. *D. L. Moody. A Worker in Souls*. New York, 1927.

BURR, AGNES RUSH. *Russell H. Conwell and His Work*. Philadelphia, 1917.

CAREY, HENRY C. *A Memoir of Stephen Colwell*. Philadelphia, 1871.

CHADWICK, J. W. *William Ellery Channing, Minister of Religion*. Boston, 1913.

CHANNING, W. H. *The Life of William Ellery Channing*. Boston, 1882.

COMMAGER, HENRY STEELE. *Theodore Parker*. Boston, 1936.

COMMONS, JOHN ROGERS. *Myself*. New York, 1934.

DEWEY, ORVILLE. *Autobiography and Letters of Orville Dewey, D.D.* MARY E. DEWEY, ed. Boston, 1883.

DODGE, D. STUART, ed. *Memorials of William E. Dodge*. New York, 1887.

EARHART, MARY. *Frances Willard, From Prayers to Politics*. New York, 1944.

ELY, RICHARD T. *Ground Under Our Feet, An Autobiography*. New York, 1938.

EVJEN, J. O. *The Life of J. H. W. Stuckenberg*. Minneapolis, 1938.

GATES, ISABEL SMITH. *The Life of George Augustus Gates*. Boston, 1915.

GLADDEN, WASHINGTON. *Recollections.* Boston, 1909. (Probably the most important single document of the early Christian social movement.)

GORDON, ANA A. *The Beautiful Life of Frances E. Willard. A Memorial Volume.* Chicago, 1898.

HALE, EDWARD E., JR. *Life and Letters of Edward Everett Hale.* 2 vols. Boston, 1917.

HALL, ARETHUSA. *Life and Character of the Reverend Sylvester Judd.* Boston, 1854.

HARLOW, RALPH VOLNEY. *Gerrit Smith, Philanthropist and Reformer.* New York, 1939.

HIBBEN, PAXTON. *Henry Ward Beecher: An American Portrait.* New York, 1927. (Impressionistic, perceptive, highly critical.)

HODGES, JULIA SHELLEY. *George Hodges. A Biography.* New York, 1926.

HUNTINGTON, ARRIA SARGENT. *Memoir and Letters of Frederick Dan Huntington.* Boston, 1906.

KEYSER, HARRIET A. *Bishop Potter, the People's Friend.* New York, 1910.

LEOPOLD, RICHARD W. *Robert Dale Owen.* Cambridge, 1940.

LINN, JAMES WEBER. *Jane Addams.* New York, 1935.

LLOYD, CARO. *Henry Demarest Lloyd.* 2 vols. New York, 1912.

MARTYN, CARLOS. *Wendell Phillips.* "American Reformers Series." New York, 1890.

———. *William E. Dodge, The Christian Merchant.* "American Reformers Series." New York, 1890.

MOODY, WILLIAM R. *D. L. Moody.* New York, 1930.

MORGAN, ARTHUR E. *Edward Bellamy.* New York, 1944.

NEWTON, WILLIAM WILBERFORCE. *Dr. Muhlenberg.* "American Religious Leaders Series." Boston, 1890. (Casts some light on early Episcopalian reform movements.)

PARKHURST, C. H. *My Forty Years in New York.* New York, 1923.

PERKINS, A. J. G. AND THERESA WOLFSON. *Frances Wright, Free Enquirer. The Study of a Temperament.* New York, 1939.

Phillips Brooks as his Friends Knew Him. Boston, 1903. (Reprinted from the *Congregationalist.*)

POST, LOUIS F. *The Prophet of San Francisco.* New York, 1930. (Henry George.)

POWDERLY, TERENCE V. *The Path I Trod.* HARRY J. CARMAN, HENRY DAVID and PAUL N. GUTHRIE, eds. New York, 1940.

———. *Thirty Years of Labor.* Columbus, 1890.

RAINSFORD, W. S. *The Story of a Varied Life.* Garden City, 1924.

RUSSELL, CHARLES E. *The story of Wendell Phillips.* Chicago, 1914.

SALTER, W. M. *Channing as a Social Reformer.* Pamphlet. N.p., 1892.

SCHLESINGER, A. M., JR. *Orestes A. Brownson, A Pilgrim's Progress.* Boston, 1939.

SCUDDER, VIDA D. *Father Huntington.* New York, 1940.

———. *On Journey.* New York, 1937. (Autobiography.)

SESSIONS, RUTH HUNTINGTON. *Sixty Odd, A Personal History.* Brattleboro, 1936. (Contains occasional information on author's brother, J. O. S. Huntington.)

SHARPE, D. R. *Walter Rauschenbusch.* New York, 1942.

SHELDON, C. M. *Charles M. Sheldon, His Life Story.* New York, 1925.

SINGER, ANNA M. *Walter Rauschenbusch and his Contribution to Social Christianity.* Boston, 1926. (Less adequate than Sharpe.)

STRONG, E. AND. M. "Biography of Josiah Strong." Unpublished. (Consulted through Professor C. H. Hopkins.)

TALMAGE, T. DE WITT. *T. De Witt Talmage, D.D.* London, 1912. (Concluding chapters by Mrs. T. DE WITT TALMAGE.)

TAPPAN, LEWIS. *The Life of Arthur Tappan.* New York, 1870.

TAYLOR, GRAHAM. *Pioneering on Social Frontiers.* Chicago, 1930.

TITUS, ANSON. *Edwin Hubbel Chapin, D.D., Ll.D.* Pamphlet. Boston, 1884.

TROWBRIDGE, LYDIA J. *Frances Willard of Evanston.* Chicago, 1938.

TUCKER, WILLIAM JEWETT. *My Generation.* Boston, 1919.

[TUCKERMAN, JOSEPH] *A Memorial to the Reverend Joseph Tuckerman.* Worcester, 1888. (Includes selections, bibliography and biographical notes.)

WATERMAN, WILLIAM RANDALL. *Frances Wright.* New York, 1924.

WILLARD, FRANCES E. *Glimpses of Fifty Years.* Boston, 1889.

WRIGHT, G. FREDERICK. *Charles Grandison Finney.* Boston, 1891.

II. SECONDARY MATERIAL

A. CHURCH HISTORY

ABELL, A. I. "The Impact of the City on American Protestantism, 1850-1900." MS Ph.D. thesis, Harvard, 1938. (MS version, consulted through Mr. Abell's permission, is fuller than published thesis on some aspects).

———. *The Urban Impact on American Protestantism 1865-1900.* "Harvard Historical Studies," LIV. Cambridge, 1943. (Detailed and authoritative account of expansion of church philanthropic institutions. Contains considerable comment on Social Gospel theory).

ADAMS, J. C. AND OTHERS. *The Religious History of New England.* Cambridge, 1917.

ADDISON, D. D. *The Clergy in American Life and Letters.* London, 1900. (Includes critical essays on Bushnell, H. W. Beecher, and Phillips Brooks.)

ALLEN, J. H. *Historical Sketch of the Unitarian Movement since the*

Reformation. PHILIP SCHAFF AND OTHERS, eds. "American Church History Series," X. New York, 1894, 1-249.

ATKINS, G. G. *Religion in Our Times*. New York, 1932. (Includes chapter "The Church Discovers the Social Gospel," pp. 46-68.)

ATKINS, G. G. AND F. L. FAGLEY. *History of American Congregationalism*. Boston, 1942. (One of the most valuable denominational histories.)

BACON, L. W. *A History of American Christianity*. "American Church History Series," XIII. New York, 1897. (Older point of view, valuable.)

BARNES, GILBERT HOBBES. *The Antislavery Impulse, 1838-1844*. New York, 1933. (Valuable and controversial interpretation of part of American religion in moral-reform movements as well as antislavery.)

BARNHART, KENNETH EDWIN. "The Evolution of the Social Consciousness in Methodism." (MS Ph.D. thesis, Chicago, 1924). (Fragmentary and inaccurate.)

BASS, A. B. *Protestantism in the United States*. New York, 1929.

BATES, ERNEST SUTHERLAND. *American Faith. Its Religious Political and Economic Foundations*. New York, 1940. (Stimulating interpretation of the role of religion in America.)

BEARDSLEY, F. G. *A History of American Revivals*. 2nd ed. New York, 1912.

BUCKHAM, JOHN WRIGHT. *Progressive Religious Thought in America*. New York, 1919. (An excellent survey.)

BUCKLEY, J. M. *A History of Methodism in the United States*. "American Church History Series," V. New York, 1896.

CARROLL, HENRY K. *Religious Forces in the United States*. "American Church History Series," I. Rev. ed. 1912 (cop. 1893). (Optimistic survey emphasizing statistics.)

COFFIN, HENRY SLOANE. *Religion Yesterday and Today*. Nashville, 1940. (Evaluation of recent religious trends, including the Social Gospel).

COOKE, GEORGE WILLIS. *Unitarianism in America: A History of its Origin and Development*. Boston, 1902.

DEXTER, H. M. *Congregationalism of the Last Three Hundred Years Seen in its Literature; with a Biblical Appendix*. New York, 1880.

DOMBROWSKI, JAMES. *The Early Days of Christian Socialism in America*. New York, 1936. (Pioneer study, including several elements of Christian radicalism other than the avowed Christian Socialists. Expresses great admiration for George D. Herron.)

DORCHESTER, DANIEL. *Christianity in the United States*. Rev. ed. New York, 1895 (cop. 1888). (Important early summary.)

———. *The Problem of Religious Progress*. New York, 1881. (Optimistic survey, emphasizing and somewhat exaggerating statistical gains.)

EDDY, RICHARD. *History of Universalism*. "American Church History Series," X. New York, 1894, 253-493.

EDDY, RICHARD. *Universalism in America.* 2 vols. Boston, 1886.

ELIOT, SAMUEL A., ed. *Heralds of a Liberal Faith.* 3 vols. Boston, 1910. (Brief biographies of Unitarian leaders.)

ELLSWORTH, C. S. "American Churches and the Mexican War," *American Historical Review,* XLV (1939-40), 301-326. (Important as a careful attempt to assess church influence.)

EVERETT, JOHN RUTHERFORD. *Religion in Economics.* New York, 1946. (Illuminating study of J. N. Clark, R. T. Ely and Simon Patten, emphasizing the relation between the religious and social ideas of each.)

FARISH, HUNTER DICKINSON. *The Circuit Rider Dismounts. A Social History of Southern Methodism 1865-1900.* Richmond, 1938.

FAULKNER, HAROLD U. "American Christianity and the World of Everyday," *Essays in Intellectual History* (dedicated to James Harvey Robinson by his former Seminar Students, New York, 1929), pp. 127-143.

FOSTER, FRANK HUGH. *A Genetic History of the New England Theology.* Chicago, 1907. (A classic survey, marred only slightly by the change in the author's theological opinions which occurred while the book was under way.)

————. *The Modern Movement in American Theology.* New York, 1939. (Illuminating, critical.)

GARRISON, WINFRED ERNEST. *The March of Faith.* New York, 1933. (Valuable summary of American church history since the Civil War.)

GLADDEN, WASHINGTON. *Pioneers of Religious Liberty in America.* Boston, 1903.

GORDON WALKER, P. C. "Capitalism and the Reformation," *Economic History Review,* VIII (1937-38), 1-19. (Valuable summary and critique of the Weber-Tawney controversy.)

GREENE, EVARTS B. *Religion and the State. The Making and Testing of an American Tradition.* New York, 1941.

HALL, T. C. *The Religious Background of American Culture.* Boston, 1930. (Controversial interpretation.)

HARRIS, GEORGE. *A Century's Change in Religion.* Boston, 1914.

HEININGER, HAROLD RICKEL. *The Theological Technique of a Mediating Theologian—Horace Bushnell.* Chicago, 1935. (Valuable insights into the theological crisis of the nineteenth century.)

HENDRICKS, ROBERT J. *Bethel and Aurora.* New York, 1933. (Account of some of the later Christian experimental communities.)

HOLT, ARTHUR E. "Organized Religion as a Pressure Group", HARWOOD L. CHILDS, ed. *Pressure Groups and Propaganda* (American Academy of Political and Social Science, *Annals,* vol. 179, May, 1935), pp. 42-49.

HOPKINS, CHARLES HOWARD. "Rauschenbusch and the Brotherhood of the Kingdom," *Church History,* VII (1938), 138-156. (Authoritative.)

————. *The Rise of the Social Gospel in American Protestantism 1865-1915.* "Yale Studies in Religious Education," XIV. New Haven, 1940.

(The most scholarly and complete account of the subject. Very favorable estimate of the Social Gospel's contribution.)

HOYT, A. S. *The Pulpit and American Life.* New York, 1921.

JACOBS, LEO. *Three Types of Practical Ethical Movements of the Past Half Century.* New York, 1922. (Discusses English and later American social Christianity, pp. 1-53.)

JAMESON, J. FRANKLIN. "The American Acta Sanctorum," *American Historical Review,* XIII (1907-1908), 286-302. (Early revaluation of the importance of American church history.)

JOHNSON, R. H. "American Baptists in the Age of Big Business," *Journal of Religion,* XI (1931), 63-85.

LATTA, M. C. "The Background for the Social Gospel in American Protestantism," *Church History,* V (1936), 256-270. (Excellent brief summary.)

LOUD, G. C. *Evangelized America.* New York, 1923.

LUCCOCK, H. E. AND P. HUTCHINSON. *The Story of Methodism.* New York, 1932.

MANROSS, WILLIAM WILSON. *A History of the American Episcopal Church.* New York, 1935.

MATHEWS, SHAILER. "The Development of Social Christianity in America," G. B. SMITH, ed. *Religious Thought in the Last Quarter-Century* (Chicago, 1927), pp. 228-239.

McGIFFERT, A. C. *The Rise of Modern Religious Ideas.* New York, 1887.

MILLER, SPENCER, JR. AND JOSEPH F. FLETCHER. *The Church and Industry.* New York, 1930. (Valuable summary of the Episcopalian social movement.)

MONROE, PAUL. "English and American Christian Socialism: an Estimate," *American Journal of Sociology,* I (1895-96), 50-68.

NEWMAN, A. H. *A History of the Baptist Churches in the United States.* "American Church History Series," II. Rev. ed. New York, 1915.

NIEBUHR, H. RICHARD. *The Social Sources of Denominationalism.* New York, 1929. (Contains valuable insights.)

NOBLE, W. F. P. *1776-1876. A Century of Gospel-Work.* Philadelphia, 1876.

RAUSCHENBUSCH, WALTER. *Christianizing the Social Order.* New York, 1912. (Includes some account of the Christian social movement's early days.)

RECKITT, MAURICE B. *Maurice to Temple. A Century of the Social Movement in the Church of England.* London, 1948. (Stimulating survey.)

ROWE, HENRY K. *The History of Religion in the United States.* New York, 1924.

SCHLATTER, RICHARD B. *The Social Ideas of Religious Leaders, 1660-1688.* Oxford, 1939. (Useful background material.)

SCHLESINGER, ARTHUR MEIER. "A Critical Period in American Religion,

1875-1900," Massachusetts Historical Society, *Proceedings*, LXIV (1932), 523-547.

SELDES, GILBERT. *The Stammering Century*. New York, 1928. (On revivalism.)

SMITH, G. B. "Theological Thinking in America," G. B. SMITH, ed. *Religious Thought in the Last Quarter-Century* (Chicago, 1927), pp. 95-115. (Valuable summary.)

SPARGO, JOHN. "Christian Socialism in America," *American Journal of Sociology*, XV (1909-10), 16-20.

STRONG, JOSIAH. *Religious Movements for Social Betterment*. H. B. ADAMS, ed. "Monographs on American Social Economy," XIV. New York, 1900.

SWEET, W. W. *Methodism in American History*. New York, 1933.

———. *The Story of Religions in America*. New York, 1930.

TAWNEY, R. H. *Religion and the Rise of Capitalism*. London, 1926.

The Church Through Half a Century. New York, 1936. (Essays in Honor of William Adams Brown. By Former Students.)

THOMPSON, R. E. *A History of the Presbyterian Churches in the United States of America*. "American Church History Series," VI. New York, 1895. (Valuable.)

TIFFANY, CHARLES C. *A History of The Protestant Episcopal Church in the United States of America*. "American Church History Series," VII. New York, 1895. (Like other Episcopal histories, largely outdated by Manross.)

TROELTSCH, ERNST. *The Social Teaching of the Christian Churches*. OLIVE WYON, trans. 2 vols., New York, 1931. (Indispensable for its insights into church history in Europe and America.)

VANDER VELDE, LEWIS G. *The Presbyterian Churches and the Federal Union, 1861-1869*. "Harvard Historical Studies," XXXIII. Cambridge, 1932. (A contribution to church history method.)

VEDDER, H. C. *The Baptists*. New York, 1902.

VISSER 'T HOOFT, W. A. *The Background of the Social Gospel in America*. Haarlem, 1928. (Brilliant comment by a European scholar on many aspects of American religious development.)

WALKER, WILLISTON. *A History of the Congregational Churches in the United States*. "American Church History Series," III. New York, 1894.

WEBER, JULIUS W. *Religions and Philosophies in the United States of America*. Los Angeles, 1931.

WEBER, MAX. *The Protestant Ethic and the Spirit of Capitalism*. TALCOTT PARSONS, trans. New York, 1930.

WEIGLE, LUTHER A. *American Idealism*. "Pageant of America Series," X. New Haven, 1928.

YINGER, J. MILTON. *Religion in the Struggle for Power*. Durham, N. C.,

1936. (Very helpful sociological interpretation, briefly covering present as well as earlier developments.)

B. OTHER SECONDARY WORKS

BERNARD, L. L. AND JESSIE. *Origins of American Sociology*. New York, 1943.

BROOKS, VAN WYCK. *New England: Indian Summer 1865-1915*. New York, 1940. (Contains some data on decline of social reform after Civil War.)

BRYSON, GLADYS. "The Emergence of the Social Sciences from Moral Philosophy," *International Journal of Ethics*, XLII (1931-32), 304-323.

CHAMBERLAIN, JOHN. *Farewell to Reform: Being a History of the Rise, Life and Decay of the Progressive Mind in America*. New York, 1932.

CURTI, M. E. *The American Peace Crusade 1815-1860*. Durham, N. C., 1929.

———. *The Growth of American Thought*. New York, 1943. (See especially "The Theoretical Grounds of Christian Socialism," pp. 629-632.)

DAVIS, EMERSON. *The Half Century*. Boston, 1851. (Early historical survey emphasizing reform and religion.)

DESTLER, CHESTER MCARTHUR. *American Radicalism 1865-1901. Essays and Documents* (Connecticut College Monograph No. 3). New London, 1946.

DORFMAN, JOSEPH. *The Economic Mind in American Civilization 1606-1865*. 2 vols. New York, 1946.

———. *Thorstein Veblen and His America*. New York, 1934.

FISH, CARL RUSSELL. *The Rise of the Common Man 1830-1850*. A. M. SCHLESINGER and D. R. Fox, eds. "A History of American Life," VI. New York, 1927.

GABRIEL, R. H. *The Course of American Democratic Thought*. New York, 1940. (See especially, "Protestantism Moves toward Humanism and Collectivism," pp. 308-330).

HAYNES, F. E. *Third Party Movements Since the Civil War with Special Reference to Iowa*. Iowa City, 1916.

HOFSTADTER, RICHARD. *Social Darwinism in American Thought 1860-1915*. Philadelphia, 1944. (Very valuable.)

HUBBART, HENRY CLYDE. *The Older Middle West 1840-1880*. New York, 1936. (Useful for background.)

HURLBUT, JESSE L. *The Story of Chautauqua*. New York, 1921.

KOCH, G. ADOLPH. *Republican Religion*. New York, 1933. (On deism and rationalism.)

LESLIE, T. E. C. "Political Economy in the United States," *Fortnightly Review*, XXVIII (1880), 488-501.

LOEWENBERG, BERT JAMES. "The Controversy over Evolution in New England," *New England Quarterly*, VIII (1935), 232-357.

———. "Darwinism Comes to America, 1859-1900," *Mississippi Valley Historical Review*, XXVIII (1941-42), 339-368.

MERRIAM, CHARLES EDWARD. *American Political Ideas*. New York, 1929.

NOYES, J. H. *History of American Socialisms*. Philadelphia, 1870.

O'CONNOR, MICHAEL J. L. *Origins of Academic Economics in the United States*. New York, 1944. (Valuable account of clerical school.)

PHELPS, CHRISTINA. *The Anglo-American Peace Movement in the Mid-Nineteenth Century*. New York, 1930.

POST, ALBERT. *Popular Freethought in America, 1825-1850*. New York, 1943.

POWER, RICHARD LYLE. "A Crusade to Extend Yankee Culture, 1820-1865," *New England Quarterly*, XIII (1940), 638-653.

SCHLESINGER, ARTHUR MEIER. *The Rise of the City*. A. M. SCHLESINGER and D. R. Fox, eds. "A History of American Life," X. New York, 1933.

SCHLESINGER, ARTHUR MEIER, JR. *The Age of Jackson*. Boston, 1946. (Useful for early anticlericalism.)

SCHMIDT, GEORGE P. *The Old Time College President*. New York, 1930.

SMALL, ALBION W. "Fifty Years of Sociology in the United States," *American Journal of Sociology*, XXI (1915-16), 721-864.

TAYLOR, WALTER FULLER. "On the Origins of Howells' Interest in Economic Reform," *American Literature*, II (1930), 3-14.

TOLMAN, WILLIAM HOWE. *Municipal Reform Movements in the United States*. New York, 1895.

VEBLEN, THORSTEIN. *Theory of the Leisure Class*. New York, 1899. (Chapter XIII, "Devout Observances," pp. 293-331, is a devastating attack on American religious institutions and customs in Veblen's time.)

WHITNEY, EDSON C. *The American Peace Society. A Centennial History*. Washington, D. C., 1928.

INDEX

Abbott, Lyman, 138, 194, 207
Addams, Jane, and Social Gospel, 226-227
Advertising, of religious press, 55 n.
Allibone, Samuel Austen, on Colwell, 19
Altgeld, John P., on Chicago clergy, 157
American Congress of Churches, 194, 219
American Economic Association, organization of, 138
American Institute of Christian Sociology, 225, 253-254
Anderson, M. B., cited, 52
Andrews, E. Benjamin, economic doctrines of, 139-140
Anticlericalism, in Jacksonian democracy, 8-9, 24-25
Antislavery, and "Benevolent Empire," 24; and clergy, 29
Anti-tenement House League, 242
Atkinson, Edward, criticizes Social Gospel, 21
Atwater, Lyman H., cited, 56, 59

Bacon, Leonard, on early Social Gospel movement, 202
Baird, Robert, on American history, 5; on socialism 11
Ballou, Adin, and socialist communities, 10; and reform movements, 33; on postwar disillusion, 73-74
Banks, Louis A., on city conditions, 118
Baptist Congress for the Discussion of Current Questions, discussions of, 191-192
Baptists, and Social Gospel, 190-193
Bascom, John, early economic doctrines of, 20; on John Fiske, 48; sociology of, 49-50; and evolution, 145; on labor, 145-146
Batchelor, George, 168
Batten, Samuel Zane, 190, 226; cited, 226
Beecher, Edward, on First International, 58
Beecher, Henry Ward, and Civil War, 40; on political preaching, 40; social and economic opinions of, 67-72; theology of, 68, 86-87; and strikes of 1877, 93-94; and Herbert Spencer, 142
Beecher, Lyman, and New York Workingmen's Party, 9
Behrends, A. J., social doctrines of, 166-168; criticism of, 244

Bellamy, Edward, and Protestant thought, 157-158; and Christian Socialists, 242
Bemis, E. W., economic doctrines of, 140
"Benevolent Empire," 22-25
Bierbower, Austin, Biblical interpretation of, 236-237
Bliss, William Dwight Porter, cited, 134; on early Social Gospel movement, 200; and Howells, 211; career of, 241-242; organizations led by, 241-242; social doctrines of, 243-244; and followers, 244-45; effectiveness of, 245-247
Boardman, George N., cited, 53; and laissez faire, 60-61
Bourne, Theodore, cited, 131; on Christian communism, 236
Bowen, Francis, economic doctrines of, 17; conservatism of, 33
Bowne, Borden P., ethical doctrines of, 195-196
Brace, Charles Loring, and city conditions, 62, 112-113
Bradford, Amory H., 223
Bright, Edward, cited, 191
Brooks, Phillips, and Civil War, 41; social outlook of, 64-67
Brotherhood of the Carpenter, 242
Brotherhood of the Co-operative Commonwealth, 260-261
Brotherhood of the Kingdom, 190-191, 225
Brown, C. O., and strikes of 1886, 100; attacks Herron, 255-256
Brown, T. Edwin, social doctrines of, 179-180; on early Social Gospel movement, 200
Brownson, Orestes A., social doctrines of, 32
Bryan, William Jennings, and Social Gospel, 230
Buchanan, J. R., and clergy, 222
Bushnell, Horace, cited, 5; on charity, 53; on hours of labor, 56; theological influence of, 84-85
Business ethics, Protestant discussion of, 54-55, 130-132
Butler, Benjamin F., 74, 96

Cadman, H. W., social doctrines of, 180
Campbell, Helen, on city conditions, 117
Campbell, S. M., cited, 42

Carey, Henry C., economic doctrines of, 17-18

Carnegie, Andrew, on "Wealth," 132-133; church reaction to, 133-134

Carroll, Henry K., 204

Carwardine, William H., on Pullman strike, 109-110

Casson, Herbert N., activities and doctrines of, 247-249

Channing, William Ellery, and reform movements, 30; social doctrines of, 30-31

Channing, William Henry, and socialist communities, 10

Chapin, Aaron L., edits Wayland's text, 136

Chapin, Edwin Hubbell, social doctrines of, 34-35

Charity, Protestant discussion of, 53-54, 59, 122-123

Chautauqua, Social Gospel at, 206-207

Cherouny, Henry, social doctrines of, 236

Chinese, immigration of, Protestant discussion of, 57; Washington Gladden and, 171

Christian anarchism, 237-239

Christian Labor Union, activities of, 77; later recognition of, 256

Christian Social Union, in England, 149; in America, 149, 185, 242, 246

Christian socialism, English, 148-149; French and German, 152

For American, see Christian Socialists, Society of, and names of individuals

Christian Socialist Fellowship, 260

Christian Socialists, Society of, Frances E. Willard and, 127; on Carnegie's "Wealth," 134; and Nationalist movement, 157, 242; organization and activities of, 242-247; Labor Church and, 248-249

Church and state, relation of in America, 3-6, 42-44, 125-127

Church Association for the Advancement of the Interests of Labor (CAIL), 184-185, 239, 241, 242

Church Congress, Episcopal, on depression of 1873, 59; and Social Gospel, 183-184

Churchill, Winston, 213

City conditions, Protestant discussion of, 61-62, 112-124

Civil War, Protestant view of, 39-41

Clark, Charles Worcester, on shortcomings of Social Gospel movement, 223-224

Clark, John Bates, economic doctrines of, 139

"Clerical laissez-faire," development of doctrines, 13-16, 44-45, 136-138

Colleges, church control of, in pre-Civil War period, 12-13

Collens, T. Wharton, social doctrines of, 78

Colton, Calvin, 17

Colwell, Stephen C., economic doctrines of, 18-19; church critics of, 19-20

Comfort, George C., cited, 58

Commons, John R., economic doctrines of, 139; and the *Kingdom*, 254

Commune, the Paris, Protestant discussion of, 58; Henry Ward Beecher on, 72; Wendell Phillips on, 74

Communism, Jesse H. Jones and, 75-76; R. J. Wright and, 77; religious press on, 58-59, 95-96

Communities, socialist, Protestant hostility toward, 9-11

Comte, Auguste, Protestant hostility toward, 46-47

Conant, William C., cited, 43

Congregationalists, and Social Gospel, 187-188

Conservative social Christianity, basic doctrines of, 163-164; early spokesmen of, 164-169; and American thought, 264

Conwell, Russell H., rejection of Social Gospel, 199-200

Cooley, Harrison R., 226

Cook, Joseph, social doctrines of, 164-166; criticism of, 244

Co-operation, Protestant discussion of, 58

Corporations, regulation of, Protestant discussion of, 132

Coyle, John P., 254

Crafts, Wilbur F., and Sabbatarianism, 130; and business success, 130; cited, 181

Crosby, Howard, on single tax movement, 155

Darwinism, and American Protestantism, 46-50, 142-147

Dawn, the, 245-247

Debs, Eugene V., and Christian radicalism, 260, 261

DeCosta, B. F., 241

De La Matyr, Gilbert, 222

Depressions, of 1873, 59-60; of 1885, 98-99; of 1893, 107

Dixon, Thomas, Jr., 192

Dole, C. F., cited, 168

Dorchester, Daniel, 120, 204

Dowling, George T., cited, 98

Economics, academic
  See Political economy
Ely, Ezra Stiles, 25
Ely, Richard T., 194, 215, 238, 254;
  cited, 130; and American Economic
  Association, 138; economic doctrines of,
  140-142; on socialism, 152; on early
  Social Gospel movement, 201; and
  Christian Socialism, 246
English Christian Social movement, and
  Andrew Carnegie, 133-134; develop-
  ment of, 148-149; influence in America,
  149-151, 186-187
Enlightenment, and Protestantism, 7
Episcopalians, and Civil War, 40-41;
  British influence on, 150; and Social
  Gospel, 182-187
  See also Church Congress, General
  convention
Equity, 77
Ethical economics, development of doc-
  trines, 138-142
Ethics, clerical teaching of, 20-21; Social
  Gospel and, 195-196
Evangelical Alliance, 52, 125; Ely and,
  141; Social Gospel and, 194; Herron
  and, 255
Evans, George Henry, 8

Farnam, Henry W., cited, 197
Faunce, W. H. P., 192
Finney, Charles Grandison, 11; and re-
  form movements, 22-23
Fiske, John, 48, 144
Flower, B. O., and Social Gospel, 227-228
For the Right, 190
Fourierism, and religion, 10-11
Free Religious Association, social outlook
  of, 81-82
Fremantle, W. F., 150
Frickstad, Taral T., attacks clergy, 220
Frothingham, O. B., social doctrines of,
  81-82
Frontier theory, 55

Gates, George A., and George D. Herron,
  253-254
Gates, M. E., cited, 125
General Assembly, Presbyterian, on Civil
  War, 39; and depression of 1873, 59;
  and Social Gospel, 192-193
General Conference, Methodist, on Civil
  War, 39-40; on church and state, 43;
  and Social Gospel, 188-189
General Convention, Episcopalian, and
  Social Gospel, 182-187

George, Henry, and Protestant thought,
  154-156; at Church Congress, 184; at
  American Congress of Churches, 194,
  220; and Tom L. Johnson, 226; and
  J. O. S. Huntington, 239-240
Gibson, Monroe J., on Spencer, 145
Gilman, Nicholas Paine, on co-operation,
  215; on Christian Socialism, 258
Gladden, Washington, 194, 207, 227,
  238, 254; on Chinese immigration,
  57 n.; on impact of city, 124; in American Economic Association, 138; on
  Spencer, 147; early life of, 171-172;
  developing social doctrines of, 173-174;
  influence of, 174-175; reports on capital and labor, 187-188, 222; criticism
  of, in Nation, 215; by labor spokesman, 219; by Charles Sotheran, 220; by
  F. M. Sprague, 244; and civic reform,
  226; and Theodore Roosevelt, 228
Gompers, Samuel, attitude toward clergy,
  220-221
Grant, George Monro, cited, 156
Greeley, Horace, and Universalism, 33
Gronlund, Lawrence, social doctrines of,
  259

Habberton, John, cited, 205
Haddock, Frank C., on prohibition, 128-
  129
Hadley, Arthur T., 102
Hale, Edward Everett, on organic society,
  178; and Social Gospel novel, 267; and
  Howells, 211
Haley, William D., economic doctrines of,
  21-22
Harris, Samuel Smith, cited, 122
Harrison, J. B., cited, 168
Haven, Gilbert, cited, 41
Haven, Joseph, ethics text by, 20-21
Haydn, Hyram C., cited, 98
Haymarket affair, Protestant discussion of,
  100-102
Haynes, Emory J., and Social Gospel
  novel, 207
Henderson, Charles R., 144
Henry, C. S., on political preaching, 41
Herron, George D., 215, 227; on Sumner
  and Spencer, 147; early career of, 249;
  theological doctrines of, 250-251; social
  doctrines of, 251-253; followers and
  organizations, 253-256; and Socialist
  Party, 260
Hill, D. J., cited, 168
History, clerical view of, 5
Hitchcock, Roswell D., social doctrines
  of, 166

Hoadley, James A., cited, 122
Hodges, George, 207, 241; social doctrines of, 181; on early Social Gospel movement, 201
Holbrook, Z. S., cited, 109
Hours of labor, Protestant discussion of, 56, 104
Howells, William Dean, and Social Gospel, 210-213
Huntington, Frederick Dan, 226, 239; early economic doctrines of, 35-36; later views of, 180-181; and CAIL, 184
Huntington, J. O. S., 220, 221, 227; and Homestead strike, 106; and Henry George, 155; and Howells novel, 211; social doctrines of, 239-241
Huntington, William Reed, on government by wealth, 132
Hyde, William DeWitt, cited, 168

Immigration, churches and, 42, 57, 123-124; Josiah Strong on, 114
    See also Chinese, immigration of
Interdenominational Congress, 194
Interdenominational organizations, early conservatism, 22-25; and Social Gospel, 193-194
    See also particular organizations
International, First, 58-59, 60; Henry Ward Beecher on, 71-72

Jacksonian democracy, and Protestantism, 7-8
Jarrett, John, 194, 219
Jefferson, Thomas, clergy and, 7
Johnson, Samuel A., on Wendell Phillips, 74-75
Johnson, Tom L., and Social Gospel, 226
Jones, Jesse H., social and economic opinions of, 74-77; and followers, 77-79; and later Protestant opinion, 79, 256
Jones, Samuel L., and Social Gospel, 226
Judd, Sylvester, opposition to radicalism, 32

Kearney, Dennis, Protestant press on, 96
Keil, William, 11
Kingdom, the, policies of, 254-255
Kingsley, Charles, 148, 149
Knights of Labor, Protestant press on, 99-100, 102-103; Frances E. Willard and, 127-128; J. O. S. Huntington and, 240; Bliss and, 242

Labor
    See Hours of Labor, Knights of Labor, Strikes, Trade-unions, Wages
Labor Balance, 77
Labor Church, the, 149; beliefs of, 247-249
Labor movement, British, influence of in America, 151
La Follette, Robert Marion, and Social Gospel, 228
Latham, H. J., and business success, 131
Laughlin, J. Lawrence, economic doctrines of, 137
Laveleye, Emile de, on socialism, 152
Learned, J. E., cited, 197
Little, Arthur, cited, 187
Lloyd, Henry D., and Frances E. Willard, 128; and Protestant thought, 158-159; and Brotherhood of the Kingdom, 191; and Howells, 211; and J. O. S. Huntington, 240; and Christian radicalism, 259-260
Loomis, Samuel Lane, on city conditions, 116-117
Lorimer, G. C., cited, 178

McGlynn, Father Edward, Protestant attitudes toward, 156-157
Machar, Agnes M., and Social Gospel novel, 208-209
MacVicar, D. H., cited, 168
McVickar, John, economic doctrines of, 13
Massachusetts Congregational Association, report on industrial relations, 187-188
Maurice, Frederick Denison, 148, 149
Mears, John W., on socialism, 11
Methodists, and Social Gospel, 188-190
    See also General Conference
Millennial sects, and Social Gospel, 199
Mission of the Carpenter, 242
Monroe, Paul, on Christian Socialism, 258
Moody, Dwight L., 42, 83
Morality, church supervision of, 3-4, 125-127
Morse, C. M., 197
Moxom, Philip S., 207; cited, 178; and Brotherhood of the Kingdom, 191
Murray, W. H. H., on religious individualism, 83-84

Nash, Joseph, on strikes, 93-94
National Reform Association, 42
Nationalism, *see* Bellamy
Newcomb, Simon, economic doctrines of, 137

Newton, R. Heber, 221, 225; social doctrines of, 176-177; at Church Congress, 183-184
New York Workingmen's Party, Protestant hostility toward, 8-9
Noyes, John Henry, 11

Order of the Holy Cross, 239, 241
Owen, Robert Dale, 8

Parker, Theodore, social doctrines of, 31
Parkhurst, Charles H., 225
Parliament of Religions, 141, 144, 194
Parsons, E. S., cited, 168
Peabody, F. G., 195, 207; cited, 194
Peace movement, and clergy, 26-27
Pentecost, Hugh O., 191; social doctrines of, 237-239
Periodicals, secular, and Social Gospel, 206
Perry, Arthur Latham, economic doctrines of, 45
Phelps, Elizabeth Stuart, and Social Gospel novel, 207
Phillips, Wendell, attacked by church press, 74-75
Political economy, religion in teaching of, 13-21, 44-46, 136-142
   See also American Economic Association, "Clerical laissez-faire," Ethical economics, Protectionism, and names of particular economists
Politics, churches and
   See Church and state
Populism, 107 n., 254
Porter, Noah, ethical doctrines of, 195
Potter, Alonzo, economic doctrines of, 15, 16
Potter, Henry C., 220, 226, 238, 241; on Carnegie's "Wealth," 134; pastoral letter by (1886), 178-179; on Christian Socialism, 246
Poverty, Protestant discussion of, 52-54
   See also City conditions
Powderly, Terence V., Protestant Press on, 99; and American Congress of Churches, 194; attitude toward organized religion, 216-219
Prall, William, cited, 181
Prentiss, George L., cited, 43
Presbyterians, and Social Gospel, 192-193
   See also General Assembly
Prescott, W. B., on clergy, 221
Progressive social Christianity
   See Social Gospel
Protectionism, 16-20, 45-46, 136-137

Radical, the, 81
Radical social Christianity, definition, 235-236; early development of, 236-256; and American Protestantism, 256-257; conservative hostility toward, 257-258; and progressivism, 258; and American socialism, 259-260; conclusions on, 261-262; and American thought, 264
Rae, John, on socialism, 151-152
Rainsford, W. S., 228; and J. P. Morgan, 186; on early Social Gospel movement, 201
Rauschenbusch, Walter, 203, 226; and Henry George, 156; on Episcopalianism, 185-186; and early Baptist social movement, 190-192; on strength of early Social Gospel movement, 201
Reed, Myron W., 222, 260
Reform movements, pre-Civil War, 22-23
Rerum Novarum, 153
Revivalism, social influence of, 83-84; and Social Gospel, 198-200
Revolution, American, Protestant historians on, 5
Revolutions, of 1848, refugees from, 11-12
Rhodes, Dudley Ward, attacks Cincinnati streetcar company, 177-178
Richardson, Charles, proposal of, 236
Richmond, J. F., cited, 63
Roads, Charles, cited, 181
Robins, John B., on Strong and Loomis, 117
Rogers, Edward H., social doctrines of, 78; mentioned, 128; and Evangelical Alliance, 256 n.
Roosevelt, Franklin Delano, 230
Roosevelt, Theodore, and Social Gospel, 228-229
Ruffner, William Henry, on Colwell, 19
Rylance, J. H., on co-operation, 178

Sabbatarianism, 25, 129-130
Salter, W. M., 101
Savage, Minot J., 168
Schaff, Philip, on relation of church and state, 6; on Jacksonian radicalism, 7; on revolutions of 1848, 11-12
Science, influence on theology, 85
Scott, J. E., cited, 193
"Scottish realism," and American political economy, 13-14
Scudder, Moses L., cited, 214
Scudder, Vida D., and Christian Socialism, 241
Seeley, Sir John, 150

Seminaries, theological, Social Gospel in, 194-195
Sessions, Arria Huntington, cited, 183
Settlement movement, influence on social opinion, 123
Sheldon, Charles M., and Social Gospel novel, 210-211
Small, Albion W., 144, 216
Smith, Joseph T., 193
Smyth, Newman, cited, 178; ethical doctrines of, 196
Social Christianity, definition, 170 n.
   See Conservative social Christianity, Progressive social Christianity, Radical social Christianity, Social Gospel
Social Gospel, definition, 170 n.; basic doctrines of, 170-171; early development of, 171-181; and Episcopalians, 182-187; and Congregationalists, 187-188; and Methodists, 189-190; and Baptists, 190-192; and Presbyterians, 192-193; and interdenominational organizations, 193-194; in theological seminaries, 194-195; and ethics, 195-196; Protestant opposition to, 196-198; early estimates of, 200-202; in 1895, 202; later development, 202-203; in secular periodicals, 206; at Chautauqua, 206-207; in novels, 207-213; lay criticism of, 213-216; labor movement and, 216-223; weaknesses of, 222-224, 231-234; and progressivism, 224-225; and civic reform, 225-228; and political leaders, 228-231; conclusions on, 231-234; and radical social Christianity, 235-236; and American thought, 264-265
Socialism, church attitudes toward, 11, 58-59; European, influence in America, 151-152; American, and Christian radicalism, 259-260
   See also Christian Socialism, Commune, Communism, Communities, International
Sociology, and Protestant thought, 46-50, 142-147
Sotheran, Charles, criticism of clergy, 220
Spargo, John, 261
Spencer, Herbert, and American Protestantism, 47-50, 142-147
Sprague, F. M., cited, 200; and Christian Socialism, 244-245
Sprague, Philo W., and Christian Socialism, 244; reception of, 246
State, relation to church
   See Church and state
Statistics, religious, 42, 120, 204
Stead, W. T., on Chicago, 118-119

Steele, George M., economic doctrines of, 136-137
Stelzle, Charles, 207
Strikes, in general, Protestant discussion of, 56-57, 59-60; particular: railroad (1877), 91-95; telegraphers' (1883), 97; Cleveland Rolling Mill (1885), 98; southwestern railroad (1886), 99-100, 102; New York coal-handlers (1887), 103; C. B. & Q. (1888), 103; New York Central (1890), 103; Spring Valley (1888), 103; London dock (1889), 104; Homestead (1892), 105-107; coal (1894), 108; Pullman (1894), 108-110
Strong, A. H., on political economy, 44; on Rockefeller, 131
Strong, Josiah, 194, 207, 254; on city conditions, 113-116; and Herron, 255
Stuckenberg, J. H. W., on social ethics, 178
Sturtevant, J. M., cited, 154
Swift, Morrison I., 237
Swinton, John, criticisms of clergy, 121, 219
Sumner, William Graham, social doctrines of, 143-144; Herron on, 147

Talmadge, T. DeWitt, on strikes of 1877, 95; on Vanderbilt, 131; on capital and labor, 198
Tappan, Arthur, on antislavery, 24
Taylor, Graham, 195, 207, 227
Theology, liberal, and social opinion, 80-87, 231-232
Thomas, Norman, 261
Thompson, Joseph P., on church wealth, 42; on labor, 166
Thompson, Maurice, cited, 153
Thompson, Robert Ellis, economic doctrines of, 45-46; and strikes of 1877, 93; new edition, 136; criticizes Social Gospel, 215-216
Tocqueville, Alexis de, on American religion, 3
Tolstoi, Leo, and American Protestantism, 153-154
Tourgee, Albion W., and Social Gospel novel, 208
Tower, F. E., and Christian Socialism, 244
Toynbee Hall, 149
Trade-unions, and clerical economists, 15-16; Protestant discussion of, 56-57, 95-96; attitudes toward clergy, 215-223
Tucker, William Jewett, 195; on Carnegie's "Wealth," 134
Tuckerman, Joseph, social doctrines of, 31

Twentieth Century, and Christian anarchism, 238-239
Tyler, R. H., cited, 5

Unemployed "armies," 107-108
Unemployment, Protestant discussion of, 60, 96, 98-99
Union for Practical Progress, and Social Gospel, 227-228
Unitarian Review, social opinions of, 80
Unitarianism, and reform movements, 29-33; influence on other denominations, 35-36; and postwar conservatism, 80-81; and conservative social Christianity, 168
United Labor Party, Protestant discussion of, 155-156
Universalism, and reform movements, 33-35

Van Amringe, H. H., cited, 11
Vethake, Henry, economic doctrines of, 13, 15, 16
Vrooman, Walter, 227

Waffle, A. E., cited, 168
Wage-earners, alienation from churches of, 61-62, 119-121
Wages, Protestant discussion of, 55-56, 61
Wainwright, Jonathan, economic doctrines of, 21
Walker, Amasa, economic doctrines of, 45
Walker, Francis Amasa, economic doctrines of, 137-138
Wallace, Henry A., 261 n.
Ward, C. Osborne, historical interpretation of, 236
Ward, Julius H., on Sabbatarianism, 129; social doctrines of, 181
Ward, Lester F., social doctrines of, 144

Ward, William Hayes, cited, 120
Warren, Josiah, economic doctrines of, 76-77
Washburn, George, cited, 53, 178
Wayland, Francis, 26, 44, 91, 111, 136, 195; economic doctrines of, 13-14; books of, circulation, 16; ethics textbook by, 20
Wayland, H. L., cited, 52
Wealth, Protestant discussion of, 52-54, 130-135
  See also Business ethics, Carnegie
Webb, Edwin B., cited, 178
Weeden, William B., cited, 168
Welfare work, of churches, 121-123
Wendell Phillips Purchasers League, Wendell Phillips Union, 242
White, William Allen, and Social Gospel, 229-230
Willard, Frances E., sympathy with organized labor, 127-128
Williams, Leighton, 190, 191
Wilson, J. Stitt, 261
Wilson, W. D., cited, 59
Wilson, Woodrow, and Social Gospel, 230
Women's Christian Temperance Union, and organized labor, 127-128
Woods, Katherine P., and Social Gospel novel, 208
Woolsey, Theodore D., on socialism, 151
Wright, Carroll D., economic doctrines of, 138-139
Wright, Frances, Protestant hostility toward, 8-9, 24
Wright, R. J., social doctrines of, 79

Yeomans, Alfred, cited, 122

Zabriskie, F. N., cited, 178